MOST SECRET

The Hidden History of

ORFORD
NESS

MOST SECRET

The Hidden History of

ORFORD NESS

Paddy Heazell

in association with National Trust

For the people of Orford and its Museum
which keeps alive the story of the place

The National Trust at Orford Ness would be interested
to hear from anyone with memories, photographs,
documents or other material relating to its 'hidden'
history. Please get in touch via www.nationaltrust.org.uk

First published 2010

The History Press
The Mill, Brimscombe Port
Stroud, Gloucestershire, GL5 2QG
www.thehistorypress.co.uk

Text © The National Trust, 2010
Foreword © Dick Strawbridge, 2010
pp.237-238 © Heather Hanbury Brown, 1995

British Library Cataloguing in Publication Data.
A catalogue record for this book is available from the British Library.

ISBN 978 0 7524 5741 3

Typesetting and origination by The History Press
Printed in Great Britain

Front cover: Shingle leads up to the pagodas at Orford Ness,
© NTPL/Joe Cornish. Inset: The three aviation pioneers: Charles
Fairburn, George McKerrow, Bennett Melvill Jones. (*Goldsworthy
Collection*). Back cover: Please see Plate Section for details.

Contents

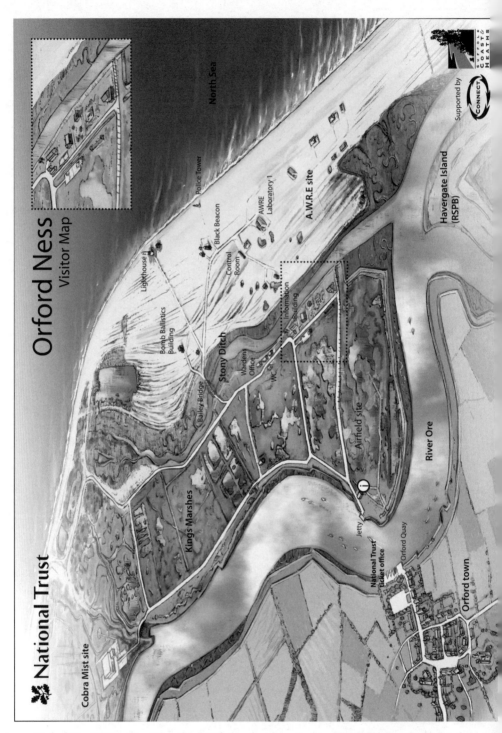

Orford Ness Visitor Map. Note the shingle beach, where the bombing range was once located and the distant Cobra Mist site. It is also easy to appreciate how cut-off this experimental station was from the real world, no wonder the local inhabitants nicknamed it the 'Island', it would have been even more appropriate to call it 'Boffin Island', as it became in its heyday. (© The National Trust/Orford Ness)

Foreword

Orford Ness is just the right place for keeping secrets; the stories of Bletchley Park and Bawdsey Manor have been told, but Orford Ness has held out.

For centuries it was mainly known for its hazardous shore and to some it is only a desolate piece of land, barely above sea level, that is exposed to bitter easterly winds. However, the War Office's procurement of the Ness as the home for an experimental establishment, in early 1914, was the start of a period that shaped Britain's military capability throughout the twentieth century. This book provides a long overdue look at how the top secret trials and experiments that took place in this remote part of East Anglia played a key role in the three great conflicts of the modern age: the First and Second World Wars and the Cold War.

Paddy Heazell brings the story of Orford Ness to life, in this the first book on this subject to be written since the secret and inaccessible military property was opened to the public by the National Trust in 1995. Fifteen years of association with this very special place, ten of which involved painstakingly digging through archives and hunting down those who worked there, have allowed Paddy to piece together the jigsaw so we now get a full picture of what really went on. His investigations, and obvious respect for those who have lived and worked on the Ness, have produced a compelling book in which every chapter makes you swell with pride at the achievement of our forebears.

The figures that have shaped the activities at Orford Ness have been a heady mixture of notable academics, high achievers and, in many cases, extremely brave men. The anecdotes, lots of which come from the first hand accounts of those involved, are frightfully British. Some of the names will be familiar, but there are a lot whose exploits have not previously been written about and their stories would remain untold but for this book.

The detail here is enthralling and it is a very rich story indeed where some of the main players provide links to the birth of radar, vulnerability of gas turbine engines, earthquake bombs and even post-Project Manhattan tests of the ballistics of early nuclear weapons. I remember years ago watching archive films of early radar trials that were being carried out by very English gentlemen, wearing tweeds and smoking their pipes, and marvelling at how business was conducted in the inter-war years. Here, such trials are put into context and allowing you to appreciate what our 'boffins' were really up to. Interestingly, today we all have our own image of what a 'boffin' is, but it was in the context of the pioneering activities that took place on the Ness that the term was coined during the inter-war years. It was really one of appreciation, as a boffin was a scientist or technician, who could liaise with the military to understand service requirements and who, not only had the skill and imagination to create wonderful gadgets, but also, had the energy and drive to build them. Far from the pejorative way the word is used today!

There are so many stories about the projects conducted at Orford Ness; every page brings more facts and information about the men who worked there. That said, it was not all glamour and you get a real sense that there was a lot of hard work conducted which would have been mundane, repetitive and even fruitless. However, it is worth noting that the effects of what was learnt at Orford Ness have had long term impacts, for example, work in the later stages of the First World War to determine how to bomb and destroy railways provided lessons applied 65 years later when a Vulcan bomber bombed Port Stanley airfield during the Falklands conflict, and without some of the significant work on aerodynamics, influenced by time on the Ness, we may have been too late to gain sufficient expertise to design the Spitfires and Hurricanes that were so vital for the Battle of Britain.

The teams who have worked at Orford Ness have been a mix of academics, engineers, military men and support staff. They have made an outstanding contribution to the winning of war and keeping Britain safe. The test pilots who lived and worked on Orford Ness were the elite of their profession; we can only marvel at the bravery of the test pilot who took off for the first time on a towed, floating platform only 21 feet wide and 48 feet long. There was undoubtedly a true daredevil spirit among the men and women of the Ness.

This book is ultimately a celebration of real people doing amazing things. It is also a timely reminder that we should never forget those splendid boffins, who alongside our soldiers, have devoted, and often sacrificed, their lives over the years without seeking glory or reward.

Dick Strawbridge, 2010

Author's Note and Acknowledgements

I first visited Orford Ness as a newly recruited National Trust volunteer in June 1995. There were four full-time staff wardens working on the property at this stage, busily occupied with the land management necessary to turn a military site into a nature reserve while also dealing with the demolition and tidying essential for making the property safe for visitors. The latter tasks were placed in the hands of the dozen or so somewhat bemused volunteers, whose understanding of what on earth Orford Ness was all about was often rather nebulous. The staff had little time to brief us. Excited visitors, fascinated by this hitherto secret place, bombarded us with a host of questions we could not easily deal with. It was sometimes tempting to make up our answers. How misled some of those early visitors were. It was in this context that I decided to exercise the skills I had acquired reading history at Cambridge. I began to find out just what had gone on in this secret site. This book is the product of ten years of mounting curiosity that led to five further years of more directed research.

Two issues of nomenclature. In referring to the place, I have been faced by a question of consistency. It is often referred to as the Ness (meaning 'nose' that sticks out into the sea), or even, by locals, as the island (which it isn't, yet). It can be written as a single word: Orfordness. Throughout this book however, I have adopted the convention of the formal geographical title 'Orford Ness' in two words.

One other word I have felt free to use throughout the book is 'boffin'. To call anyone before the Second World War a 'boffin' is incorrect. As I reveal, the word sprang out of work begun at Orford Ness and was coined only after 1940. Yet it has become so much part of our language that it seems perfectly reasonable to retrospectively describe the scientist/airmen of earlier decades, especially as they were so clearly doing exactly what boffins were famed for doing. The first boffin was a former Ness man. Indeed, Orford Ness might well have been renamed Boffin Island.

My research has stemmed from three chief sources. From the time of acquisition in 1993, the National Trust, with commendable foresight, began to assemble a comprehensive archive of material and pictures at their East of England Regional Office, now at Westley Bottom, near Bury St Edmunds. The second main source of information has been the National Archives (Public Record Office) at Kew. The third source has been the only other study of the place: *Orford Ness: Secret Site* by Gordon Kinsey, which was locally published in 1981. Kinsey of course was gravely handicapped in his enterprise. The Ness was still a secret and inaccessible military property. He could never visit it at the time of writing. Most files in the National Archives were similarly unavailable to him. However, he was able to contact a number of people who had served on the Ness and his work in identifying whatever was then in the public domain has provided an invaluable starting point for my rather fuller account of events between 1913 and 1993. I have 'borrowed' much from Kinsey and do so with his permission and blessing.

Is there any call for a history of Orford Ness? Apart from satisfying inevitable curiosity that stems from anything that has the magic word 'secret' attached to it, surely the nation owes a debt to those who served it in unpublicised – and in this case, largely unpublished – ways. For three quarters of a century, work was done on the Ness of real importance. The stories of Bletchley Park and Bawdsey Manor have been told. Now it's Orford Ness's turn.

A history of Orford Ness can be justified on three basic grounds. The very nature of its existence makes it a geographical phenomenon of real importance. The string of extraordinary military research projects it hosted only adds to its significance. This in turn has made it a place of unique atmosphere. It has a rare beauty, whatever the weather. Few people that visit it are unaffected by its wildness which only enhances the sense that history was made there.

Much background material has been culled from various published works. In some cases and where appropriate, these sources are quoted in the text, either as authorities and or as participants in the events described. I make no apology for including no bibliography, but I can assure the reader that I have authority for every fact quoted. If I have been in doubt, I have said so (as for example, in the role of Barnes Wallis' alleged visit and trials on the Ness). Though hidden away in remote East Suffolk, much that happened in secret on the Ness was most relevant to contemporary world events. Conclusions I have drawn as to their significance are based on informed judgements, for which I alone am responsible. Inter-war pacifism and consequent subterfuge is a case in point.

I regard this as a general historical study. Coverage of events and activities is representative rather than comprehensive. Moreover it is designed very much for the non-specialist reader. I have managed to discover much (though not all) about what happened on Orford Ness, when, and in most cases, why. I am not a technical expert, however, and the reader needing to discover the details of how weapons work is recommended to look elsewhere. I am of the generation that finds the science involved totally mystifying and have made little attempt to search this out for myself.

The National Archives holds many files relating to work done on the Ness. I am grateful to staff for pulling out many dozens of them over the course of a number of visits to Kew. Not far short of twenty sections have yielded information on the Ness, especially sections AIR and AVIA.

The following libraries and similar institutions proved most helpful:

The Imperial War Museum, London
The National Maritime Museum, Greenwich
The Cambridge University Library
The Orford Museum
The RAF Air Historical Branch
The RAF Museum, Hendon
The Radar Museum, Neatishead, Norfolk
The Royal Aeronautical Society Library
The Suffolk Wildlife Trust
The Suffolk County Library and Record Office services

The National Trust has created an audio archive and I record my indebtedness to the work of a volunteer, Roger Barrett, who assembled a significant collection of taped interviews. These have provided useful information and in some acknowledged instances, material which I have been able to quote verbatim.

I record with just as much gratitude the following (and many others doubtless omitted), who have given me first-hand information or pointed me in the right direction to discover it.

Jane Allen, John Anderson, John Backhouse, Len Beavis, Pat Bishop, Brian Boulton, Gordon Bruce, Brenda Carter, Maggie Cooper, Ken Daykin, D.F. Farrant, Chris Fisher, Lord Freeman, Vicky Gunnell, Charles Haynes, Harry Holmes, Chris Howard, Prof. Sir Bernard Lovell, Dennis Knights-Branch, Prof. Geoffrey Melvill Jones, David Miller, Iain Murray, Valerie Potter, Dr Ernest Putley, Brian Riddle, Clive Richards, Peter Rix, Bill Roberts, Ron Richardson, Keith Seaman, Margaret Shepherd, Bert Smith, Prof. Ramsay Spearman, Mary Stopes-Roe, Frank Tanner, Alistair Taylor, Geoffrey Taylor, Jane Timmins, Geoff Twibell, Adrian Underwood and Mike Vincent.

This project would have been out of the question but for the National Trust, which in its generous wisdom agreed to undertake its production. The Orford Ness wardens have been brilliant: Duncan Kent, Dave Cormack and Countryside Manager, Grant Lohoar. No less encouraging and helpful have been the Regional Director, Peter Griffiths and Archaeologist, Angus Wainwright. The Publishing Manager, Grant Berry at Heelis, Swindon and his counterpart at The History Press, Jo de Vries, have undertaken a mammoth task in making sense of the mess I submitted for publication and for the vital tasks of editing and proofreading.

For errors of fact or interpretation however, I am entirely to blame. A final word of thanks to a long-suffering family which has tolerated my interminable preoc-cupation with this story and the monopoly I seemed to assume over the family computer.

I fully recognise that the story of Orford Ness and with it, the revelation of its many secrets, is far from complete. Indeed, I am hoping that this book will provoke the unearthing of much more that I have failed to discover. The National Trust at Orford Ness will most warmly welcome further information, pictures and artefacts relating to this remarkable place. Contact should be made direct to the property, via: www.nationaltrust.org.uk.

Setting the Scene

As a place for keeping things secret, Orford is a good choice, for it is unexpectedly remote. In many respects, its contact with the rest of the world has relied on water as much as land. East Suffolk itself can seem very much off any beaten track with its relatively sparse rural population. Between Felixstowe to the south and Lowestoft on the Norfolk border lies some 40 miles of Suffolk's Heritage Coast, today an almost unbroken nature reserve. With no coastal road to link the intervening towns and villages, it remains a remarkably unspoilt and undeveloped corner of England.

There is only one classified road to Orford. The B1084 takes a distinctly circuitous route from Woodbridge, 10 miles to the west. This road ends uncompromisingly at a riverside quay. For quite a small place, it is quite a big quay. Its very size provides a real clue as to Orford's importance, particularly during nearly eighty years of military occupation of what locals often refer to as 'the island', the extensive stretch of marsh and shingle on the far side of the river Ore. Moreover, there is no way to continue on from Orford, except by boat. This so-called island is in fact a peninsula, narrowly and somewhat precariously attached to the Suffolk mainland at Slaughden, just to the south of Aldeburgh, some 6 miles, as the gull flies, to the north. This is Orford Ness.

There are good reasons for giving the means of communication with the outside world a prominent place in this history. Twisting roads and narrow lanes have always been an endearing feature of this part of the county. The railway from Ipswich to Lowestoft to the north passed 9 miles distant from Orford. Communications – or rather, the lack of them – have inevitably shaped the development of the village. Even the major trunk road to this part of the county, the A12, was only modernised years after secret operations on the Ness were over. Between 1915 and the early 1970s, enormous volumes of traffic, some of it very heavy, made its way along this inadequate route. That such considerable and complex projects were contemplated at such an inaccessible place is not the least of the mysteries of the Ness.

ORFORD BACKGROUND

Orford does not appear by name in the Domesday Book, and hence cannot claim quite the ancestry of some of its neighbours, like Snape or Iken or Sutton. It was no more than the coastal outlet for Sudbourne, now no more than a scattered village, but then a substantial and great estate, 2 miles inland. With a small but secure harbour, then much more open to access from the sea, Orford was a very suitable spot for Henry II to establish a base for exerting royal control. The castle was built to deal with various challenges to the King's rule, including possible threats from the exiled Thomas à Becket, as well as troublesome sons and rapacious local baronage, led in this district by Hugh Bigod of the nearby Framlingham Castle. Though Henry never visited Orford himself, his garrison must have stabilised the state of East Anglia and it certainly turned Orford itself from an insignificant fishing village into what was for a period, a notable town.

The power and dignity of Orford reached an early zenith in the reign of Elizabeth I, but even then, there were the first clear signs of impending decline. During the later medieval period, Orford had gained a charter entitling it to send two members to Parliament, a right that, disregarding the years of the Protectorate, only ended with the Reform Bill of 1832. The town's powers were extended by a series of Royal Charters, which gave it land and privileges.

Trade was under pressure, not least because of the shifting shingle spit, which increasingly blocked the harbour entrance. By the early eighteenth century, Orford came to be described by a noted visitor, Daniel Defoe, as 'once a good town, but now decayed'. Poverty and corruption marched hand in hand, making Orford a classic eighteenth-century rotten borough.

During the eighteenth century, the Seymour-Conway family acquired and developed the estate of Sudbourne Hall. With their title of Earls of Hertford their principal seat was in Warwickshire, at Ragley Hall. They added the manors of Iken and Gedgrave to their existing Suffolk estate, which included Orford village, the castle and the very quay on which all local trade relied. In 1793, the then Earl was created 1st Marquess of Hertford. The Sudbourne estate was attractive for much more than just its game sport. With the ownership of Orford came the lucrative patronage provided by its two parliamentary seats. The Hall was developed by the great architect James Wyatt and became notable for its art collection. The 4th Marquess was succeeded by his illegitimate son, Sir Richard Wallace, who sold the estate in 1884. The family treasures were transferred to their London house, now famed as the Wallace Collection.

Orford had benefited greatly by the generosity of the Hertford family, who built both the school and the Town Hall. With no railway and poor roads, the community was cut off from the rest of the county and was pretty self-reliant. Under its new owners, the Clarks, the estate was to give Orford another thirty years of relative prosperity. However, come the First World War, Orford was indeed fortunate that a new source of patronage appeared: the War Office.

Apart from the castle keep, another tower dominates the Orford skyline. This belongs to St Bartholomew's Church, which stands rather massively above the road that zigzags past it. Orford's church was originally no more than a chapel, the daughter church to Sudbourne, some 3 miles away. However, in 1295, with wealth rapidly increasing in the place, an Augustinian Friary was founded and the church in Orford expanded accordingly. Not all of its imposing structure has survived, and today little more than half of the original building remains. It is blessed by fine acoustics making it a favoured location for concerts and was chosen by Benjamin Britten for the première of *Noye's Fludde* and church parable operas.

Shortly before the only road enters Orford, it passes the edge of Sudbourne Park. The Hall, once a great focal point for grand society gatherings, was requisitioned by the military during the Second World War. Together with much of the countryside along this coast, the estate became part of a vast military training area in preparation for D-Day. The Hall, occupied by the Army, never recovered. Too damaged to be worth repairing, it was knocked down in 1951.

This sad event does not alter the fact that the village was a source of rest and recreation and indeed of hospitality for countless Ness personnel, both military and civilian. Its hostelries provided accommodation, venues for meeting and social gatherings, and at times, Officers' Mess facilities. Its church tower was a navigational marker for many of its airmen, and its churchyard, sadly, a resting place for a few of them. Personnel from the Ness learned to regard this area as their 'home from home'. It is remarkable how many preferred to stay in this part of Suffolk when their appointments at the Ness came to an end. Orford is an essential part of the story of Orford Ness, however secret the activity there was supposed to remain.

Whatever the season, the scene on the quay is seldom dull and in summer, 'fishing' for crabs provides endless excitement for the young. The observant may spot a highly significant craft, usually moored on the further bank, a substantial battleship-grey landing craft, which periodically crosses from its home on the Ness to run vehicles on and off from a ramp which slopes into the water. This vessel more than any other provides a graphic reminder of a military past.

For centuries, Orford Ness was known chiefly for the hazards of its notorious shore. It was always posing a potential threat to the busy passing traffic, shipping goods and raw materials down to London, as well as to the local inshore fishing trade. The call for some sort of aid to navigation reached a point in the seventeenth century when the need for action became irresistible. King Charles I was happy to grant a 'patent' to a private speculator rather than to Trinity House, one assumes because he could thereby benefit his Treasury.

A long sequence of pretty unsatisfactory wooden beacons followed, all in turn burnt down or washed away. The last of these was destroyed in a fierce storm in October 1789. The then owner, Lord Braybrooke, aware that this was a profitable asset that deserved a more robust construction, decided to construct a mighty new tower in stuccoed brick. It was completed in 1792. This is the lighthouse that has survived to the twenty-first century.

During the nineteenth century, the Orford Light was developed under the demanding stewardship of Trinity House, which acquired it by an Act of Parliament in 1837. Technical improvement followed, notably in the 1860s, when the eminent contractor James Timmins Chance installed new lenses and mirrors. Chance brought with him his consultant engineer, John Hopkinson, the inventor of a system for light flashing. His son was Bertram Hopkinson, who would play a vital role in the history of the Ness.

Further major development was undertaken during the decade before the outbreak of the First World War. The Orford Light was thus as advanced as any in the land when war broke out and the keepers found their whole way of life altered for good. From then on, they would have to share the Ness with new neighbours, both military and civilian.

This prelude to the Ness story aims to explain the setting and the context for events that took place there over the course of nearly eighty years when it was a secret place. Forbidding notices along the riverbank throughout this period used to warn people off: 'WARNING: This is a prohibited place within the meaning of the Official Secrets Act. Unauthorised persons entering this area may be arrested and prosecuted'. Perhaps all this hardly welcoming message did was to stimulate an added curiosity as to what was really going on. Its new owner, the National Trust has, for obvious reasons, found itself seemingly only a little less forbidding. 'Please keep out', run its notices. 'This site is not open to the public.' The notice explains this apparently qualified welcome: 'All the structures are very unsafe: There may be a risk from contamination and unexploded ordnance.' Sadly, access to the secret site has to be managed and controlled, even as visitors are encouraged and warmly welcomed.

When the National Trust purchased the Ness in 1993, it rescued the site from serious neglect. Such neglect would not only have destroyed the intrinsic value of the place, but would have constituted a disgraceful insult to the memory of a legion of people who gave great service to their country. For the secret researches and tests carried out on Orford Ness played no small part in the resolution of the three great wars of the twentieth century: the First, the Second and the Cold.

So, even now that it is in the custody of the National Trust, Orford Ness may still give an impression of being essentially a secret place. There are no brown signboards with the familiar oak leaf logo to point visitors from far and wide in its direction. By design and by circumstance, the place maintains its obscurity. Only the determined and discerning press their way to the quay. They may quickly come to regard their passage across the river as an adventure into a land of secrecy, privacy, 'cover stories' and mystery; of curiosity, challenge, danger, discomfort, enterprise and invention. One thing is frequently observed and has often been repeated by those who worked on the site over the years. Here is a place with an amazing atmosphere, a bit of magic and, in its unique fashion, an unmatched beauty.

When the Ness was officially opened to the public in June 1995 it ceased to be quite the mysterious and secret site of the previous eight decades. Visitors at the rate of up to 7,000 a year come to satisfy their curiosity, and see the place for themselves. For a National Trust property, the numbers are small: a great house would welcome that many over a few weeks in summer. The Ness is not a grand landscaped estate or ornamental garden and it provides no stately home. Its charm is its seclusion and loneliness and the fact that many of its past activities can only be imagined.

VISITORS' VOICES

This coast in general and Orford in particular has always enjoyed a long tradition of folk-tale and legend, of ghosts (M.R. James (1862–1936) the noted Cambridge scholar and writer of celebrated ghost stories, was greatly affected by East Suffolk), of smugglers and of violence. Here is the venue for the nineteenth-century romance of Margaret Catchpole and the smuggling fraternity. Latterly it has been the land of military secrets, and it has regularly provided inspiration for artists and writers.

The first and perhaps greatest interpreter of the Ness shore was J.M.W. Turner, who painted a number of watercolours as part of his important 'East Coast' collection during the 1820s.

Until it was opened to the public, descriptions with a Ness setting have been understandably rare. An exception appeared in 1938, when the thriller writer Richard Keverne, a former Royal Flying Corps (RFC) pilot, published his book *The Havering Plot*, set in a thinly disguised Ness. In 1992, shortly before the Trust takeover, the atmospheric writer and scholar W.G. Sebald paid a visit. A description of an afternoon on the site appeared in his memorable book *The Rings of Saturn*. He chose a rather gloomy day and was in a rather gloomy mood. Tellingly, and he was far from being alone here, he sensed what might be termed an 'Ozymandias' reaction to these evocative silhouettes on the seaward horizon:

> Look on my works, ye Mighty, and despair!'
> Nothing beside remains. Round the decay
> Of that colossal wreck, boundless and bare,
> The lone and level sands stretch far away.
>
> (P.B. Shelley)

The Ness was open to the general public only from 1995 and so the opportunity for artists and writers to be inspired by the place has inevitably been restricted. In recent years, the Ness has proved almost irresistibly attractive to artists, writers and photographers, actively encouraged by the National Trust.

Essential to the cultural heritage of Orford is the medieval myth of the 'Merman of Orford'. The story, as related by Ralph of Coggeshall, tells of the creature, half man and half fish, caught in Orford fishermen's nets and forced by torture to reveal who or what he was. Terrified that they had captured a devil who might corrupt them, they hurled him back into the sea off the Ness, and he was never seen again. This legend inspired the then Poet Laureate, Sir Andrew Motion to a write a major poem, published in the *Independent on Sunday* in July 1994. Here he subtly interpolates the Merman tale into his interpretation of the twentieth-century military activity.

As to other writers in recent years, these have largely been journalists, who have struggled to find sufficient information about the Ness, many sources remaining classified. Travel writer Christopher Somerville penned a portrait which appeared in *The Sunday Telegraph* in January 1998 and offers the best possible alternative to actually visiting the Ness. 'It was', he argues, 'probably the nearest you can come in England to walking in the desert...' The description given by the National Trust is 'the last coastal wilderness in southern England'. Somerville explains how the unique feature of the ridges and furrows in the shingle beach, which appeared 'to have had a giant's comb dragged lengthwise along it', were the product of centuries of wild storms. His is a brilliant picture in words.

Somerville reminded his readers of another feature of this Suffolk shore: its association with one of the great musicians of the twentieth century. Benjamin Britten, living locally most of his life, loved the characteristic sound of the Suffolk coast, and wove it into the fabric of *Curlew River* and *Peter Grimes*. For those with an ear for such a fantasy, the music of Britten and ghost of Grimes 'at his exercise' is never far away. For even if the air is still, there is the constant lap of water rolling up and down the shingle. The cry of swooping gulls is seldom absent. The constant winds blow through the railings on the staircase up to the Bomb Ballistics building's viewing platform. It makes a steady whistle and hum, varying in pitch and volume, like some eerie invisible orchestra.

The First World War and the RFC comes to the Ness

The first manned flight by a powered fixed-wing aircraft took place in 1903. The significance of this momentous achievement by the Wright brothers in remote Kitty Hawk, North Carolina may not have been appreciated at the time. Indeed, initially it was scarcely acknowledged in the United States and in Europe. While the Royal Aeronautical Society in London had inaugurated a lecture series in honour of Wilbur Wright as early as 1913, no equivalent event happened in America until 1937. A guest speaker at this inaugural event in the US was an Englishman, Professor Bennett Melvill Jones. He was one of many brilliant men whose flying career had been launched on Orford Ness in 1917. This curious lack of appreciation of the Wright brothers' achievement in their own land can be illustrated by one other extraordinary fact. Their pioneering biplane spent all its early years on display in London, at the Science Museum. It was transferred to Washington's National Air and Space Museum only in 1948.

The year 1903 was a significant year for other reasons. While a European war may not have seemed imminent, there were signs, on land and sea if not in the air, that an international war was a possibility. The very idea seemed to enjoy quite a degree of popular support. Jingoism was widespread. A German High Seas Fleet was being built, and a spy-thriller, published that same year, further provoked the fear that Britain could be attacked. *Riddle of the Sands* by Erskine Childers aroused some widespread interest, and was noted in official circles. It forecast a surprise invasion on the East Anglian coast by German barges. For a decade, similar wild plans were indeed in circulation around the German High Command, chiefly in order to curry favour with the anglophobe Kaiser. The idea was largely debunked by the more realistic Count von Tirpitz, architect of the Imperial German fleet and for nearly twenty years State Secretary of the Navy Office.

The main preparations for war on both sides of the North Sea did indeed tend to focus on naval developments. As early as 1909, the Royal Navy began to realise that the aeroplane might well have a useful part to play in future warfare. That year, Prime Minister Asquith set up an advisory committee under Lord Rayleigh to guide the War Office. He brought in professional academics to work with the military and the government, a cooperation that would be a major feature in the Orford Ness story over succeeding decades. Two years later, a generous bene-factor, Frank McLean, presented the Admiralty with the site of its first air station at Eastchurch, to enable aviators to be taught to fly. In some respects, therefore, the Navy took the lead in aerial warfare. With an easily excited and air-minded First Lord of the Admiralty in Winston Churchill, this was hardly surprising.

The War Office created its air wing in 1911, the same year as the Admiralty. The Army was much more conservative however. There was widespread suspicion of noisy machines, which 'might frighten the horses'. Initially, this air wing was to be no more than a branch of the Royal Engineers. Nevertheless, the recruitment of eager volunteers truly excited by the novel experience of flying led it to evolve rapidly into a unit in its own right: the newly designated Royal Flying Corps (RFC). It was founded in a formal and identifiable sense in April 1912 and was in operation a month later.

By 1913, it had established its headquarters at Farnborough and acquired a further station at Netheravon in Wiltshire, close to the vast military centres at Tidworth and Larkhill. It was also near what in May 1912 had become the Central Flying School for pilot training at Upavon, used by Army and Navy alike: its first commanding officer was in fact a naval officer, Capt. Godfrey Paine RN. He was appointed by an enthusiastic Churchill, and given just two weeks to learn how to fly in order to prepare him for his new role as Commandant.

At the same time, the Army was beginning to take the part the RFC might play in warfare more seriously. RFC requirements came to be given proper consideration. By the early autumn, various memos were in circulation defining the current state of the Corps, as well as indicating the priorities in realising its immediate needs. In particular, there was talk now of making provision in the military estimates for the purchase of land and the construction of barracks and special buildings. A plan was revealed, expanding the RFC to at least eight squadrons of aircraft by 1914. Of course, at that stage, the timing of the outbreak of a full-scale war could only have been surmised. A survey of resources around the British Isles was undertaken. This indicated just how few aircraft and airfields there were at this juncture. The bulk of these were in the hands of private amateur enthusiasts. The Army spelled out various criteria for selecting suitable sites for its airfields. The emphasis was clear: the RFC was to be seen largely as an adjunct to the land Army. Air stations must be near to existing concentrations of troops and used in their support. This perhaps explains the apparent preoccupa-tion with sending RFC squadrons to Ireland, where the political tension was by then serious.

In view of the primitive and hence unreliable nature of the aircraft of the day, these air stations were to be 'in the countryside and suitable for flying over'.

Urban locations might be too dangerous. A 15-mile radius of open fields with low hedges and the minimum of woodland were suggested requirements, with the odd lake or proximity of the sea – 'not less than 3 miles distant' – to assist in navigation and orientation. A level strip a mile in length would be needed, with a site for accommodation barracks not less than 3 miles away. Just to complicate matters, and for fairly obvious reasons, a nearby town to supply a repair base was considered important. Railway access was also a recommendation. Reflecting on these recommendations, it is interesting to note how relatively few seemed to apply to Orford Ness.

In the light of this sense of increasing urgency, officers were dispatched around the country to recommend suitable sites. Perhaps typical of these tours was that by Major Brooke-Popham, who surveyed the area between Fareham and Cosham and other localities round Southampton Water. Major Brooke-Popham was to become a senior RFC officer and by 1919, a Brigadier-General and Director of Research, and thus closely involved in work on the Ness. By the 1930s he was the Air Chief Marshal who helped make the RAF ready for the next world war, but in 1913, following his tour of the countryside, he was unable to recommend a single possible site for the RFC. In addition, it was evident that during the last few months of pre-war calm, the landed classes were far from willing to consider sacrificing their private interests to any sort of national requirement. 'Nimbyism', a feeling of 'not in my back yard', was alive and healthy. In November 1913, a conference attended by no fewer than three Major-Generals (Cowan, Van Donop and Scott-Moncrief) was held to discuss the situation. A number of suggestions were put forward, like taking over the Dover Prison buildings to hasten the provision of an airfield in a strategic location, obviating the need to build barracks. By now, the southeast corner of England was identified as the crucial area for RFC deployment.

Shortly before this, in September 1913, correspondence within the War Office revealed the promise of a third air station, following on from Farnborough and Netheravon. 'Purchase of some land at Orford Ness is about to be completed', reported the RFC commanding officer, Brigadier-General David Henderson[*], 'and I propose to establish at least one squadron there. This station, which is on an island, [sic] is required to enable certain experimental work to be carried on in privacy. It is within reasonable distance of the troops at Colchester, Ipswich and Norwich.' This same letter, with its very first reference to the Ness in the War Office files, mentioned a number of other places that were being targeted by the RFC, including sites in Chatham, Lydd, Hyde, Shorncliffe and Dover. One air station not listed was already established on rented property at Montrose in Scotland. It was from here that an early notable achievement by RFC aircraft is recorded. Six planes successfully flew the considerable distance to take part in summer manoeuvres in southern Ireland in 1914.

---

[*] Henderson, with Hugh Trenchard, was a founding father of the RAF.

When war broke out, the Army operated just seven stations, a number that had risen to over 300 by 1918. Orford Ness had become a military site, and remained so for another eighty years. It can thus claim the distinction of being one of the very oldest air stations in England. However, for legal reasons, the acquisition was not totally straightforward, and this explains the considerable delay between the War Office statement in September 1913 and the actual arrival of the first aircraft over two years later.

The title deeds, now in the hands of the National Trust, show that the initial purchase was of some 155 acres of King's Marsh, and is dated as early as 16 August 1913. The named vendors of this section of the site were Edward Moberly and Mary Louise Tyler. They appear to have been occupying tenants of what was a property quite seriously compromised by what the legal documents refer to as 'adverse matters'. These were traditional grants in support of local parishes, manorial rights and customary agreements. One of these was a right to extract from the beach 150 tons of shingle per annum. The complicated business of dealing with tenancy rights and all other similar obstructions to acquiring the total freehold delayed matters until 13 December 1914. It had involved a certain amount of wrangling. Thus, the making of the grazing marshlands ready for use by aircraft was delayed and work cannot have begun until early 1915.

The main sale of the Ness was dated 20 January 1914 and referred to the bulk of the site. The price for the 1,500 acres of 'Saltings' and 'Orford Beach' was £9,250. A further £500 to obtain release from free rent and other commitments meant that the War Office ultimately paid a total of £13,750 for their Ness property. Eighty years later, the MoD's asking price was a twenty-fold increase on this original purchase cost.

This land formed a peripheral part of the 11,000 acre Sudbourne Estate and its sale marked the beginning of its break-up, a fact of life for many large agricultural holdings during these years. Now owned by a very wealthy but improvident and extravagant Scottish industrialist, Sudbourne Hall was enjoying a terminal flourish of Edwardian splendour. Kenneth Mackenzie Clark restored the Hall, making it the happiest of homes for his noted son, Kenneth, later Lord Clark, of *Civilisation* fame. His grandson, historian and politician Alan Clark, will in turn appear later in the story of the Ness in his role of Defence Minister. The writing was on the wall and the decline of the estate culminated in the abandonment and demolition of the Hall in 1951.

So Orford Ness, well over 2,000 acres in all, for so long just an appendage to a great estate across the river, began to develop a significance and identity in its own right. This was based in large measure on the very fact that it was cut off from the mainland, affording, as the War Office described it, 'privacy'.

For the reasons described above, there was an apparent hiatus before more frenetic military activity could begin in late 1915. What had in 1913 seemed ideal for the purposes of an experimental station from the viewpoints of location and availability was certainly not so ideal in terms of terrain. The marshland had to be transformed from its uses as grazing for livestock and as a playground for affluent sportsmen. There were channels and ditches and humps and bumps, all of which had to be transformed into a flat and essentially dry field suitable for take-off and landing. In fact from the outset it was more accurate to say 'fields', for a channel was left for the roadway (and later a narrow-gauge railway) leading from the jetty on the river to the station's buildings. In effect there was a pair of airfields. Such an arrangement was not so uncommon in the early days: one thinks of Croydon or Lulsgate at Bristol. An accident on one side would not necessarily cause closure of the other.

There seems to have been no sign of any impatience at the delay in gaining access. It was always scheduled to be an experimental station and it could be argued that the RFC needed time to discover just what experiments actual warfare conditions at the Front would necessitate.

The arrangement of Britain's air forces in 1914 was very much at a formative stage. The RFC, and the naval wing, the Royal Naval Air Service (RNAS), each had a distinct area of responsibility. For a while, defending the coastline was seen as a job for the Navy: home defence was just a part of the RNAS brief. It was therefore Churchill from the Admiralty who defined the tactics for dealing with aerial attacks. This was the position in September 1914, at a time when the nation was defended by only seven operational RFC air stations; the prime responsibility of the RFC was to support the Army in the field, and not to protect the civilian population at home. The Navy and Army had scarcely 120 aircraft in service, less than half the number available to the numerically much larger armed forces of France, Germany and Russia.

The Admiralty directives argued that if possible, enemy aircraft be engaged at, or near, their bases, and that priority for locating anti-aircraft guns would go to military installations. Cities should receive no such protection but rely on blackout. The success of the first Zeppelin raids from 1915 prompted a more methodical defence arrangement, necessitating the creation of RFC's so-called Home Defence squadrons, to work with the RNAS. This all resulted in various rivalries and inevitable conflicts. Home Defence squadrons for example did not take kindly to an experimental station like Orford Ness involving itself in its sphere of responsibility. There was a marked and fierce rivalry between the RNAS and the RFC.

When work on preparation of the military facilities began on the Ness, the Central Flying School had been established at Upavon. In late 1914, a unit known as the Armament Experimental Flight, commanded by Capt. A.H.L. Soames, M.C., was created, also at Upavon, to develop techniques and equipment for the effective tactical use of aircraft as weapons of war. This was the unit that was transferred to the Ness. Its functions shaped the sort of work that Orford Ness would be undertaking for the rest of its existence as a military site.

In an almost lyrical passage in his book, Gordon Kinsey suggested that the impact on the servicemen involved in the move to East Anglia must have been pretty shattering, even by wartime standards. It will have seemed: '... a scene of complete desolation. After the rolling hills of Wiltshire this flat, lonely marshland, barely above sea level, with its bitter easterly wind, must have made the new arrivals wish they had been posted anywhere else but here.'

Initially, it seems that accommodation had to be found for many of the troops in Orford itself and the officers used the Crown and Castle Hotel as their 'mess'. This was to be far from the only time that this hostelry was to play its part in the work done on the Ness. Orford's fine Town Hall, the gift to the community of the 4th Marquess of Hertford, was for a while used as station headquarters.

Gordon Kinsey quotes a recollection of an Orford inhabitant, Lou Anderson, the village tailor:

> We were all excited one day to see the arrival of six large RFC lorries, as our village was at that time a backwater and large lorries were not an everyday sight. They were loaded with large bales of canvas and long poles, which turned out to be portable hangars for aeroplanes. Other large and small items of equipment could be seen piled up on the backs of the vehicles as they trundled through the village down to the quay.

The recreation ground was commandeered for marquees and bell tents, while the officers were billeted in the hotels and other larger houses. Mr Friend's Garage was used as the motor transport depot and boats were acquired to ferry the men across the river each day until more permanent facilities were constructed. The sight of so many servicemen must have come as both a thrill and a shock to the local population.

Primitive buildings, mostly of a pre-fabricated wooden type, were erected for the troops and for administration, while the aircraft were initially housed in canvas hangars. These were essentially tents, shaped to accommodate the wings and fuselage of a single aeroplane. During 1916 larger canvas hangars and rectangular wooden Bessoneau hangars (a type named after its inventor) were erected, to be followed later by two even larger and more permanent structures, the so-called Belfast Truss constructions. In 1918, a pair of the largest hangars of all was built to house twin-engined aircraft. These seem to have been to a design unique to the Ness and they were sufficiently strong to give many decades of service.

All these buildings were arranged in a long sprawl on the eastern side of the fields, about 1 kilometre from the river jetty. On the seaward side of these buildings was the tidal creek, Stony Ditch, which separated the marshland from the great shingle spit, at this point around 800 metres wide. A very clear picture of how these buildings were arranged is provided by a series of aerial photographs taken in 1917 and 1918 (see Plate Section).

The actual opening of Orford Ness took place during October 1915. The official commissioning of the Ness station came the following year, on 15 May 1916. The first squadron to arrive was given the number 37, and came from the Experimental Flying Section from within the Central Flying School in Upavon, but it would be a mistake to describe the personnel or planes on the station in terms of defined or fixed squadrons. A constant flow of aircraft and people came and went, constituting the Orford Ness Armament Experimental Flight.

From early 1917, there was an added complication over nomenclature and staffing. The Experimental Flight, which had begun work on the Ness in 1916, was to grow into a greater and more imposing organisation. The Ness was no longer quite extensive enough. Two important officers were dispatched from the Ness to Ipswich to look for another airfield site, to extend the trial facilities. These were Lieutenant Henry Tizard and Captain Bertram Hopkinson, both archetypical Ness figures, high-powered and extremely brave, and very notable academics. They observed that a field on Martlesham Heath, part of the Pretyman estates, which stretched northwards from Orwell Park at Nacton to the east of Ipswich, was already being used as an aircraft landing field. Their recommendation was that the whole site be acquired.

Martlesham Heath opened in January 1917 as the RFC Aeroplane Experimental Research Station. The Ness meanwhile had its title defined as the RFC Armament Experimental Research Station. From 1920, the word 'Establishment' replaced 'Station' and in 1924, with the reopening of Orford Ness after a temporary suspension, the whole organisation of the two stations was officially called the Aeroplane and Armament Experimental Establishment (A&AEE).

For several reasons Martlesham immediately assumed the 'senior' status. Martlesham was considerably bigger than the Ness. It was closer to a large urban centre, Ipswich, and located beside the A12 road and just a mile from Bealings station[*] on the Lowestoft branch of the Great Eastern Railway. Over the years, the two air stations shared research projects and the personnel to conduct them. Indeed, it is almost impossible to claim that a Martlesham pilot was not also an Orford Ness pilot. Similarly, another smaller research field was established a year later, in January 1918, at Butley, a heathland site in the Rendelsham estate.

A host of trials and experiments took place at all three stations, and indeed at a fourth, attached to the seaplane base at Felixstowe. So, by the end of the war, four of the seven experimental air stations in the hands of the RAF were located in this cluster in east Suffolk, and further south, beside the Medway in Kent, was the naval equivalent, the Isle of Grain Research Station, also transferred from Upavon.

The two stations at Orford and Martlesham rapidly established an enviable reputation for skilled flying, meticulous attention to detail in their researches and for bare courage in what could be a highly dangerous occupation. Moreover there was a constant turnover of personnel, with plenty of interchange between the two stations. Describing these pilots, the historian (and former Women's Auxiliary Air Force (WAAF) officer) Constance Babbington Smith wrote: '... the

---

[*] Bealings was closed by British Rail in 1956, well before the Beeching 'axe' removed so many country stations during the 1960s. The closure coincided with the running down of RAF Martlesham Heath.

very name Martlesham came to stand for everything that was most accurate and thorough in test flying. A Martlesham pilot was by definition one who could turn his hand to testing any variety of aeroplane and a Martlesham report meant a report that indicated an analysis of unprecedented detail and comprehensiveness.' Gordon Kinsey confirms that 'to be a Martlesham test-pilot was to be one of the elite of the profession'. These tributes applied no less to an Orford Ness test pilot. To be an Orford Ness scientist, boffin or pilot was to demonstrate the highest standards of research, worthy of any great university. This is indeed where so many of these men came from.

It would be perhaps a mistake to attempt to define a tidy or conventional hierarchical structure for the operation of these stations. In the case of Orford Ness, there was a Commanding Officer, in the rank of Major or Lieutenant-Colonel. His job was to become increasingly administrative, running the organisation of the station, which by 1918 on the Ness was to grow into a sizeable unit, with over 600 men and women on site. He also held overall responsibility for conducting the trials. His signature would follow that of the trials officers in the official reports. Major Wanklyn was the inaugural Commanding Officer (C/O) until early 1917. It is significant, just to indicate how blurred the lines of authority were, that he was a regular pilot in trials and clearly wanted to be involved. Wanklyn was followed by Major J.B. Cooper, whose appointment coincided with a number of changes in personnel. In spring 1918 he was replaced by Lieutenant-Colonel Shackleton, who presided over the transfer from RFC to RAF in April 1918. By the end of the war, Lieutenant-Colonel Boddham-Whetton had taken over.

Above the C/O was the highly significant figure of Major, soon promoted Lieutenant-Colonel Bertram Hopkinson, who acted as mastermind and liaison with the War Office. The naval analogy would be that of the Commodore in his relationship with the Captain of a flagship. Hopkinson helped set up both the Ness and Martlesham. Sadly, he died shortly before the end of the war, and no replacement was appointed to fill the post.

Hopkinson was a very remarkable man indeed. He took a first class degree in Mathematics at Trinity College, Cambridge and promptly decided to train for the Bar to become a barrister. Before completing this course of study, his father died in a climbing accident. His father was an eminent engineer, who had invented the system of light flashing used in the lighthouse and who had installed it on site half a century earlier. Bertram immediately abandoned all thoughts of a legal career and took over his father's engineering consultancy business. He was only twenty-four, but he was so able that he was elected a Fellow of King's College, Cambridge despite having taken no higher degree. At the age of twenty-nine he was made Professor of Mechanical Engineering at the university. His experience as a teacher enabled him to select the brightest students, often his own pupils, to work on the Ness. One of the most outstanding of these was Bennett Melvill Jones, a man whose achievements as a boffin were destined to match those of his tutor.

On the outbreak of war, Hopkinson joined the Royal Engineers and was directly instructed to organise the fortifications of the UK to deal with any attempted invasion. He admitted that this was a science about which he knew nothing. Fortunately, any serious threat of sea-borne attack rapidly disappeared. He was then transferred to the RFC to lead research and development, a field to which he was eminently more suited.

His function was to provide the interface with the War Office and ensure that the research stations in Suffolk were properly resourced and given assignments appropriate to their facilities. His family, which included seven daughters, lived in Crag Cottage, 3 miles or so out of Orford. Mrs Wooley, one of the seven, has given the National Trust an interview, recalling childhood memories of her imposing father, a man she associates with a loud laugh and a terrific sense of fun. She vividly remembers the occasion of a 'rest and recreation' swimming gala, when the children were brought over to witness the airmen having fun and games in a special 'lido', a swimming enclosure created in the river. They travelled in a large staff motorcar.

Hopkinson felt that he should share the dangers of trials flying which he required of his test pilots. By now over forty, he learned to fly. It was evident that he relished the opportunity to take part himself in some of the experimental flights. This was a risky undertaking: some referred to the RFC as the 'suicide club'. In August 1918, he took off for a meeting at Farnborough and encountered fog in the Home Counties. He was flying solo, lost his way and suffered a fatal crash. His loss was a deeply felt blow. Many considered that the nation lost the services of a man who could have made a major contribution to aeronautical development over the decades that followed. Sir Henry Tizard went as far as declaring that, had he not been killed, 'the chance of a second world war breaking out would have been greatly lessened'. An immediate consequence was a curtailment in letting scientists become pilots.

THREE GREAT MEN OF THE NESS

By 1916, the Orford Ness RFC station had already taken on three pre-eminent academic pilot/scientists from Upavon, in Henry Tizard, Frederick Lindemann and Bennett Melvill Jones. All three were recruited from the universities and destined to reach the highest positions in their academic fields either as university heads or professors. They commanded the three sections of research activity:

- Fighters, bombers, reconnaissance aircraft
- Bombs and bombing releases
- Tactics and enemy aircraft

They were responsible for coordinating the work done by the three flights of aircraft that corresponded to these areas of research, with specific service demands, which came through the War Office's RFC Headquarters at Adastral House in London and its base at Farnborough.

They were therefore essential and regular members of the Ness research and trial teams. They were never there exclusively however, and all three were also Martlesham pilots. Indeed, Martlesham's reputation for brilliant research flying was attributed very much to Tizard's leadership. Lindemann was particularly involved in bomb technology. One of the so-called 'Chudleigh Mess' – named after the billet in which they were accommodated at Farnborough – he was a notably brave and skilled pilot, developing as infallible techniques of flying out of hitherto fatal spins as could be defined in those days. Spin and stall were the lethal hazards for inexperienced pilots of primitive aircraft with uncertain engines. In a single month, May of 1918, forty-one of the 108 recorded flying accidents arose from uncontrolled spins. Trying to remedy this problem was largely a Farnborough responsibility, but, as will be shown, Orford Ness boffins were involved.

Lindemann was also a pioneer in the development of early bomb sights and improving the ballistics of bomb cases, and this was very much Ness territory. He supplied the link with the Royal Aircraft Factory (as it then was titled)[*], at Farnborough, which would manufacture the equipment. Lindemann's character was a strange mix of courage, persistence and eccentricity. He would fly from Hampshire to Martlesham and before going on to the Ness, would change out of his flying gear into a long velvet-collared coat and bowler hat, sporting, of course, a rolled umbrella. During these early years, Tizard and Lindemann were colleagues and friends. They had first met in Germany before the outbreak of war.

Tizard came from a naval family but poor eyesight led to his commitment to an academic career. From Westminster School he went to Magdalen College, Oxford where he gained distinction as a mathematician and chemist. He worked on high performance fuels, in particular the development of high octane rating. He was eventually to be elected Provost of the college. Recruited into the RFC by Hopkinson, Tizard proved to be less of a great pilot than a great administrator and organiser, and a brilliant judge of ideas that would work. He was to make an unmatched career as a coordinator of military research, in the Department of Scientific and Industrial Research and as Rector of Imperial College, London. The importance of his judgement in backing Watson Watt's work with radar, the gas turbine engines of Frank Whittle and the bouncing bombs of Barnes Wallis goes without saying. Tizard and Lindemann are to return to the Ness story, but as bitter rivals.

The Melvill Jones family, as father and son, proved to be uniquely important as scientist/boffins at Orford and Farnborough, once again typifying over the years the brilliance of the men the RAF had available to them. Bennett grew up in Birkenhead, the son of a barrister who was also an amateur engineer. At school,

---

[*] The Factory changed its name to Establishment in 1918, to avoid confusion with the newly created RAF.

his enlightened headmaster allowed him to miss cricket to pursue his enthusiasm for engineering. This led to his election to an exhibition to the family college, Emmanuel, Cambridge. Here, he was taught by Bertram Hopkinson, and his future as a boffin was almost preordained. Via Woolwich Arsenal and the National Physical Laboratory Aeronautical Department at Teddington, he qualified for a further research scholarship at Imperial College, where he undertook some remarkable work before the First World War on airflow over wing surfaces. 'Bones', as he was known, led work on air armaments, air gunnery and instrumentation and after training to fly in 1915, he had some fighting experience during 1918, winning an AFC (Air Force Cross) and ending the war as a Lieutenant-Colonel. After a few months working for the RAF, he returned to Cambridge as a lecturer, whereupon he was elected to a Fellowship in his old college, Emmanuel, and shortly after, at the age of only thirty-three, to the newly founded Chair of Aeronautical Engineering.

This proved to be a difficult assignment, chiefly because his work was grossly under-funded. However, despite this, he conducted research of the highest significance on aerodynamics, which led to the concept of the 'Ideal Streamline Aeroplane' and directly influenced aeronautical design, particularly that of the Spitfire and Hurricane. Writing in the *Journal of the Royal Aeronautical Society*, A.V. Stephens has commented on the visionary quality of this work: 'The case for the streamline aeroplane came at just the right moment.' Such ideas, smacking of H.G. Wells, would have been dismissed ten years earlier. Designers were set to invent cantilever wings and retractable undercarriages, variable pitch propellers, landing flaps and duct cooling. 'These problems would have been solved in any case. But it is possible that without the timely lead from Melvill Jones there would have been no Spitfires and Hurricanes to win the Battle of Britain.' Was it entirely a coincidence that at just this time the railway companies were introducing streamlined locomotives to haul crack expresses *Silver Jubilee* and *Coronation Scot*?

The three sections of research activity each operated a flight of aircraft allocated to particular specialties. A group photograph taken in January 1917, shows just eight pilots in all*, with the two Commanding Officers, Hopkinson and Cooper, seated in front. The Section Commanders, Tizard, Lindemann and Melvill Jones would be 'on business' elsewhere. Each section had a flight of aircraft, not necessarily the latest types, since speed was never as important as reliability and stability. The three flights were assigned to arming and equipping smaller and medium-sized aircraft, to bombs, bombing and bombers, and finally to tactics. Added to these were what later came to be described as 'vulnerability and lethality' testing. More than that, specific projects could always be rushed their way in response to particular military requirements. Any demarcations seem therefore to have been far from strict and moreover a pilot might find himself required to fly more than

---

* These eight pioneers were Bourdillon, Holder, Barrett, Clarke, Oxley, Collett, Gribble and Brown.

one type of plane in a single day. This was years before the need for specialist training or 'conversion courses'. The records show that a spectacular range of research projects was accepted, especially as airmen on active service, from practical experience at the Front, volunteered suggestions for solving the technical problems they encountered in action.

Wartime Pioneers

In October 1916, the Advisory Committee for Aeronautics, part of the Department of Scientific and Industrial Research, sent a team to inspect what was happening at the Ness. They reported that there were currently eight specific trials being conducted. These included machine-gun firing at targets towed from an airplane or hung from balloons, and flying model aircraft for testing guns sights. Phosphorous bombs for attacking balloons as well as incendiary bullets for dealing with Zeppelins were under test, as were various different types of high explosive for standard bombs. Being tried out was a new type of bombsight, the so-called 'Lucas' sight. Also under survey was a hydraulic timing gear for gun firing. Finally, they were exploring means of producing artificial clouds.

THE HOLDER CONTRIBUTION

Who were the pilots who did this work, much of it dangerous and even more of it tediously repetitive, and all of it in what could often prove a lonely and unattractive environment? From historic photographs and documentary evidence, many of their names are known. One of them has left a detailed account of his experiences, recalled from his personal flight log. In his article published in the specialist journal *Cross and Cockade International* in 1977, Squadron Leader F.D. Holder, OBE, MC, JP, DL provides a vivid and extensive picture of work on the Ness between early 1917 and the culmination of trials in 1919.

Frank Holder joined the East Kent Regiment at the start of the war, and soon transferred to the RFC, gaining his wings at Upavon, whence, after being interviewed by Hopkinson in London, he was sent to the Ness, joining in January 1917. His experience was to be unusual: he was not moved on elsewhere but spent the rest of the war working there. Rapidly promoted to be I/C (In Command)

'A' Flight, he was in a position to see the whole of the station's development and witness most of the ever-widening range of trials that took place.

His first impression was clearly of the remarkably high calibre of his colleagues. Humphrey Raikes, Bennett Melvill Jones and Ralph Griffiths were Oxbridge dons. Robert Bourdillon was another Oxford academic, destined to be knighted for his services to medical research. Five other colleagues were to end their service careers as Air Marshals.

Much of the work that Holder and his fellow airmen did was mundane, repetitive and fruitless flying. Added to this was the constant hazard of flying fragile and unreliable machines in which he and his fellow airmen had to entrust their very lives. Seldom if ever were all the aircraft scheduled for a trial fit to fly, and often flights had to be hurriedly aborted. He describes how in 1917, his former colleague, Bourdillon, returned to the Ness to investigate a serious structural failure in the DH9 aeroplane, a number of which had suffered a broken tail when in a spin. 'He suggested I should take him up', recalls Holder, 'and try a few spins to see what happened. We spent a cheerful half hour spinning at 10,000 ft and all went well. It was not until a year later that I heard the cause of the bother was the shortage of ash. Other wood was being substituted, which could not take the strain.' Clearly the aircraft they had taken up was constructed with appropriate and safe materials. The potential for disaster that faced these men needs no elaboration.

An early task assigned to Holder involved machine-gun firing, using new types of gun mounting. This included devising gun-sights and effective techniques for firing at oblique angles (not just straight ahead) and using appropriate – that is, not so bright as to dazzle the gunner – tracer ammunition to assist in targeting.

One particular trial of interest was designed to permit firing through the arc of the propeller to enable a single-seat scout pilot to shoot straight ahead from his cockpit. This necessitated an 'interrupter' mechanism, invented by Rumanian inventor and engineer, George Constantinescu. He came to the Ness in the spring of 1917 to demonstrate his idea and supervise the test. The mechanism operated by controlling the firing of the gun through a link with the pulsations of the oil in the engine. Shortly afterwards the system was put to the test in action by Holder, flying a Bristol Fighter during a raid by Gotha bombers attacking London. Like almost every fighter pilot, he was never able to lay a finger on these formidable adversaries.

Another visitor that spring of 1917 was the unfortunate inventor, Everard Richard Calthrop, who had poured his own money into his 'Guardian Angel' parachute apparatus. He had been inspired to develop this gadget by the death in a flying accident in 1910 of his friend, Charles Rolls, the pioneering motorist and aviator and first man to fly across the channel and back in a single uninterrupted flight.

It was RFC policy to show no more than polite interest in the device, echoing the sentiments expressed by *Flight Magazine* in September 1913: '... we see very little future for the parachute as a life-saving apparatus in emergency on planes.' Rather patronisingly, the editorial went on: 'We nevertheless are far from discarding the ingenious invention'. Indeed, articles in later issues of this magazine were to express disbelief that the authorities were so reluctant to adopt it. Moreover, Calthrop was no casual amateur. A highly qualified and experienced construction engineer, he was responsible for building narrow gauge railways both in India and at home. The notable Leak and Manifold line was his brainchild.

Early in 1914, the first successful Guardian Angel parachute jump was made at Hendon from 2,000 feet. The RFC went as far as taking the apparatus to Farnborough to design a reduction of its excessive weight. It was not until 1917 that an attempt was made to give it an operational trial for use in military aircraft. The Ness teams castigated the system as being dangerous, physically harmful and totally impractical under battle conditions. Holder describes the whole episode:

> … the gear was carried from Woodbridge in a Leyland lorry with the two assistants beside the driver. On the way the flywheel burst, fortunately without any injury to personnel but leaving two badly shaken mechanics.
>
> The parachute was packed in a container and fastened to a hinged bracket under the nacelle [of the aeroplane]. The packing was very complicated and took the two men most of the morning to do. The parachutist wearing a harness had to climb out onto the wing, being careful not to twist the connecting cords, and jump between the main and tail planes. The effect of his weight pulled the parachute out of its container. Collett [a very experienced pilot, shortly to leave the Ness] was chosen to do the jumping with Captain Gribble flying a BE2c. It was entirely successful and repeated under rather blustering conditions for the benefit of Adastral House [RFC HQ] on the following day.

Collett was the first RFC airman to make a parachute descent from an aeroplane over the Ness. Calthrop's invention was never adopted by the RFC for aircraft, much to his chagrin and financial hardship. The reaction of the Ness staff was that it was quite impractical for use in emergency – which of course would be the circumstance of its usefulness. The report indicated concern that it was liable to cause a damaging jerk on the body of the escaper. Moreover, the bracket with the chute in it would impair aircraft performance.

Holder would later try out the 'Mears' parachute. Captain Mears had been in charge of the dogs on Scott's Antarctic expedition and no doubt used his knowledge of dogs' traces to make a parachute harness that would be safe and easy to manage. This could easily have been adapted for use on a larger scale but was rejected by the leaders of the RFC and RNAS because they thought it would impair the fighting qualities of pilots and cause needless destruction of aircraft as it would encourage cowardice. Officials were concerned that when attacked or damaged, pilots might choose to bale out rather than continue to fight or nurse their valuable aircraft home.

The policy of disregarding the use of parachutes, also adopted at this stage by the French and German air forces, shows an extraordinary attitude to the value of human life and the apparent priority given to fragile and far from efficient aircraft over expensively trained aircrew. By the last few months of the war, the Germans did widely adopt parachutes. A trial conducted in September 1918 on the Ness involving another Guardian Angel concluded that the RAF would really be advised to look at German practice. It may be surmised that the purpose of conducting this further trial was to provide a means of dropping agents or scouts behind enemy lines. Meanwhile, Allied pilots were being lost in large numbers and it was estimated subsequently that 500 lives could have been saved in active service had parachutes been issued. To that total of lost young lives must be added many more still, killed in flying training. The RAF finally relented, ordering some 500 kits in late 1918, too late for the war. During 1919, trials of an American Holt system took place over the Ness, although no report on its outcome has survived. When in 1926, parachutes were made standard issue, the US Irvin pattern was adopted. A year later, aged seventy and a disappointed man, Calthrop died.[1]

The irony of all this was not lost on RAF personnel during the '20s. For while so many airmen were lost, on the false understanding that 'no case is known of any officer wishing to provide himself with a parachute', 800 lives had been saved by parachutes issued to crews of observation balloons. Sholto Douglas was one of many RAF officers to express their fury at this official policy when its true implications were revealed. The tragedy of this misguided policy was made evident within weeks of the Armistice. In December 1918, an article appeared in *Flight* magazine confirming just how many German lives had been saved by their use of albeit relatively primitive parachutes.

In this context, it is interesting that Holder and his colleagues were testing two other pieces of equipment. Holder himself took part in early attempts at using oxygen for high altitude flying. In retrospect, it may appear extraordinary that the possible benefit of this support for pilots was not further investigated. Flying at 15,000 feet and above puts pilots under severe strain. Since Zeppelins' ability to climb even higher was their sole sure means of escape from RFC defence fighters, this policy appears almost negligent. At the time however, the general consensus was that the chief difficulty was not lack of oxygen but extreme cold. Sadly, a similar negative approach was adopted towards electrically heated flying suits being used at the Ness. At extreme altitude, in open cockpits, aircrew could easily suffer serious frostbite and hypothermia, but the authorities were more concerned about the safety of their aircraft and feared the possibility of an electrical fault causing fire. Heated suits were not routinely adopted until many years later.

More personnel were being sent to the Ness, not all necessarily pilots. One such was Walden Hammond. He is described as 'a real enthusiast', who flew whenever the opportunity to take the spare seat arose. He was a pioneering photographer of technical brilliance and rare imagination. That so much is known about Orford

Ness in these early years is in part due to the wonderful pictures he took and to the fact that his family preserved so many of them. Hammond and Holder were close friends and much of Hammond's work was done with Holder as pilot. A notable example is the series of pictures of the Theberton Zeppelin, shot down in June 1917 (see Plate Section). Hammond's pictures of aircraft in flight were far in advance of anything previously attempted, including a sequence showing Vernon Brown looping the loop in a Sopwith Triplane.

Of greater military significance were Hammond's researches. He tried to find a means of compensating for inevitable vibration when photographing from an aeroplane. He experimented with new ideas, one of which was for taking aerial reconnaissance shots at an oblique angle. He then attached a perspective grid to indicate range. The Army always required that for intelligence purposes their pictures were taken from vertically overhead, ignoring the fact that this was an extremely dangerous procedure. Hammond's perfectly practical solution was rejected on those grounds by the Army and was not officially adopted for military intelligence purposes until 1941. When it was, no recognition was ever accorded to its first inventor. Another technique he pioneered was night photography, notably achieving shots of Wickham Market railway station in the late summer of 1918.

Hammond soon moved his photographic operations to Martlesham, but research on making night pictures continued on the Ness. The inventor of a special flare was Bertie Harper, and trials used a pair of parachutes to delay the 75,000 candlepower light in its descent from 1,500 feet by upwards of 6 minutes. Here again, an idea pioneered on the Ness was not adopted by the military until well into the Second World War. A reason for this is said to have been the Army's anxiety that it upset the soldiery to have a sudden brilliant light disrupt the relative security of the darkness at night, when so much movement was undertaken. Once again, here were trials that were to be repeated, at a new level of technical performance, twenty-five years later.

Accurate navigation posed considerable problems for early aviators. They had to rely on telltale indicators like railways and rivers to work out where they were. Map reading was an essential skill and this could be difficult, especially for a pilot with no observer. Holder introduced a system for making existing maps much more usable by highlighting key features such as the shape of woods and fields as well as rails and roads. It was an idea widely taken up.

Navigation by day was hard enough. At night, it was so difficult and dangerous that for a long while, most aircraft were not permitted to take the risk. Holder was involved in the development of lighting for cockpit instruments. This, and better runway flares, meant that from 1917, night flying was expanded. It was made the more necessary by the need to counter Zeppelins and Gothas, which were increasing the frequency and potency of their bombing raids on London and the East Coast.

THE ZEPPELIN MENACE

There was one particular aspect of the conduct of the First World War, which was never forgotten, even in times of peace. This was the horror of indiscriminate bombing of civilians, particularly by Zeppelins. It was worse than the shelling of coastal towns by the German High Seas Fleet as Royal Naval ships dealt with that. The problem with Zeppelin bombing was that there seemed to be so little effective defence. Meeting the widespread and mounting public fear of a barbaric, random aerial attack on a defenceless civilian population during the inter-war years was to become a part of the Orford Ness story.

From 1916, Ness boffins had of course been working on ways and means of dealing with Zeppelins. By 1917, following the first raid by Gothas on Folkestone, the need to deal with German aerial attacks reached critical proportions. It led to an instruction that if the opportunity occurred, all aircraft should be used, even if not fully equipped for the task. In June 1917, such an opportunity arose.

Initially, German air attacks were clumsy, strategically inept and, for the year of 1915, almost totally unimpeded. Aircraft flown by both the RNAS and RFC were unable to detect the enemy or reach the height at which Zeppelins flew and had limited methods of destroying them. By 1916 however, there evolved a quite elaborate Home Defence system, including searchlight and anti-aircraft batteries and designated squadrons, both RNAS and RFC, specifically allocated to the task. Zeppelins were relatively slow, susceptible to the weather and with far from reliable engines or navigational aids at such great altitude. Altitude was almost their sole and decisive means of defence. The threat to the nation's morale was growing serious, however. Almost always they hit non-strategic, random civilian targets and often at night. Their threat was the source of fear out of all proportion to the damage done or even the actual number of casualties caused. This was the first time British homes and families had been directly subjected to the realities of modern warfare. Indeed, the damage to morale in the Home Front was the declared principle aim of German air attacks. It was a tactic that looked like proving all too successful

By the standards of what was to come in future wars, the actual damage was not in fact that grim. Certainly, by comparison with the slaughter on the Western Front, civilian losses were minute. Just over 100 German air raids by Zeppelins, Gothas and Giant 'Staaken' aircraft caused losses valued at £2 million. Around 1,400 people were killed and 3,400 injured, but compared with the traumatic consequences of Second World War strategic and 'area bombing', these numbers appear a mere trifle. In July 1943, over 40,000 were killed in Hamburg on a single night. The total number of civilians killed in Britain throughout this war was 51,500.

The euphoria that followed the successful destruction of the first Zeppelin, L37, by Flight Sub-Lieutenant Warneford, RNAS, in June 1915, illustrates this public feeling of fear and anger, fanned by vocal and overhyped newspaper head-lines. He was awarded his Victoria Cross in record time, within just thirty-six hours. A Cross of the Legion of Honour followed. His courage, flying a totally inadequately armed and equipped Morane scout plane justified such rewards. It went to his head and he died in an accident ten days later, caused largely by his own impetuosity. He flew without any securing seat straps.

A new breed of heroes was being created and with it a public hunger for seeing Zeppelins brought down. Two of the kills that followed were to directly or indi-rectly involve Orford Ness pilots and technicians. The first occurred on the night of 16/17 June 1917, when a recently commissioned prototype of a new design of Zeppelin, L48, made its first – and last – attack.

The German plan was for a fleet of six airships to make a coordinated raid on London. In the event only two achieved the English coast. L42 flew well, hoping to hit London from the south. However, fearing thunderstorms, it was decided that any delay should be avoided by going for the first target encountered. It thought it was raiding Dover when it dropped its load of bombs on Ramsgate, causing, by a rare fluke, a direct hit on a naval ammunition store. It then headed northeast up the coast, shaking off attempted attacks on it as it clawed its way back to base. It was by now out to sea, where it witnessed at some distance the fate of the only other airship of the six to reach England.

L48 was the first of a new breed of super-craft, a 'U' type, designed with improved buoyancy and a reduction in weight so as to achieve even greater altitude – up to 20,000 feet – as well as pace of ascent, all to escape the attention of defence fighters. Its greater ceiling slowed its speed and increased the risk of instrument failure through icing up. The engines used were not upgraded sufficiently to match the stress that they were subjected to. Her hull was enormous, three times the size of a Boeing 747 'Jumbo' jet. Her speed was about ten times slower.

L48 carried the Deputy Chief of the German Naval Airship Division on this trip, Captain Victor Schutze. Intending to approach London from the north, it crossed the East Anglian coast directly over the Ness. It was a clear summer's night. This made it distinctly both audible and visible to those on the ground. Orford Ness despatched three planes and contacted the nearest RFC Home Defence Station at Goldhanger, south of Harwich. A plane from its No. 37 Home Defence Squadron also took off and gave chase. By chance, this was the very squadron that had briefly served on the Ness in 1916. The ill-fated L48 was encountering increasing power and navigational failures. It drifted over Wickham Market to the northwest of the Ness, and then swung southeast, planning to attack Harwich. It missed that target by a few miles, unloading its bombs over two villages inland from Felixstowe. By now in serious mechanical trouble, it swung back towards Leiston while desperate efforts were made to right its problems. Meanwhile, the RFC aircraft had gained sufficient height to tackle the intruder.

One of the Ness pilots was Frank Holder. He explains that night-flying exer-cises were at this stage being regularly conducted. Several Orford Ness aircraft were equipped for the purpose. These were not the fastest of planes; speed was not the crucial factor in developing instruments for flying at night, nor indeed for dealing with Zeppelins. Moreover, lack of speed was at that time deemed essential for safety in the dark. His aircraft was the ageing FE2b, no. B401, the locally built plane* which gave valiant service during the war. As a two-seater pusher type, with excellent all-round visibility and properly equipped with night-flying instruments, it was ideal for the purpose. Holder explains that 'though not strictly a home defence station Orford Ness was on call in the event of hostile action, and suitable aircraft were equipped with machine guns, and for use against airships, the ammunition included Brock and Pomeroy explosive and incendiary cartridges.'

There was no rota for home defence, and Saturday afternoons were the only periods of free time they had. 'I had been playing tennis about three miles inland and did not return to the Station until the evening of June 16th and I was immediately ordered to stand by to fly. Neither of the officers, Lieutenants Musson and McKerrow, from the machine gun section, was available, so Sgt Ashby took their place. And Capt Clarke flew solo in the BE2c to save weight, owing to its limited range'. Holder's account of what happened next follows:

> Ashby and I finally took off at 1.55 a.m. on a perfect summer night with exceptional visibility. The Zeppelin was almost overhead and we had no difficulty in locating it and keeping it under observation. The FE2b climbed slowly, all the while keeping abreast of the target, until we reached our ceiling of 14,000 feet on the altimeter (probably about 13,500 actual) only to find it still out of range but obviously losing height and still moving slowly just inside the coast line by Aldeburgh. As it descended we opened fire with both guns firing obliquely but my gun jammed and Ashby was unable to correct the fault. As the airship continued to lose height, and only the observer's gun firing, I altered course so that Ashby could use the easiest aim, firing straight ahead without deflection and approached the airship's starboard rear, still slightly below. Ashby, with a clear view of the target, fired three drums, the last at a range of about 300 yards, at which point we were aware of tracer bullets coming from the direction of the enemy. I started to take evasive action, but as we did so we saw flames appear at the point at which we were aiming. The time was 3.25 a.m.

Clarke was unable to get higher than 11,000 feet and though he fired a couple of drums of ammunition, he was definitely out of range. Saundby (Captain I/C 'C' Flight, and later to become Air Marshal Sir Robert) was given permission to fly a DH2 at 2.55. His aircraft was not equipped with instrument lights or landing flares, but it was felt that his great experience of the type of machine, plus the

---

* This particular aircraft was built by Ransome, Sims and Jefferies, the agricultural engineers in Ipswich.

fact that they would be landing after daybreak, made it a fair risk. He climbed as quickly as possible and fired three drums of ammunition from below. Holder continues his account:

> Meanwhile 2nd Lt Watkins in a BE12 from 37 Sqn., stationed at Goldhanger on the Blackwater Estuary in Essex, took off at 2.03 am and reached his maximum height at about the same time as we did. He fired several drums of ammunition and it is possible that the tracer we saw came from him, and not the Zeppelin, if his attack was from the opposite side.
>
> With three experienced pilots attacking such a large target, then almost stationary, it was difficult to allot the credit to the action, and the final award of the MC to Saundby, Watkins and myself and the MM to Ashby was probably the right decision. It is clear that the unexpected size of the target made us all under-estimate the range at first and we had to approach closer to be effective. A German survivor, Machinist's Mate Ellerkamm, who witnessed the attack, stated that the fire broke out at the starboard rear panels, the point which we had attacked.
>
> The flames spread with amazing speed until the whole airship was ablaze and falling slowly, pulled down by the weight of its gondolas and engines. I was able to circle round as it fell until it finally ended in a field at Theberton, near Leiston.

The giant airship crashed in flames, tail-first, its nose-cone acting as some sort of parachute, slowing the rate of descent. This accounted for the rare event of three members of its crew surviving the impact.

Ellerkamm had a miraculous escape – he was almost unhurt. The executive officer Leutnant Otto Meith survived with broken legs and one other, the machinist's mate Van Stockum, died two days later. The rest of the crew of seventeen lost their lives and were buried in Theberton churchyard. The only wreath was from the officers at Orford Ness – for which they met some criticism. It was, however, normal to do this in France, when enemy flyers were shot down over British territory, and vice-versa.

The burial of the dead German crew took place on 20 June, and was attended by a contingent from the Ness. There was a real sense of camaraderie among airmen from both sides, each respecting the courage of the other. The inscription on the wreath from the Ness read: 'To a very brave enemy from the RFC officers'. Such sentiments were not entirely shared or understood by the local civilian population. Holder goes on:

> While it may not appear a great feat of arms to destroy such a vulnerable target, we had to do as we were ordered… The psychological effect was out of all proportion to its merit. Even those who were not afraid of raids felt frustrated at the insolent way the Zeppelins dropped their bombs and returned home. Here was positive proof that things were going to be different. It was estimated that 30,000 people visited Theberton on the days after the crash and this, in a remote

part of Suffolk, before the days of radio news. Petrol was in short supply and the majority of the people must have come by horse transport, cycle or on foot.

A consequence of Saundby's achievement was the decision to permit more night flying. Holder claimed to be a pioneer in this field. In fact, the only other major Zeppelin raid, in October 1917, ended in disaster for the attackers, scattered by North Sea weather.

The L48 affair was not quite over however. Holder was probably unaware of the intense police activity that followed the crash. Part of the popular response to a downed Zeppelin was to rush for souvenirs and these were duly seized, until a military guard was posted. To this day, there are numerous households in the locality where the taking of trophies from the crash has become part of family history and bits and pieces of the craft are preserved as family heirlooms. The wreckage of all airships was always made available to RNAS for analysis, and because L48 was known to be a new type, special attention was paid to ensuring that no bits were removed. The file now lodged at the National Archives in Kew is inches thick with police reports on their endeavours to locate all the 'stolen' items. A young Flight Lieutenant, Victor Goddard RN, was placed in charge of salvaging the wreck. To protect his property, squadrons of men from the nearby Cheshire Regiment appeared, closely followed by hundreds of troops from the Suffolk Cyclist regiment and later, the London Cyclists. Admiralty Intelligence officers soon followed, to sift through documents and other equipment that survived the crash. The bulk of the looting seems to have occurred after the wreckage left the crash site, falling off the backs of the fleet of RNAS lorries despatched to and from Leiston railway station.

The story of shooting down the 'Theberton Zeppelin' rapidly entered local folklore. From time to time, other records of the affair come to light. In 2007, the local newsletter, *Ebb and Flow,* published a letter written exactly ninety years before by a twenty-year-old Cambridge undergraduate, then staying at nearby Blaxhall. It gives us a graphic contemporary account of the victory, as seen from the ground: 'The minute the Zepp was down half the population of Blaxhall went off on bicycles to see where it was and of course they got there before there was a proper guard and got lots of souvenirs.' Another anecdote emerges from the newsletter's next issue. Captain Saundby was apparently lodging with the correspondent's mother in Daphne Road, Orford. 'That night, when he heard the commotion, he got up, rowed across the river, got to his aircraft, took off and proceeded to fly round the Zepp, with his guns blazing.' The story went round that 'he was later court-martialled because he was still in his pyjamas'. There is no record of this, of course, and it certainly had no bearing on Sir Robert's future distinguished career as an Air Marshal. What is certain is that whatever he had on underneath, he would have donned proper flying kit: the temperature at about 12,000 feet would have seen to that!

This was not quite the end of the campaign against Zeppelins as it affected the Ness. The Navy was increasingly anxious to bring the attack to the enemy coast to prevent German reconnaissance by Zeppelin. The best tactic was to catch their airships at their moment of greatest vulnerability, namely when taking off or returning to their bases. Not having attack aircraft with the endurance to fly across the North Sea, scout for a victim and then get back, the idea was mooted by the Harwich Command, under the resourceful Admiral Tyrwhitt that a crude form of aircraft carrier could be created by fitting a deck on a submersible lighter. These latter were currently being built at Richborough in Kent and designed to be used for transporting seaplanes.

The somewhat hair-raising idea was to tow this crude carrier with a Sopwith Camel aboard to within range of a Zeppelin base, and by steaming at full speed – over 30 knots – launch the plane for an immediate attack. Once the mission was completed, the pilot would ditch close by the barge. The pilot would be rescued, and if possible the plane, or at least its engine lifted back aboard by the destroyer's crane.

The first experiments were conducted by the charismatic RNAS pilot Commander Samson, the pioneer aviator who had made the very first takeoff from the deck of a ship. In a Short Boxkite flying boat, he had flown from a runway fixed to the quarterdeck of the King Edward VII class battleship HMS *Africa* back in January 1912. The Sopwith Camel was attached to the lighter with a release arrangement, which the pilot operated once the deck crew had started his engine. The deck was sloped so that once full speed through the water was achieved and the bow correspondingly lifted, his take-off deck would be level. The whole operation was clearly highly precarious, since the width of the deck was only 21 feet and the length just 48 feet. Samson, a daredevil personality, proved somewhat too reckless for this new experiment and crashed his Camel. Sub-Flight Lieutenant Stuart Culley was chosen to continue the trials. On 31 July 1918, HMS *Truculent*, one of four high-speed 'R' class destroyers allotted to these trials, towed the lighter No. H3 out of Harwich and up the coast to the Ness.

That July afternoon, a perfect take-off was achieved in less than 40 feet of runway. Culley flew safely over his naval escorts, across the Ness and back to land at Martlesham. So promising was this operation that an immediate order was placed for more such converted lighters, with the plan to operate a fleet of twelve. Ten days later, Culley was launched to attack L53 and achieved the last Zeppelin 'kill' of the war. He won the DSO, deservedly; many of his colleagues thought he had earned a VC for such a demonstration of outstanding courage. Tyrwhitt's delight in his young eighteen-year-old pilot's feat was evident.

The episode gave rise to one those cryptic signals so favoured by commanding officers in the Royal Navy. A signal went out to the whole squadron, which read *Hymns Ancient & Modern, no 224, v. 7.* This ran: *O happy band of pilgrims, / Look upward to the skies, / Where such a light affliction, / Shall win so great a prize.* Tyrwhitt later presented Culley with a cigarette case, with 'Hymn 224, verse 7' engraved on it.

His plane was rescued. Even more remarkably, it has survived. In pristine condition, it is on public display hanging from the roof at the Imperial War Museum in London.

NIGHT FLYING

Accurate navigation in the dark was a permanent problem for these early aviators. In part this was because of the inadequacy of relying solely on RFC compasses. Frank Holder's good friend F.W. Musson suggested the idea that at a given distance between airfield and target, a pair of vertically directed searchlight beams should be set to guide the plane on its proper course. This would indicate not just the correct bearing but also the range to the intended destination. Keeping to a steady altitude and speed, a stopwatch could be used to indicate when the aircraft was due to reach the target – unless of course the weather upset the calculations. Holder discovered that this system could work amazingly well. He used it to navigate the considerable distance from Orford to Cranwell in Lincolnshire, where a new system of electric runway lights had been installed.

Of greater concern was the lack of any means of judging height above the ground during hours of darkness. The Ness solution was again the use of light beams focused downwards. When the beams met, the exact height would be known. Almost inevitably, this idea was rejected for security reasons. Again, the military distrusted any lights at night. Airmen too were well aware that such light would offer too easy a target. The principle was never forgotten however, and was revived in dramatic circumstances in April 1943. The bombers from 617 'Dambusters' Squadron had to approach their targets at an exact height above the reservoir water. Two light beams were fixed beneath them, focused in such a way that they met at exactly 60 feet above the surface. The fact that the light beams would give the defending gunners the exact position of the attacking aircraft was felt in the circumstances to be an acceptable risk.

A major area of research by Ness pilots lay in developing tactics for night flying and fighting. Recommendations were made for ideal heights for spotting enemy planes and looking for ways of using searchlights to direct fighters towards them. No clear conclusions were drawn here. Little more than twenty years later, work on the Ness and at nearby Bawdsey would provide the solution to the problem: it was called Air Interception (AI) radar.

Night operations led to the development of camouflage, a novel concept which gave rise to a new word that entered service vocabulary during the First World War.[*] The Army's urgent need to make its troops less conspicuous had emerged directly from the Boer War, where troops' bright red uniforms clearly stood out in the dusty African bush. On the Western Front the value of making military installations less obvious to observation and recognisation from the air soon became evident. The need for aircraft to be rendered invisible at night led to the invention of a dark green varnish, which was to be painted on their upper surfaces. It was given the acronym

---

[*] Camouflage, a word that now has entered the general vocabulary, was then so novel that many a dictionary in the inter-war years would not have included it.

NIVO, standing for 'Night Varnish Orford Ness'. This paint was widely adopted and remained in use until well into the Second World War. As for daytime camouflage, experiments on the Ness were extensive. Some were useful and adopted. Others were somewhat fanciful and were rapidly dropped. One such was an idea to make it difficult to focus on a scout aeroplane by using a so-called 'dazzle' design (see Plate Section) and which worked by painting multi-coloured shapes and odd patterns on ships, buildings, etc to make it hard to determine range, speed, direction and shape. This made targeting and firing on them much more difficult, particularly for submarine commanders aiming torpedoes at enemy shipping. The idea was quickly identified as being quite inappropriate for aerial warfare. [2]

Darkness was far from being the only hazardous environment a pilot would encounter. Clouds could be a haven for escape, but more often were a cause of serious disorientation. A special flight was set up in 1917 to develop systems for training pilots how to cope in cloud. The development of essential cockpit instrumentation was a continuing responsibility for the scientists at Farnborough. As a means of testing the pilots' skills at flying solely by instruments, hoods would be fitted over the cockpit, a tactic that was used in pilot training during the Second World War and beyond.

The whole business of tight and accurate formation flying was still in its infancy. Only by means of trials, which took place over the Ness, could the most effective formations be discovered, especially for bombing. The recommendation was for what they described as a half-moon arrangement that placed the formation commander's aircraft in the lead, responsible for locating the target and directing when to release the bomb load, with the remaining aircraft forming a semi-circular ring behind their leader, to provide a protective screen from enemy counter-attack.

HITTING THE TARGET

Frank Holder's flight had as its principal area of research, bombs and bombing technique. This work included somewhat tedious 'quality control' tests on consignments of bombs. A sample from each production batch was dropped on the shingle range. If there was a dud, it had to be extracted from the shingle and a pilot like Bertie Harper would be required to discover the cause of the failure. Why such an obviously dangerous task was assigned to a valuable airman rather than a munitions specialist is far from clear.

Holder tested various types of bombsight, at times flying at a considerable height. On one notorious occasion in late 1917, he had achieved 17,000 feet, unaware of the strength of the southerly wind. Intending to release just north of the lighthouse, he had drifted towards Aldeburgh. His bomb-aimer delivered the four bombs for testing beside the Martello Tower, which was occupied by an Army detachment. The Army wanted the aircrew to be put under arrest! Holder escaped, with a lesson learned. This was that meteorological aids were an important element in successful targeting.

Much of Holder's work revolved round assessing the effectiveness of a variety of bombs and the bombsights. From this he was able to evaluate bombing strategies, particularly with reference to hitting railway lines. These were proving to be a favoured target for attack on the Western Front. The Ness teams could offer little positive encouragement. It was widely appreciated by airmen that it was a singularly difficult task to hit a strategic target, a bridge or tunnel, for example, with any certainty of doing lasting or decisive damage. During the Gallipoli campaign in 1915, supply lines to Turkish forces were attacked, chiefly by RNAS seaplanes. Erskine Childers, a brilliant navigator/observer (and author of the successful 1903 spy novel *Riddle in the Sands*), took part in these raids. He was decorated for his exceptional skill. The jingle that the resigned and slightly sceptical pilots would repeat explains it all:

> There's a game that some play for the whole of a day
> Of dropping a bomb from the air,
> And men grin with delight if they drop it aright,
> A contingency only too rare.

No less than three separate Ness-based trials took place to discover the most effective means of disrupting rail traffic. A direct hit was the ideal, but being entirely realistic, there was a need to provide indications as to the value of proximity hits; how close should a near miss be to cause meaningful damage? A disused stretch of track at Medbourne in Leicestershire was 'attacked' on 22 December 1917. To achieve up to 25 per cent success, dangerously low level flying was essential and then possible only for very experienced and resolute pilots. Throughout the war, it was shown that to cause any significant damage that would disrupt rail traffic, a standard 112-pound bomb had to strike within 4 yards of the track. For heavier 230-pound bombs, the proximity should be no more than 8 yards. Flying across the line at an oblique angle increased the likelihood of at least one bomb being effective. This lesson also applied sixty-five years later when a lone Vulcan bomber was sent to put the Port Stanley airfield out of action in the Falklands conflict of 1982.

Trials were conducted on the Ness itself, where a stretch of shingle south of the Martello Tower was marked out to simulate a railway line. The purpose here was to attempt accurate high level, and therefore safe, bombing, at 12,000 to 15,000 feet. These 1918 trials proved even more unsuccessful than the Medbourne experiment. Half the bombs dropped were at least 140 yards off target. The report concluded that 'it is impracticable to cut a rail line by high level bombing'. The only sure and safe way to achieve a useful result, it was suggested, would be at low level, flying down the track, using a pusher aircraft with its superior sight line, and probably at night.

Efforts to solve the problem continued. Another test was conducted to the north of Debenham, some 20 miles away, on an unfinished branch of the

Mid-Suffolk Light Railway. Analysis of the results of bombing in France proved even more discouraging. Only 8 per cent of bombs being dropped fell within 200 yards of their target, and less than a quarter within 800 yards. A damning conclusion in the Ness report suggested that the 'amount of damage seems scarcely commensurate with the cost of such raids'. The raids continued nonetheless and the loss of planes and aircrew and the relative ineffectiveness of the raids were never questioned. The truth was that accurate bombing was all but impossible; certainly there was as yet very little science to it. This was the conclusion reached by the remarkable aviator and RNAS air mechanic, Henry Allingham, the last survivor from action in the First World War, who died in 2009. In 1917 he was posted to the Western Front. He writes in his autobiography: 'In the air I was an observer, by now armed with a machine gun. I also used to sit behind the pilot and drop bombs – there was no art to this, just plain luck'.

Holder's flight tested various types of explosive and fuses. They had to invent effective bomb carriers and workable release mechanisms. They were presented with specific problems, like bomb penetration into soft mud that absorbed all the blast. This all raised the issue of an effective height for a bomb to detonate and the relative merits of explosive blast and shrapnel. Ingenious ideas were constantly being sent over from the Front – the Gidino 'bouncing bomb' for example. This involved a double charge, one to detonate as the weapon hit the mud to blow it upwards into the air, whereupon the second charge would go off. It totally failed to impress the Bombing Section on the Ness. The Marlin shrapnel bomb was no more promising. Named after the exotic fish with a long beak, this weapon had a long spike in its nose, which would penetrate the mud, leaving the explosive charge above the ground. To test the depth a bomb might sink into soft ground, a site was requisitioned on the heath land of Tunstall Common, 5 miles or so north of the Ness.

A trial involving Holder was concerned with protecting low-flying trench-strafing aircraft from enemy gunfire. The AE3 'Farnborough Ram' was a very experimental machine, heavily armour-plated for protection. This however made it very difficult to lift above 1,000 feet as with every turn it tended to drop by 100 feet. This was an experiment that was quickly aborted, but this trial anticipated remarkably the work that Holder's successors on the Ness would do twenty or so years later.

Likewise were the trials to test fireproof and self-sealing fuel tanks, which were started in July 1917. Again, work in this field would continue on the Ness over the next thirty years and beyond. Petrol-resisting putty was tried and found wanting. Naval unvulcanised rubber was found to be inadequate. A senior officer, Lieutenant-Colonel Cave-Brown, came up with an idea. His new type of fuel tank was tested in April 1918, but the tests conducted in February of 1918 seem to have been the most promising. An RE8 aircraft was fitted with tanks filled with 15 gallons of petrol. It was sealed with rubber and shot at, at 40 yards range. 'The protection against leakage afforded by this system of covering is considered very satisfactory', ran the official report dated 14 February 1918, and signed

by the Section Commander Captain W.G. Mitchell, Major H.R. Raikes, Chief
Superintendent Officer, and the C/O, Colonel Bodham-Whetton.

Tests with fresh materials continued. In September 1918, a new type of tank
using vulcanite was deemed too heavy and too brittle to be practical. So important did this safety aspect for aircraft prove to be, that nearly forty years later,
the Ness would still be conducting similar experiments, albeit with vastly more
sophisticated aircraft.

Many tests drew from the Ness boffins the comment that it would be useful to
know exactly how the Germans were solving the selfsame problems.

The Constantinescu interrupter gear suffered from jams in the ammunition
feed. In August 1918, a captured German Albatros was delivered to the Ness. Its
interrupter gear was very impressive. Likewise, when German incendiary ammunition was fired into a British unprotected fuel tank, it never failed to ignite. Such
reliability was sadly not so evident in every item of RFC weaponry.

Holder mentions some of the visitors to the Ness, many of whom he was clearly
proud to meet. Perhaps the most notable of these was the Air Minister of the day,
Winston Churchill. This was not to be the last time he was to show interest in the
work at the Ness. Another memorable occasion involved a visiting pilot, for a trial
inspired by Roderic Hill, later to become Air Marshal Sir Roderic. He wanted to
see whether specially fitted aircraft could fly straight through a balloon barrage
by severing the cables. Holder describes how they fixed a protective wire to the
faithful old machine, FE2b no. B401, which he had flown against the Zeppelin
L48. Hill insisted on flying it himself. This was not altogether an unexpected
request: Hill was chief test pilot at Farnborough. The result was a flash as the FE
and cable met. The balloon cable held and the FE2b got into as near a spin as the
stable old lady ever did, and then flew on unharmed.

Work on the Ness was steadily expanding in scope and quantity, and somehow
the horizons of the place were widening similarly.

Widening Horizons: RFC to RAF

Photographs from *c*.1918 show around forty officers involved in the host of trials on the Ness. Not all were pilots: observers were just as important and just as brave as the men who actually flew the planes. There were other scientists too by then, men conducting experiments in, for example, sound detection and silencing of aero-engines. Often such work involved a brief assignment from another station. In one case at least, the officer was not in the RFC.

When it came to academic credentials, Lieutenant Arthur Milne RNVR was academically every bit the match of Bertram Hopkinson. Indeed, it was largely through Hopkinson that Milne was despatched to the Ness to conduct special trials. His calibre as a scholar may be judged by the fact that he was elected a Fellow of his Cambridge College, Trinity, at the age of twenty-three, without ever having completed his B.A. degree and on the strength of no less than four dissertations, all to PhD level and largely derived from his wartime work. He was to become Professor of Mathematics at Oxford and an astrophysicist of world renown.

Milne's recruitment into military research straight out of the undergraduate body of a Cambridge college well illustrates Hopkinson's role. Milne was sent to research with the Anti-Aircraft Experimental Section of the Department of Munitions, working at HMS *Excellent* on Whale Island, Portsmouth. The purpose of this work was to provide gunners with binaural sound trumpets to assist in detecting enemy aircraft and direct searchlights and gunfire at them. Given the speeds and altitudes involved at that time, these sound detectors were valuable aids to accurate direction finding for gunnery. Indeed, this technology, refined with more accurate amplifiers, was to remain in operational use into the Second World War. Milne's contribution to this early research was considered so important that the Captain of *Excellent* issued strict orders to the gate sentry: any Army recruiting sergeant trying to enter to grab this young man for the draft was to be immediately arrested. Milne was hastily appointed to the rank of

Lieutenant, RNVR. Some months later, he was on the Ness. His precise task is not recorded, but that such an expert in acoustics was present just at this time cannot be coincidental.

THE BUTLEY OUTSTATION

The motive for seeking more effective silencers initially was to prevent the enemy from identifying approaching aircraft. Various tests failed to achieve any marked reduction of noise without significantly reducing the power of the engine's output. The report that followed the original Ness researches noted that 'there will continue to be considerable noise however carefully the engine is silenced (and thus reducing power) even when throttled back, owing to the swish of the prop, the clatter of the valves and valve tappet gear, and the humming of the wires'. Clearly, these required to be silenced too. This report indicated the need for a move to a quieter specialist trial site.

The work being done on sound and silencers was transferred to a remote – and hence relatively tranquil – site 4 miles inland, on sandling heath (poor, sandy soil) in the Rendlesham estate, near the small village of Butley. A modest camp for an estimated establishment of ninety-four personnel was built on one side of the road from Orford to Woodbridge, and on the other side, about 200 yards further up the road to the west, a grass field was prepared. It was land similar in character to the Martlesham site: heather, bracken and scrubland. Not a trace of it survives. The location of the encampment is still an open space, surrounded by mixed woodland. The airfield is deep in what is now Rendlesham Forest and extreme imagination must be exercised to appreciate that airmen flew in and out, conducting what must be admitted were somewhat bizarre and often rather inconclusive experiments.

Operations at Butley lasted little more than a year. By the end of the war, there were two canvas hangars and a motor transport shed there, as well as quarters for twenty-five officers, ten NCOs and sixty-nine other ranks. Much of the construction work for the accommodation was still not completed and there can have been no case for keeping the station open after the immediate researches were complete, in late 1919.

Butley Acoustic Research Station, as it was officially described, was presented with two problems to resolve. One was the creation of effective engine silencers, something that had so far defeated the teams on the Ness. The other idea was rather more curious. This was to develop workable sound signalling systems for air to air and also air to ground communication.

The aims of the Butley team's researches were clearly defined. Added to the already explained issue of power loss were several new reasons for developing more effective reductions in noise. These included increasing comfort for aircrew while at the same time making access to servicing the engines easier for the ground crews. It was also recognised that aircraft were identified not just by their sound but also by the sight of their exhaust flames at night. A reduction in flame visibility was therefore necessary, and improving the aerodynamics of the whole engine casing was very desirable.

The final report on all the work done at Butley was presented in August 1919 over the signature of Brigadier-General Brooke-Popham (RAF officers were continuing to retain their Army rank at this stage), by then the Director of Research. It confirmed that the noise of airflow over the wings and through the rigging would always make silencing an engine purposeful only in terms of the comfort of the aircrew. More research was required however, and the construction of a new subterranean soundproof bunker was recommended, capable of allowing for fully accurate acoustic measurement. This would also avoid the need for more costly aerial testing. Not surprisingly given that the war was over, this recommendation was never implemented.

The other field of investigation concerned sound signalling. The standard Klaxon horn in use on land was proving ineffective when used by or for aircraft. Again, a schedule of requirements was drawn up. The new system had to be capable of use for Morse code. It should be audible at heights up to 10,000 feet in calm weather. It should be what was nicely termed as 'foolproof': easy to use and durable under service conditions. It must be light in weight, between 12 and 40 pounds, and it must have a 'suitable' source of power. Chiefly, it must operate even if the engine was not running. Finally, it must be adaptable for use in any type of aeroplane.

No less than fifteen types of assorted horns were trialled, variously operated either manually by aircrew, or mechanically by wind, gas or electrical power. The researchers tried using reeds as well as horns and even looked to discover what was the most acoustically effective note for the horn to be tuned to. Some systems unsurprisingly proved to be useless, while others did work, after a fashion. As a result, trials were conducted on the Western Front in July 1918. The oddest of all the ideas was the so-called Stentorphone, which claimed to be able to transmit aerial broadcasts of gramophone records. It is perhaps with the wisdom of hindsight that one judges the inadequacy of even using horns for signalling.[1]

Although a small station, Butley inevitably witnessed flying accidents. So did the Ness. Holder possibly underestimated just how many there were. Detailed records remain slightly hazy, but it would seem that at least half a dozen airmen were fatally injured, probably more. Two of these deaths are particularly poignant since the pilots involved were the closest of friends.

Ness pilots flew in and out of Butley. One of them was Oliver Wills. His letters give posterity a valuable insight into the life of a Ness aviator. Wills was quite a late arrival on the Ness, arriving from the Western Front in 1918. 'This is a lovely place,' he enthused, 'It is more like coming for a lovely holiday than going to Netheravon or France.' He confirms that he was assigned to Holder's flight, trialing bombs and bombsights: 'I am experimenting on bombs and have dropped eight already, nearly killing as many fishermen. But it seems rather absurd wasting perfectly good fishermen when food is so scarce. I just must be more careful next time.'

Extolling the happy environment on the Ness, Wills refers to another feature of the station by 1918. So heavily committed to flying and testing duties were the RFC and RAF personnel that twelve members of the WAAF were despatched to take over various ancillary tasks like driving and running the offices. 'We have girl motor drivers attached to this squadron who seem to have a splendid time of it...' In fact, Holder confirms that despite their rough and unfeminine uniforms, these young ladies did indeed have a good time. Two of them married Ness airmen.

Mention of the sea level prompted a comment on the forthcoming late summer high 'spring' tides. 'All last night we were expecting to be flooded out and special guards were put to watch the walls, which are only about an inch above high tide in places, and in the event of the sea coming over we were each to fly a machine away to safety (in a freezing gale and in the middle of the night). But much better than lying in bed until the icy water crept in.'

Wills had the closest links to the Jones family. He was made godfather to Bennett Melvill Jones's daughter, Margaret. Thus Bennett's younger brother 'Toddy' Jones was a particular mate of Wills. Known by the nickname 'Toddy', Benedict Henry Melvill Jones was described by Holder as 'a brilliant pilot'. He was wounded in action on the Western Front, and once he had recovered was brought over to the Ness through the influence of his elder brother, so they could fly together. Bennett was deeply involved in air-to-air gunnery experiments at the time, a matter that was enormously complex, given the many variables involved at a time when instrumentation was still relatively crude. He needed a talented and reliable pilot 'up front' to assist him.

Alas, disaster struck the family in April 1918. Conducting trials on negotiating spin conditions in a two-seater Bristol Fighter, 'Toddy' announced that he felt he was solving the problem and was determined to go up again for one last time: tragically, that it is what it proved to be. It was thought that somehow his observer inadvertently caused the controls to become jammed. This explanation may well have been put about to soften the blow to elder brother, Bennett. Within the family, the real truth of the matter could not be disguised. 'Toddy' was working on a theory about the impact of airflow over tail-plane surfaces on a spinning aircraft, as proposed by his elder brother. Clearly, the theory was flawed. Bennett always felt that he was ultimately responsible for the terrible crash that killed his brother.

The local tailor, Lou Anderson, made a new uniform for Toddy's funeral. The old one was retained by the Anderson family, and Toddy's original buttons and insignia have, remarkably, survived as a result, and are now in the possession of the family of Lou's grandson, the late John Anderson.

As his closest friend, Oliver Wills designed a simple memorial stone, with a plane depicted at the intersection of the cross. Seven months later Wills himself was dead. He suffered the tragic misfortune of losing his life on the Butley airfield on the very day before the Armistice, in November 1918. On the occasion of the crash, he was flying as a passenger, excellent pilot though he was. The two friends are buried side by side some 20 yards to the north of the great tower of Orford Church, a landmark both pilots must have come to know so well. Their crosses are identical.

AUXILIARY FORCES

There were other residents on the Ness that Wills might not have expected. He wrote: 'There is about an 80 per cent Hun population on the island.' These were the German Prisoners of War housed on the King's Marsh, initially in a tented camp, as photographed by Hammond, and later re-housed in a more substantial hutted encampment. Wills exaggerates their number, relishing an evident touch of sensationalism. Helpfully, he goes on to explain the reason for their presence on the site: maintenance of the airfield, including keeping sluices and ditches clear and assisting with the construction of the so-called Chinese Wall sea defence. 'The aerodrome and our camp are well below sea level. It sounds amazingly dangerous but I suppose is all right. The Huns haven't taken us prisoner yet but in the event of a Hun naval landing things might become rather priceless...'

The slightly surprising fact that POWs could be employed to work on military establishments was governed by a private convention between Germany and Britain. Each undertook that prisoners on both sides would never be employed within a zone 30 kilometres from the front line. This explains how POWs from the camp in Woodbridge were to be seen marching over to Martlesham where they built hangars and concrete aprons. So it would seem that making use of them in this way was not uncommon and was an acceptable practice.

Four prisoners tried to escape from the Ness but were recaptured. The so-called Spanish influenza pandemic struck just at the time of the Armistice and thirteen prisoners died. Several of the luckless German prisoners were also buried in Orford churchyard. Their remains were eventually transferred to the German military cemetery on Cannock Chase.

The other labour force on the Ness for a while was Chinese. Tough men from northern China had been used in Canada to build the transcontinental railways. They were ideal for construction jobs in Europe, and many were employed in the heavy work, manning the ports, building ammunition dumps or trench systems, laying down railways or even acting as mechanics. In all, a total of 96,000 members of a Chinese volunteer labour corps arrived in Europe between January 1917 and the end of hostilities. They provided the best and most reliable of all the labour force companies, which included men drawn from every continent as well as British conscientious objectors.

Some Chinese were diverted to such jobs such as sea defences, as at Orford Ness. Gordon Kinsey quotes the reminiscences of B.G. Goldsmith, who as serviceman and civilian was employed on the Ness on and off from 1916 to 1970.

In particular he worked with both the Chinese and the Germans. He was working with the German prisoners in their daily tasks of draining the marshes and raising the seawalls to protect the site. The POWs dug ditches, which were filled with shingle he brought over across the slender bridge over Stony Ditch in his horse and cart. He recalls two of the Germans, typically named Fritz and Hans, the latter with a large drooping moustache and a loud gruff voice that rang out, especially when singing Teutonic songs over the stillness of the flatlands.

Goldsmith also worked with the Chinese Labour Force who were billeted in the old balloon shed at the northern end of the range of hangars, and close to where they were put to work. They were all volunteers and although it was a somewhat international assortment of labourers, the Chinese were in the majority. They carried out ditching and draining works and their efforts are known to this day as the 'Chinese Wall'. Cutting out cubes of 'pug' (solid blocks of clay) they piled them up to form a strong sloping wall, employing the 'human chain' method of carrying the material from the excavation site to the builders. Some thirty to forty men were engaged in this task. The majority of them owned bicycles, which they used on their days off to tour the local villages buying all the chickens that they could find. As they did all their own catering and cooking it can be assumed that chicken figured largely in their diet. They would enlist the help of local schoolchildren to collect grasshoppers and crickets, telling the youngsters that they needed them so that they could hear them sing. No one appeared to be quite certain whether or not they served a culinary purpose.

Only the faintest trace of that original wall survives. The great floods of 1953 completely demolished it. One monument to those First World War labourers remains. By the roadside is a large concrete block about 5 feet high with a large vertical groove in one face. In the event of a flood warning, wooden baulks were slotted across the road to another similar block – no longer surviving – to complete the barrier that stretched from the river Ore all the way to Stony Ditch. The original Chinese Wall was eventually replaced with the present anti-flood embankment, which is still referred to as the Chinese Wall. Of course, it was constructed to twice the height of the original, using mechanical diggers and bulldozers: not a Chinaman involved.

MCKERROW'S CONTRIBUTION

It is easy to suppose that the pilots were the key boffins in all this research work, but they needed assistants, observers in the second cockpit of the various two-seater aircraft. Of all the men accompanying Holder, unquestionably, the most significant was George McKerrow. Fortunately, the records of his two-year service on the Ness have survived, held in the archive of the Liddle Collection in the Leeds University Library. In addition, friends he was to make in his later years in Ayrshire were to receive from him a large collection of his photographs in two volumes, many of which depict his time at Orford. Some of these pictures were copies of Hammond's great collection; the rest McKerrow took himself.

George McKerrow came from south-west Scotland. His father was a doctor, who sent him to Clifton College in Bristol, and on to Cambridge, where he attended Caius College, taking a double first in Maths and Mechanical Engineering. Here was yet another brilliant young Orford Ness boffin in the making. He did not follow his elder brother into a medical career, and though his abiding passion was in fact sailing, the outbreak of war saw him join the Physics Department of the Royal Aircraft Factory, as it was then called, at Farnborough, researching early bombsights and the allied problem of aircraft stability. In 1915, his father's illness caused him to move north to Scotland and he became an aircraft inspector in the Glasgow factory of G. & J. Weir, building BE2s for the RFC.

After his father's death, he moved back to Farnborough and decided to enlist. Sadly, poor sight in one eye meant that he would never be permitted to train for front-line flying. For a while he was assigned to what must have been the appallingly mundane tasks of an Equipment Officer, dealing with stores and supplies. He gained some recognition in setting up the air station at Thetford in Norfolk, and following the death of his brother near Ypres in late 1916, he was anxious to find a more challenging role in the RFC. Happily, an ideal one was found for his energetic and creative talents, with his appointment to join the growing team of researchers on the Ness, where he arrived in early 1917.

McKerrow's logbook suggests that he led an amazingly active life, both socially – the Ness provided ample opportunity for his sailing – and as a boffin. Three different flights in a single day were not uncommon for him. His expertise and versatility were clearly invaluable, and his courage unquestioned. He never missed a chance to go up in the observer's seat, flying with almost all of the pilots on the station. He even took the opportunity to learn to fly himself, though the indications are that he was more attuned to the managing of boats than planes. Such was his reputation that on two occasions he was the obvious choice when a crew was needed to observe or test systems on active service in France.

It would be a somewhat tedious exercise to provide a blow-by-blow description of the myriad pieces of equipment that he personally tested, particularly since many, if not most, were quickly discarded as being impractical, useless or positively lethal. Many of the reports emanating from the Ness and now available at the National Archives feature the judgements formed by McKerrow.

McKerrow's previous experience at Farnborough stood him in good stead with his continuing experiments on bombsights, and he must have relished the chance to look for more sophisticated systems than what he referred to as 'nails and wire' which were in vogue when he started. It would be possible to list upwards of a dozen different types that he personally tested in his time and equally it was fairly evident that not one of them was very satisfactory. Indeed, this very fact explains why the Ness bombing range was going to be such a necessary facility for the RAF from 1927 onwards.

However, McKerrow's first few weeks on the Ness involved ground testing and looking for improved accuracy in bomb dropping. For this purpose, a *camera obscura* (referred to by some who operated it, like Vernon Brown, as the '*camera lucida*') proved a useful piece of equipment, crudely unsophisticated yet something that researchers would continue to use for the purpose in the Bomb Ballistics building well into the 1950s.

The *camera obscura* as adapted for bombing research was in effect a large pin-hole camera which could project the image of an aeroplane flying overhead onto a ground-glass screen, permitting its course to be plotted on a suitably inscribed overlay. From this could be identified the effects of drift, steering errors and the accuracy of simulated bombing runs. For the officers recording the data and stationed for long periods in uncomfortable and inhospitable bunkers down the range, often in uncertain weather, this was the least popular of duties.

After a few weeks, McKerrow graduated to more attractive assignments. His first flight in May 1917 was with the senior flight commander and veteran from Upavon, Captain Vernon Brown. He also flew with Frank Holder in the FE2b B401, the plane which helped shoot down Zeppelin L48. Indeed, McKerrow was scheduled to fly with Holder on that memorable flight, but it was a Saturday, and he was absent on some social engagement – probably a tennis party or a sailing trip – which is why Sergeant Ashby was taken up instead.

In addition to experiments with various different types of bombsight, a search was being made for improved means of locating targets at low level at night. So-called Bombsight Lamps were tried, a pair of beams projected to intersect at 500 feet, a development of the idea for using beams to ascertain altitude. McKerrow accompanied 'Toddy' Jones to France in late June 1917 to test this idea under battle conditions. Squadrons at the front were unhappy with the idea because, however carefully screens were placed to hide the source of the light, it was felt that the beams would be far too likely to attract enemy fire.

One particular bombsight gadget was designed by one of McKerrow's colleagues, Captain Jenkins. The 'Jenkoscope' was a large contraption fixed to the side of the aircraft. It resembled an unwieldy bicycle frame and was far from reliable: Jones and McKerrow flew one series of trials and were disparaging about it; just one of many Heath Robinson-esque ideas thrown up by serving airmen during this war.

McKerrow would be expected to operate the observer's guns for experimental purposes, or for real if the enemy was encountered. To start with, he naturally found this quite hard, particularly since his pilot would often be deliberately flying in a far from smooth or level pattern, but his prowess earned him several calls to fly in action when Zeppelin or Gotha attacks led to Ness machines being 'scrambled' to engage the enemy.

Once the Gotha bombing campaign was underway (there were eight daylight raids that summer, involving 142 sorties), aircraft from the Ness were available to join in the counter-attack. This also led to research into ways and means of dealing with these formidable enemy weapons. On the night of 4/5 September 1917, a raid by a Gotha saw the only enemy bombs to fall on the Ness site. Exactly how many were dropped or where they fell is not recorded, but it is recalled that the craters were nearer the jetty than the hangars. Certainly the Ness was not the intended target. The same plane dropped bombs on Aldeburgh: the Gotha could carry a 2,200-pound bomb load. This particular raid, the first bomber attack under cover of darkness, was intended for London, as were the vast bulk of such attacks. A fundamental imperfection of this style of warfare in 1917 is illustrated by the fact that of eleven bombers that took off, only nine made it across the sea and only five found the intended target. The raiders scattered their bombs from Dover and Margate in the south to central Essex and Suffolk in the north. About ninety bombs fell on London. The shrapnel scars on the base of the obelisk by Cleopatra's Needle on the Embankment were caused by this attack. No planes took off from the Ness that night. None of eighteen RFC aircraft that were sent against the Germans found their targets, let alone fired at them.[2]

One young pilot who might have been involved in attacking these German aircraft was Lieutenant Cecil Lewis. That evening, he was off duty and took advantage of the close proximity of his Home Defence station at Hainault to party in London. He was in the Savoy Hotel, and was a first-hand witness of the damage the bombs inflicted. One of them penetrated through four floors of No. 2, Savoy Hill, a matter of feet from the hotel.

Cecil Lewis was the author of perhaps the finest autobiographical account of the RFC war, both at home and over the Western Front. His book *Sagittarius Rising*, published in 1936, is a classic and provides ample confirmation of the many operational problems facing those pioneer pilots that the Ness boffins were trying to resolve.

Following action at the Battle of the Somme, Lewis was sent back home for a period to test new aircraft. He was posted to Upavon and on from there to Martlesham. He describes the excitement of trying out a variety of aircraft, waxing particularly enthusiastic over the flying qualities of the Sopwith Triplane. This, the only one in RFC hands, was based at Orford Ness and it demonstrates that during his brief spell in Suffolk, he was indeed just another of those fleeting visitors to the Ness.

It would have been at this period too that another air ace, Albert Ball, flew in, presumably to catch up on latest equipment research and combat techniques and pass on information drawn from battle experience. Ball in fact turned his aircraft over onto its back on landing and was photographed being escorted away from the scene of this somewhat undignified arrival (see Plate Section). He was by all accounts a shy and retiring person and preferred to be spared the hospitality of the Officers' Mess, staying overnight in Orford. He was not the reckless extrovert that so many young fighter pilots seemed to be. His recreational joy was playing the violin. Lewis explains: 'His favourite after-dinner amusement was to light a red magnesium flare outside his hut and walk round it in his pyjamas, fiddling!

He was meticulous in the care of his machines, guns, and in the examination of his ammunition. He never flew for amusement… He never boasted or criticised, and his example was tremendous.' The two of them were shortly to be recruited into the crack No. 56 Squadron and despatched to the front with new SE5 aircraft to deal with von Richthofen. On the evening of 7 May 1917, the squadron, eleven aircraft strong, took off for an offensive sortie. Only five, including Lewis, returned. Ball was never seen again. Lewis was the last to see him. He had forty-four 'kills' and was regarded as an especially brave and effective leader and most talented fighter pilot, often flying machines that were at the time inferior to those of the enemy. He was awarded his VC posthumously.

The raids by the Gothas prompted several new experiments on the Ness. One was to discover the best angle for a fighter to spot an enemy while at the same time remaining unseen. New guns and ammunition were researched too. It is a quaint sign of those times that permission up to Cabinet level had to be obtained to use anti-Zeppelin weaponry, notably Brock and Pomeroy explosive shells, against enemy aeroplanes. It was feared that these more lethal weapons could be seen as being disproportionate and in breach of international agreements. It is often held that the decision to amalgamate the two air wings into the single RAF, which was effected by April 1918, sprang in great part from the crises involved in dealing with Gothas.[3]

McKerrow was meanwhile delving deeper into various problems and experiments involving instruments and equipment. The silencer trials that took place on the Ness that late summer of 1917 involved him and 'Toddy' Jones. It was their relative failure to achieve results that led to the decision to open up Butley Station (see p.50). During August, he conducted research into a more aeronautical issue, namely, the matter of the 'angle of incidence' for various types of aircraft (the pitch of the aircraft in relation to the wind flow). This was all to ensure level and steady flight at varying speeds and heights. His tests led him to use a pair or more of different altimeters to compare results. His pilots on these trips were either Holder or Jones. He was also looking at gyros to establish more accurate performance with bombsights. This early mention of the use of gyroscopes to solve gun- and bomb-aiming problems anticipated the crucial development of this technology by Melvill Jones twenty years on.

Another problem became evident during his work on formation, cloud and high flying trials. A section of novice trainee pilots were drafted in to assist. It became clear that the very compasses on which all relied were far from reliable and often worryingly inconsistent. So, during the late autumn of 1917, McKerrow would take off with a selection of compasses on board, flying up and down the range over the *camera obscura*, with the plane twisting and turning at varied altitudes. It was tedious but important work, conducted with the meticulous attention to detail for which the Ness was by now already noted. The lack of any positive recommendations in the reports suggests that the matter was analysed, but no immediate improvement was identifiable. In fact, research work reverted to Farnborough, where Dr S. Keith Lucas, another Cambridge graduate and inventor of the Lucas bomb sight, was a formidable boffin and would-be pilot. Lucas was a neurologist by training, and was responsible for taking up this Ness problem: disorientation caused by flying in the dark or through cloud. His determination to solve it by becoming a pilot himself was to prove fatal: he was killed in a crash over Salisbury Plain. Increasingly, valued scientists were forbidden to risk their lives by trying to become pilots themselves.

Keith Lucas demonstrated that the cause of 'disorientation' was not 'pilot error', but what came to be defined as 'inherent compass turning error'. His mathematical and observational research led to him realise that the main problem lay with the current type of RAF magnetic compass. The nature of the workings of the North Pole's magnetic field when flying over the British Isles was shown to be such that the compass would seem to go haywire whenever it pointed to the north. When flying in the dark or in cloud, pilots could easily become disorientated, unwittingly going round in circles, since they could no longer check on the general direction they were taking. The outcome could be disastrous. The result of his trials was the Keith Lucas Air Compass, tested on the Ness, and in use by the RAF until replaced in the 1920s by gyroscopic compasses. Lucas's Cambridge colleagues, including future Nobel Laureate Lord Adrian, were always to lament his loss, a potential neuroscientist of the highest promise. His name is commemorated in that area of Farnborough given the nickname of 'Rafborough': Keith Lucas Road still survives.

During these months in late 1917, various new aircraft found their way to the Ness via Martlesham, and McKerrow duly assisted in their evaluation for fighting purposes. One model had the curious name of Sopwith 1½ Strutter and was the replacement for the aging BE2s.

A classic confusion occurred when McKerrow was airborne in Strutter No. A1067, on 27 December 1917. This had been fitted with dual controls, to make for the improved performance of trials. Tactfully, he omits the pilot's name in his log. Each thought the other was in control, and for the ten minutes during which the plane 'flew itself' on a somewhat erratic course, each thought the other was having difficulties with the compasses that were under test in the flight. Only after the pilot safely landed did a realisation of this potentially fatal confusion emerge. The need for improved communications between pilot and observer that this little episode clearly illustrates was yet another area for Ness research. Voice pipes were tested and later, crude telephones. These ideas were widely approved by the Ness boffins and recommendations were passed on for further action to the appropriate Air Ministry authority.

The compass problem clearly remained a serious worry and inspired some truly bizarre ideas. In January 1918, McKerrow, with Wills, flew in a new RT1 type plane with a sundial to test against a compass! He was impressed, as he records, by the plane rather more than by the idea of using a sundial. Doubtless the far from certain East Anglian weather may have prompted doubts as to its practicality.

McKerrow by his own admission was not a 'natural' pilot himself. He was officially licensed on 18 March 1918, with a medical certificate, which declared him 'Fit to fly as a pilot for experimental work only, not to carry a passenger', (implying one supposes that he was at liberty to kill himself but not a luckless colleague!). He records flying only one plane, an FK3 and then always very much round the Ness area.

Searchlights had been used as navigational aids, as Holder had demonstrated. In January 1918 came the idea of using them for directing bombers to their target on dark and moonless nights. McKerrow took part in two trials during the month, the latter using Holt flares attached to the bomb to act as a 'tracer' marker, anticipating the idea of Second World War pathfinders. It was successful but like a number of Ness trials, seems never to have been taken much further.

One last series of trials to perfect more accurate bombing techniques at greater altitudes involved an important new instrument, the 'Turn Indicator'. For much of McKerrow's work in 1918, Lieutenants Francis and Barrett were his pilots in a variety of aircraft. They flew at between 10,000 and 15,000 feet, encountering the challenges of such altitudes, despite using heated suits, which of course did not always prove reliable. They dropped standard bombs and new types of incendiaries. The dropping areas to the north of the airfield must have been saturated with ordnance, not all of which exploded. From time to time relics of these trials continue to emerge. One, an Amatol-filled 112-pounder, came to the surface in the shingle north of the lighthouse almost ninety years later. Bomb disposal squads will probably need to be on hand to tidy up from these trials for many years to come.

In view of the primitive nature of bombing techniques available to the RFC in the early days of the First World War, it is interesting to reflect on the mounting appreciation of its potential impact on the enemy. In late 1915, months before bombing research began on the Ness, a flight of RFC aircraft was despatched to the North-West Frontier of India. Its purpose was to impress the tribesmen on the Afghan border during a highly sensitive period with a threat of an anti-British insurrection stirred up by German agents. The natives had never seen a flying machine and were mightily impressed by the evident power of these bombers. A tribal elder was quoted at the time as stating to the Army officers that 'those flying machines are worth at least 20,000 troops to you'. The urgency of the work on bombing, one of the main thrusts of Ness research, can be understood in the light of this experience in a far-flung corner of the Empire.

In March 1918, Francis and McKerrow were selected for deployment to the Western Front, to demonstrate the various bombing techniques that they had been exercising on the Ness. This assignment arose out of a report submitted by the Ness, curiously given the official title 'Night Flying in the Air' (The Ness perhaps had in mind that the future might reveal possibilities of flying elsewhere than in the air!). This report described their findings on long-range shooting from beneath enemy targets and night visibility trials. The two young men took a Bristol Fighter, departing for France on 17 June 1918. Their detachment ended on 14 August, when they returned to resume various trials back at Orford Ness.

Interchange between Ness boffins and front-line pilots was a very regular feature of these final two years of the war. Albert Ball had made an ill-starred visit in 1917, as has already been described (see p.57). James McCudden, another legendary ace, was also a fleeting visitor who nonetheless was able to take the opportunity to participate in an anti-Gotha sortie, sadly without success. Other ex-Orford men found themselves at the front. One was Captain Wackett, whom McKerrow and Francis met up with, now Flight Commander of No.3 Squadron.

It would be appropriate to sum up their experience in France as one that could only be seen in the light of 'the fog of war'. They found no lack of commitment in aircrew, despite poor communications, seriously unreliable machinery, unhelpful weather and a general lack of uniformity in any application of tactics and technology. They attended several funerals.

Squadrons were generally eager to learn what Ness trials were showing up, but somewhat reluctant to abandon their current methods. Bravely, the two boffin visitors joined in with active squadrons to share in night attacks. McKerrow blazed away his ammunition more in hope than expectation. As he put it, this 'made him feel slightly better'! They learned that attacking railways was a favoured pastime, and came to see for themselves just how impossible it was to locate these targets or to hit them. They were able to impress their hosts with the idea of using large mirrors to trace the movement of smoke from shells fired upwards into the upper air where aircraft were flying. The information this provided aided accurate navigation at these altitudes.[4]

It was an intensely busy two months and the two ambassadors from the Ness impressed High Command. The general officer commanding, Major-General Salmond was pleased enough personally to authorise McKerrow to be awarded the observer's brevet, the half-wings that he thereafter proudly sported on his uniform.

The two had to draft a report. This must have been a pretty anodyne affair. Neither officer was senior enough to voice serious criticisms of what they found. McKerrow's own diary certainly could not be quoted. So, for both of them it was back to routine trials, tests and bombing runs, including renewed railway line targeting. They also tested a gadget originally designed for the RNAS for low level bombing, the 'Wimperis Course Setting Bombsight'. Wimperis was a name to re-emerge some years later in the Ness story.

McKerrow flew with Major Charles Fairburn in experiments involving using cloud flying as a tactical weapon. In their joint report dated less than a month before the end of the war, they stressed the vital need to train pilots to use their compass and navigational instruments with total accuracy. The idea being propounded as late as October 1918 was to devise an attack strategy to take advantage of cloud cover: 'On days when there is a continuous layer of cloud low down, it is possible to fly in the cloud until over the objective, when the pilot can dive down, drop the bombs and climb into the clouds before the enemy can retaliate.' It all sounds somewhat simplistic and one must assume that the idea was never put to the ultimate test. Fairburn was just another of the star performers to come to the Ness. He was the very first Oxford student to gain a First degree in Mechanical Engineering. He was a railway man, ending his career as Chief Mechanical Engineer for the LMS Railway, dying prematurely in 1945.

Another exercise that involved the pair was carrying out mock attacks on the newly arrived large Curtis flying boat, which was equipped with gun positions on its upper wings. These trials became the subject of one of the last major reports to come out before the Ness closed down.

McKerrow was dropping bombs with Holder onto the shingle from up to 15,000 feet right up to the close of hostilities in November 1918. His last bombing flight was on 7 November. Francis was the pilot for his very last trip the following February in what was a joy ride. Two months later he was demobilised, with his flying log giving him credit for 360 hours in the air, twenty-five of them at night, and only six as a solo pilot. His qualities and experience assured him ready employment wherever he chose. He turned down promising offers in government-linked agencies, and instead went into industry, ending as Head of Research at Metropolitan Vickers.

McKerrow was just one of many enterprising and talented men who helped to create an RAF which despite many vicissitudes, emerged as a truly formidable fighting force by 1940. This was in no little measure due to work done on the Ness. Vernon Brown describes some of the trials he helped to conduct:

> Hair-raising stories are told of the exploits of the De Havilland 4, in which 'Bones' [nickname of Bennett Melvill Jones] had installed a specially engineered harness attached to the aircraft's cockpit floor by a swivel so that when the aircraft was flying inverted, the gunner could still hang upside down and use the gun! Some gunners attained considerable skill in this art, much to the astonishment of pilots who arrived from the Western Front in France to demonstrate the latest combat techniques. One of the German's latest dodges was to attack with two fighters each passing in a dive alongside their victim at short intervals, and invariably out of the sun, thus giving rise to the saying 'Beware of the Hun in the Sun'.

Jones acted as Vernon Brown's gunner in some test firing, leading to a near disaster.

> After one or two practice runs which brought us as close as possible to the target, he [Jones] signalled that he would fire on the next run. All went well, we turned, there was a short burst of Lewis gunfire and then I felt a rap on my shoulder. He then instructed me to lose height as slowly as possible, to turn neither to port nor starboard and to make a landing in any direction as long as we got down and last but not least, not to ask any stupid questions.

I obeyed these instructions to the letter making an almost down wind approach and touch down with a resultant long run as we had the wind behind us and only the tailskid to apply braking pressure.

It transpired that the tail fin and rudder had been all but shot through and the whole thing was held together only by two bracing wires. Recounting this episode in the *Royal Aeronautical Society Centenary Journal* many years later, Vernon Brown recalls that 'when riggers and fitters arrived on the scene, they found two young officers sitting on the grass doubled up with laughter'. Such a comment speaks volumes for the courage and the carefree attitude of these pioneer aviators.

Vernon Brown, one of the most significant figures in the Ness story, was the pilot who first drew attention to the medical impact of blacking out when under extreme acceleration and consequent G-forces. He was a particularly close friend of Bennett and the Melvill Jones family. When young Geoffrey Melvill Jones (Bennett's son) was a medical student during the Second World War, he lived with the Brown family in London. Brown was Bennett's preferred pilot for many trials, including those involving extreme tight turns, which caused temporary blackout. It was also a remarkably dangerous procedure. The medical aspects of high performance in aviation were to form a major feature in Geoffrey Melvill Jones's future career. He was to be recruited to Farnborough in the 1950s as a member of the Institute of Aviation Medicine. Here his work focused on high altitude oxygen deprivation and pressures on the lung leading to anoxia. The science involved here was quite misunderstood until well after the Second World War.

There was a steady stream of visitors to the Ness over these wartime months, airmen under training, airmen calling in from the Front or, occasionally, pilots calling in from action over the sea. One such who arrived under somewhat more severe circumstances was someone destined for a distinguished service career. In October 1917, on anti-submarine patrol over the North Sea, Flight Commander Douglas RNAS (to eventually become Air Marshal Sir Sholto Douglas RAF) in his Porte flying boat out of Felixstowe was attacked by three German fighter seaplanes. Two were shot down by the Porte's gunners but Douglas found himself trying to nurse a disabled plane back home, with a gunner badly injured. Landing on the sea, he began a long, slow taxi towards the coast. Regularly stopping his engines to let them cool, he eventually made landfall on the Ness and ran his plane up onto the shingle beach, only to be confronted by a zealous Army patrol that disbelieved his story and actually arrested him until he could prove his identity. The Porte was towed back to its base shortly after. The Ness with its prominent, albeit camouflaged, lighthouse, would prove a blessed haven for many a damaged plane in the Second World War.

Some visitors were clearly not welcome. These were aircraft that came over from Martlesham for experimental and testing trials. The suspicion arose that the Ness experience might provide decisive evidence that they were simply unfit for their purpose. One such has already been described, the so-called 'Farnborough Ram'.

Another such was the Wight Quadraplane. This unwieldy beast had four stubby wings, intended to give sufficient lift with the reduced span that the Navy required. Only one reached the Ness, was found to be dangerously difficult to fly and ended its days being used for machine-gun vulnerability and lethality tests. The National Archives holds a fine photograph of the stricken monster suspended from the jetty crane so that it could be shot at from underneath.

Twin-engined planes seemed to pose problems in the early days. Avro's first twin was a long-distance reconnaissance machine, designed to take two observers. Holder wrote: 'No one liked flying it and all rejoiced when I ran it into a tree in a fog, writing it off without injuring the crew.' In view of the notable shortage of trees on the Ness, this was quite a feat. Likewise was the destruction of a DH10 twin-engined prototype, which Holder's friend Barrett took off only to encounter total engine failure and crashing rather neatly with the cockpit nacelle sliding between a hangar and a supporting concrete buttress. The wings were smashed beyond repair. Holder records the famous Vickers Vimy as being the easiest twin to fly. It was for these aircraft that the two big specially designed hangars were erected in 1918, the only ones that survived the closure of the station in 1921. They were given end doors 80 feet wide and were 170 feet in length. The Ness was never to receive any of the super bombers, the four-engine Handley-Page aircraft, intended for long-distance raids on Berlin in November 1918. The Armistice intervened and this extravagant gesture was cancelled.

An astonishing variety of tests and experiments were conducted on the Ness during the two and a half years of its full-scale operations. Some not already referred to, merit brief mention. Some are significant for their obvious practical simplicity. For example, a pilot needed to be able to break open and reload his 'Very' pistol, a vital piece of signalling equipment. How to do it using just one hand and not taking both hands off his controls? The Ness was invited to design a trigger mechanism for firing off twin machine guns together and for safety belt buckles. The drawing in the report held in the National Archives seems to show remarkable similarity to the design that every airline passenger is familiar with today.

Safety tests, for fireproof clothing and protection of oxygen cylinders or electrical accumulator batteries from enemy gunfire, all earned their solemn reports. By contrast, the boffins were instructed to devise means of destroying an aircraft, which having made a forced landing could fall into enemy hands. There was a curious preoccupation with securing the secrecy of the instruments and gadgets being fitted to planes. The irony of this was that many trials amply demonstrated that the Germans were all too often producing superior equipment and probably had little to learn from the RFC. There remains an abiding impression that during the First World War, the fate of men came a poor second to that of material.

Amid the plethora of experiments with new bombs, bullets and shells, searches for ever more effective explosive mixtures, and for effective means of delivering them all, come references to fascinating but glorious failures. One of these was an attempt that amazingly anticipates Second World War trials, with a curious link to the legendary flaming beach at Shingle Street twenty-four years later. The Army invited the boffins at the Ness to create a means of dropping an oil and petrol mixture onto the rivers in the Mesopotamian campaign in what is now Iraq. The purpose was to set fire to the Turkish pontoon bridges, half a dozen of which had been constructed for vital reinforcements and re-supply. Unsurprisingly, attempts to create a mixture that would ignite on water totally failed. The Ness was not provided with the expertise that this science needed. In 1940, an Admiralty Fuel Experimental Unit was established at Langstone Harbour, staffed with specialists in the field, including this author's own father. It took them over a year to perfect the idea. Back in 1917, the search was in vain.

THE ORFORD NESS RAILWAY

A lack of easy transportation to and over the Ness has been a high price to pay over the decades for its 'privacy'. Quite apart from the river crossing, there was a long passage from the jetty to the airfield buildings, a distance of over 1 kilometre. In 1917, the War Office decided to construct a railway to supplement the roadway.

The track was eventually laid to run for over 1.5 kilometres up to Stony Ditch and then on and across it to the ammunition stores on the shingle. The order for two petrol driven 0-4-0 locomotives was placed in February 1917, and delivery came nearly a year later, in January 1918. There seems to have been little sense of urgency here.

The War Office ordered a considerable number of these 60 centimetre gauge locomotives during the First World War. The Western Front was often so static that railways became a realistic means of supply. The manufacturer was Baguley Cars Ltd of Burton-on-Trent. and the Ness pair boasted maker's numbers 719 and 720. Weighing just over 1 ton each, they were quaintly designed to appear like steam locos, with a cylindrical cover to the motor and a mock chimney at the front.* A spur in the jetty area ran across an irrigation channel to stores long since demolished, and to a substantial concrete-block building with corrugated asbestos roof that still stands. For years, it has served as a cattle shed. The permanence anticipated for this structure is indicated by the existence on the southwest corner pilaster column of a benchmark. This was clearly designed to be a significant building, with an office/workshop at the western end and a suspended wooden floor. It is not easy to see now exactly how the tracks led into the shed. This is undoubtedly a building contemporary with the construction of the railway but there is some doubt as to its original purpose. The complex of tracks at the jetty confirms the usefulness of the line, for before the Second World

---

* The War Office stipulated that internal combustion, not steam, was to be employed. This was because the military were anxious that no bright light at night, arising from opening a firebox door, should ever betray signs of the railway being used.

War as many as four sidings were built, to give access from a heavy crane, to bomb stores, a paint store and a fuel store.

The civilian driver of the locomotives in the early days was Jim Meadows. Gordon Kinsey noted that his tasks included shifting shingle from the proximity of the bomb stores in some hopper wagons, thereby relieving a horse and cart of the task.

The line was built alongside the existing roadway to the airfield buildings, rather in the fashion of a tramway. It followed the curve of the road to the north-east towards the hangars of the northerly airfield. The branch line to the bomb stores reversed back from the hangars across the Stony Ditch by way of the rather fragile-looking wooden trestle bridge, some small parts of which have survived. Evidence of this First World War railway is most clear on this eastern end of the route, with an embankment to raise the line above flood levels and the very evident imprints left by the sleepers. By the northern store, there is a tangled pile of rail and discarded sleepers, the only material remnants of the original track.

All too few hard facts exist regarding the fate of the railway on the Ness. Of the quaint petrol locomotives of 1918, one, No. 720, was certainly sold off to a local dealer, Walter Boynton, and was stored at a dump he set up, by ironic chance, on the site of the former RFC satellite of Orford Ness at Butley. By then only scrap, No. 720 was last seen – and photographed – in the yard of Malcolm Bloomfield at Debenham some years later.

TO CARE AND MAINTENANCE

On the day the Armistice was signed, Frank Holder was flying a captured German LVG fighter up from Lympne in Kent to the Ness to compare its performance with a Bristol Fighter.

Activity rapidly and inevitably slowed down from this point on. The influenza pandemic hit the RAF personnel too and the staffing was rapidly reduced. By the summer of 1919, Holder was the senior officer and the only pilot left. Shortly afterwards a team led by Wing Commander H.J. Sanders arrived to effect the closure of the station. Sanders was an expert in this business, having already dealt with Feltwell and Narborough. On arrival he found this vibrant place reduced in numbers from over 600 to just one. Sanders explains that his brief time on the Ness involved receiving Vickers Vimy twin-engined bombers flown over from their factory. There was a shortage of Rolls Royce aero-engines. His job was to remove these engines for future use and return the aircraft bodies for scrap.

There were plans afoot to develop an Experimental Station on the Ness, but nothing came of them. Dumping grounds were designated for unexpended ammunition and bombs, out to sea, 13 miles offshore from the Ness. The last trial reports were completed and duly submitted. All service personnel were withdrawn and a civilian warden appointed to oversee its Care and Maintenance status. However, in no time the Ness would be back into action.

Inter-War Years

TRIALS RESUME

Having been among the very first airfield sites to be acquired by the War Office before the outbreak of war, Orford Ness emerged as one of the few dozen stations to be retained. It was actually closed down but retained under a 'Care and Maintenance' regime. The one activity that clearly occupied these first few post-war years was the removal of many of the buildings that had housed all the military, civilian and POW personnel. Most of the accommodation huts at both ends of the site were removed. It is more than likely that these were auctioned off at local disposal sales and that some of these historic buildings lingered on in East Anglian backyards for some years.

Reports on trials in progress during the final months of the First World War came out during 1919. The last, on air-to-air gunnery, was dated January 1920. It was signed by Bennett Melvill Jones, and was one of the most 'scientific' and technically complex to come out of Orford Ness. It was written during a six-month holiday, prior to his return to Cambridge, largely spent in a cottage at Wasdale Head, in the Lake District and it proved to be, for its time, the definitive document on the subject.

These Ness reports were designed to advise the RAF on the technical developments to be anticipated for the next generation of larger and more heavily armed aircraft. The continuation of such researches was to be the feature of Orford Ness work during the inter-war years. In practice, actual developments were slow to materialise, since expenditure on the armed services was severely restricted and for much of the 1920s, the only aircraft available for trials were largely obsolete First World War models.

In the place of the eleven huts occupied by other ranks which are clearly evident in the aerial photographs taken by Hammond and McKerrow, one much larger and more distinctive building was erected. This was a prefabricated clerestory-style barrack, which still stands to this day, the last complete survivor of its type.

They were mass-produced during the war by the National Slab Factory at Yate, north of Bristol. It must be assumed that its installation indicated a very positive future for the Ness: a substantial and permanent building to replace wooden and clearly temporary ones. This new barrack was designed to accommodate up to eighty-six airmen. By 1928, it was still being used for this purpose but by the 1930s, it appears that this ceased to be so and it was designated as a 'service store'.

The RAF retained an experimental unit after the war at the former RNAS station on the Isle of Grain. In May 1924, it was decided to concentrate all the work involving aircraft and their armaments at their Suffolk bases. The Martlesham station, which had great advantages in its size and location, was designated the Aeroplane and Armament Experimental Establishment (A&AEE). Simultaneously, Orford Ness was reopened as its satellite, and classified as a research station. For the next fifteen years, the Ness was officially titled Orford Ness Research Laboratory. With the Marine Aircraft Experimental Establishment air station at Felixstowe only a few miles distant, the proximity of the three bases was to prove flexible and entirely useful. Martlesham had much longer runways, which were suitable for larger aircraft. The Ness remained conveniently 'secret'. Until about 1937, only one of its two grass fields was used for flying purposes, the other lapsing back to grazing meadow condition. However, the northern field was in regular use, as pilots often landed to consult the boffins on the ground about their particular trial, before returning to their home base, usually Martlesham.

This development inevitably relegated Orford Ness to somewhat subsidiary status. Indeed, so far as its service operation and management was concerned it was always from here on to be under the wing of either the RAF at Martlesham, Felixstowe or Bawdsey, or of the RAE (Royal Aircraft Establishment) at Farnborough. It was designated an RAF station in its own right only when, and if, circumstance demanded, even though the number of service personnel might be in single figures. Its title, and even the ownership of the lease of the property was to change with confusing frequency over the years, with one Ministry transferring or selling it on to another. The single fact remained however that it was a mightily useful secret location for whatever experiments the government of the day deemed necessary. It was merely that the department responsible for them was to vary over the years.

Thus, for much of the 1920s and '30s, the station was very much at the 'beck and call' of its larger neighbour. Whatever was being researched at Martlesham might well involve trials at the Ness. This work included the development of guns and their ammunition, or bombs and the improvement of bombsights.

Initially, No. 15 Squadron was assigned to this work equipped with obsolete De Havilland DH9a planes. This arrangement was something of a subterfuge. It was a squadron only on paper. The government was anxious to give an impression that in theory anyway it was retaining sufficient operational squadrons, despite the cutbacks in defence expenditure.

These older types of aircraft were satisfactory for the purposes of testing gun and bombsights, since speed was, at this early stage, less important than stability and reliability. However, over this period, many new types of aircraft made their appearance over the Orford Ness ranges. Their improving performance made it essential that the whole science and technology of the range was radically improved, evidenced by the construction of a specialised new building for the bombing range in 1933, given the title of the Bomb Ballistics building.

Steadily, the volume of work involving bomb and gunnery testing was increasing. These tests took place largely over the shingle to the north and west of the lighthouse and involved both land- and sea-based aircraft from Martlesham and Felixstowe respectively. The virtue of this arrangement was that, having fired off their ammunition or released their bombs, the landplanes could descend on the Ness's northern field to receive immediate reports on the trial. This procedure was tougher for seaplanes; the crew had to land on the sea and paddle ashore in a rubber dinghy – weather conditions permitting.

This procedure offered another less publicised advantage. On their return flight, the larger aircraft were able to replace their bomb loads with a very different cargo. It was the custom to take quantities of turf dug from the lush areas of grazing marsh to enhance the sports fields and Officers' Mess lawns at the rapidly developing Martlesham. Another welcome task was to ferry off-duty personnel from Martlesham to the Ness for recreational purposes. This of course was possible only when aircraft were made available from trials and other operational requirements allowed and, of course, when the weather was sufficiently friendly.

FIRST OF THE BEAMS

Not all experiments on the Ness were at the behest of Martlesham. This was the time of great strides forward in the field of wireless communications and a beacon was erected at Orford Ness for use – well, by whom?

The true purpose of the five-year long trial of a rotating-loop beacon system which took place from 1929 until it was summarily aborted in 1934, was for several decades never fully appreciated. The idea here was to use a radio signal as a beam from which ships and aeroplanes could work out their position. This was to be a rapidly evolving technology during the 1930s and '40s, once RDF (radar)[1] and IFF (Identification Friend or Foe) had been perfected. This project was one of the most carefully disguised of all Orford Ness experiments; so well disguised that until the archive documents were reviewed, it had been assumed that the 'cover story' was its true purpose and that this beacon was indeed designed as an electronic substitute for lighthouses, to provide a superior navigational aid for shipping.

Radio-generated navigation systems had been established during the First World War for the Navy, and this facility was left in operation for a few years after the Armistice for the benefit of merchant shipping. Such systems for aircraft remained very rudimentary however, largely for practical reasons: necessary apparatus was too heavy and bulky for planes to accommodate. By the mid-1920s the RAF began to take an active interest in developing direction finding (D/F) systems, using the Vickers Vimy bomber for their trials. As early as 1918, mindful of the need to bring academic and industrial expertise to bear on the requirements of the military, the government appointed a new body, the Department of Scientific and Industrial Research (DSIR), under the chairmanship of Lord Balfour (this was the body that Henry Tizard joined following his service on the Ness). In turn, the DSIR created a Radio Research Board. By 1925 it had set up the Committee on Wireless Direction Finding. Trials began on a rotating-loop beacon system, a form of radio compass, involving a transmitting aerial that rotated through 360 degrees.

This work was undertaken by the RAE at Farnborough. RAF equipment was set up at Gosport for preliminary tests. The technology was neither new nor original; it had been used by the German Navy for vectoring U-boats back to base. For RAF use, it did represent something that was both new and of considerable tactical importance.

A special sub-committee was set up to supervise this work, and by February 1928, it was able to report that experiments had shown promise. A station to undertake full-scale trials was now needed, at a suitably located site. For reasons that will rapidly become apparent, the proximity of marine traffic was seen as a requirement for their purposes.

A margin note in a report at the National Archives indicates that Orford Ness had been considered from the outset as a possible location for trials. In February 1925, it was rejected on the grounds that the site was too waterlogged, too remote and difficult for civilian access, too far from other stations which could supply cross-bearings and above all lacking in suitable accommodation. Three years later, this judgement was totally reversed. The Ness was selected as being ideal. The Committee had looked at an alternative at Dungeness, and discarded it on the grounds that the purchase price for the land – £14,000 – would be beyond the projected budget. Throughout this whole operation finance never ceased to be a prime consideration.

At this point it has to be explained that a major element of duplicity was integral to the whole project. In 1928, there was little public support for military expenditure. In the light of the 'jingoism' that preceded the First World War, and the fervour that Churchill had inspired by 1940, it is perhaps hard to appreciate just how adamant everyone was that come what may, peace must be preserved. This sentiment was very evident at the highest levels of society. Notably, King George V was outspoken in his attitude to armaments, the very existence of which he blamed for causing war. Patriot though he undoubtedly was, and a former active senior naval officer, he controversially was known to favour abandoning all but the simplest of weapons, including battleships. As noted by the Air Minister, Sir Samuel Hoare, 'he was strongly prejudiced against flying, the Air Ministry and the Air Force'. He hated aeroplanes as being both noisy and dangerous. He never even boarded one.

Three government departments were involved in the negotiations over cost: the Air Ministry, the Board of Trade and the Treasury. Two other organisations were responsible for implementation: RAE, Farnborough and Trinity House (responsible for lighthouses). As the Treasury understood it, the purposes of the Ness beacon trial were fourfold: to test practical utility for shipping and aircraft, to discover power requirements for varying wavelengths, to learn what the limitations were with varying sites and locations, and to estimate what levels of staffing and maintenance the system would require for full-scale operation. The costs were to be shared on an exact fifty-fifty basis between the RAF and the Trinity House Lighthouse Fund, which was in fact met by a direct Treasury grant to the Board of Trade.

In all the documents in the archives, references to ships and shipping were underlined, as if for emphasis – or was it for deliberate misinformation? There is no doubt that this whole project was intended to be seen essentially as a complement to the lighthouse service, hence the involvement of Trinity House. The elders agreed to this arrangement with reluctance, and the ship owners with suspicion and even hostility. For these reasons, it was accepted that the trial would operate for 6 months only and then only during daylight hours, when the ships would have radio operators on duty. This limitation was rapidly removed once the system began to prove itself.

Power for operating the transmitter and the rotating mechanism was to be supplied by the existing First World War 30 kilowatt DC generators, driven by Tangue semi-diesel engines in the powerhouse located beyond the MT building on the northern airfield. Power lines had to be extended via cables through the shingle or, as it is described, 'the beach'. The Treasury noted that 'a building fitted with six bunks, cupboards and small cooking range exists near the coastguard look-out station and could be utilised for crew. Other buildings exist on the RAF aerodrome. Water and lavatory accommodation are available.' One suspects that conditions were pretty rugged. It was stated however that all were content that the site would be very suitable, that there was plenty of passing shipping and that work should proceed to construct a beacon 'on a temporary basis, for the dual purpose of value for air navigation [on this occasion underlined] and marine navigation'. In March 1928, agreement was reached to proceed and a statement, the first of many, was released to the national press. There seems no question but that this was to be a very publicised venture. Any implications of sinister military use were carefully disguised.

The system needed rigorous testing. Feedback from civilian shipping and aircraft was required. The true importance of what was going on was downplayed. Press reports, statements to Parliament, notices to mariners and invitations to European users (including both German and French) suggested that this was just a useful experiment involving a rather simple gadget. A reminder that ships would need an accurate stopwatch suggested that this was scarcely 'high tech' (ironically, subsequent experience demonstrated that the RAF did find problems with the use of their stopwatches). Aircraft moved far faster than ships and the practical operation of the system was always going to be easier at sea than in the air. The Air Ministry went as far as to admit that they foresaw relatively little application for civilian aircraft. Press stories about it seemed to be open and unsecretive.

All was being revealed. Such was the theme of a news report in *The Times* of 14 October 1928.This was fully eight months before trials began.

Yet a secret memo from the Air Ministry to the Treasury in July 1928 indicated a somewhat different reality.This trial was *not* being undertaken 'in the interests of shipping and civil aviation' at all, it ran, 'but on account of its vital importance to the navigation of service aircraft'. Even if it proved to be of little use to civilian operators, 'it would be necessary to carry out the proposed experiment for RAF purposes. It was vital for direction finding in the dark and would obviate the need for heavy D/F equipment on aircraft ... or for aircrew to calculate navigation at night and in war conditions'.

This rather uncompromising declaration was greeted with some surprise by the Treasury spokesman: '... it is difficult to square with the documents we have in file, which suggest that the genesis [of the trials] was in shipping requirements, and that air requirements only came in by a side wind... Nevertheless, I do not think we can dispute it, and we should now sanction...'

Work on the building that would house this rotating-loop beacon apparatus was not to begin for several months, until January 1929.This delay was caused in part by poor weather conditions.The structure was deliberately to be without any metalwork. A brick basement was topped by two storeys in timber, in the shape of an octagonal-sided windmill.The building contractor was W.C. Reade & Co. from Aldeburgh, and the labour force was drawn largely from Orford. It was at this juncture that the existing railway was extended across the shingle to this new building site. It was further extended past the Bomb Ballistics building and across to the large lagoon by the shore, from which shingle was being extracted.

The machinery was officially inaugurated on 26 June 1929. From the outset, it worked well and earned widespread commendation from mariners from far further afield than was originally expected. Indeed, it worked so well, that by October the demand for twenty-four-hour operation was met and the trial extended, in the first instance, for a further six months.The cost of working it continued to be shared between the Air Ministry and Trinity House. Its so-called Lighthouse Fund was of course really Board of Trade money, but sensitivity to the issue of funding continued. Significantly, a Treasury memo of July 27 1928 had stated: 'Ship owners do not care a cent about this research...They have fallen in with this half division [of costs] to avoid bother. If we press for more they may well say:"The government want this research, we don't. Let the government pay the whole bill!"'

Kept under much higher levels of secrecy was the research conducted by the RAF itself. A full week before the official inauguration of the beacon on 20 June 1929 the first squadron of RAF aircraft was fitted for trials and took part in researching the efficacy of the apparatus for military purposes.

In March 1931, after some twenty-one months of seemingly successful operation, the DSIR's Radio Research Board issued its 'Special Report No. 10', which indicated that the project, though still regarded as a research trial, was performing most satisfactorily. Significantly, every indication was reaffirmed that this was indeed a programme designed to benefit the shipping industry, with the active and positive backing of Trinity House. After the briefest reference to the RAF's role in setting up the equipment ('on behalf of the Board of Trade') and early work at Gosport, the entire document concentrates solely on its benefits to marine navigation. In the concluding section of the report, it is stated that the beacon 'has achieved a large measure of success among those for whom it was intended, viz., the Mercantile Marine.' It was almost as if both the DSIR and Trinity House were quite determined to take themselves in by their own deception. A table of results of the reception of the beacon's signals by various light vessels at ranges of up to 45 miles from the Ness recorded as early as August 1929, showed that the accuracy of the signal's bearing was never more than a single degree out. A similar table of results from shipping, both civilian and military, recorded up to April 1930, was impressive. Significantly, the report made no mention at all of any results from RAF aircraft or ground stations.

On the other hand, most remarkable long distance signals were evident. The record was the case of the SS *Bangalore,* which heard the Ness beacon off Algiers in the Mediterranean – a range of over 900 miles. The Flower class sloop HMS *Rosemary* reported clear signals at 550 miles. Accuracy was less certain at these distances and the report suggested that, while the system would work satisfactorily at up to 200 miles, a margin of error of 2 degrees or less could be expected within a range of 100 miles. The indication too was that as other beacons were set up, ships would be able to obtain even more precise accuracy by averaging their results or taking cross-bearings.

The report provides a brief but succinct description of the way the system worked. The radio signal was transmitted via a closed loop or frame coil, about 10 feet square and mounted on a vertical shaft that stuck up into the roof of the beacon building. It was rotated at an even speed, clockwise through 360 degrees. The signal's effective strength varied during the course of the rotation. Thus, the ship's operator would hear a sound, the intensity of which moved from maximum to minimum strength as the radio beam traversed in the direction of the receiver. Two cardinal points during the beam's rotation were specially marked. At due north and due east, a Morse signal for letter V and B respectively interrupted the beam signal. As the beam passed the receiver, signal strength would decline. As the report explains, with the coil of the aerial moving through exactly 6 degrees for every second, exact and true location of the signal source could be determined by measuring the lapse of time from the loudest signal to the quietest. Each second of rotation represented 6 degrees of bearing. This necessitated the use of an accurate stopwatch. A specially designed type, which combined a second hand with a compass rose, was made available via the Board of Trade. A further refinement was an automatic recorder, which operated in a similar way to a barograph.

Operating on a wavelength of 1,040 metres and a frequency of 288.5 kilocycles, the beacon's transmission lasted for a 5-minute burst, alternating with a

5-minute pause. The call sign 'GFP' would be sent in slow and deliberate Morse for a full minute, immediately followed by a 4-minute continuous signal. There would then be 5 minutes of silence.

The outcome was less than entirely satisfactory and certainly from the outset doubts arose as to its suitability for the services in wartime. Somewhat pathetically, some initial operational difficulties were encountered with service stopwatches; standard RAF issue proved inadequate! There was little sense of urgency, and the airborne radio equipment remained rudimentary: it was still undeveloped from ten years earlier. Human error in using the stopwatch could also lead to serious inaccuracy. In 1929 there was no obvious 'enemy' to drive forward research. The contrast with events six years later is stark. There were quite serious difficulties with night time reception, and it was this that prompted a decision to extend research for longer than was apparently necessary for its maritime purposes. That the trial lasted five years in all was at the instigation of the Air Ministry.

The programme of trial by inviting shipping to record the effectiveness of the signals continued through 1930 and 1931. In an appendix to the report was listed a long recital of 'satisfied customers'. Many noted the merit of the system during adverse weather conditions, either fog or heavy seas. Let the opinion of the master of the SS *Newton Abbot* stand for many others: 'These observations were taken by ordinary watch and found correct on all bearings. I strongly recommend that more of these beacons should be erected round the coast. I consider they are the finest aid to navigation established.' One other commendation was received from another significant source. The German Ministry of National Defence confirmed that Ness signals were observed by their principal W/T (wireless telegraphy) stations at Norddreich and Cuxhaven.

A team of four civilian staff was recruited as operators, paid what was conceded to be a modest weekly wage of between 60s and 75s each (£3 to £3.75). The response from maritime sources was positive enough to warrant not just continuation but expansion of the trial service. There was always a potentially serious objection to the whole thing, however. A future enemy would all too easily be able to jam the signals. During this period, however, the RAF's potential opponents were relatively unsophisticated Third World tribesmen in the Himalayas or Mesopotamia. Curiously, the only sour note in feedback came from the Navy: both HMS *Repulse* and *Glorious* reported grave doubts as to its potential, perhaps deliberately. Was this a subtle way of disguising the military purposes that lay behind the whole thing? Or perhaps it was a demonstration of the senior service's sceptical and jaundiced attitude to new-fangled innovations. The new fast minelayer cruiser HMS *Adventure* demonstrates this suspicion: at almost point-blank range and in sight of the Orford Ness light, she recorded some of the worst bearing results. To be 5 degrees out at 3 miles range was shameful: or deliberately contrary.

In May 1931 a full-scale operational trial was held in what might be termed a security experiment, with three RAF bombers notified of a shift in the signal frequency and three not. The results were disappointingly inconclusive. More work was needed. So, in October, the RAF compared three possible options for High Frequency Direction Finding: the existing rotating-loop beacon, a First World War system, using improved Adcock aerials on ground stations equipped with what were transmitters of a type dating back to 1907, and a rotating coil system mounted inboard on aircraft.

In April, the Air Ministry had confirmed its decision that the Ness beacon was still needed and announced a plan to build a second beacon at Cove, near Farnborough, just by the present M3 motorway. Eighty years later, there is still a signals station operating on the site. A letter to the Treasury dated 14 April 1932 seemed to remove all doubts about this equipment: '…Air Council are now satisfied that the beacon will be required to remain in operation as an essential adjunct to the Home Defence Force, at any rate for several years, and that even when the respective merits of various systems of D/F [direction finding] have been ascertained, it will probably be necessary to retain the rotating loop system for specific functions irrespective of any value it may possess as an aid to marine navigation.'

The full significance of this equipment needs an explanation. The issue here was the recovery of aircraft, enabling pilots to locate the bearing of a home airfield following the completion of their mission. This was clearly an important facility, the provision of which would be crucial to the successful conduct of any future aerial warfare.

At this point, in mid-1932, consideration was given to moving the Ness beacon to a more substantive building, possibly by the Orford Light itself or to a dedicated site near the south coast or an existing inland air station. Another issue here was the cost implication of the whole project. Trinity House was quite unimpressed by any idea of replacing its present systems of fixed beams attached to lighthouses. It was made abundantly clear that any move from Orford Ness would lead to an ending of the current funding arrangement. It would mean that the Air Ministry would pay for it on its own.

In early 1933, cost reductions were in mind when an application was made to the Treasury for a sum of £1,650 to build a dedicated new powerhouse, to avoid the continued use of the old and expensive generators. This was immediately agreed and the powerhouse building that stands to this day was built in a matter of weeks to house a small, heavy oil engine-driven generator, which it was reckoned would cost just £400 a year to run, a fifth of the cost of operating the old machinery. Since a new bomb range was also being built at this moment, this new cheaper power supply could serve a dual purpose.

That autumn, Trinity House backed out of its part in the beacon, and trials began to adopt an increasingly military slant. The Treasury wondered whether civil aviation might benefit, and if so, whether the airlines would contribute to the cost. In fact, they were all too small in scale to feel able to provide funds, and in any case, they had never indicated any good need for the service. Besides, the RAF wished to focus on its own requirements.

The doubts over security and vulnerability, which had plagued the project from its outset, remained unresolved. All RAF trials failed to point to any solution. Somewhat peremptorily, on 16 October 1934, a decision was taken to scrap the whole thing, even though at that stage no obvious alternative was immediately available. The official history of the RAF comments that, effectively, five precious years had been wasted, since the doubts about it had long been known, and no serious attempts had been made to resolve them or discover a workable substitute. Another beacon had been constructed at RAF Tangmere. It was scrapped too. A new sense of real urgency had emerged.

The story of its solution, in time for the Battle of Britain, is a postscript to this part of the history of Orford Ness, except in one respect. The RAF had realised that the fatal flaw in a station-based beacon was that it could be hijacked by an enemy, directing their aircraft just as easily. The solution was to put the trans-mitter on the aircraft and place the receiver on the ground, which would make such hijacking extremely difficult. All that was now required was an IFF system (Identification Friend or Foe), which was in place by 1940.

A plan to supply a complete network of receivers at all fighter stations was imple-mented by 1939. The inaugural bases were set up at Biggin Hill and Hornchurch as early as 1935. By the outbreak of the great air battle of 1940, aircraft needing a bearing to get back to base would transmit their by now VHF signal and three receivers would pass the bearings to the appropriate fighter control plotter who by means of triangulation would calculate the exact location of the 'lost' aircraft and direct it back to its home station. By 1940, the whole procedure took less than half a minute, and saved the lives of many hundreds of aircrew.

This story is so characteristic of inter-war activity: dedicated researchers battling with miserly budgets, uncertain targets and, until latterly, with only a half-hearted sense of serious urgency, yet under a cloak of almost confusing secrecy. The legacy of the trials in Black Beacon (a name given to the structure by the National Trust) is highly significant. The technology was admittedly wanting, though the purpose was indeed of great moment. By 1940, structures identical in shape to Black Beacon were to be seen on airfields all over the country, octagonal windmill-like towers, protected by high bomb-blast walls. They played their key role in the winning of the ensuing battle. The Orford Ness contribution may be seen as architectural, if not scientific. By what was not entirely a coincidence, as work ended on one scheme for dealing with the German bomber threat on one part of the Ness, a new and even more significant project was about to start on another. This would be a beam that did work.

'THE BOMBER WILL ALWAYS GET THROUGH'

A legacy of the Great War was the grim determination that such a bloodbath would never be repeated. This surely had been the 'war to end all wars'. The inevitable consequence was more than a decade of financial cutbacks in military expenditure, affecting all three services. Successive governments were managing a fragile national economy through a period of worldwide recession. Just as important was the popular post-war attitude that this reflected. Deep-seated pacifism was widespread, illustrated by the notorious Oxford Union debate of February 1933. The motion being debated was that 'This House will in no circumstances fight for King and Country'. It was passed by 273 votes to 153, a result denounced by Winston Churchill as 'abject, squalid, shameful'.

Unfortunately, the future enemy seriously misinterpreted such sentiments. The great traveller, Patrick Leigh Fermor, was in Germany a few months later, and he confirmed the very real belief that 'England was too far gone in degeneracy and frivolity to present a problem'. German hostility had become the more implacable by a sense of injustice over the terms of the peace that had been imposed on their proud nation and the demoralising collapse of political and economic institutions that followed.

This is the context in which the truly remarkable researches conducted during the inter-war years on the Ness are to be understood. If there was ever need of absolute proof that Britain – or certainly, the Air Ministry – was not entirely asleep during what Churchill referred to as his 'wilderness years', Orford Ness provides it. What was being undertaken there, during the '30s especially, was of a historical importance almost beyond calculation.

Many people never forgot the mounting sense of terror and frustration that resulted from the aerial bombardment by the Gotha and Giant bombers during 1917 and 1918. The impact of the far fewer Zeppelin raids was less, although these vast lumbering machines cast a particular spell. Berlin was never attacked as London was. The RAF possessed no aircraft capable of reaching it.

The seriousness of the situation became increasingly evident from 1933 onwards as Germany developed new and impressive aircraft. Stanley Baldwin, at this point merely the Leader of the Opposition, had already made his memorable statement in a House of Commons debate in November 1932: 'The only defence is offence, which means you have to kill women and children more quickly than the enemy if you want to save yourselves.' In other words, in any future war, the civilian population were likely to be effectively in the front line, unless, of course, some new method of protective shield could be devised. The Air Ministry in particular realised that here was an issue to be taken seriously. During 1934, matters rapidly came to a head: a large-scale air exercise to test current systems of advance warning totally failed to detect incoming aircraft. This was despite the fact that their route and targets, including Buckingham Palace, the Air Ministry Building and the Houses of Parliament no less, were all known in advance.

Cecil Lewis, who had briefly been a member of a Home Defence Squadron back in 1917, must have shared this pessimistic view. In his *Sagittarius Rising*, written nearly twenty years later, he recalls vividly his sense of frustration at the near futility of trying to find enemy aircraft at night, 'like trying to see a fly in a dark room'. He must have been very aware of Baldwin's stark warnings, for in a tone of resignation he concludes too that 'the bombers would always get through'. He was unaware of what by now was going on at remote and secret research station in east Suffolk.

Precautions for identifying incoming aircraft had been in place for some years. The Observer Corps was set up in 1925, and significantly, Orford Ness provided an early station, set up in 1929. This was seen as of limited value in giving early warning of an aerial attack however.

Meanwhile, a motley assortment of ideas to meet the problem was being considered, including elaborate balloon barrage systems, aerial mines and improved searchlight networks. These were all extensions of largely inadequte tactics from the war. The most elaborate and potentially costly proposal being investigated revolved around fairly crude acoustic early warning systems or so-called 'sound mirrors' ranging from 200 feet long walls 25 feet high, to circular cones some 30 feet in diameter. From 1934, a network of these reflectors to be fitted with amplification was scheduled for the south coast. Under favourable conditions, these just might provide as much as 5 minutes warning of an incoming aerial attack. No idea of numbers or altitude of incoming enemy aircraft could be more than guessed at.

This was the only option presenting itself to the Air Ministry at the time and there seemed little alternative than to give it due priority. By now appointed to a very significant position as Director of Scientific Research, Dr Henry Wimperis despatched his assistant, A.P. Rowe, to inspect a structure on Romney Marshes prior to a trial demonstration before Air Marshal Dowding, the senior RAF officer in charge of research at the time. It is related that as Rowe was being conducted around the site, a milk cart came rattling past. The milkman was stopped and asked by the director of the system, a Dr Tucker: 'You won't be here this afternoon will you?' The noise completely wrecked the effectiveness of his equipment! Remains of these primitive constructions survive along the south-east coast, a notable example being at Lydd in Kent. In retrospect, they may only go to show just how little progress or technical development had been achieved since the researches by Ness boffins at Butley in 1918. The reaction of the Air Ministry was to prove positive and productive, though not before it had investigated a far-fetched alternative. This particular idea might well perhaps have owed something to the imagination of that former RFC pilot, Captain W.E. Johns, creator of 'Biggles', the then aviation hero of children's fiction[*]. In 1934, the RAF (seriously) offered a £1,000 prize to the inventor of a death ray capable of killing a sheep at 100 yards range. The idea here was to find the means of targeting the bomber pilot. The sheep population was not decimated and no claim on the prize was ever made.

Johns was by then a far from uninfluential figure in the debate over aerial defences. As editor of the magazine *Popular Flying*, he wrote an article in January

---

[*] In 1935, Johns published his new tale, *Biggles Hits the Trail*, set in Tibet. Our hero solved the problem of a mysterious blue ray that paralysed unsuspecting victims.

1934 headed: 'Where Stands Germany?' He warned his readers: 'In the matter of personnel, Germany is a nation of fliers. Flying has become a national sport. Vast crowds attend aviation meetings. Even a gliding meeting is attended by everyone, young and old...' These anxieties were well founded. In 1934, plans for a grand new airfield were announced for Berlin-Tempelhof, described by the British architect Lord Foster as 'the mother of all airports'. Its significance was unmistakable. The mammoth terminal building, with 280,000 square metres of floor space was to make it the largest free-standing building in the world in its day, a spectacular platform for Hitler's megalomaniac ambitions. Such a statement of intent could scarcely be ignored.

The death ray idea took some time to disappear completely. Right up to the war, the rumour persisted in the Suffolk coastal locality – and pointedly was left unchallenged – that motor car engines mysteriously cut out in the neighbourhood of the great masts being erected at Bawdsey for the so-called 'secret radio station'. This neatly combined a useful cover story with effective security, to deter unwelcome nosey-parkers.

In the light of mounting anxiety, the scientists at the Air Ministry were about to come up with very much more technically exact and operationally effective solutions. The outcome, of course, was to be Radio Direction Finding (RDF), or to give it the name by which the system was later to become known: radar.

SCIENTISTS TAKE OVER

In August 1934, a figure who has already made his mark in these pages reappears. In a letter to *The Times*, Frederick Lindemann, by now an eminent academic, the Professor of Experimental Philosophy at Oxford, entered the controversy over aerial defence. His contribution was the weightier for his having a track record as a distinguished and courageous scientist and pilot on the Ness seventeen years before. Moreover, he was not without political ambition and had the ear of politicians, notably Churchill. He was subsequently to become Churchill's wartime Chief Scientific Advisor with a seat in the House of Lords, as Lord Cherwell.

Lindemann could have been an invaluable ally in driving forward a fruitful programme of research. Indeed, he began positively, by countering the widely held assumption that attack was the best means of defence. Such a policy was just an invitation to an unprincipled enemy – what he termed 'gangster governments' – to launch a pre-emptive strike. It implied, he argued, that our only means of deterrence was reliance on mere reprisal and counter-attack, which could well prove to be too late. He went on: 'To adopt a defeatist attitude in the face of such a threat is inexcusable until it has definitely been shown that all the resources of science and invention have been exhausted.' This was a direct challenge to the government to throw all its weight behind a concerted drive to find a solution to what was rapidly growing into a serious threat. The expansion of Germany's national airline, Lufthansa, was clearly a thinly disguised front for building a military aircraft fleet, in theory something that was prohibited under the terms of the Peace Treaty of Versailles.

Sadly, having set the ball rolling, Lindemann was to threaten the whole operation with his almost fatal interference. Mercifully, the Air Ministry had access to powerful minds, men who easily matched Lindemann in expertise and were his equal in practical research experience from earlier days on the Ness. Foremost among these was Sir Henry Tizard, a former colleague on the Ness. By now Rector of Imperial College, London, he had never severed his links with the RAF and while he resisted any temptation to abandon his academic career, he pressed the government to fund the creation of a Scientific Research Department for the RAF. It was at his insistence that Harry Wimperis had been selected as its first Director. He had been an RNAS pilot. He was an expert on bombing techniques and the inventor of an early type of bombsight, frequently in use at Orford Ness.

The importance of applying scientific techniques to this problem will have been clear to him and to his assistant, A.P. Rowe, another ex-Ness man. In June 1934, Rowe had sent a memo to Wimperis with a dire warning: 'Unless science evolves some new method of aiding our defence, we are likely to lose the next war if it starts within ten years.' Rowe had just returned from a holiday in Germany.

By the autumn, the Air Ministry had decided that positive measures were now required and again turned to the man whose wisdom and sound judgement could be entirely relied upon: Henry Tizard. By December 1934, a new body had been set up: the Committee for the Scientific Survey of Air Defence. Tizard agreed to be its chairman. Lindemann was not invited to join it. A few months later, the government, not appreciating that the Air Ministry's Tizard Committee was up and running, agreed with Lindemann – and Churchill – to create within the existing Committee of Imperial Defence, a new sub-committee for air defence. It was all rather clumsy and inefficient. The setting up of this second body was altogether too late and it played only a minor role in future events. The increasingly fierce rivalry of Tizard and Lindemann, formerly such close colleagues and friends, may be seen to stem from this moment. Lindemann was later invited to join the Tizard Committee, in the pious hope that constructive cooperation might ensue.

There were fundamental differences between the approaches of the two camps. Lindemann and Churchill believed that research and development should be driven forward by political initiative and pressure, and hence be answerable to Parliament. They had little confidence in the Civil Service – the Air Ministry, that is. They feared it would tend to be too slow and too cautious.

The Ramsay Macdonald government was about to relinquish power and hand over to Baldwin's coalition National government. Meanwhile, it set up a new committee to review the situation. The Air Minister, Lord Swinton, was its chairman and one of its purposes was to mollify Lindemann and swing his support behind Tizard. In apparent desperation to find something Tizard had not thought of, he persisted in promoting the idea of aerial mines suspended from barrage balloons, hoping these would deter incoming bombers. At a scientific level, he was determined to question the approach being so painstakingly investigated by the team Tizard had been responsible for assembling, insisting that the secret lay in heat detection by infrared rays. This idea was not new and had been tested during the 1920s. Both range and effectiveness were clearly very limited even at that stage. In the context of long-range aircraft detection, it was a fatally flawed idea.

So, what was Tizard's team researching? Actual work on what would eventually be called radar began on the southern end of the Orford Ness airfield site in the early summer of 1935. The success of this whole project was to prove an amazingly close run thing. Britain had the system in place to win the crucial aerial battle of 1940, but only just in time and against many odds. Lord Swinton later claimed that:

> ... radar was the greatest achievement of the scientists... We could not hope that we should have a monopoly of this discovery. What we could fairly hope was, that by getting off to a flying start and by concentrating the most experienced scientific and operational minds together on the problem, we should be first in the field, be ready in time, and retain our lead in future developments. And happily so it proved. Such was the debt which the RAF and the country owed to these men of science. It was another example of the debt the many owed to the few.

However, as what followed shows, achieving effective results was to be far from straightforward. The extraordinary ingenuity, imagination and perseverance of a tiny bunch of very young scientists, and their resolution to combat interference, interruption and a fearfully inadequate provision of resources and equipment, were rather remarkable. They benefited from the visionary talent of a gifted leader. Robert Watson Watt is the next great name to appear in the Ness story.

If Watson Watt was an outstanding name to be associated with the development of radar, A.P. ('Jimmy') Rowe, Watt's assistant, was to prove no less important. Indeed, in the minds of many, he was the most significant figure in the story of early radar. A Cornishman, he was a highly qualified scientist, as well as an expert in the field of aerial navigation. He was an academic and an administrator, but unlike a number of those around him at this time, not an aviator. He was to play a major wartime role as Chief Director of the Telecommunications Research Establishment (TRE). The importance of their respective roles has been well defined by Dr Ernest Putley. The final designs by 1937 for the crucial radar network, given the name 'Chain Home' were described as: 'Conceived by Watson Watt, with Jimmy Rowe filling in the details'.[*]

As Secretary to the Tizard Committee, Rowe was desperate to move things forward on the issue of the threat from the enemy bomber. In the autumn

---

[*] Correspondence with the National Trust, 2007.

of 1934, he consulted a colleague working at the Radio Research Laboratory, part of the Department of Scientific and Industrial Research at Ditton Park, Datchet, near Slough. This was the Superintendent, Dr Robert Watson Watt. He in turn introduced yet another name to the Orford Ness story, A. F. Wilkins. He was the scientist who dismissed the death ray idea and made the first tentative suggestion that led to effective and workable radar as the means of solving the Air Ministry's problem.

Wilkins explains how, in the autumn of 1934, he was first involved. He was asked to calculate the amount of radio frequency power that would need to be radiated to raise the temperature of eight pints of water from 98 degrees to 105 degrees Fahrenheit at a distance of 5 kilometres and at a height of 1 kilometre. Wilkins quickly realised that enormous power would be needed, and would prove fruitless when screened by the fuselage of the aircraft. Accepting that a 'death ray' was out, Watson Watt then wondered how they might be able to help. Wilkins reminded him of the phenomenon being encouraged by Post Office engineers who had noticed that VHF signals were often disturbed by the passage of over-flying aircraft. This might provide the clue to detecting enemy planes. 'I remember Watson Watt interrupted me and suggested that some calculations might be useful'.

It has to be emphasised here that the idea that Wilkins proposed was not entirely novel or original. He and his boss, Watson Watt, had been working on the distant detection of thunderstorms by means of radio. They were working on radio direction-finding systems using directional aerials and cathode ray tube displays and were quite familiar with pulse techniques for ionospheric measurements. They were following original research done in the USA in 1925. Further, the whole principal of reflecting radio waves and monitoring the return signal was far from new. As early as 1904, the German scientist Christian Hulsmeyer had patented (in London) such a system, for use by river craft on the Rhine to avoid collisions. In 1922 Guglielmo Marconi was working on the reflection of radio signals off hard surfaces, an idea taken up by the French who installed a similar apparatus in their luxury liners for detecting icebergs. The USA had already begun to develop interference-based radars for the military. Germany had elementary gun-laying radar by 1934.

So neither Watson Watt nor Wilkins can in truth lay claim to having invented the idea. Where their work put British development months ahead by the time war broke out was the brilliant application they devised for its effective use. Radar helped win the two absolutely crucial battles of the Second World War, namely the Battle of Britain in the late summer and autumn of 1940 and the Battle of the Atlantic in the early summer of 1943. The loss of either would have made every other victory and campaign either impossible or irrelevant.

Early in 1935, Wilkins was drawn further into the business of radar. It was to occupy him for the rest of his working life. A man of enormous original flair and meticulous attention to detail, he was just the man Watson Watt would need to consult. A few weeks later, Wilkins recalls, he was posed another question.

Wilkins later could not recall the exact terms of Watson Watt's query but in essence it invited him to calculate the power required on the 50-metre VHF radio waveband to illuminate a target aircraft at a height of 5 kilometres. Wilkins obliged with some figures, which seemed surprisingly favourable. His boss could see no flaws in his work and began to plan how these findings might be put to good use. Wilkins wrote: 'We had no doubt at all, even at this first conversation, that the method of range measurement, azimuth [bearing] and elevation could be made by techniques existing at Slough.'

By February 1935 Watson Watt had drawn up a memorandum for the Air Ministry, which was shortly presented to the inaugural meeting of the Tizard Committee. Its reception was entirely favourable and it was agreed that facilities should be made available to pursue research. However, the cautious Air Member for Research, Sir Hugh Dowding wanted an immediate demonstration to prove the feasibility of the idea. Watson Watt, not for the last time, had to contain the impatience of his masters. Preparation of a suitable short-wave transmitter with short powerful pulses could not be rushed.

Wilkins had noticed during his work at Slough the performance of the BBC short-wave transmissions from Daventry, and in particular on the appropriate 49-metre waveband. He suggested that it should be possible to set up an installation to monitor, by a cathode tube display, any radiated signal from an overhead aircraft. All they now needed were some readily prepared aerials. The suggestion was promptly accepted and Wilkins instructed to set up the apparatus. A minor problem then occurred to Wilkins, as he recounts:

> I said, 'These activities are going to arouse the curiosity of the Station. What must I say when people ask me what I am doing?' 'Oh,' he said, 'just say you are doing a DF [direction finding] experiment.'
>
> The next day I started loading my apparatus into the van and was spotted by Barfield who was in charge of the D.F. work at the Station and who immediately posed the dreaded question. I knew it would be useless to tell him that I was going to do a D.F. experiment, but I did nevertheless, expecting that he would suspect something of a confidential nature and be astute and considerate enough not to enquire further. This fortunately is just what happened.

So occurred a truly momentous and, in the event, epoch-making trial. As might be expected, there was something of an element of 'cloak and dagger' about it. It is not recorded what Barfield thought his colleague was up to. He was in fact being driven to rural Northamptonshire in a small van, an ambulance converted into mobile laboratory, with a civilian staff driver named Dyer. The site selected for this trial was a field just seven miles from the BBC short-wave transmitter. The surrounding hills channelled the signal in the direction of their aerials. The following morning of 26 February 1935, Watson Watt and 'Jimmy' Rowe from the Air Ministry were to join them.

Today, a black plaque stands beside a minor by-road that joins the busy A5 just south of the village of Weedon, near Daventry. It reminds the occasional passer-by that history was made in this rural backwater. The plaque is titled: 'BIRTH OF RADAR MEMORIAL', and beneath is an inscription:

> ... in the field opposite Robert Watson Watt and Arnold Wilkins showed for the first time in Britain that aircraft could be detected by bouncing radio waves off them. Later known as radar, it was this invention, more than any other, that saved the RAF from defeat in the 1940 Battle of Britain.

Arriving at their chosen site, Wilkins and Dyer hastily erected the aerials before finding a hotel for the night. It was dark and cold when, after dinner, they returned to tune the receiver. Unfortunately, the somewhat primitive vehicle had no interior lighting and all the apparatus was connected by the light of matches. It was almost midnight, when Daventry would be shut down, before everything was set up and tuned satisfactorily. They did not notice that during their frenetic activity a hard frost had set in and their van had become frozen to the ground. Happily, they found a spade to extract themselves.

The next morning, Watson Watt and Rowe joined them. To their relief the aerials were still in place, and, with everything ready for operation, they awaited the approach of their aircraft. Only one fault had transpired. The equipment for recording their signal had become disconnected. So, much to Wilkins's regret, no physical record survived to demonstrate their triumph.

A delightful element of Heath Robinson is apparent in Wilkins' recital of mishaps and difficulties, typical of much of the saga of radar development. This spirit of making do against the odds was to characterise their experience at Orford Ness. The wonder is that radar research ever achieved anything. It is inconceivable that scientists in Germany or the USA would ever have tolerated such primitive conditions or facilities as were offered Watson Watt's researchers. Indeed, this 'making do' approach was to be a reason for Lindemann's hostility to the team's efforts.

Meanwhile, a Handley-Page Heyford bomber had been directed to fly from the RAE at Farnborough on a track up and down the signal. The BBC was persuaded to suspend the normal short wave broadcasting transmissions to Australasia scheduled for that time. Wilkins continues his narrative:

> We did not have long to wait for the Heyford bomber to appear. On its first approach it flew well away to the east and no re-radiated signal was detected. The second approach was nearer the beam's axis but still some way off and this time rhythmic beating of the re-radiated small direct signal allowed through the receiver was noted. As the aircraft subsequently flew off to the south, good beats were observed, and, calculating from the time interval from the closest approach to us until the beats could no longer be detected and from the

airspeed requested (100 mph) we estimated that we had followed the aircraft to about eight miles.

I was highly elated and not a little relieved that, after all, the calculations I had made were not far off the mark, and, knowing how rudimentary the receiving apparatus was, much better results could readily be obtained with better facilities. I realised that we were 'on to a good thing' for air defence. I could not however disclose any of my thoughts to Dyer who was not in the secret and who had been sent away to a remote corner of the field during the test.

Doubtless the bomber crew also may have wondered what this strange assignment was all about. Pilot Officer R.S. Blucke, who flew the aircraft that morning, was to be the first of many RAF personnel who were to be similarly puzzled over the next few years. A silhouette of his Heyford is included in that memorial plaque on the roadside. It appears to be a clumsy dinosaur of a machine, but it helped to make history. For a trial of such significance, it is amazing that its precise location might have remained unrecorded but for the researches of local enthusiasts, who worked out where the site was, sought local planning permission for a commemorative monument and raised the money to achieve it. Mrs Wilkins contributed substantially to the cost, and rightly she was invited to unveil it just 50 years after the event it records; Arnold Wilkins himself had recently died. He was essentially a humble and retiring man and would possibly have shied away from such immodesty. This stone is thus a fitting memorial to him and to all his fellow boffins.

Wilkins mentions one quite significant anecdote relating to the Weedon experiment. He spotted a letter in the weekly journal *World Radio* from a reader living in Northampton. He had often listened to the short-wave transmissions from Daventry and noticed a fluttering of the signals when aircraft were in the vicinity. He wondered whether this was a phenomenon that the readers of the paper had also noticed, and felt that it might warrant further investigation. Wilkins immediately showed this letter to Watson Watt, with the result that the paper was firmly requested not to publish anything more on the subject. Radar research was to remain a closely guarded secret.

Rowe immediately recognised the implications of that day's work and reported accordingly to the Air Ministry. Approval was given some two weeks later for a £10,000 budget towards the cost of an initial full-scale trial. Watson Watt was invited to select a team from his young scientists at Slough. The suitably secure site that was recommended was already familiar to members of the Tizard Committee. That it was already in military hands was an obvious advantage, and its 'privacy' made it ideal. Thus, radar came to Orford Ness.

Wilkins does not recall receiving any formal invitation to join the team; Watson Watt just assumed he was part of it already and would wish to carry on. Nor does he recall the exact date of his visit to inspect the Ness. A file at the National Archives confirms that it was 20 March 1935. Also in the file is the actual blueprint map of the whole site with the potential location for the aerials marked.

Watson Watt and Wilkins inspected various (mainly wooden) buildings surviving from the First World War and hence in a state of some dilapidation. Presumably, their construction was preferred because wood would cause no interference to radio signals. He chose to use two smaller structures, one to be the transmitting station and the other to house the receiver and hold their stores. These two huts still survive. The southernmost began life as the Officers' Mess but by 1935 had been translated into the other ranks' dining and recreation building. This was where the early glimmers of radar were first witnessed. The transmitter building was about 150 metres further north and had originally been known as the Regimental Institute. It is preserved as an historic site, re-roofed to keep the weather out, but is now somewhat forlorn and overgrown.

Watson Watt stipulated that a new, smaller, hut be provided, though for what purpose was not recorded and it appears never to have been built. Altogether six wooden lattice aerial masts, 75 feet high, were commissioned to the design of a Slough staffer, Fred Lutkin. Some of the concrete bases for these, or their successors, have survived. Later, when it became abundantly evident that the height of the aerial made a crucial difference, three more 250-feet masts, also made of wood, were erected for the transmitter to a design that went back to the 1920s. Little trace of their bases remains. These were telescopic, in three sections. They were erected by hauling them up from a horizontal position to the vertical. They were not free-standing but had to be supported by guy ropes. Two of these masts were erected by the transmitting hut on the Ness and the third of this type was to be used at Bawdsey, following the move there in 1936.

The proposal to erect these masts caused some upset to the station's residents. The RAF was just in the process of recommissioning the southern airfield. The senior officer, Squadron Leader Foster, was concerned that these new structures might interfere with flying. An estimated £10,000 was being set aside for the survey of the southern field and the provision of fresh subsoil for a new runway surface – a sum that nearly matched the amount to be allocated to the whole radar project. However, arrangements to flood-light the aerials when so required seems to have settled this issue, particularly in respect of possible developments and night-flying in particular.

The capital costs allocated at this stage to getting Watson Watt's research under way was initially set at £12,350. On 8 May, a memo to the Tizard Committee (by now given the full title of the Committee for the Scientific Survey of Air Defence – CSSAD) indicates that preliminary preparation was in danger of falling way behind schedule.

The initial research team had been selected. There were just four of them. Two things stand out. This truly pioneering work was to be in the hands of a very small group. They were all amazingly youthful. Watson Watt himself later reflected on the gamble he had taken in picking so few and such young men.

Labouchere Hillier Bainbridge-Bell was one of the first of them. He was a Senior Scientific Officer, described as 'the most talented circuit designer at Slough', a truly inventive and original boffin, to be responsible for the assembly of the receiver and the design of the cathode ray tube direction finder, all very advanced for its day. His very name hints at a degree of faintly precious eccentricity and he proved to be a less than perfect 'team player' and was described as 'somewhat cranky'. He was a perfectionist and easily inclined to pessimism, liable to assume the worst and look for problems and difficulties even where they didn't exist.

Wilkins was by contrast a bit of a leg-puller and given to inventing nicknames: Bainbridge-Bell failed to see the funny side and it was a matter of mutual relief when, in July, Watson Watt sent him back to Slough to work out technical solutions there rather than on site. Significantly, Wilkins's own nickname was 'Skip', which shows the respect in which he was held: he was seen as Watson Watt's deputy.

E.G. 'Taffy' Bowen was the third of the original quartet. He was a Welshman with an engaging sense of humour. This youthful exuberance is illustrated by the photograph of the team in front of one of the huts on the Ness, in comic pose and wearing silly hats (see Plate Section). He was a product of University College, Swansea and then a pupil of the great Professor Appleton at London University, who himself became involved as a member of the Tizard Committee. Bowen was another truly original mind, the creator of the pulse transmitter, so powerful for its day that, in his own words, 'it scared the living day-lights out of Bainbridge-Bell'.

The fourth member of the team was George Willis, an expert on aerials, whose talents rather blossomed once the restraining influence of Bainbridge-Bell had departed. Bainbridge-Bell's successor was R.H.A. 'Nick' Carter, an expert and highly industrious technician, destined to play a major role in developing airborne radar at Bawdsey.

So by mid-May, the first members of the team had packed their bags and made their way to Suffolk. A technician, A. Bidland, and a lab assistant, Alec Muir, were to join them. A pair of RAF 10-ton lorries brought up the equipment, including a suitably modified ionosphere receiver and a new transmitter. Shortly afterwards, the team was joined by more technical experts from Slough, including Joe Airey. Airey was described by colleagues at Bawdsey as 'a remarkable, practical man, small in stature but high on wisdom'.

There was by now a real and novel sense of urgency, notwithstanding the fact that there was a serious shortage of supplies and equipment. The team was shamefully under-resourced. Bowen demonstrates this frustrating fact when he admitted that the transmitter he had to design had 'many of the parts purloined from discarded equipment from Slough and Teddington'.

Once on the Ness, they would find that tools that had to be borrowed from the Air Force could only be acquired along normal service procedures. This was tiresomely bureaucratic and slow. The radio parts they needed had to be begged or borrowed from whatever sources that could be approached. In particular, finding valves capable of delivering sufficient power necessitated recruitment of manufacturers able to meet these new demands, under a deep screen of secrecy. The Navy helped out with a supply of its most powerful valves, the NT 46, ideal for pulse operation. At the same time, with significant restrictions on funding, the team found itself lumbered with generous gifts of useless and condemned apparatus, much of which ended up dumped in Stony Ditch.

All who worked on the Ness were referred to as 'islanders'. They felt they were something of an elite and were proud of their pioneering role. No facilities for living there were provided. They were expected to find their own accommodation in Orford and Aldeburgh, though often during that busy summer, they seem to have had to 'camp' on the site. The ferry service across the river posed problems, but Rowe firmly rejected a request for a boat of their own. He also denied any of them a security pass to any relevant RAF establishment. One detects in the correspondence a distinct sense that Watson Watt was pushing his luck on these sorts of issue. He had yet to prove the full significance of his team's work. Rowe might equally have worried that the blanket of total security might be compromised.

It was 13 May 1935, a perfect spring day, when Wilkins arrived at Orford. Work began immediately on ferrying across their equipment. The next day was foul, with hail and thunder, but they managed to transport all of their kit without mishap. The RAF had prepared their chosen buildings, but the wooden aerial towers were not yet ready. The two erectors from Harland and Wolff at Woolwich were being delayed by the fierce weather. 'Their faces bore witness to the severity of the elements' recalled Wilkins.

Watson Watt still worked at Slough but most weekends he would travel to Suffolk to monitor what progress was being achieved. He stayed at the Crown and Castle Hotel, seizing the lounge for their exclusive use as a sort of Officers' Mess. His team met there and brainstormed their ideas, speedily resolving problems and developing their vision for future development. Aircraft from Martlesham and flying boats from Felixstowe were used for early tests. Among their number was a noted type; it was the first operational Short Sunderland flying boat. 'The information obtained in these early experiments,' wrote Wilkins, 'encouraged us to believe we were on the right track.' One suggestion they put to the test even at this early stage was to see what the effect would be of shortening the wavelength of their signals. The significance of this reduction, first to 26 metres and then in 1936 to 13 metres was that it was pointing their researches in the direction of centrimetric wavelengths that were to make airborne radar possible.

These weekend meetings in the hotel in Orford were a major feature of Watson Watt's leadership and management technique. Throughout this summer, he remained on duty at Slough and was yet to be appointed to a full-time position as Director of Radar Research. The merit of these meetings was that it inspired all these very young boffins by giving them ample opportunity to share and pool their views.

On 27 May Watson Watt reckoned that operational trials were ready to start, and the Tizard Committee members were invited to make an inaugural visit on 15 June. This was arranged before in fact any aircraft echoes had even been detected. Wilkins recalls this somewhat inauspicious first visit to test their achievements:

I thought on hearing this that maybe they just wanted to see the accommodation, hear our plans and witness any echoes good fortune might provide. A test flight was arranged for the Saturday afternoon of the visit and at the appointed hour, the Valentia aircraft flew overhead at 15,000 feet regardless of the fact that a thunderstorm was brewing. Atmospherics were very strong and signal interference was also much worse than had previously been experienced. Watson Watt was observing the cathode ray tube and claimed to see a glimpse of an echo at 27 kilometres. No other echoes were seen and we subsequently heard that the pilot had abandoned the flight because of the storm. When the flight log was received it was found that Watson Watt's observation could well have been genuine.

Notwithstanding their disappointment, it was decided to repeat the trial early on the Sunday, hoping that at 7 a.m. they might avoid the adverse atmospherics. Again, no signal was received. It was later shown that that particular period in June 1935 saw exceptionally violent weather conditions. This conveniently hid the fact that they were far from ready to show off their equipment. Wilkins and Watson Watt would later agree that the trial should never have been attempted. Wilkins bemoaned the fact that they were constantly being 'pushed into demonstrations for which they were not prepared'.

From the outset, security was seen as being of the utmost importance. A cover story was widely advertised. This new activity across the river was all in connection with further ionospheric radio research. This was not so far-fetched, since Watson Watt and his scientists were known to be involved in this field of study at Slough. It was not incidentally the only time this particular cover story was adopted for work on the Ness. There was only a slight problem it. As another radar expert, Robert Hanbury Brown, was to point out, none of that original team was actually a radio specialist. As well as their youthful enthusiasm, Brown regarded the fact that they were all pure physicists as being the key factor in their successes. They greatly enjoyed being stimulated by what they regarded as an academic and intellectual challenge.

Another cover story put out to RAF personnel was that this programme involved a radio system for locating aircraft by monitoring the magnetos in aero-engines. A typically smart pilot who gave no credence to the idea called their bluff. He had already observed that engine ignition systems were screened, and no noise from them was audible on an aircraft's own radio. How could it be detectable at Orford Ness, miles away? On one trip, he switched his engine off and glided some 30 kilometres to Orford Ness. He knew full well that whatever it was the boffins were up to, it had nothing to do with magnetos. The story never got further than the Sergeant's Mess at Martlesham.

They soon were observing genuine echoes from their trial aircraft however. A favoured route, best suited to giving strong echoes, was from Orford to Bircham Newton in north Norfolk. Pilots were given precise instructions over height, speed and altitude, but nothing about the purpose of these seemingly aimless flights. These were among the best in the service, and they found their assignments tedious and frustrating.

At this early stage, the chief area of research lay with reducing the length of the pulse and simultaneously increasing the power. They modified the valves they scrounged from their contacts in industry (without revealing the precise purpose), by introducing heavier filaments. As a result, the aerials began to give off sparks and bangs. Wilkins explains how they solved the problem: 'The sparking was so strong that I recall hearing it one calm afternoon while standing on the quay at Orford, about half a mile away. We soon cleared up this trouble by soldering a copper lavatory cistern ball-cock at each end of the aerial.'

New ideas were constantly thrown up for sharpening the signal and improving the scope of the system. Bainbridge-Bell's return to Slough was part of this pattern of progress. It led to the development by 1936 of a cathode ray tube direction finder capable of stable operation on high frequencies.

Other discoveries occurred more by chance than design. One such happened on 24 July 1935. Wilkins has described an unexpected breakthrough during a weekend visit from Rowe and Watson Watt. They were observing the oscillograph during a test flight by a Westland Wallace aircraft along the normal Orford Ness-Bircham Newton path. At one point, an unmistakable variation in the signal was evident. Wilkins guessed that they had detected a formation of aircraft. The Wallace echo duly reappeared at 34 miles range and was followed back to Orford Ness. When the pilot of the Wallace arrived to give his flight-log he was asked if he had seen any other aircraft during his run. By the greatest stroke of luck he had spotted a formation of three Harts, one of which subsequently broke formation and went away in a different direction. Both Watson Watt and Rowe were very impressed by this lucky observation, the former because it supported a statement he had made to the Tizard Committee about the possibility of counting aircraft by RDF, and the latter because he realised that there was now some hope of being able to estimate the size of bomber formations.

All sorts of questions had to be addressed by the team as the days went by. Would wooden-constructed aircraft reflect a signal? An example of such a plane was duly tested and the inferior signal noted. Most Fridays, Watson Watt would appear, often with new ideas. Sometimes, Rowe would join them, usually posing challenging questions with regard to practical applications for air defence. Watson Watt would be eternally optimistic, making claims that Wilkins and Bowen felt were little short of 'line-shooting'. One of these related to the estimated accuracy of gun-laying anti-aircraft RDF, which in 1935 was merely a possibility. Watson Watt claimed to be achieving accuracy in bearing and altitude to a matter of the odd degree and of range down to just yards, at a time when this microwave RDF was a vision only.

As performances steadily improved, discussions took place about the way ahead. During brainstorming sessions that summer, the ideas of a chain of coastal stations as well as gunnery control and mobile early warning RDF systems emerged. They even conceived of the possibility of airborne RDF. Reports of their progress circulated around defence circles, and various visitors would join in the debates. One of the earliest was Charles Wright, Director of Scientific Research at the Admiralty. Wright regarded metre-wave RDF as an interim device for naval vessels, because, by using it, they would be acting as beacons for the enemy. He saw that microwaves were essential for the future and that work would have to be done to produce powerful radiation at such wavelengths.

This link with the Navy was significant, confirming the importance of inter-service cooperation. The senior service had already helped with the supply of powerful valves. The move towards less conspicuous wavelength radars arose from an appreciation of the snag raised by the Navy. Fundamental research into powerful substitutes for valves, necessitated by shortening wavelength, led to the cavity magnetron that was to be the key invention in the achievement of operational centrimetric radar. The three Birmingham University Professors, Randall, Sayers and Boot, who created it were indeed true inventors.

Airborne radar was very much in mind even at this early stage in radar development. It was a project that was set up almost immediately after the main team left the Ness. 'Taffy' Bowen from that team was appointed to lead it, with Hanbury Brown, another ex-Orford Ness 'islander' and other pioneer researchers, including Keith Wood, Gerald Touch and Percy Hibberd. But this is still in the future. Meanwhile, Wilkins was reporting some local troubles:

The presence of the research team was not always popular with the local villagers when they found their radio reception was interfered with by our pulse transmissions. When investigated by the Post Office it was found that the receivers concerned were all very old models and I think that their owners were advised to buy new ones. At any rate we did not have to take any action.

Another complication was 'surges' on the electricity mains. I forget how these manifested themselves but the Electricity Company deemed it advisable to insert a large filter in the mains at our switchboard. This probably did nothing useful but we heard nothing more of the complaint.

Fortunately neither of these two complaints caused any speculation as to what was going on in our huts. If anyone asked what we were up to our reply about ionosphere research seemed to satisfy the questioner. It was to a small extent true!

RADAR WINS THE ARGUMENT

The island team was growing as the range of work extended. Bainbridge-Bell, who seems to have had a pedagogic streak, was back in Slough training up a string of new recruits who would staff the great new expansion about to be made possible. It was clear that the Orford site was no longer adequate for the developments being envisaged. During a visit in July 1935, Watson Watt took Wilkins and 'Taffy' Bowen in his rather grand Daimler to explore the locality for a likely alternative site. They first looked at the Martello tower at Slaughden, which was immediately dismissed. Earlier in the summer, Wilkins and Airey had gone for an exploratory drive round the locality and hit upon Bawdsey. In brilliant weather the whole place looked exotic and both agreed there and then that it would make an ideal location for their research work. They learnt that the grand manor and estate belonged to Sir Cuthbert Quilter.

Wilkins mentioned this trip to Watson Watt, who promptly drove straight there and immediately fell in love with the place. With characteristic energy he set wheels in motion to acquire the property and to the delight of all, it soon tran-spired that it was in fact for sale.

Wilkins understandably is vague in his account of events as to the date of this important development. In fact, Harry Wimperis received a request from Watson Watt as early as 6 August 1935 to see if the Quilter estate could be acquired. He was also unaware that it was already on the market. Watson Watt spent the rest of the month putting forward a case for immediate purchase, explaining that it was uniquely well placed for inaugurating a whole chain of such stations. The Chief of Air Staff was persuaded. Comments by the Secretary of State for Air included a pressing statement: 'This must be done. Treasury are as anxious as we are to pursue this investigation', adding: 'Mr Watson Watt's requirements on land, plant and personnel should be met as quickly as possible.' Luckily, the vastly extravagant Quilter family had begun to feel an economic pinch and were only too happy to take the money.

This decision marks the acceptance in principal by the Air Ministry of the whole idea of a chain of coastal RDF stations every 20 miles. This remarkable defence early warning system came to be called Chain Home, and by the outbreak of war it stretched from the Isle of Wight (Ventnor) to the Shetlands (Scapa Flow). The final settlement over Bawdsey Manor and its estate involved a partial move in on 17 January 1936 and a final completion of the possession on 1 June. This settlement was slower – and £10,000 more expensive – than had been hoped and explains the need to keep Orford Ness up and running until Bawdsey operational.

Wilkins seems to have made little reference to his feelings about working on the Ness. Bowen is less reticent. He writes: 'These were idyllic times, one of the happiest periods of my life.' He is far from sentimental however:

> Rowe described the Ness as surely one of the loveliest places in the world. His views are heavily biased; to us the Ness was a very forbidding place, a land of freezing winds, shingle, mud flats – and comfortless huts. By contrast, Orford was a delightful spot – a seductive paradise – with a population of the most charming people it was possible to imagine.

Bowen had 'digs' in Orford, which was clearly a most happy arrangement. The other three, in his words, 'settled for the more opulent streets of Aldeburgh' motoring over each day to take an RAF ferry across the Ore at 8.30 a.m. each morning.

Some nights, they would camp by their machines, their supper and breakfast little more than 'a piece of cake and a bottle of beer'.

Their work they found 'enormously satisfying' and 'they cared not a jot about the absence of refinement'. Bowen cannot avoid commenting on Lindemann's attitude to their crude facilities. Lindemann had joined Tizard's committee during that summer, and scarcely ever failed to find fault with everything, including their primitive conditions. 'He had fastidious tastes', observed Bowen, a characteristic evident from way back during his First World War days.

Arnold Wilkins confirms that work was continuing apace on the Ness right through the autumn of 1935. There were still major areas of difficulty to be overcome, notably in the apparatus for direction finding.

These masts presented Watson Watt with a frustrating delay, his first experience of the inflexibility of the civil service machine in action – or in this case – inaction. He was clear that added height for the aerials was essential for improved performance. Three 250-foot lattice steel towers were ordered, only to be delayed because of a shortage of materials. None were ever supplied to Orford, and indeed it was not until late 1938 that work on construction was put in hand by the Air Ministry Works Directive. By the outbreak of war, at considerable cost, including some human lives, the familiar 350-foot metal towers were in place for transmission, four per each Chain Home station, plus two lower ones for the receivers. Meanwhile, the lower wooden towers had to suffice on the Ness. Their shape, with feet splayed, clearly influenced the design of later steel masts. The heavy bases for the masts were problematic as they tended to sink unevenly into the shingle and marsh at the Ness. Eventually, the first six-tier array was attached to a mast, with its radiating and reflecting elements duly calculated and the aerials hauled up into position. The team were suitably proud of their handiwork. One man, Alec Muir, did this erection work single-handed.

Nick Carter was to play a major part in the development of operational radar. He joined the team on the Ness in July 1935 and recalled some of the practical difficulties facing them:

> We had a beautiful summer, and our daily working period was governed partly by two factors. First, the Ministry of Works ran a motor-driven ferry from Orford capable of carrying a ton or so across the river to the Air Ministry site on Orford Ness. This ferry departed from the quay at 8.30 am and made the last return journey at 4 pm. We just did not accept this early return time, so one of their boatmen met us at 7.00 pm with a rowing boat. This timing was kept up all summer, and well into the autumn. Secondly, there were no shops on site, so all food, drinks etc. had to be taken over at 8.30 am, or else one had to go without refreshment for the day.

Carter was allocated to the specific task of developing height-finding techniques. The first practical trial took place on 21 September 1935 and immediately produced another example of the curiosity that tantalised RAF aircrew. The aircraft involved had been instructed to fly to East Dereham and back at about 9,000 feet. Everything seemed to go well, except that when some distance from Orford, the aircraft appeared to lose height down to scarcely 1,000 feet. Carter checked his apparatus. As it reappeared it had climbed back to the instructed height. The pilot as usual landed on the northern airfield on the Ness, to check with the boffins that all was well. Carter confirmed that the run had been satisfactory and noted that the pilot's log made no reference to losing altitude. He duly reported the apparent anomaly and thought no more about it. A few months later, at a social gathering when one of the Ness boffins was entertained by the RAF at Martlesham, the truth emerged. As Carter explains:

> During the evening he learnt of the various very intelligent tests the pilots had made in an effort to find out what we were trying to do. Security was of the maximum category. We did not advertise that any secret work was in progress by enclosing the site in barbed wire with sentries on the gate. The pilots were not told anything of our work. It was at the time when the pilots handed in their flight logs that we had to be extremely careful what we said. We wanted to be as open as possible and to talk with the chaps who were working with us.

This whole episode is particularly significant. The pilot in the September trial admitted he had indeed dropped down to 1,000 feet. Carter's measurements proved to have been entirely accurate. The curiosity of the pilots was understandable. Above all, the subtle policy of maintaining the security of the Ness by means of 'privacy' rather than by impenetrable barriers and armed guards was amply demonstrated. This may well have fooled the Germans through two wars. Only when the Americans became involved from the 1960s did this policy change.

From September, work began on another aspect of radar, with the secondment of a new scientist, Harry Dewhirst, from RAE Farnborough. This was the creation of transportable radar, for use at mobile bases.

Not everything was going smoothly. Typically, the usual problems encountered when the team was pressurised to produce results before they were ready would arise when the Tizard Committee descended on them expecting results. Signals would suddenly fail and only its more informed members could appreciate their difficulties. The fact was that the whole radar programme was still very much on trial, and failure to perform could have led to cut backs or complete cancellation. The team were well aware of this and they often had to achieve accordingly. A visitor in October 1935, a Wing Commander from the RAF Signals Department, made some pertinent and sobering comments. He was worried about the jamming aspects of the proposed network of RDF (radar) transmitters: 'If I am correct it will be obviously unwise to start the engineering development until the possibility of jamming has been completely eliminated.' In fact, he was not correct, but such observations by senior serving officers threatened the smooth progress of the research. Indeed, Wilkins had successfully operated the transmitters under severely adverse conditions. Watson Watt won the arguments and persuaded the Tizard Committee that the 1936 chain of RDF stations programme should proceed.

This sort of threat was far from being the only one. The influence of Frederick Lindemann was damaging the very Tizard Committee itself. Bowen described it as being 'riven with strife'. Lindemann was beginning to oppose the very concept of radar, insisting on a switch to his own ideas. So acute did this controversy grow that during the autumn, with the entire CSSAD (Tizard Committee) threatening to resign, Lord Swinton, as Air Minister, was forced to disband it and re-establish it with Professor Appleton installed in Lindemann's place. This eased matters in the short term, though as Bowen himself observed, there were 'ominous developments later...' While not relevant to the Ness story, this indicates just how difficult it was for Watson Watt to keep everything running productively.

Wilkins describes the day-to-day business of work on the Ness:

> To get to work we were ferried across the River Ore usually in the Air Ministry motorboat, but occasionally in a rowing boat. The rest of the journey was either by Trojan van or hanging onto a Hucks Starter [an old motorised mechanism mounted on a Ford Model T, used for rotating the propeller of an aircraft to start its engine].
>
> Sometimes we had to walk across the aerodrome – not very pleasant in wet weather... As we frequently stayed late at work we had to row ourselves back to Orford. At certain states of the tide the current ran very fast and it took some time before we mastered the art of crossing in these conditions. On one such occasion when Bowen and I with Watson Watt as passenger were rowing over we overshot the quay and had to row back against the powerful ebb tide. I am sure that Watson Watt thought his last day had come!

Reading Wilkins' account of these exciting months of pioneering work, an undertone of faint disapproval of Watson Watt comes to the surface every so often. It all seemed to turn on the ultimate recognition accorded Watson Watt for his 'invention'. Wilkins felt that he and others in the team were the true inventors. There is some justice in this. A sense of mounting bitterness would re-emerge with greater force after the war, and this in a man universally regarded as having a notably amiable and placid temperament. However, a more immediate issue arose, most clearly illustrating the differences between Watson Watt and his loyal colleague. Wilkins provides an explanation of the issue that divided them.

It was quite early in the time at the Ness that Watson Watt had perhaps rather off-handedly mentioned to Wilkins a seemingly tiresome instruction from the Air Ministry. They wanted him to take out a secret patent on RDF. Asked if the others in the team would wish to be named as co-inventors, it seemed apparent that they would not be exactly welcome to do so. Had this been a matter of intellectual property for academic publication, Wilkins and Bowen would have felt insulted not to be shown as co-authors. However, as this was a mere patent, Wilkins was content not to press for any involvement. Bowen, perhaps more reluctantly, accepted this course of action. That this matter was to rankle in Wilkins' mind is very evident from later events. He made the following observation: 'At a later date, Watson Watt also patented IFF [Identification Friend or Foe] before any trials had been made of this device. His patent included the passive keyed dipole, a method which I claim to have suggested to him, although he denied it...'

This somewhat sour tone is in some contrast to the generally genial spirit shown by the team as a whole, and the undoubted deep respect and appreciation they held for their leader. This tension was only to grow as work at Bawdsey expanded. There is little doubt that in truth it arose out of a sense of quite deep-seated grievance over the levels of recognition accorded the radar team after the war. The fact here however, was undeniably that Watson Watt owned the patents and thus could justifiably claim the greatest prize. However, Watson Watt could come up with some bright ideas. He focused on establishing the altitude of aircraft. They were soon measuring heights from about 1,200 feet upwards. Then, in November 1935, Watson Watt himself came up with an answer to the problem of precise direction finding. Sitting in the train he suddenly wondered whether crossing two dipoles would offer a workable solution. Wilkins was impressed by the simplicity of this arrangement, and with his aerials expert, Joe Airey, he had a trial arrangement rigged on the Ness upon the 75-foot towers.

Wilkins completes his account of the Orford Ness phase of his radar work:

By December 1935, after seven months work at Orford Ness we had developed a transmitter of 100 kw (nominal) peak pulse power, which worked with a pulse width of about 10 microseconds. Performance on aircraft range-finding with this equipment was such that, on a single aircraft flying at 7,000 feet, detection could be achieved at 70 km to an accuracy of half a kilometre; the corresponding range at 15,000 feet flying height was 85 km. Ranges to which aircraft could be followed were somewhat greater and these results were all obtained using 70 foot masts. Such was the situation, when on the 19th December, we were told that the Treasury had sanctioned a chain of RDF stations for use in defence of London.

The radar facilities at Orford Ness remained in operation as an outstation for Bawdsey until 1937, and the rapidly expanding number of scientists found themselves moving from one station to the other. Wilkins tells of the old Crossley staff car that transported team members from Bawdsey (where all now were accommodated) the dozen or so miles via back lanes to Orford. This somewhat lavishly appointed vehicle was given the nickname of the 'Gin Palace'.

Watson Watt was appointed Director at Bawdsey in 1936, and initiated a host of the developments that were to play a vital part in the war that followed. The role in this story taken by Orford Ness was gradually diminishing, though for some eighteen months, research work on the Ness continued. Some new 'islanders' were recruited. George Willis of the initial team was joined by Henry Dewhirst from RAE, and young men like Donald Preist, Bill Eastwood and Robert Hanbury Brown. Their tasks were largely to test equipment 'in the field'. New masts were regularly being erected for these purposes. Adding to the height of the array of masts was at this stage a continuing requirement.

A major air exercise was held in September 1936, in part to put this new radar technology to the test and impress the powers that be. Bawdsey was the only station in anything like a semi-operational state – the other pioneering Chain Home stations were still in the course of construction. Even here, Bawdsey had but a single mast in commission, and on the crucial day it seriously malfunctioned. The great and good came to watch the operators (Hanbury Brown, Wilkins and Harry Dewhirst) monitor the approach of 'enemy' aircraft and report their position and range to Fighter Command. The trial was a complete washout, for a variety of reasons, not least because of the intense rush involved, which meant that the signals proved far too weak.

The Orford Ness transmitter was still in place. The next day, Hanbury Brown and a newcomer straight from Oxford, Gerald Touch, were despatched to the Ness. The transmitter operated with total success and rescued Bawdsey's reputation. At stake was the possibility already referred to that work on other research might be suspended, especially as there was considerable competition for limited resources then available. One of Watson Watt's greatest qualities was his ability to be persuasive! Tizard and the RAF were duly persuaded, and in this, the 'old' Orford Ness transmitter proved handy. All thoughts of persevering with the south coast sound reflectors were abandoned from this moment.

It should be noted that this episode came at a highly critical stage in the infighting that had been raging with increasing fury during the summer of 1936. This struggle for influence in the conduct of radar research may crudely be defined as Lindemann and Churchill versus Tizard and Wimperis. It became even more critical when the rumour emerged that Lindemann was seeking election to Parliament as a Tory candidate for the University of Oxford seat. This implied an ominous threat of political interference. It came to nothing.

Tizard and his sympathisers were in fact winning, although a disastrous practical demonstration was the last thing that Watson Watt needed. They were still however encountering technical problems, which was hardly surprising in view of the immense pace of development and the very uncertain, not to say unreliable, equipment and materials available to the team.

All pioneering radar research at Orford Ness ended during 1937, with the completion of work on 13-metre wavelength transmission. The team was sent down to Dunkirk, near Canterbury, to set up one of the first Chain Home stations. This was very far from being the end of radar at the Ness.

THE WATSON WATT LEGACY

There is a significant and intriguing footnote to this account of early radar research. The word 'boffin' is regularly applied to the astonishingly inventive folk who worked on Orford Ness and at Bawdsey. Dictionaries remind one that the word was indeed coined 'during World War II'. Its creation is attributed to a senior RAF officer, Wing Commander, later Air Vice-Marshal, Peter Chamberlain, who was involved in the fitting of Air Interception (AI) radar into RAF aircraft. He is generally given credit for inventing the word, though where he got it from is not recorded. He reckoned that 'boffins' were the scientists and technicians who not only had the skill and imagination to create wonderful gadgets but also had the get-up-and-go to make them work and who would liaise with the military to see that they were practical and useable and met service requirements. Watson Watt records that the first man to be so defined and described was Robert Hanbury Brown, who spent a year at Orford Ness and whose departure in 1937 marked the end of the site's involvement with radar research.

Professor (as he was to become after the war) Hanbury Brown titled his autobiography *Boffin*. Given that the word boffin has become rather degraded in more modern parlance, suggesting some sort of reclusive absent-minded professor, it is worth repeating here the definition Watson Watt gave to it:

> A boffin is a researcher of high scientific competence who has learned that a device of great technical elegance, capable of remarkable performance in the hands of a picked crew, is not necessarily a good weapon of war. He is the instrument for building into the design provisions which depend on close analysis of the vehicle in which the device is to operate, the field conditions in which it is to operate, and above all things, the competence of those who are to operate, maintain and repair it.

The truth is that Hanbury Brown was just one of a host of boffins that worked on a variety of trials and experiments over the decades, all of whom well deserved the title 'boffin'.

Few can possibly doubt that the 'invention' of advance-warning radar was a defining technical achievement of the era. The threat of the bomber was never removed but its scale was dramatically reduced and the damage to civilian morale greatly lessened. The significance of this may be judged by what happened on the Monday afternoon of 26 April 1937 at the small market town of Guernica, cultural capital of the Basque country of northern Spain, during the Civil War. A totally defenceless civilian population was bombed and strafed by waves of Heinkel He111s and Junkers Ju52s. There were devastating casualties. No less than 1,654 civilians died that afternoon, more, it will be noted, than the entire fatal civilian casualties suffered by Britain during the First World War. A further 889 were wounded. This sounded a fearful warning of the possibilities of the bomber getting through. Had no system of defence and counter-offensive systems been available, it is undoubtable that Fighter Command would not have been able to defend Britain in the summer of 1940 and much more of Britain would have been destroyed. The role of radar was crucial in giving early air-raid warnings that helped both defending aircraft and reduced civilian casualties. Watson Watt and his research teams at Orford Ness, and then Bawdsey, Dundee, Worth Matravers and ultimately, Malvern, deserve grateful recognition.

This is to see Watson Watt's role in the broadest of historical perspectives, however. He was indeed an inspirational leader during the key years of 1935 to 1940. He was highly respected by his people because they were well aware of the importance of both his vision and his driving energy and political skill. Hanbury Brown for example described him as 'a delightful person to meet. Nowadays he would, I suppose, be called charismatic.' The particular talent he recalled was that of the supreme salesman. However, there is no doubt that a certain degree of bitterness was generated at times over his behaviour.

Radar was developed under immense pressures. Impatient and demanding expectations by the military were accompanied by tight-fisted scrutiny from the Treasury. All the while, there was a mounting sense of the imminent threat of war. Necessity being the mother of invention can seldom have been better demonstrated. Much also hung on the happy combination of the creative imagination and the faintly amateurish expertise of those youthful and enthusiastic pioneering boffins, and the leadership and management skills of their director.

This latter factor alone justified Watson Watt's claim to fame. As team leader and political fixer, he was a winner. He was also blessed with the gift of a vision to see just how radar could be made to be effective and useful in practice. Two events early in the war illustrate the importance of this point. The Germans had gun-laying radar on their pocket-battleship, *Graf Spee*; the US had radar at their naval base at Pearl Harbour. In the final analysis, when facing crushing enemy attack, neither had the means or technique to apply their radar and make it useful.

The *Graf Spee* episode presents a particularly poignant reflection on the immediately pre-war surge towards technological supremacy by the two protagonists. This so-called pocket-battleship was conceived as a commerce raider. Long-range detection of shipping would have been a valuable facility. She was the very first warship to be fitted with sea-borne radar equipment. Its range was very limited however – a maximum of 10 or so miles. Meanwhile, her optical range finders were so superior, capable of accuracy to the horizon, that the radar was not developed as a tactical weapon, being used only when visibility was severely limited.

The consequence of this was that the German warship could not determine the nature of the reception it might receive if it ventured out of Montevideo harbour following the battle off the river Plate estuary in December 1939.

A significant postscript to the battle relates to the Ness. This was the determination by the British to acquire the wreck of the *Graf Spee* so that lessons could be learned about its equipment. The British Naval Attaché in Montevideo, Captain Henry McCall, was instructed to negotiate with the pro-British Uruguay government for the purchase of the wreck, ostensibly for scrap. In February 1940, one of the notable Ness radar pioneers, Bainbridge-Bell, was despatched by Sunderland flying boat from Marseilles to Rio de Janeiro and on to Montevideo to look at and if possible, retrieve, the radar. He spent three days in early March aboard the all-but-submerged wreck, and was able to remove several important components, notably from the antennae and the display tube. Throughout this trip, an element of 'cloak and dagger' persisted; travelling with a cover story, he was supposedly the agent for Thomas Ward Ltd, a firm of Sheffield scrap merchants. Was it worth the effort? A year later, the Admiralty received a characteristically frigid letter from the Treasury, requiring a justification for the cost involved. The Navy responded:

> The examination of the *Graf Spee* was most valuable in establishing the use of RDF [as at this stage it was still called] by the enemy. It provided sufficient technical detail to guide us in the search for enemy RDF in general and the revising and preparation of equipment and counter-measures.

Ness boffins were to go on proving their worth in what can only be described as front line intelligence. In February 1942, Donald Preist, another Ness 'islander' was summoned by the Air Ministry from his research work on Chain Low (1.5 metre) radar at Langton Matravers to take part in the intensely risky Bruneval Raid. The purpose here was to capture intact the vital components of the German 'Würzburg' direction-finding radar, which was responsible for the unacceptable losses by then being sustained by Allied bombers. German technology appeared to have caught up. A substantial operation was launched by Combined Operations*, which put Flight Sergeant Cox into the enemy base, enabling him to grab the key parts of the installation. Preist, regarded as too valuable to risk capture, was left on the beach, to confirm that they had what they were looking for. Under enemy fire, the whole party managed to escape in naval gunboats, leaving only two dead behind. The research done on the captured items proved both alarming and crucial. It demonstrated that the Allied technological lead was all but lost. The boffins were, however, able to detect operational flaws in the German design that permitted the use of a jamming device, WINDOW (small, metallised strips, like tin foil, that were designed to be dropped in bundles from the sky and confuse the German signals) to neutralise the whole system. The Germans never discovered why 'Würzburg' ceased to be so effective thereafter. Preist seems not to have been decorated for his

---

* Combined Operations Directive was created in the gloomiest months of 1940 by Churchill to develop the concept of Army-Navy-Air Force inter-service cooperation. It generated the skills and techniques of counter-attack on the mainland of Europe, ultimately leading to the D-Day landings. The most significant Director was Lord Louis Mountbatten of the Royal Navy. The testing of Army tanks, etc on the Ness site, which was primarily an RAF-associated station, in 1944 typifies the Combined Ops in action.

courage under enemy fire, surely well beyond the normal call of duty for a radar boffin. Did he realise that should he be in danger of capture, his bodyguards were instructed to shoot him dead?

Back in 1940, the RAF possessed a system entirely fit for its purpose. In analysing the reasons why the RAF won the Battle of Britain, it is commonly presumed that the famous 'few' had superior aircraft and although outnumbered, they fought more brilliantly. In fact, the Messerschmitt 109 was in most respects a superior fighter and German fighting tactics were more up to date having been honed in battle conditions as the German Condor Legion provided assistance to General Franco during the Spanish Civil War. The crucial factor in negating these shortcomings was intelligence and communication. The notice British squadrons had of the identity of incoming attacks, and the up-to-the-minute information supplied by the network of Observer Corps volunteers, all focused through an efficient centralised information network, gave Allied pilots a vital advantage. The RAF wasted no time (or fuel) in searching for their enemy. The Germans were operating towards the limit of their effective range. They lost many fighters who simply ran out of fuel!

Watson Watt's most significant legacy was how radar was organised. Watson Watt had the grand concept of a network of radar stations, which became Chain Home[2] and Chain Home Low. Moreover he realised that they could only be effective if linked to a central point, a sort of clearing house to define priorities and direct operations. This was manifest in the familiar image of tireless WAAF operators and plotters in the Filter Room at Fighter Command HQ Bentley Priory, taking in reports and directing fighters to their targets from a list of hitherto unknown places, which rapidly became part of the Battle of Britain story: Tangmere, Biggin Hill, Manston, Kenley, North Weald, West Drayton and a string of others. This was a crucial element in Watson Watt's 'invention'.

One other element in the success of the Battle of Britain however was very much Tizard's contribution, not Watson Watt's. This was the training given to RAF pilots from as early as 1936 in ground to air radio communications. Directions from fighter control went against the current spirit of pilot independence. Moreover, the source of intelligence information had to be kept secret or the significance of radar would be revealed. It was Tizard, the virtual inventor of the concept of the crack test pilot, who drove through what came to be called 'The Biggin Hill Experiment'. Fighter pilots became used to accepting without question instructions from their base, in the sure knowledge that they would be effectively directed to their targets, and the system became further refined throughout the summer of 1940.

So what is to be made of the role and reputation of Sir Robert Watson-Watt? A key to assessing his true worth and evaluating his obvious self-esteem is the fact that he was a direct descendent of another monumental figure in the history of British invention, James Watt. Robert, who from the conferring of his knighthood in 1942, assumed a rather grander title by hyphenating his name, must have been aware that he was another Scot whose 'invention' changed the world. Yet Wilkins in particular, and others too perhaps, can well have had grounds for feeling somewhat aggrieved as they beavered away, often with too few resources and somewhat imprecise instructions. They may well have reflected on the outcome of the post-war Royal Commission on Awards to Inventors, which was set up to give financial reward and recognition to those whose inventions had particularly benefited the nation and contributed to eventual victory.

One such name to be considered for an award was Sir Frank Whittle, inventor of the jet engine. He was recommended for a prize of £100,000, (generous, and to be multiplied by a factor of twenty-five to give a value to it fifty years later), and perhaps not a little surprising because it never seemed to occur to him even to apply. Watson Watt on the other hand applied early and persistently. The Commission questioned his role as an actual inventor, in contrast with the three Birmingham scientists whose genuinely groundbreaking cavity magnetron really was crucial to the development of radar. They were each given £12,000. 'Jimmy' Rowe was consulted and submitted the following, quite revealing opinion:

> There was nothing particularly brilliant about the early work on ground radar...
> In general, I would not put Watson Watt [or Watson-Watt as he was by then
> calling himself] in the first two dozen radar inventors. In my opinion however,
> he did a splendid job in the early days of radar in arousing enthusiasm, getting
> in touch with the Service people and in rapidly absorbing the nature of the
> problems... His influence was great before the war, although less in the role of
> inventor than as a 'seller' of a new field of applied effort.

The opinion of another member of the Tizard Committee, Professor E.V. Appleton, sums up both the value of Watson Watt's work and the relative significance of his team's contribution. He reported to the Commission:

> When I came in touch with the practical radar work I found Bowen and
> Wilkins hard at work on the technical side ... but the biggest effort of all was
> being made by Watson-Watt in pleading, advocating, getting stores, masts and
> buildings. It was above all due to his drive and powerful advocacy that we had
> radar stations around our coast when war broke out... He had the vision of what
> it all implied, he just burned with it. I think that Watson-Watt deserves a very
> substantial award for his work in turning scientific radar into practical radar but
> I would like to see others, especially Bowen and Wilkins rewarded as well.

It was perhaps a surprisingly contested issue, possibly made so by the contrasting aspirations of the various beneficiaries. On 19 December 1951, Sir Robert Watson-Watt was awarded a very handsome sum of £50,000. At the same time, his two leading pioneer boffins, Bowen and Wilkins, neither of them knighted, got just £12,000 each. Ten other members of the team received between £2,400 and £750. By way of comparison, Barnes Wallis, for various reasons, received a somewhat grudging £10,000.

Pre-War Research

THE SCIENCE OF BOMBING

Just a few hundreds of yards to the north of the Black Beacon, an important new bombing range was being established. The need to refine the techniques first introduced during the First World War became evident as the performance of aircraft was developing during the later 1920s. This prompted the establishing of a fully equipped facility to analyse trajectory and accuracy of bomb flight as much as explosive effectiveness. This became a Bomb Ballistics Unit, a dedicated site for which was laid out as early as 1927.

At first, this range provided no more than a fairly deep pit, or as the civilian operators described it, 'an improvised dugout' in the shingle a few hundred yards west of the lighthouse. This was distinctly uncomfortable and somewhat dangerous, with minimal shelter overhead. It was, at that stage, far from sophisticated, and very little more advanced than the facilities Frank Holder had endured back in 1917.

The trials were all now under the aegis of RAE Farnborough, with aircraft flown over from Martlesham. In 1932, the decision was taken to build a far more substantial base building for the following season of trials and what from then on came to be called the Bomb Ballistics building was hastily designed for operation from 1 March 1933. This was – and still is – a substantial concrete and brick structure, designed to withstand the vibration caused by the impact of bombs without damaging or upsetting the array of cameras and recording equipment housed in and on it. Reports on this new facility noted that 'it was drier and gave a better view'.

That same year, 1933, appeared what was rather grandly referred to as the Orford Ness Beacon Power Station. It was always assumed that the decision to install such a generator was taken to provide solely for the beacon. In fact, the coincidence of this supply with the opening of an improved bombing range was no accident. Perhaps it was a deliberate ploy to ascribe its construction to the supposedly civilian beacon project, thereby disguising its application to this new, solely military, facility.

In June 1943, a report was submitted to the Air Ministry which was designed to summarise the current position on bombing technology, at a moment during the war when a major leap forward in the science involved was being anticipated. This document provides some detailed background information on the evolution of British bombing technology from the earliest period of military aviation. The importance of Orford Ness in this story emerges very clearly.

At the start of the First World War it had been accepted that bombs and bomb releases were so crude and undeveloped that the science of ballistics could have little bearing on the accuracy or effectiveness of bombing. Some quite primitive early trials did take place at Upavon and at RNAS Calshott before the Ness itself was opened. A disused coalmine shaft at Rossington in Yorkshire was used for timing the fall of a bomb, and other tests took place at the Isle of Grain, where pairs of bombs were dropped to see what the difference in flight between a known model and a new variant might be. This was all in respect of flying at relatively low altitude and slow speeds. A boffin involved in much of this work was Henry Wimperis, a distinguished scientist and Air Ministry civil servant, whose name has already cropped up in relation to RNAS bombs.

When, in 1925, Martlesham resumed full-scale operations, Orford Ness became the chief location for ballistics testing and bomb sight development. Trials were undertaken involving pairs of bombs dropped from 10,000 feet, where 'known' characteristics of an established type of bomb would be compared with the performance of a new one. It all remained relatively crude and unsophisticated. The whole science of bomb ballistics required far more elaborate apparatus and with it, mathematical expertise. Thus, when the formal range became fully operational in 1928, one of its first tasks was 'to check the validity of the particle trajectory theory based on the quadratic drag law.' This was the stuff of real boffinry, and total comprehension of some of the reports sent from the Ness required a degree of superior mathematical understanding.

Throughout these years, the trials, conducted during summer months, and then only when the weather was favourable[*], were designed to develop a standardised test for all types of RAF bomb and discover just what the factors were that would enable aircrew to achieve any sort of reliable accuracy. Moreover, an important element in all this work on the Ness was more than just the development of bombs; it supplied a means of training bomb aimers and pilots. So, bombs were produced for practice and exercise purposes, constructed to give performances

---

[*] It was reckoned during the 1940s that fully reliable weather conditions would occur on average for only forty days per year. On such occasions, the team would operate double shifts to take advantage of the window of opportunity.

identical to the real thing, yet avoiding the expenditure on precious and costly materials, including explosive charges. They were 'dummies'.

This work, which was begun in the late 1920s and continued through the '30s, was immensely valuable in creating a bomber force capable of waging war. It has indeed been claimed that the bombing range on the Ness was quite as important a facility as any located there during all the decades of military occupation.

The 1943 report observes that 'with small modifications from time to time, the original equipment is still in use today'. What is even more significant is that the Ness's pre-eminence in this technical field was sustained, and when after the war, new bombing ranges were opened at West Freugh in Scotland, and at Woomera in Australia, it was the Orford Ness model that was adopted.

By 1933 and with the opening of the new range, it was established that the bomb aimer needed to know his air speed, height above the target, wind speed and his 'trail angle' or the pitch of the plane. The gadgetry on the Ness had by now developed a system for precise coordination between plane and ground in order to calculate the time of the bomb's flight. A series of ground cameras could record the precise course of the aircraft, and monitor, again by cameras, the entire passage of the missile from bomb bay to 'splash'. The Bomb Ballistics building was fitted with a *camera obscura* to follow the passage of aircraft, a super-high speed 'Vinten' 35-millimetre movie camera, and still cameras, all coordinated by an electrical link and mounted on the roof. Out on the shingle, a string of painted markers running from south to north at irregular intervals were again designed to enable photographs taken from the aircraft to establish its exact altitude. Other fixed cameras were located along the shoreline to monitor the splashes of bombs dropped out to sea.

Reports in the archives reveal the existence of two distinct bombing lines, each with clear ground markers for the pilot to follow. A sea bombing line was directed from the north of Orford village in a south easterly direction, leaving the lighthouse 100 or so yards to the north. A second ran southwest to northeast, designed for bombs being dropped into either shingle or the sea towards Aldeburgh. Both tracks ran directly over the ballistics building.

During the 1930s, communications between ground and aircraft were still far from reliable. A wireless hut some 800 yards from the Bomb Ballistics building established a link between air and ground, but puffs of smoke and large white painted visual signals had always to be used. These latter indicated to the pilot the need to shift his run either to the left or right, to stand by, or to abort and go home. The signals comprised large arrows or rings. The camera points were linked by loudspeaker 'philcophones'.

Out of this painstaking work emerged ever more accurate bombing tables essential for bomb aiming. With new speeds and altitudes achieved during the pre-war years, this was something that could no longer afford to remain a mere 'hit or miss' affair. Of course as aircraft performances were dramatically increased over the succeeding two decades, so Farnborough's need for continuing research was to remain.

Significantly, the number of personnel working on the Ness at this time was quite small. Gordon Kinsey quotes the experience of a B.G. Goldsmith, who had served there during the previous war. He returned to the Ness in 1929 for a three-year tour of duty in the RAF:

> The scientific work was under the supervision of a civilian Scientific Officer, Mr Rowe, who was responsible for all the ballistic trials carried out on the Island. Mr Jay looked after the Works and Maintenance side and this was directed from Farnborough, whilst a local night watchman, Mr Smy [member of a notable Orford family], looked after the security after dark, and another civilian, Mr Harold Gibbs * was the Motor Transport driver... When tests were carried out additional personnel were flown over from Martlesham in one of various aircraft. Another Scientific Officer, Mr Pritchard was also engaged in these duties.

Although the work was dangerous, no records exist of any serious injuries incurred during these trials.

Goldsmith provides a characteristic example of Rowe's organisational powers. He admitted that official procedures often left much to be desired. Invariably during the hand-over (between plane and ground) the sighting was lost and the aircraft had to be signalled to abort the run, as it could not be recorded. This necessitated another run or runs. 'Mr Rowe quickly amended the whole course of action so that valuable time was not lost...'

Another reminiscence comes from Flight Lieutenant J.R. Bennett who was stationed at the A&AEE Unit at Martlesham for an unusually long spell, from 1932 to 1938. He recalls how they would fly over in a Vickers Valore twin-engined transport, with their bombs lashed down to eyelets and shackles to steady them and without their detonators, which came over by road. They would row back across the river for a ploughman's lunch, taken at the Jolly Sailor, or, as they liked to call it, 'The Frivilous Matelot'. He comments on the potential dangers, but equally on the sense of fun they clearly enjoyed. 'Unfortunately, as is always the case with experimental flying, we lost some splendid chaps, but there was a great spirit of cooperation throughout the whole unit and for me Orford Ness has always been a happy experience and a valuable one.'

The question of casualties on Orford Ness over the years remains shrouded in a certain degree of mystery. Certainly, no precise list is available in the National Archives. It seems that the authorities were reluctant to advertise accidents at their research station. The secret site still managed to retain some of its secrets. A report appeared in the *East Anglian Daily Times* of 27 November 1933: commenting that: 'Three airmen were severely injured in a mysterious RAF aeroplane crash yesterday.' Bennett was one of the pilots involved. He was testing

---

* Gibbs was to achieve notoriety two decades later when he drove his mobile crane into the main door truss of the southern hangar.

an electro-magnetic bomb release on a Fairey Gordon. He spent the best part of a year in hospital ... where he met his wife-to-be when she was nursing in the Accident Ward.

Aircrew logbooks over these busy months spent developing more efficient and effective aircraft record a relentless programme of trials. Some of these would prove immensely significant in the light of events after 1939. One such was the work done by a newly commissioned pilot, H.J. Sanders, who recalled his involvement in the checking the effect of the ice on bomb release units and machine guns:

> This also happened when the eight guns in the first Spitfire were fired at altitude, and on one such trial, the pilot found that the ammunition had frozen. On encountering warmer air at lower altitude, the guns thawed and fired a burst on their own. We had a block electric heater made to fit inside the hollow of the breech mechanism and also a rate of fire recorder.

This invaluable research was all undertaken well before the exigencies of actual warfare could expose any serious design weaknesses in these new machines. Another experiment, which involved Sanders, interestingly anticipates work taken up on a far greater scale by the lethality and vulnerability testing a few years later. They fired guns at engines as they ran, to discover how long they would continue to run under fire.

New, more sophisticated bombsights and novel bomb designs were introduced; small hexagonal incendiaries for example were developed by Squadron Leader G. Crawford of the Armament Design Department. Based on a German model of a 1-kilogram bomb being used with great effect in the Spanish Civil War, this weapon allowed for more compact stowage. The body was made of cast magnesium and was thus light and easily ignited. The hollow centre was filled with Thermite incendiary compound. They would be packed into a small container and released in highly effective showers.

Dropping trials would be conducted by the Armament Flight Officer, Flight Lieutenant Davies, who used to amaze the assembled officials by standing right in the trials' dropping zone in order to observe the flight and scatter of the dummies used for the tests. He was thus following the example of Henry Tizard some twenty years earlier.

A standard task for the Armament Section was the 'proofing' of bombs and pyrotechnics. The purpose here was to test every batch of bombs held at store depots by taking a random sample for test purposes, to check they were still functioning correctly. A failure would lead to another sample being taken. Should that too fail, the whole batch would have to be condemned as unserviceable. This job was routinely undertaken on the Orford Ness range, the aircraft of course using Martlesham as their base.

While an extensive range of tests on new types of bomb was conducted, as so often in the story of Orford Ness, financial constraints were a source of difficulty.

Bombs, or rather a lack of them, were no exception to this climate of parsimony during these years. This meant that existing war stocks had to be used and development of new types held back. Using obsolescent material was no way to create the modern RAF. A new type of 1,000-pound general-purpose bomb was being developed until work was cancelled in 1932. In a state of some panic, work on producing and testing this weapon resumed as late as 1940. Some new design 250-pound and 500-pound general-purpose bombs were meanwhile being trialled on the Ness.

By the later '30s, whole squadrons would be posted to Martlesham in order to practice on the Ness range. Most of the bombs they dropped were in fact 'inert', and explosives were rarely used, which of course saved money and made life that much easier for all concerned.

One of the armament workshop personnel of this period worked at Martlesham but travelled over to the Ness for trials, from 1935 to 1937. He and his team would fly over in a Valentia transport in advance to set up the marks on the range. His job was to spot the fall of the bombs. He has described how they would then await the arrival of the Hawker Demons of No. 64 Squadron from Martlesham to carry out their bombing practice. As a bomb was dropped, they each recorded the point of impact so that they could estimate how far or near to the target the bomb had fallen.

Operations were controlled from the tower by means of the *camera obscura*. The aircraft was tracked across the mirror on its run up to the target. When the operator was satisfied it was on the correct course and in the right position he gave the signal for the bomb-aimer to release the bomb. Inevitably, accidents would occur, happily not always with fatal results, as when a bomb release would be fractionally delayed such that staff on the ground very narrowly avoided being hit. Yet, as always, they all regarded their time on the Ness range as 'happy days'.

AIR GUNNERY

The Ness range was used for testing the armaments with which new aircraft were being fitted. This involved fresh types of gun, improved ammunition, and more effective mountings and distribution of weapons, with more powerful propellants. It seems however that a lower priority was given to armament than to the design of more aerodynamic aircraft and more powerful engines. Thus, armament research received less funding, which in turn discouraged the scientists. Lack of finance was always being used to delay any ambitious – and hence expensive – schemes. To a large extent, armament needs of aircraft were catered for by RAF officers rather than by expert civilian scientists. Progress was therefore slow.

However, during the 1930s the RAF was establishing its freedom to consider its own specialist needs and not rely on weapons supplied by the Army. The Vickers gas-operated machine gun, which had been inherited from the Army during the First World War, had become redundant, and the RAF stock was returned to the

Army. These weapons were to be used to good effect in such campaigns as the desert battles of North Africa.

A good example of the value of the technical research work done on the Ness was the discovery that standard Army-issue .303 ammunition was no longer any good for RAF use. With aircraft now flying at greater speeds, serious levels of inaccuracy were experienced, caused by the increased airflow slowing the flight of the bullet. Thus, a modified design was created specially for RAF guns, to reduce drag and velocity loss and hence increase range.

Weapons available for operation by the observer/gunner in two-seater aircraft needed to be upgraded. In earlier days they had operated lightened Lewis guns. Research was taken up by Vickers. The Ness held a trial of a French-designed Berthier, modified by themselves and known as the Vickers Berthier, or later as the Vickers 'K' gun. Another type of gun came from the Coventry Ordnance Works firing a 37-millimetre calibre shell – the COW gun – and was mounted rather as an artillery piece. Aircraft manufacturers submitted new models of plane designed to accommodate these new weapons. The Westland F29/27 fighter was called the 'Cow Gun Fighter'. It was powered by a Bristol radial engine, and had an open cockpit with the cannon mounted at one side. Vickers submitted an even stranger aircraft, the Type 161, a pusher biplane – almost the last such plane to carry RAF colours – with pilot and gun housed in a monocoque nacelle mounted forward of the upper mainplane. The gun was fixed to fire upwards, raked at a 50-degree angle. This somewhat unlikely arrangement had been trialled even during the First World War as an anti-Zeppelin weapon. It was later adopted by the Luftwaffe, fitted to their night-fighters for dealing with the vulnerable and unprotected undersides of Lancasters and other heavy bombers.

Evaluation trials on the Ness developed from 1933 and 1934 as world events began to cast darker shadows. Guns from UK, USA, French, and Czechoslovakian manufacturers were compared. As a result, the American Colt Automatic machine-gun, renamed as the familiar Browning, became the standard weapon for the RAF. In June 1931, an Armstrong Whitworth Siskin single-seat fighter had carried out armament trials fitted with two .303 calibre Browning machine guns, which proved promisingly successful. This was perhaps the start of a process of gun layout, which evolved into the eight-gun fighter of only a few years later.

Firing trials on the Ness would have taken place in and around the northern field and over King's Marsh to the north. Plans for a more specific range set up in 1936 have survived in the National Archives. This was an 800-yard specialist facility for a particular project on the southern field. The cost was to be £800. Records invariably include detailed estimates for costs, evidence, if any was needed, of the severe budgetary control exercised by the Treasury. This new range stretched from the river wall to the south of the jetty in a south easterly direction towards the derelict ancient oyster beds by the exit of Stony Ditch into the river Ore.

A platform was built with an array of eight Brownings in a line. The relatively small target butt was filled with sawdust, a fact that agitated the authorities, concerned that a fire hazard might arise. Of more significance was the string of marker flags, erected every 50 yards along the firing line so that the spread of bullets from the eight guns fired simultaneously could be monitored and analysed. Trials began in February 1937, using Mark V .303 ammunition. This range remained in service for several years in conjunction with lethality and vulnerability tests. It was, for example, used for testing duraliminium, the metal used for protecting the wings of Blenheim bombers.

The significance of this range is obvious. The Spitfire and Hurricane began to appear over Suffolk from 1935. The fitting of the guns and more especially, the research relating to the most effective use of them, required many months of testing. The aircraft were based at Martlesham, but many of the gun-firing and other flying trials took place over the Ness. In November 1938, firing trials at Martlesham produced some scientifically expert recommendations for the harmonisation of the eight guns, indicating that the maximum impact of their fire would be achieved at a range of 400 yards.* The report also drew the armourers' attention to the very significant difference in the placing of the guns for these two types of Battle of Britain fighter.

Professor Bennett Melvill Jones had by now returned to the Orford Ness scene as the result of a pressing appeal from the Air Ministry; he seemed to be resuming where he had left off back in 1920. In August 1936, it was proposed that RAF research should begin to assume a more positive role, looking to develop offensive weaponry quite as much as defensive. The newly established 'Committee for the Scientific Survey of Air Offence' was given the brief 'to consider how far recent advances of scientific and technical knowledge can be used to strengthen present methods of offence against hostile aircraft'. The idea was for an Armament Experimental Station, to be based at Orford Ness as an outstation for RAE Farnborough. The busy Professor initially had grave doubts as to his availability to help, but was persuaded. Clearly a building programme was envisaged and the southern runway at the Ness was being reopened. Martlesham would provide airfield services until the Ness was ready. In the event, no grandiose building project ever materialised.

After twenty years absence, Melvill Jones was pretty dismayed to discover that almost no progress had been made during the intervening years. His research was in much the same fields as it had been back in 1919 on the Ness – the problems of accurate air-to-air gunnery. By 1939 he was able to advise the Air Ministry on the best means of attacking enemy bombers in terms of speed and range, angle of attack, and the value of tracer ammunition. This research also included techniques for dealing with an enemy taking avoiding action by weaving. Very high-powered mathematics was involved, with evidence based on the use of camera guns in aircraft flying out of operational stations, notably at Duxford.

---

* From their first encounter with German bombers in September 1939, it became immediately apparent that an effective tange for their fighters should be reduced to 250 yards.

The summer of 1939 saw his younger son, Geoffrey, a seventeen-year-old schoolboy, enjoying a family holiday at Felixstowe. This was nearer Martlesham than their Cambridge home. One afternoon, basking on the beach, they had spotted a twin-engined aircraft flying low over the sea, firing its guns into the water, close by the shore. This was Bennett, trying out an experiment he had used off Orford Ness in 1918. He would photograph the bullets as they hit the surface, from which he could compare the experimental data with theoretical predictions of the effects of orthogonal wind forces (i.e. approaching at right angles). Geoffrey's recollection of what happened a few days later follows:

> I vividly recall listening gravely to the declaration of war at 11 a.m. on September 3rd. After the news, father decided we must all dash out for a picnic on the sandy coast, since this might be the last time we'd all be together ... ever! So off we toddled in the ancient Morris Cowley. On return to our holiday lodging, there was a service car waiting to take Pa away on his war work, day one of the war. He was whisked by air to Boscombe Down, the new location of A&AEE, where he worked on air-to-air gunnery for the first year of the war. He took one of the family great danes (of which we had 5 at that time) as his pet-guardian, living in the mess till my brother and I drove a clapped out old caravan down there, in which he and Mother plus the danes lived till the Gunnery Research Unit was moved to Exeter.

Melvill Jones commanded this unit, developing advanced gunnery equipment. His research was so important that he was knighted for his services in 1942. He had been awarded a CBE in 1938, and the following year he was given the highest accolade his colleagues could offer and was elected to be a Fellow of the Royal Society. His achievement with gyroscopic sights produced dramatic results during the final months of the war, and led to his award by President Truman of the highly prestigious Medal of Freedom in 1947. He continued his aeronautical research and travelled the world as a highly respected scientist and was retained as an adviser to such bodies as the Aeronautical Research Council. The fact that he was always a delightfully eccentric and slightly chaotic figure only added to the deep affection with which this great man was held. Truly, he was as significant a boffin as any to have come from the Orford Ness stable.

PREPARING FOR WAR

In 1935, the attention of the Air Ministry was drawn to the absence of any research work on the protection of airfields, particularly of the key strategic buildings located on them. It was realised that any information drawn from First World War experience would be totally irrelevant for a future war. Technology had moved on. So trials were scheduled for the Ordnance Experimental Station on Shoeburyness in July 1935. Unfortunately, facilities could not be made available and so the trials were transferred to Orford Ness.

The 'island' therefore again shook to the impact of 500-pound general-purpose bombs. Target buildings, constructed to Air Ministry standards, were hastily erected, for the purpose of assaulting them at just 10 yards range. The objective was to assess the damage done by blast and impacting bomb fragments, and to discover how much steel plate and shingle revetments would help reinforced concrete walls. During the following two summers, further trials continued which included tests to see just how proof against gas attack standard service windows were. This trial was conclusive: they weren't! They also tested the effect of impact on roofs, thereby anticipating further wartime trials conducted on behalf of the Department of Civil Defence's ARP (Air Raid Precautions). Shoeburyness too was already by now being employed for research on the impact of bomb blast on civilian buildings, at the instigation of the Home Office.

These trials in this immediately pre-war period of intense activity included the effects of armour-piercing and semi-armour-piercing bombs. The objective was to provide protection for such sensitive and vulnerable airfield buildings, fuel and ammunition stores, standby powerhouses, operations buildings, W/T stations and gas decontamination centres. Information on potential enemy weapons was unsurprisingly almost non-existent and the RAF found itself working virtually in the dark. Intelligence was sought from French and German sources, and further trials took place out of RAF bases in Malta and Egypt. An RAF officer was despatched to Germany in 1937 and came back with depressing news. He felt that the Germans were some two years ahead. Meanwhile the Chemical Research Station at Porton Down was brought into the picture to look into anti-gas protection for airfields.

By 1939, decisions were taken to protect airfield personnel by digging slit trenches and solid underground shelters. In the event, airfields were attacked rather less often or effectively than had been anticipated, and the RAF never bothered even to record the number of casualties sustained on their airfields. The impact of bombing on civilians by contrast was quite enormous. No personnel were even injured by enemy action on the Ness site during the Second World War, unlike the people of Orford itself. However, protective measures were in place, and blast walls were to be a feature of all stations. Examples are evident still at airfields like Duxford (now part of the Imperial War Museum) which illustrate the fruits of Orford Ness trials in the immediate pre-war period.

Over these years, a whole string of novel aircraft found their way from Martlesham to the range on the Ness. The purpose here was largely weapons evaluation, as well as suitability for the demands of actual warfare, including engine performance. Many proved unpromising and never progressed beyond the prototype stage. Most were speculative commercial ventures put forward by hopeful manufacturers. These were known as 'private ventures'. The hope was that a profitable contract might ensue.

Many types that were to be developed arrived for a brief showing from a multiplicity of manufacturers. Others that had made an early appearance here were to become household names, like the Westland Lysander. The old 'warhorses' continued to be used for trials, slow perhaps, but stable and reliable and quite suitable for the work they had to do. They were based at Martlesham, flying across the Ness for bombing, gunnery and gun-mounting trials. When in 1939 A&AEE was moved from vulnerable Suffolk to more remote and secure Wiltshire, many of them were transferred.

The intense activity in the skies above the Ness in those pre-war days of mounting tension is well described by Gordon Kinsey. As a small boy he attended scout camps in the grounds of Gedgrave Hall, across the river from Havergate Island. He writes of what were clearly cherished memories:

> ... scanning the skies as a succession of aircraft passed over the site on their way to the ranges, only a short distance away. What a magnificent sight they would make today, the Sidestrand resplendent in all-over silver finish with bold red, white and blue roundels and dark green top decking to the fuselage to prevent sun glare to the crew. Hawker Harts and Fairey Hendons, NIVO Green on top and sides and black underneath, broken only by the large underwing serials in white. The following year the prototypes of the new breeds flew over in their brown and green camouflage finish on top and black undersides, the Bristol Blenheim, Fairey Battle, Westland Lysander, Hawker Hurricane, Vickers Wellesley and the Supermarine Spitfire.
>
> From the 'island' came the stutter of machine-gun fire, the crump of practice bombs, and in the sky the dull thud and resultant trail of white smoke as a smoke puff burst, or the comet-like trail of a Very Light. What an environment in which to pass the Boy Scout's Airman's Badge; and we even had an instructor from Martlesham Heath to assist us in the task.

Dennis Knights-Branch too was a youngster during Orford at this period. He was greatly intrigued by noting the aircraft flying overhead and all the bumps and bangs audible from the Ness. The villagers were warned when experimental bombing 'raids' were to take place. A few years later, having joined the Merchant Navy, he happened to be on leave from his ship, the *Orontes*, on the morning when Orford was attacked for real by German bombers. His recollection is of the clouds of feathers that were sprayed high and wide over the Square and rooftops of the houses, from the down-filled mattresses that were commonly used in those days.

Charlie Underwood was a schoolboy during these years of intense flying activity over the Ness. He has recalled his impressions of what this meant to him, particularly during night trials. He remembers lying in bed as the Vickers Virginia bomber would drone over, waiting for the bang of its bombs, which would rattle his bedroom windows. By day he would lie on his back to watch Hawker Harts in mock battle. It all gave him invaluable knowledge of aircraft for when he joined the RAF. Charlie Underwood was to be a major player in the unfolding story of Orford and the Ness.

The last military aircraft to use the runway officially was a De Havilland DH86, a new biplane airliner, taken into service as the precursor of the four-engined aircraft in the RAF. Its function was as a senior staff transport, and on 10 June 1939, it delivered the Chief of Air Staff up from Hendon on a leg of an inspection tour. Landing and taking it off from the short grass field of the Ness was no mean feat. This proved to be the only four-engine plane ever to land on the Ness. The Lancaster and other aircraft that found themselves parked on the Ness in later years came over in bits and were assembled on site, for trial purposes.

It was, as ever, a place for play as well as work. The attractions of the Ness for the personnel stationed at Martlesham were not confined to 'other ranks'. 'Other ranks' would hitch a lift to enjoy swimming off the beach. Dennis Knights-Branch recalls a particular task in which he was sometimes asked to be involved. '... on Saturdays, now and again,' he wrote, 'the job was given to us to act as beaters for the RAF officers' and friends' shooting parties from Martlesham Air Base. We collected the hares and pheasants as we went and hung them on long sticks over our shoulders, and by the time we had finished the morning shoot, our legs and shoulders were bending and a bit sore'. The gamekeeper was a Mr Thirkettle, who provided notable lunches and strong tea. 'At the end of the day we got the princely sum of two shillings and six pence (12½ p.) and a pair of hares'.

At the outbreak of the war, the Ness grew briefly quiet. Mighty work had been done, often against the odds. The RAF had spread new wings and had begun to make them effective. All the calculations for the creation of ordnance tables for bombing, and the calibration of aircraft gunnery was now available. What perhaps only the boffins and the politicians behind them really understood was that it had been a close run thing. Had the country been forced to go to war in 1938, it would in all probability have lost, through being seriously ill-equipped to tackle a better-armed opponent.[1]

The Research Station at War

The outbreak of war in 1939 came as no surprise to those working on the Ness.
The previous decade had seen the Orford Ness Research Laboratory, as part of
the Aircraft and Armaments Experimental Establishment, working on projects
that took it for granted that sooner or later, there would be a war.

The location of the Ness was exposed and considered vulnerable to enemy
attack. The lighthouse beams were dimmed and as in the First World War,
operated only when directed by Naval authorities. The Aldeburgh building
contractors, W.C. Reade, were commissioned to disguise the tower with camouflage paint. Keepers were of course retained, but it must have been a lonely and at
times dangerous occupancy. Indeed, in 1940, keeper Frank Layton, beachcombing
or just wandering along the shore, detonated an item of ordnance that killed
him instantly. While this tragedy was only to be expected in a place that had, for
over twenty years by then, seen a constant rain of assorted weapons, it is in fact
amazing how few of such accidents, fatal or otherwise, were ever to occur.

Machine-gunned and scarcely maintained, the lighthouse must have been a
melancholy place. In 1944, a V-I flying bomb landed near the tower, doing plenty
of superficial damage, as did shrapnel splinters from the light AA (anti-aircraft)
battery set up on the Ness. This damage, and routine wear and tear, including the
faded paintwork, necessitated urgent repair once the war ended and full lighthouse operations were resumed.

Meanwhile, the important decision to transfer the whole of experimental
operations to an alternative site in Wiltshire had been taken some months earlier.
Wing Commander Bilney, Deputy Commander at Martlesham, was responsible
for all operations on the Ness at the time. The order to move was given on 1
September, when, in Bilney's words, 'the whole A&AEE packed up its bags and
moved lock, stock and barrel to Boscombe Down'.

Boscombe Down had been a First World War air station, but was closed
down until 1930. Its proximity to military ranges on Salisbury Plain and secret

establishments like Porton Down prompted a decision to re-open it and eventually extend the runway. By 1939 there were trials ranges at Crichel Down near Blandford and Ashley Walk in the New Forest, though they were without any sort of ballistics testing facilities. That apart, it was an ideal location for experimental work to continue. There, the Martlesham tradition has continued to this day. Very much by now in the front line, Martlesham soon received its fighter squadrons, and with them, some pilots of considerable note, including at various times, Douglas Bader, Peter Townsend, Manfred Czerin, 'Bob' Stanford Tuck and Larry Forrester.

So, very briefly, the Ness and its experimental range and test facilities ceased to operate. Any sort of formal link with Martlesham was severed until the situation became clearer, which, by as early as November 1939, it did. Boscombe Down's lack of immediately available bomb range analysis facilities proved a serious handicap and the need to resume ballistics trials outweighed concern over vulnerability to attack.

In these days, inhabitants on the east coast will have been awaiting the expected Blitzkrieg invasion with some apprehension. Along the Suffolk shore, defences were hastily erected, beaches mined and barricaded, and inland tank traps excavated. Likely coastal invasion points were flooded and networks of pill-boxes constructed. Over sixty years later, the evidence of such frenetic activity still remains.

Invasion never came, but the so-called 'phoney war' proved to be far from a joke for those sailing offshore. The war at sea was fought in earnest from day one. The losses of Allied and neutral shipping mounted. During a five-day period in November 1939 alone, eighteen ships were sunk, and others badly damaged. Ironically, this total includes vessels flying Italian and Japanese flags: neither of these countries had yet declared war. These losses were largely the victims of mining, especially by the newly devised magnetic mines. Often dropped by aircraft, this prompted a lively increase in aerial warfare, in which Martlesham was involved. Inshore convoys had to make perilous journeys up and down the coast, subject to regular Luftwaffe attack. The Orford Ness lighthouse proved to be a useful navigational beacon for the RAF. The Ness was indeed photographed by German air intelligence and its location in relation to Ipswich noted, but not once was the Ness an actual target for formal air attack, apart from sporadic strafing of the lighthouse tower. Nor was there bombardment from the sea. In August 1940, Martlesham was twice attacked. Bombers hit Aldeburgh and Orford village later in the war. Bawdsey received considerable attention from June 1940 onwards, presumably because it was thought to be a radio station, but no serious attention was paid to the fairly obvious military target on the Ness.

It must be a matter of pure speculation to explain why this was so. Was it perhaps that the absence of any anti-aircraft defences argued that there was nothing there of sufficient significance to merit them? Or perhaps aerial reconnaissance showed that lines of communications with the Ness were very poor and were evidently not being improved. German intelligence must surely have deduced that this was a place of very little importance. Yet over a period of months, reconnaissance photographs would have shown military aircraft lying around the airfield site. Some of these might have been identified as German. Two large aircraft hangars remained in place throughout the war, which cannot have been missed, unless the Luftwaffe had concluded that nothing was going on at the Ness.

They were very mistaken as to its innocence. By the end of 1939, the decision was taken to 'reactivate' the site, with a view to an immediate resumption of gun firing trials and a few months later, the reopening of the bombing range. A number of the pre-war scientists were brought back. This initiated a staffing policy that differed radically from First World War practice. Then, the entire establishment had been under military command. From 1939, the key scientists and directors of the trials were to be civilians. The airmen stationed on the Ness were entirely technicians, mechanics and fitters, riggers and weapons specialists, with a substantial number of support and admin staff and an RAF Regiment detachment for defence. They were all 'other ranks' or NCOs. A group photograph of 1942 reveals that the C/O, Flight Lieutenant Quinlan, was the sole commissioned officer responsible for the work on the site. The numbers employed on the station were a fraction of the 1918 total: the average complement of service and civilian personnel was about 120 in all.

As part of this new look for the Ness, it had a new title and was under a new authority. Now called Orford Ness Research Station (ORS), it was to be at the disposal of the government's overall war effort, under the direction of the Ministries of Supply and of Aircraft Production. The fact was that ORS was to be a mightily useful place for any sort of experiment the exigencies of total war might require.

THE SHINGLE STREET MYTH

Almost exactly a year after the outbreak of war, a curious episode occurred, affecting, if not Orford Ness, then certainly its southerly neighbour, Shingle Street. The myth is that an attempted German invasion took place at Shingle Street, only to be repelled by intrepid defence forces, assisted by a boom barrage that set the sea on fire, leaving burnt bodies to drift in on tides along the coastline. This was something which ever after has aroused unceasing curiosity; and among those determined to look for a sinister explanation for the non-disclosure of the relevant files, fierce controversy. It certainly roused grave apprehension in the mind of Sebald when he paid his illicit visit in 1992. The questions arise: what happened and why were files kept secret for so long? Did something sinister take place which the authorities were at pains to hide and for which official documents still remain classified?

It simply cannot have occurred as recounted, invariably only by folk who were not actually in or even near Shingle Street at the time. Not a single shred of concrete evidence to prove it has yet been produced. There was a large contingent at the radar station at Bawdsey throughout this time. Not one person stationed there has ever mentioned any sort of military action a mile or so away. The technology for setting the sea alight had not been developed (and when it was, Shingle Street would count as about the least likely spot for it to be installed). As telling as anything is the absence of any record even from German sources of a raid. There is no case for supposing that this was an attempted raid on the secret radar station at Bawdsey. The Germans believed at this stage that it was nothing more than a radio station. The failure of the Luftwaffe to identify the significance of British RDF during the Battle of Britain was not the least of its fundamental tactical errors.

The most probable explanation is that the whole affair was another example of 'black propaganda', a deliberately contrived false story, put about to discourage the enemy from even thinking about launching an attack. The lack of any access to a file was because it was, entirely empty.[1] Black Propaganda was the name given to the radio warfare element in the armoury of the Special Intelligence Service. It was run by the German-speaking *Daily Express* journalist Sefton Delmer and began to operate from June 1940. Broadcasting from an immensely powerful transmitter imported from the USA and nicknamed 'Aspidistra' (the biggest in the world) at Crowborough, its function was to undermine the morale of enemy service personnel. By employing 'turned' German POWs, its messages proved most well informed and hence persuasive. By curious coincidence, Aspidistra was in due course replaced with the transmitter that was installed on the Ness in the US radar station, Cobra Mist, from 1975.

THE BATTLE COMES TO SUFFOLK

Before long, an element of the real war was to reach the island. The date was 11 November 1940 when a quite bizarre event occurred. An enemy fighter crash-landed on the shingle a short distance north of the lighthouse; this was no ordinary or familiar Luftwaffe fighter, but an Italian Fiat CR42 Freccia biplane, the equivalent of the all but obsolete British Gloster Gladiator fighter.

The explanation for this visitation lay with Mussolini's ambition to demonstrate that his *Regia Aeronautica* could be worthy fellow combatants in his new ally's aerial war with Britain. If he thought this might be an easy task, he was rapidly to be disabused. He understood even less the implications of Chain Home radar or the effectiveness of RAF eight-gun fighters in the hands of experienced pilots.

Elements of this *Corps Aerio Italiano*, comprising well over 300 fighters and bombers, all at best obsolescent, were based on the Channel coast. Despite grand claims of successes in raids on London – claims with no foundation in fact – their first and last offensive assignment for a group despatched to the Low Countries for the purpose, was to be a daylight raid on Harwich. Forty fighters escorted ten twin-engined Fiat BRL20 bombers. RAF Hurricanes at Hornchurch, North Weald and Martlesham were scrambled and were able to break up the bombing formation. All the bombs fell into the North Sea. The attackers were speedily driven off in what became something of a 'turkey shoot'. The Martlesham pilot, Flight Lieutenant H.P. Blatchford, recalls it as being 'the best party I have ever had in my life'. When he ran out of ammunition he even rammed a CR42, cutting up its upper wing with his propeller and physically driving off others with dummy attacking runs. Around a dozen Italian planes were destroyed, and the idea of using Mussolini's air force was never repeated. It is perhaps relevant to add in parenthesis that even a year later when CR42s came head-to-head with Gladiators in aerial battles over Greece, the RAF were able to score notable victories over the Fiats.

These engagements were duly recorded in the report for the day by the ARP (Air Raid Precautions, the civil defences authorities). In somewhat dispassionate terms, it noted that the 'following enemy aircraft reported to have crashed at about 14.10 hours, one in sea off Orford Ness, one Italian fighter on beach at Orford Ness, one bomber at Bromeswell, east of Woodbridge, and at 14.17 hours, one Italian fighter at Corton, north of Lowestoft.'

The twenty-three-year-old pilot, Sergeant Salvadori Pictio, was doubly shaken by the strange Ness environment in which he found himself. He is quoted as fearing that he had somehow landed in the desert and would undoubtedly die of thirst; there was also the fact that an excited crowd of airmen had rapidly rushed across to surround him, seemingly far more interested in the aircraft than in him. A severed oil pipe was the only damage, apart from the crumpled propeller. The Fiat was removed to Martlesham, where it was repaired, painted in RAF colours and then flown to Farnborough for further evaluation and both test and recreational flying. It was reputed to be a beautiful aircraft to fly. Crated up for future exhibition purposes it was in due course included in the RAF Museum display at Hendon.

The luckless pilot doubtless was happy to realise that his war was over. On his return to Italy in 1945, he became an able test pilot, dying in an air accident in the 1950s.

LETHALITY, VULNERABILITY AND BALLISTICS

After the ORS reopened in 1939, many of the trials conducted over the next few years showed remarkable similarities to those conducted during the First World War. More obviously, they continued work that had been done in the inter-war A&AEE days. These included trials to improve the effectiveness of weapons and the protective armour of aircraft. They can by summed up as being 'lethality and vulnerability' trials.

Even before the outbreak of war, the urgent need to research this whole aspect of offence and defence in aircraft seems suddenly to have emerged as a high priority. In 1938, the Air Ministry commissioned a one-off series of tests on grounded aircraft, shot at with .303 ammunition. A civilian scientist, Alan

Daniels, led this research. He sadly was to lose his life at a later date under most regrettable circumstances.

This 1938 assignment exactly anticipated what was to follow from 1940. It shows the importance attached to the scientists' findings, and confirms the usefulness of the Ness for experimental purposes. One very significant and extended set of trials involved improving self-sealing fuel tanks, following on from similar experiments during the First World War to ensure that fuel tanks punctured by enemy bullets sealed themselves rapidly, thus removing or reducing the risk of explosion, fire or fuel loss. This proved to be an on-going issue, since every new type of aircraft and every increase in performance created new problems, necessitating fresh trials. Work in this field continued well after the end of the war.

Happily, and most unusually, a complete report on one of these trials has emerged, retrieved from a proverbial family attic. The scientific officer running this trial, dated August 1943, was John Hughes-Jones, who served on the Ness from June 1940 until December 1944. On discovering a pile of his papers, his son kindly donated relevant documents to the National Trust archives. Very few such reports have survived from the Second World War.

This trial seems to typify the sort of work that Ness boffins were being instructed to conduct. They were invited to compare the effectiveness of US and British 0.5-millimetre incendiary ammunition in attacking German bomber self-sealing fuel tanks. They constructed replicas of the bomber wings and their tanks, and in one case used a real Heinkel He111 bomber wing. They fired 175 rounds of each type of ammunition into almost completely filled tanks and filmed the impact of every one. The report included the seventeen 'variables' that had to be taken into account – the size and fullness of the tank, angle of attack, atmospheric conditions etc – and then supplied a detailed analysis of every single bullet's performance. This was painstaking work, and, with possible exploding high-octane fuel involved, not without its dangers. The conclusion seemed to be that US ammunition was significantly more effective. Equally, the report drew attention to an earlier Ness trial, in November 1941, when German 7.92 millimetre nose-fused incendiary ammunition was fired into British tanks. The issue here was the importance of preventing fires becoming lethal before the self-sealing chemical process could kick in. The relative value of the soft and flexible bag-type of tank as opposed to the rigid metal covered type was the issue at stake. John Hughes-Jones was especially commended by the British Air Commission for his 'excellent work'.

Meanwhile, on its site across the shingle, the Bomb Ballistics building facilities were quickly restored and put to good use for developing flight characteristics of ever-larger weapons, dropped at ever-greater altitude and speed.

A report on the significance of the range appeared in 1948, well after the end of the war. The notable officer in charge, George Hicks, signed it. Hicks explained that the principles and procedures for trials had been established during the 1930s but that new demands were now clearly apparent: conditions for bomb release were changing, as air speed, operational altitude and types of weapon all continued to develop. They were being required to deal with 'salvo' release of incendiaries and fragmentation bombs and even ventures into chemical warfare. The Ballistics building continued to be of considerable value for many years. Technical improvements had to be made as a result. This included the use of radar and ever more sophisticated cameras to take into account the developing performance of aircraft.

As explained, routine reports on ORS researches have alas not proved as easy to locate as might be expected. Significant documents were lost on the Ness during the floods of 1953. The archive from RAE Farnborough no longer exists: some of it destroyed by fire or dispersed to unknown locations. The truth is that such reports would in all probability prove exceptionally dull reading, certainly for the layman. Many who worked in this research have admitted that much of what they did was by its nature painstaking, meticulous and in the process, pretty tedious.

Another reason for the difficulty now encountered in trying to identify the various trials being conducted was that they could be quite brief and 'ad hoc'. Personnel would appear on the Ness range to conduct some experiment at the behest of a trial laboratory at Farnborough. They might well spend little more than a day or so in Suffolk. Records of their time on the Ness have simply disappeared.

One example of a report on such a trial has survived in the National Archives. It well illustrates the typical striving for total and exemplary authenticity in the conduct of the trial by the Ness boffins. In April 1942, the ARP asked for help in supplying guidelines to the building industry for constructing roofs capable of withstanding German 1-kilogram incendiaries.

In order to research the typical angle of hit, depth of penetration and concentration of spread from a standard stick of bombs, they decided to go for complete replication of a bombing raid even to the extent of using a captured German aircraft, armed with loads of retrieved unexploded bombs. RAF Duxford kept such aircraft in operational order and supplied a Junkers Ju88A. This particular one had fallen into RAF hands the previous July via a neat trick. Its pilot was totally bamboozled by false radio signals and, much to his surprise, he found himself landing at Lulsgate, near Bristol, when imagining that he had reached his Brittany base. The bombs, all repaired, had their explosive charges replaced by plaster of Paris, and were suitably weighted with steel shot to replicate in all respects the weight and balance of the real thing. They were then dropped over King's Marsh from the two usual operational heights, 3,000 feet and 7,000 feet. The aim was to analyse every single bomb strike. In the event about 70 per cent were traceable and these supplied sufficient evidence for the purpose. A 2-inch mortar was also used to simulate the impact onto specific surfaces. The results were tabulated, bomb by bomb. It makes turgid reading, but at a grim period in the war, the issue was highly charged. The ARP was pleased to be given the facts. The Ness's skills and usefulness were well demonstrated.

However the survival of such reports is rare. What do exist are first-hand accounts by those who worked on the Ness during this period. It is from these

people that a fuller understanding of their work may be gained. Among the most
notable of these was Bert Smith, who as serviceman and later, civilian, spent
many years on the site, a unique and invaluable source of information. Smith has
presented the National Trust with authoritative accounts of the work being done
during his time with ORS between 1942 and 1955. The brief autobiographical
sketch he added serves to lend weight to the authority of his contribution:

> I was a Fitter II(E), (that is an aero engine fitter) in the wartime RAF and in June
> 1942 was posted to RAF Orford Ness from an operational bomber squadron.
> Being a young and ambitious junior NCO with sufficient seniority in rank to
> be eligible for promotion to sergeant, I was somewhat taken aback to discover
> I had arrived at a very peculiar and thoroughly atypical RAF station*. A large
> proportion of the Service personnel were corporals; there was no establishment
> for a sergeant in the skilled trades, only for the police and the admin; because of
> the specialised nature of the work, people were screened from periodic posting
> and many had already been there since 1940. Also, the specialist armament and
> aircraft tradesmen worked to the direct instructions of the civilian scientific and
> technical staff.
>
> However, the work was varied and interesting and I thoroughly enjoyed the
> years I was there. Eventually, towards the end of the war, I 'escaped' by applying
> for and getting a commission. While on demob leave in 1946 I visited the Island
> (the only RAF station I know where people came back on visits) and as the
> RAF posts were being civilianised I accepted a job in the workshops. Shortly
> afterwards I transferred to the experimental staff in the Firing Trials Section.

The Ness clearly had a very special place in his affections. He recalls that he
passed his twenty-first birthday there and, managing to scrounge a hen's egg,
he persuaded the NAAFI (Navy, Army & Air Force Institute) manageress, Mrs
Davey, to cook it for him: egg and chips, luxury indeed in 1943.

Bert Smith explains the particular significance of just what he found himself
doing during the war and after. 'The RAF (and RN) faced a fundamentally
different challenge from the Army' he writes. 'The latter met its operational needs
by "equipping men"; the needs of the first two were better met by inventing or
refining equipment and then training the men to operate it – or man their equipment'. For this, places like Boscombe Down and Orford Ness were of enormous
value. Smith emphasises too the inescapable fact that in 1939, the German war
machine was technically much superior to Britain's. This certainly confirms just
how important the re-opening of the Ness was.

Smith observes that the core of pre-war scientific civil servants were joined by
wartime entrants from a wide variety of disciplines and backgrounds: university
graduates, an ex-policeman, a former mining surveyor etc. Many had never even

---

* Of course, strictly speaking, this was not an RAF station at all.

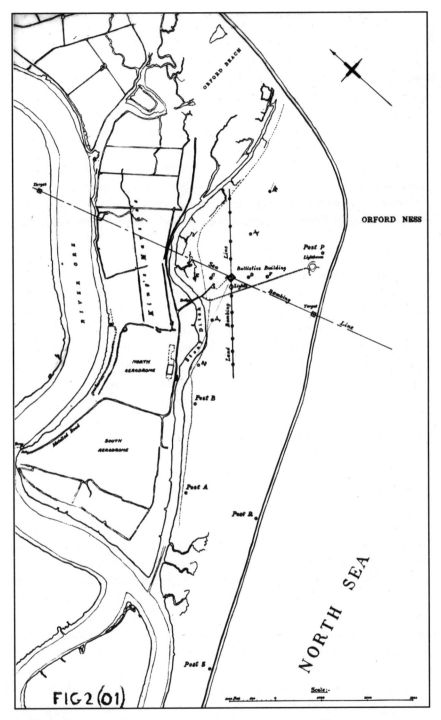

ORFORD NESS

NORTH SEA

FIG 2 (01)

This diagrammatic map from the late 1930s was drawn by Ken Daykin and shows the track of the two bombing trial runs, both passing over the ballistics building, the seaward one from the west to east past the lighthouse and the other, south to north for 'splash' into the shingle. Note the wide spread of recording camera posts. (*Unknown*) fired a gun, let alone been near an aircraft, but skilled assistance was available from the appropriate RAF personnel. Smith describes the purpose of the ORS researches with which he was chiefly involved. He explains the whole purpose of lethality and vulnerability trials, which was:

> ...to attack captured enemy aircraft with our airborne weapons and our aircraft with the enemy's airborne weapons, the results providing essential data for those responsible for identifying and meeting the operational needs of the Service. At its simplest, a trial could be carried out with just a gun and a target, but additional information such as velocity and altitude of the projectile on impact, potential to inflict damage or injury on impact, effects of slipstream etc., might also be required. Sometimes high-speed cine photography would be used to record the sequence of events after impact.

Smith goes on to describe the meticulous care taken over recording the path of each projectile. They were interested in the damage impact of both bullets and shrapnel, since the development of proximity fuses meant that near misses could be as lethal as direct hits. He recalls the vitals of German aircraft being laid out in the southern hangar, with rods from the bullet entry holes marking the path towards their vulnerable areas. From this information, diagrams were prepared to indicate where and how pilots could concentrate the fire for their guns to inflict the greatest damage on enemy aircraft. Such diagrams were reproduced for display in RAF fighter station crew rooms.

When it came to vulnerability, quite apart from adding armour plate protection, certain particularly hazardous items on board an aircraft could be identified. High-pressure oxygen bottles, for example, could explode with devastating consequences. Trials demonstrated that merely wrapping these cylinders with a layer of wire could virtually eliminate any tendency to rupture.

A firing range for this work was established at the northern end of the northern airfield, the firing being directed towards the old Chinese Wall. A First World War building next to the still surviving MT (Motor Transport) workshop building was used as an armoury to house Allied and German guns of every size. Ample ammunition was provided by the Ministry of Supply (MoS), or direct from shot-down enemy aircraft. As to the targets, partially complete aircraft were ferried across the river, or just the components required for testing, notably windscreens, cockpits and engines. These bits and pieces were stored in profusion on the concrete apron at the north end of northern hangar. The area was commonly described as the 'Graveyard'.

Tests became increasingly complex, involving measurement of distance and flight time of both bullets and metal fragments, the latter often with non-standard physical properties. The object was to establish the critical striking velocity for penetration of armour plate. The speed of a projectile was measured by means of electronic timers, or chronoscopes, linked to a pair of photoelectric pick-ups, set up under the line of flight. The stability of flight was also highly significant:

accuracy and penetration might suggest minimum yaw and instability, but equally, a broadside-on impact could cause increased rupture damage, to a fuel tank for example. One extraordinary fact relating to this quite technically advanced research was the use of a mid-Victorian handbook containing ballistics tables for firing trials. It was originally constructed by a mathematician, the Reverend Francis Bashforth (1818–1912). Smith's personal copy was dated 1904, and the 1929 version, titled *The Textbook of Small Arms* and employed for these Ness trials, remains a valid source of information to this day.

Very important impact trials were undertaken on internal fragmentation or 'spalling', characteristic of armoured plate or windscreens. Guidance was needed on whether supposedly bullet-proof materials might give rise to even worse injuries to aircrew, particularly from spicules of glass damaging unprotected eyes. There was a similarly acute problem for tank crews in the Army. One quaint aspect to these experiments was the use to which out-of-date London telephone directories were put. Since they were of uniform thickness and density, the effects of missile materials splayed from a target could be measured and compared. The number of pages penetrated gave an accurate comparative measurement. Sheets of acetate were used in a similar way for measuring eye injury from windscreen damage.

Where testing related to penetrating fuel tanks, trials were often conducted using a mock-up rig of a wing, covered with sheet metal. Very high-speed photography was usually involved, to record the effects of impact and the subsequent sequence of events. A 35-millimetre camera made by Vinten ran so fast that a reel of film lasted only a few seconds.

An additional element in validating the effects of this shooting was the creation of an artificial slipstream. This was especially important in fuel tank tests. Fire can either be extinguished or fanned and sustained by it. A damaged and no longer airworthy Spitfire, with an engine in working condition was retained and, firmly anchored to the ground, run flat out via a remotely controlled throttle. Smith claimed the precious privilege of being allowed to taxi this aircraft round the airfield to its operating station. A second Spitfire became available, when, disabled by a glycol coolant leak, it was landed onto the southern field, almost, but not quite, missing the concrete anti-glider blocks that had been placed on it in 1939. The shocked pilot confessed that this was the second aircraft he had written off in the week. He was perhaps a trifle reassured by the enthusiasm of the Ness staff who were happy to use the crippled aircraft's engine for their slipstream tests. In the event this aircraft was never reinstated and the engine was merely cannibalised for the existing Spitfire. The slipstream 'section' also enjoyed the somewhat vicarious services of two other 'aircraft in pieces', a one-engined Blenheim and a German Me109.

Varied types of armour plate came over to the Ness in 3 feet squares. Following tests, largely set up by Smith, an elaborate statistical formula was used to establish a pecking order of effectiveness. This exercise was given the grand title of a 'Figure of Merit', and was conducted by Smith's Head of Section, Bruce Gordon, a civilian scientific officer. Gordon had grown up and was educated in India, where his father was a senior engineer on the State Railways. On arrival back in England in 1939, his ambition was to seek a commission as a pilot in the RAF. His Indian education and work experience background (he admitted to taking a temporary job as a railway clerk) appeared to disqualify him from having officer-like qualities and instead he found himself employed by RAE Farnborough in the field of weapon testing. Before long he was despatched to the Ness. He led lethality and vulnerability trials with distinction and later in the war was offered a pilot's training course at Duxford, in company with a number of other civilian scientists. This invitation points to an interesting contrast with First World War policy. Then, as has been noted, 'valuable' scientists had to be stopped from attempting to learn to fly. In the event, Gordon actually failed his course!

While existing buildings were taken over in 1940 for much of this work, over the years a number of new structures were specially erected. The most evident of these is what has always been referred to as the Plate Store, dating from not later than 1941, and modified during a further building programme after the end of the war. Its original function was to store armour plate and provide the base for vulnerability firing tests and analysis. A dark and rather sinister looking single-storey building, it still stands, not accessible to the public (it is a barn owl habitat), but a grim-looking memorial to Second World War and Cold War activity.

From time to time, a fuel tank fire occurred, and the normal procedure was to smother the flames with an asbestos blanket. Any concept of health and safety at work was still unimaginable! The exigencies of war required that risks were taken, sometimes in a spirit of rash bravado. It is remarkable that there were so few serious accidents. Inevitably however, accidents there were. The most distressing of these saw the death of Alan Daniels, the civilian scientist leading the experiments on fuel tanks. Smith relates the episode:

> Having fired every variety of round into a certain fuel tank, without effect, he believed that he had proved a bulletproof tank. Gradually decreasing the distance used to fire at the tank, he ultimately stood right on the tank and fired a round point-blank into it. Tragically, the muzzle-flash ignited the fuel/air mixture in the top of the tank and the resulting explosion killed him.

Trials required that shooting at fuel tanks (and other bits and pieces of equipment) should be directed from different angles. To facilitate this, a special structure was provided, comprising two steel towers with a gantry to link them. For reasons that will become immediately apparent, this was given the name of the Incendiary Tower. In 1944, Austin Frazer was, in his own words, 'the film and photo boffin recording strikes – bullets and cannon shells of various types...' He describes his experience up the tower:

> The gantry gave superb views over the whole of Orford Ness but reaching the small platform at the top necessitated climbing the outside of the structure on

steel tubes some 18" apart. The gantry became my favourite lookout. I overcame my initial fear of heights by climbing it daily with a heavy film camera strapped to my back. The day of the first test firing I was in position, focused on the tank. I gave the order to fire.

The tank exploded and enveloped the gantry in flames, which passed over me as I crouched down. Some hours later, when the steel cooled, I climbed down unharmed...

Lethality trials involved the use of enemy aircraft. A remarkable collection of these was accumulated, retrieved from a variety of sources and ferried across the river. Setting up these trials was far from easy, given the primitive means to hand for getting the components to the quay, across the river and up to the research area.

For the purposes of trials, considerable patching up and 'cannibalism' was required and Smith, as a Mechanical Engineer, was part of the team that concocted targets that would provide a valid test of their vulnerability to attack. Smith and his colleagues were to become very competent welders, panel beaters, blacksmiths and turners. 'We all acquired skills far outside those expected in normal RAF service' he observed, 'and I think that had we lost the war I could have applied for a job in the Luftwaffe, as I knew as much about German aircraft as I did about British.'

As the war progressed, work on the Ness increased. During 1943, it became apparent that the existing buildings were no longer adequate. The contractors, Rogers Brothers of Felixstowe, were engaged to carry out an extensive programme of repairs and new construction. Their workers were still on site in 1945 when the war ended. This period saw the erection of three solid brick buildings, inherited by the National Trust. Their function back in 1944 was entirely practical. They included a maintenance and works office, a new camera section, a laboratory drawing office and engineering workshops. At the same time, a new concrete road was laid from the Stony Ditch bridge up to the Bomb Ballistics building. This replaced the existing trackway and was the first section of hard road on the shingle. The railway by then ran up past the Ballistics building, heading out towards the sea and was used for shifting loads of shingle for construction work. Short sections of this track still survive, embedded in the concrete of the roadway.

The Ballistics building was all the while carrying on with the work that had been temporarily suspended in 1939. The ballistics tables with which the RAF equipped its bombers would clearly become totally inadequate as new higher performance aircraft became available. In 1943, the Air Ministry required tables that allowed for bomb release at up to 400 miles per hour, from altitudes up to 45,000 feet. This would involve introducing into the calculations the resistance factors at rarefied atmosphere, while also allowing for a whole set of drag factors. New, heavyweight and streamlined weapons were needed for penetrating heavily armoured targets like U-boat pens.

Ken Daykin was a civilian boffin, whose time and experience on the Ness encompassed much of the trials work, spanning the war and post-war period. He arrived on the Ness in 1941 as a qualified surveyor. His employment in the roads and bridges department of East Suffolk County Council was regarded as a reserved occupation at the time. He was not permitted to volunteer for the forces but was able to wangle a secondment as a Civilian Scientific Officer (officially titled a Technical Assistant), under the Director of Research at ORS, George Hicks. His first assignment was within his professional field, surveying the whole site as part of re-establishing the instrumentation for the bombing range. He used the prominent vantage positions of Aldeburgh Church tower and Orford Castle as trigonometric points for establishing his datum line.

His work on the range began slowly, and often, Daykin has recalled, the weather interrupted all aerial activity. So, though primarily attached to the Ballistics section, he was also employed to assist in some of the vulnerability and lethality trials, which he found intrinsically rather boring and often somewhat dangerous. He confirms that health and safety was a concept seldom considered.

His first invitation to join a bomb trial flight over the Ness saw him board an elderly Handley Page Hampden, flown out of Farnborough and calling in on Martlesham. The bomb being tested was a general-purpose 250-pounder. Daykin recalls the thrill of embarking on this first flight, which quickly evaporated as he became extremely airsick! Flying in this aircraft was risky. Anti-aircraft gunners aboard coastal shipping often mistook its slim fuselage for that of a Dornier, and shot at it.

Naturally, the Ness was affected by military activity. Much of the East Anglian coast, from Shingle Street in the south to Thorpeness to the north, was taken over for battle training. Both Army and Navy liaison officers would appear on the site from time to time to coordinate various exercises that might affect the Ness. Occasionally, shells flew overhead or bombers unloaded experimental weapons. The ballistics of the 12,000lb ('Tallboy') bomb, devised by Barnes Wallis, was tested on King's Marsh. 'Tallboy' was dropped mainly on the Ashley Walks range in the New Forest and at Shoeburyness, but trials on the Ness took place during March 1944. The trials were designed to deal with the problem of spiralling, which could lead to inaccuracy. Wallis devised asymmetric fins, which increased the bomb's spin and speed of descent. Bert Smith recalls that a special mock-up of a concrete building was erected on King's Marsh. B17 bombers dropped weapons onto it. These were unlikely to have been Tallboys – the B17 bomb bay was too small for them – but probably the US so-called 'Disney' bombs, 4,500-pound weapons. An added complexity here was the scheme to improve their powers of penetration by adding rockets to increase downwards penetration. They were deployed on a number of US missions, but never as decisively as 'Tallboy'.[2]

Part of the myths surrounding Orford Ness includes the story that Barnes Wallis,[3] inventor of the infamous 'bouncing bomb' used in the 'Dambusters' raids in May 1943 was a visitor. It is likely that Wallis did visit the Ness to observe these trials,

lden Hammond was a remarkably successful and pioneering photographer. This is one of several
ws he shot of the Orford Ness site in 1917, taken before he transferred his photographic unit to the
w RFC station at Martlesham Heath. It shows the northern field, with two of its three great hangars
npleted. A narrow bridge across the tidal creek, Stony Ditch, links the fields with the bomb stores
 the shingle. Note the three canvas hangars and the drainage marks outside them in the bottom
ht-hand corner. The large white circle was an identification mark for pilots. (*Hammond Collection, by
d permission of Mrs Victoria Gunnell*)

prototype RE9 aircraft, one of only two built from 1917 onwards. The problem of engine noise,
ich betrayed the approach of attacking aircraft, as well as deafening aircrew (note the twin vertical
nausts above the engine), remained unsolved after extensive trials on the Ness and at Butley.
cKerrow Collection, by kind permission of Mrs Jane Timmins)

Top Left: The FE2b had an engine mounted behind the pilot, and the observer, with his gun, right forward. This exposed position must have been alarming but it made this aircraft extremely useful for aerial reconnaissance. The oblong 'bracket' was fitted for some sort of experimental gadgetry, exactly what is unclear.

Top Right: Close-up view of the engine of an FE2b with its pusher propeller. The silencer under test is visible to the left of the vertically pointing exhaust.

Below: Research into effective on-board instrumentation was essential for night and cloud flying, making a major contribution to the development of aviation for war and peace. The cockpit of a DH9 in 1918 is pictured below. Experiments carried out by Frank Holder revealed the need for clearly illuminated instrument panels when flying 'blind'. (All on this page: *McKerrow Collection, by kind permisison of Mrs Jane Timmins*)

A range of experiments in the new concept of camouflage were undertaken during the First World War, some of which were to be adopted as standard RAF practice. Here is a Sopwith Snipe given a pattern treatment to blend in with the ground below, protecting it from attack from above. (*McKerrow Collection, by kind permission of Mrs Jane Timmins*)

In a relaxed pose in 1918, the three aviators involved in experiments in gunnery and in hazardous cloud and formation flying. Charles Fairburn (left) was a star pilot and George McKerrow (right) a specialist observer. Bennett Melvill Jones (centre) was primarily a scientific researcher. Note that they retained regimental insignia (and ranks) even after the RAF was founded in 1918. (*Goldsworthy Collection*)

Left: The brilliant but maverick character, Frederick Lindemann, arrives at the Ness in an NE1, probably up from Farnborough. He conducted vital experiments in flying as well as bombing techniques and became an Oxford Professor, but political ambitions were to cloud his judgment at times in later years. (*Goldsworthy Collection*)

Below: Regular exchanges took place between the front-line aviators and experimental staff from the Ness. Here, the notable and much admired fighter 'ace', Albert Ball makes an undignified arrival on a wintry Ness airfield in a Bristol Scout from No. 34 Squadron between late 1916 and the first few months of 1917. Only a few months later, in May 1917, he was killed in action. (*Imperial War Museum*)

The destruction of a Zeppelin was greeted rapturously by enormous crowds. The *L48* was shot down over Theberton, near Leiston, in June 1917. To protect the wreck from trophy hunters, soldiers ringed the site. This aerial photograph was taken by Walden Hammond the following day. His pilot was his great friend, Frank Holder, who had been one of the pilots that had attacked the airship the previous night. (*Hammond Collection, by kind permission of Mrs Victoria Gunnell*)

Shooting at moving aircraft from a moving aircraft under variable weather conditions involved highly complex mathematics. The guns used were army issue, not necessarily suitable for aerial combat. The range being used here was to the north of the airfield. A group of airmen and Officers watch an aircraft towing a target drone, out of picture. (*Hammond Collection, by kind permission of Mrs Victoria Gunnelll*)

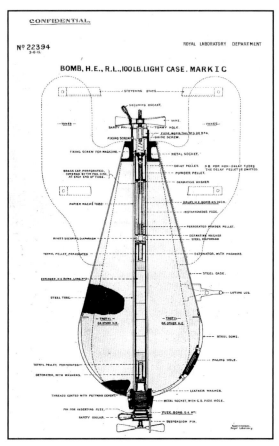

Nº 22394
3·6·15.

ROYAL LABORATORY DEPARTMENT

BOMB, H.E., R.L., 100LB. LIGHT CASE. MARK I C

Left: The development of ever more sophisticated bombs was a major objective for Ness boffins. Armed with detailed blueprints like this (for a general purpose high explosive bomb), effective explosives, fuses, bomb-case designs, bomb sights and carrier and release mechanisms were painstakingly tested. Bombing remained a singularly inaccurate business. (*McKerrow Collection, by kind permission of Mrs Jane Timmins*)

Below: A somewhat crude rack displays a motley assortment of early bombs for trial these were often weighted dummies. The science and technique of bombs and bombing was still in its infancy. Some of the experiments being conducted were positively bizarre. Many were distinctly hazardous – not even 'hit or miss' – usually 'miss or miss'. (*McKerrow Collection, by kind permission of Mrs Jane Timmins*)

For nearly twenty years important trials took place on aircraft, both Allied and enemy, under a programme titled 'Lethality and Vulnerability Testing'. Here a Bristol Blenheim bomber, brought across in sections and reassembled, has been shot at by German guns to test its weak points. (*Crown Copyright*)

Close analysis was made of the effect of gunfire on the interior of aircraft, to see how effective armour plate would be in protecting aircrew. Here is the same Blenheim after severe testing. Long rods were put through holes to plot the passage of every single bullet. (*Crown Copyright*)

Left: In November 1940, a unit of the Italian Air Force failed to return to base. Attempting to raid Harwich, this Fiat CR42 fighter was no match for RAF Hawker Hurricanes. It had to make an ignominious forced landing to the north of Orford Ness Lighthouse. RAF staff were more interested in the aircraft than in the captured pilot. (*By kind permission, Mr David Kindred*)

Below: The youthful team sent by Watson Watt to develop RDF (radar) in the summer of 1935. Carefree in appearance, they worked with immense enthusiasm and dedication. Pictured outside one of the First World War huts, wearing silly hats, 'Skip' Wilkins is left centre and 'Taffy' Bowen is far right. (*Douglas Fisher Collection*)

Top Left: Sir Robert Watson-Watt (as he called himself from 1942) is usually credited with 'inventing' radar. He was a skilled leader and his vision and powers of persuading both politicians and brass hats (senior officers) ensured that air defence radar was in operation to defend the country in 1940. (*Imperial War Museum*)

Top Right: Sir Henry Tizard was among the most important and brilliant of all who worked on Orford Ness. A fair pilot, he was primarily an academic with a sharp analytical mind. He 'found' the site for Martlesham Heath airfield, developed the concept of the test pilot and then ensured that RDF would evolve into radar. (*Imperial War Museum*)

Right: From 1917, women were regularly employed on the Ness for various tasks. During the Second World War a team of WAAFs was brought over to run all the on-site transport, often physically quite tough work. Corporal Pat Jermyn (far right) is seen here relaxing with colleagues in August 1944. (*By kind permission of Mrs Pat Bishop, née Jermyn*)

Overleaf: This cartoon drawn during the Second World War by an unknown serviceman sums up everything about Orford Ness experiments over the years. Note that there is only a single Officer (Flight Lieutenant Quinlan) ordering about a disrespectful Corporal. On the river is the notorious ferry barge, known by its number as '*Ein Ein Sieben Fünf*'. The great hangar that survived until 1987 stands serene, surrounded by unlikely explosions, with a single figure waving forlornly on the roof. (*Unknown*)

Many key staff were neither military nor high-powered academics. John Backhouse was totally unqualified when recruited to assist in operating the Askania Kine-theodilites. He is seen here in his workshop in 1955. He was later employed as a Technical Assistant by AWRE in complex work, spending twenty years on the Ness. (*By kind permission of Mr John Backhouse*)

Frank Tanner became a Ballistics Officer, conducting bombing research from 1948. He had the idea of linking captured German Kine-theodolites to mobile gun-laying SCR 584 radar, to monitor the fall of bombs under test. He is viewed here, operating one of the four machines on site. (*National Trust/Frank Tanner*)

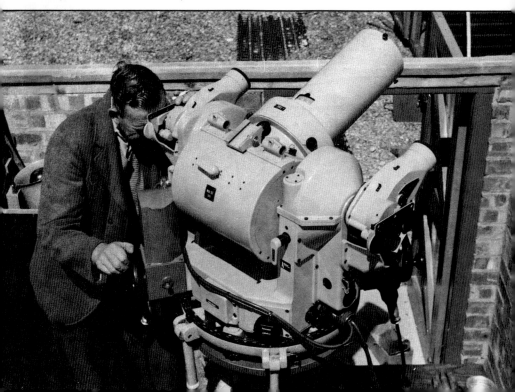

The two so-called Pagoda labs for the second phase of environmental tests were virtually identical in design. Here at work are the contractor's men from Messrs Cubitt and Goff Ltd, Ipswich. (*Crown Copyright*)

Neat and tidy, ready for trials to begin. One of the Pagodas *c.*1960. Note the plastic glazing beneath the roof, carefully designed to seal the interior, but capable of instant disintegration in the event of an accidental explosion in the testing chamber below. (*Crown Copyright*)

Left: Photographed in about 1955, the so-called Maritime Navigation building that operated between 1929 and 1934 is here seen in use for its second function, to house the AWRE telemetry equipment for testing nuclear bomb triggers. Note the 100 feet radio mast for transmitting and receiving signals from a falling bomb. (*Crown Copyright*)

Below: In 1957, Keith Wood's AWRE team was commissioned to track and monitor the Russian satellite, Sputnik. A highly effective, if somewhat Heath Robinson, device was the result, positioned close to the Bomb Ballistics building. (*Crown Copyright*)

Opposite above: An aerial view of the Cobra Mist site taken from 7,500ft on 24 March 1972 makes the 'blockhouse' appear relatively minute at the bottom left of the picture. In reality a giant building which alone still survives, it houses the BBC World Service transmitters. The jetty built for barge traffic is clearly visible in the bottom left-hand corner, although it has long since gone. (*Reproduced by permission of Ordnance Survey on behalf of HMSO. © Crown Copyright 2010. All rights reserved. Licence 100023974.*)

Opposite below: The vast array of aerial masts stretched to the north of the 'blockhouse' operations building, covering about 135 acres (equivalent to over 75 full-size football pitches). At 150 feet, the tallest masts were one and half times the height of the lighthouse. Faint scars in the marsh are all that remain of this amazing construction. (*Unknown*)

Orford Ness artefacts on display for visitors to view do not come more chilling than this WE177A nuclear bomb case. WE177 was a family of UK parachute retarded/free fall nuclear weapons with three distinct variants. WE177A, in its role as a depth bomb, could also be delivered by most UK naval helicopters of the period 1971 to 1991, when that capability was withdrawn. The WE177 weapon system was withdrawn from RAF service at the end of March 1998, and all weapons have been dismantled. This display remains as a reminder of the work that the Ness boffins conducted in the development of such nuclear weapon systems. (*National Trust*)

Not all trials on the Ness have been documented. Installed at the height of the Cold War during the early 1960s, the definite prime purpose(s) for which this substantial concrete ring was constructed remains a matter of speculation. (*National Trust/Simon Bradford*)

even if no documentary evidence exists (the Ness being a secret site, it was unlikely to be recorded by Wallis, and other documents that would have proved or disproved the fact were destroyed in the floods of 1947 and 1953). It is recorded that he often liked to take the opportunity to watch trials and tests, although his diaries reveal no confirmation of any visit to the range and no contemporary reminiscences recall seeing him on the site. The notion too that he had any part in the trial at Shingle Street in March 1943, which resulted in the total demolition of the ill-fated Lifeboat Inn, is highly dubious. The weapon involved was a Chemical Defence Research Establishment weapon, being developed at Porton Down. Mystery shrouded this episode too, for the files concerning it were not released until 1994. The idea here was to combine a blister-inducing chemical with a high explosive charge, for tactical use against specific targets where, following detonation, rescuers would be deterred from approaching the area. It was decided not to proceed with this questionable idea. To this day, Shingle Street has never had its pub replaced.

Preparations for D-Day led to other visitors to the Ness. Early in 1944 a substantial detachment of around fifty Royal Electrical and Mechanical Engineers (REME) was drafted in to conduct several trials in anticipation of the Normandy landing. One of them was Charles Haynes.

The 'need to know' principle operated as strongly as ever. Haynes had no idea what the RAF teams were up to. The Army men were billeted in huts on the Sudbourne estate and bussed in daily via Aldeburgh and down the shingle track past the Martello Tower. This was an extraordinarily lengthy route, one presumes to ensure their separation from the RAF, made odder by the fact that they shared workshop space and such facilities as the NAAFI.

Between January and June, Haynes's unit conducted a variety of trials. The fitting of 'flails' to Churchill tanks to detonate land mines was entirely successful. Less so was the attempt to fit rockets to the sides of light vehicles, including Bren-gun Carriers, to propel them across the ditches and streams of Normandy. So many occupants were seriously injured, often with broken limbs, that this far-fetched idea was abandoned. These modifications to armoured vehicles were devised by General Hobart, and were described, with that typical British talent for not appearing to take things seriously, which puzzled and irritated their American allies, as 'Hobart's funnies'.

Also made and tested were components for what were to be used in the D-Day Mulberry Harbours. Typically, they were never told at the time what their ultimate purpose was: it was 'need to know', again. The most serious failure was an experiment with material for generating a new system of flame-thrower. A mixture of nitrogen and glycerine was tested with a demonstration before a party of 'brass hats' (senior officers). When nothing appeared to be happening the officers' curiosity got the better of them and they moved in from the protective shelter of a ring of tanks. The REME men remained prudently out of range. The sudden explosion took a fearful toll, an accident that was hushed up and the experiment abandoned.

One aspect of their time on the Ness followed a pattern set by their RAF opposite numbers: private enterprise activities. Haynes cannot have been alone in the manufacturing of objects in his spare time, taking advantage of the high quality equipment and variety of raw materials lying about. He made toasting forks, cribbage boards and even metal picture frames. His memories of the six months on the Ness include trips to Ipswich, where he witnessed the great footballer Dixie Dean playing. Cricket was his game however: he was subsequently in the post-war Army team, which in those days had fixtures at Lords. He became a chartered accountant before retiring back to Suffolk.

Of course, as the war progressed and Suffolk grew into a vast air base for the USAAF* as well as the RAF, the noise of aircraft overhead must have been a constant experience. This could create problems, illustrated by another piece of rather different and clearly quite formidable hardware. Hence, the Ness was the obvious location for its trial. It was a mighty photoflood flare, designed to be fired from beneath a pathfinder bomber to light up the target. Here once again history was repeating itself: similar, if relatively primitive, experiments had been conducted during the First World War. Daykin recalls that it was extremely noisy. Setting off a trial flare on the ground, far too close to the lighthouse for comfort, caused such a bang that the lantern lamp jumped clean off the mercury bed and the light was temporarily put out of action. This awesome 'weapon' led to a complaint from an old lady in Aldeburgh. The officer in charge at this period was Maurice Helliwell, who recalls visiting her:

It appeared that her physical condition was such that an unannounced bang caused her great distress but that if she could be forewarned a few minutes before the bang, she could cope. I therefore gave instructions that she should be telephoned just before the explosion.

In 1944, a new sound was heard: the sinister chugging of the V-1 'doodlebug'. By the late summer, as the Allies advanced through northern France, the Germans had moved their launching sites to the Low Countries. German bombers were also used for aerial delivery. The route now taken was over the Suffolk and Essex coast. This brought Suffolk to the forefront of defence activity. In all, eighty-five AA batteries were hastily erected along the county's coast; the Ness thus entered the fray as an active military site for the only time in either war. This operation was code-named DIVER and was commanded by General Frederick Pile. Temporary wooden platforms were constructed for mounting the guns, using railway sleepers. Pile explained the slowness with which this work was undertaken, despite the urgency of the task. He later wrote: 'On the narrow twisting roads in that part of East Anglia where we were re-deploying, convoys

* The US Air Force was a component of the Army (USAAF) until 1947, when it gained its autonomy, as USAF.

of 10-tonners would suddenly encounter head-on a convoy of 3-tonners. The subsequent delay and confusion was enormous.'

There has long been a legend that the RAF Regiment Squadron Leader in command of this operation on the Ness was none other than Walter Hammond. Wally Hammond was one of the greatest cricketers of his generation, Captain of both England and Gloucestershire. He had certainly returned to the UK by the summer of 1944 following service in Egypt. Evidence that he was involved in Operation DIVER is not confirmed either by his county club or by Lord's Cricket Museum. Indeed, it is probable that he was already more involved in cricket, than in fighting the doodlebugs. Quite how this intriguing tradition arose is just another Orford Ness mystery, although he may have been in the locality to pay a social call upon a fellow RAF Regiment officer who lived in Orford.

The setting up of the Ness battery had several consequences. The first of these was the construction of a pontoon bridge giving direct vehicular access from Orford Quay to the island to supply the battery. This came as a great boon to the young WAAF girl in charge of transport, which she had to operate on both sides of the river. It also of course had a major impact on traffic up and down the river.

It cannot have been seen as anything more than a very temporary measure, but even so, it had its troubles. The winter of 1944 was harsh, as those fighting in the Low Countries found to their cost. Parts of the river Alde froze and ice floes and piles of frozen snow accumulated on the marsh 'flats' above Aldeburgh where the less saline water froze more quickly than elsewhere down the river. These posed a potential threat to the bridge. The Royal Engineers, who had constructed it, were happy to get rid of surplus time-expired munitions by using them to blow up the ice. Unfortunately, the operations went awry. The ice floated off carrying the explosives on it, and blew up against the pontoons, removing a section of the bridge in the process. It was repaired but was removed once the war was over – but not completely. Two of the fourteen floats on which the roadway was fixed remained at Orford, used as tenders for maintaining the mooring buoys in the anchorage. These last survivors from the Second World War could still be seen on the water up to sixty years later.

This was the only time a physical link with the Ness was ever constructed, though not the last time a full-scale bridge was to be considered. The importance of the role the river Ore has subsequently come to play in providing for recreational sailing as well as an anchorage for inshore fishing is now unquestionable. In this respect, the 'privacy' of the 'island' seems as secure as ever.

The Ness batteries assisted in defeating the V-1s. DIVER battery guns accounted for nearly 2,000 of them. The secret here were the radars linked to its guns, which, armed with proximity fused* shells, enabled a remarkably high accuracy to be achieved. In all around 10,000 flying bombs were launched, flying at about 4,000 feet and reaching a speed of up to 400 miles per hour. Over half of

---

* The invention of radio aerial proximity fuses by William Lord (1919–2008) and his team earned them the reputation as the men who 'saved London from the flying bomb'.

these reached Britain. Of the 112 V-1s that entered the Orford area, the Ness and neighbouring guns accounted for ninety-four. The Ness record was fifteen (out of a possible sixteen) in a single night. It was an Orford gun that accounted for the very last V-1, on 29 March 1945.

Another small radar unit was established during the war on the roof of Orford Castle. This was to provide Identification Friends or Foe (IFF) for aircraft returning to their bases in East Anglia. This was a curious full turn of the circle, for it represented a service that the rotating beacon had been devised to supply over a decade before. It was part of the function of a branch of the services too often given scant recognition. The Observer Corps was in fact created during the height of inter-war peace, in 1925. The Orford post was, in 1929, one of the very earliest to be established, based in the coastguard station on the quay, and using the watch house by the lighthouse as its forward lookout. During the war, the Corps recorded every movement by air, including what, in 1940, it defined as raid C7. This proved to be no enemy attack at all but a desperate escape flight by a Dutch party of refugees, who made a forced landing on the airfield. It is easily forgotten how important was the part it played in supplementing the work done by radar stations during the Battle of Britain. The Corps was granted its Royal title in April 1941 as a result, thus becoming the Royal Observer Corps (ROC).

The American-designed SCR 584 gun-laying radars used by the DIVER battery were of great interest to the Bomb Ballistics team. Ken Daykin has recalled being instructed to take a close look at these mobile units to see whether they could be useful. Their particular attraction was their capacity to predict the course and position of the target. It was quickly appreciated that this radar would indeed be ideal for monitoring the flight path of bombs being tested. Shortly afterwards, some captured ex-German Askania kine-theodolite high-speed, tele-scopic tracking cameras were introduced. Linked to the radar, it would mean that the dropping aircraft could be accurately tracked at high altitude. It also meant that trials were no longer totally dependent on clear skies. The kine-theodolite was unfailingly directed to follow the bomb to its target. Four stations were set up with kine-theodolites, at least one of them equipped with 'slaved' radar. This new equipment was to set the scene for the development of the range over the next decade (see Plate Section).

OFF DUTY ON THE NESS

Life on the Ness during the war was little different from that experienced on many RAF stations: much that was boring routine, episodes of great fun, periodic examples of service mischief, moments of elation and throughout evidence of a widespread sense of comradeship. The composition of personnel, civilian and service, was well-nigh unique. But it was a military establishment and the day began with a parade, on the concrete apron to the south of the southern hangar. This was perhaps a bit of 'going through the motions'. The senior NCO was a Sergeant Miller, who was not a technical expert but was responsible for the smooth operation of the establishment. He was to be observed prowling around, armed with a clipboard on which matters requiring his attention might be noted. It was all a bit casual. Typical of the spirit of the place was the prank to test out the efficiency of Sergeant Miller's inspections. Rifles were of course carried on parade. It was a habit to push a spider down the barrel to test Miller's powers of observation.

Much of the maintenance work was farmed out to civilian tradesmen in Orford. The Lewis brothers were often to be seen on the 'island'. Other regular visitors included members of the Smy family and the Goldsmiths, father and son.

Particularly reassuring evidence has survived that, despite all that was so abnormal about the Ness during the war, some of the old traditions survived. In the archive are copies of the Christmas dinner menus for 1942 and 1944. These could have hardly been more reassuringly traditional. Clearly, supplies of turkey and mince pies were available for an important military establishment, even in wartime.

From 1943, a small group of about sixteen WAAFs was brought in to take on some of the support duties, such as drivers and clerks. It was suggested that their hut, No. 9, would need barbed wire protection from the attentions of amorous airmen: none was ever provided. This was not of course the first time that young ladies had been introduced to provide ancillary services. Twenty-five years before, Oliver Wills had expressed his delight at finding their predecessors working on the Ness.

One of these young women was Corporal Pat Jermyn. Drafted from RAF Hornchurch, she spent the rest of the war in charge of the motor transport unit. Her recollections of the place over fifty years later remain vivid. Some people held the view that the Ness was too harsh a place to be sending girls to. She recalls that on the contrary, they proved rather more robust in coping with any unpleasant weather conditions than the men. Their living quarters were far from gentile either: Pat was allotted a minute office no more than 10 feet square, in a corner of the MT building, little more than a cupboard. The building and her 'cupboard' still remain.

The men were keen to put these girls to the test too. Pat recalls how she was challenged to have a go with a .303 rifle, since such weapons were everyday tools of the trade for the men. A dustbin lid was propped up on the further bank across Stony Ditch, perhaps 75 yards away from her quarters. She was given some brief instruction before pointing her rifle through the window. The result: a direct hit! Her account of this little challenge concludes: 'I have never fired or touched a firearm since, quite satisfied to live with this first result!'

One of her colleagues was Jack Bishop, a member of the ferry crew in the motorboat section. After they were demobbed, in 1949, they married. This was far from being the only romance that occurred on the Ness.

Pat was in charge of a motley assortment of motor vehicles. On the island, she had a couple of standard RAF service vans, a 30-cwt Bedford truck and a tractor. Her mainland collection included a Dodge 3-tonner, a Bedford 14-cwt lorry and a Hillman Minx. With this mixed bag she was responsible for providing for all the transport needs of the station. This included ferrying personnel from the jetty to and from their places of work, at start and finish of the day and for their lunch hour. The mainland vehicles were used for collecting stores, principally a 'ration run' each week to the newly opened RAF base at Bentwaters. This is where she would take anyone needing medical attention beyond the capacity of the ORS medical orderly. The Dodge was also used for the Saturday afternoon 'Lib [Liberty] Run' to Ipswich.

There were three other WAAF drivers in her team, plus the civilian Harold Gibbs. It is clear that they had a busy time. The provision of a pontoon bridge was a great boon to them. They no longer had to split up their string of vehicles on either side of the river so long as the bridge was operational.

In due course, however, it wasn't. It was winter 1944. 'At the time,' writes Mrs Bishop, 'the saltings were icing over and it was decided to use explosives to break up the ice. Good idea until one of the "punts" was punctured and down it went. It was a Saturday afternoon and the "Lib Run" was away in Ipswich. On arrival back that night ... no bridge!'

The motorboat crew had to ferry everyone back. Unfortunately, the bulk of the station's vehicles were parked on the jetty, cut off from the mainland. For some time, only the heavy Dodge was available on the quay and Pat was its only qualified driver. The recovery of the 'lost' pontoon float defeated divers and necessitated the haulage power of a friendly army tank.

One of their more taxing duties was to collect cans of petrol for the station. It is amazing that an important military establishment was reliant at this time on the crudest of supply arrangements: 'All available cans were taken over to the only petrol pump in the village: an antique hand pump with only a ½-gallon capacity each time. This took considerable time and energy, especially if a visiting Queen Mary (the articulated RAF low-loader used for transporting aircraft) said it wanted 20 gallons...'

The motor transport on the Ness was of vital importance although its quality was hardly impressive. The provision of boats for ferrying personnel and equipment across the river was if anything even more crucial, given the geography of the place. The quality available was extraordinarily unimpressive. Pat's husband-to-be, Jack Bishop, was one of the corporals involved. His views on the 'fleet' were hardly complimentary:

Our boats were a mixed lot, comprising a commandeered fishing boat, *Sunflower,* a typical estuary craft powered by a Thorneycroft 'Handybilly' engine of the chug-all-day-when-you-have-got-it-started variety, an RAF planing dinghy, a quickish little general service boat and a 30 foot scow built in about 1914. It was decked forward over the engine for about 8 feet, the rest open and this was designated by the RAF as No. 1175. It was hard to start, a pig to handle and generally known to her crew as '*Ein Ein Sieben Fünf*', since we felt it did more for the Germans than us.

This seems again a curiously inadequate provision given the volume and complexity of the job required of it. Loading vehicles and aircraft parts onto the scow by means of a hand-wound crane was indeed a challenge. It was all in some contrast with the subsequently more lavish supply of suitable landing craft, once the war was over.

The NAAFI hut was very much a social centre. There was a full-size snooker table*, as well as table tennis and darts. Parties and dances were regularly held, and monthly film shows, arranged by a character nicknamed 'Old Pop', who clearly thoroughly enjoyed being with the islanders. Occasionally, ORS was allotted an ENSA** concert. An invitation to these entertainments was extended to villagers in Orford, though Pat recalls on one occasion an ENSA party chickened out of braving the ferry crossing and cancelled.

Pat Bishop (née Jermyn) still often reflects on the happy times on what she refers to as 'that magical island. I think all the folk who were there, at least those I know, feel the same about the place.'

In 1942, the NAAFI manageress Mrs Davey, whose kindness to Ken Daykin has already been noted, recruited a nineteen-year-old school-leaver from Leiston. Irene Gilbert has provided a fascinating picture of serving the airmen: every item seems to have cost one penny. Like so many civilians working on the station, she was happy to remain blissfully unaware of what her 'customers' were up to. She never even enquired, even of her husband-to-be – romance came her way too – she married one of the airmen.

On her arrival, she had stayed with her boss in the village, until the notorious air attack of 22 October 1942. It was early morning when a lone Dornier swooped over Orford and, turning in from a southerly direction, unloaded its bombs on the totally defenceless civilian population. Chapman's shop was destroyed by a direct hit and some council houses severely damaged by another bomb, which bounced clean over Mr Friend's Garage. Two servicemen and eleven civilians, including three children from one family, the Chambers, lost their lives. Bert Smith recalls this tragic and purposeless event:

We heard and saw the aircraft through the window and recognising it immediately, I and several others made a dash for one of the gun pits located close to
the building... We were considerably 'put out' when the C/O refused permission for any of us to help with the rescue work.

---

* The snooker table was subsequently rescued from the Ness and made available to the youth of Orford.
** Entertainments National Service Association. This organisation involved many of the lead-ing variety and classical artists of the day.

Although the Army were immediately to hand in the village, the airmen on the 'island' felt they had let the villagers down by not assisting.

The attack, which in fact involved two bombers, one that jettisoned its load out to sea without pressing home its attack, was typical of the tip-and-run so-called 'Baedeker' raids. It happened so suddenly that no anti-aircraft fire could be brought to bear and the raider escaped.

A few months previously, a similar lone enemy incursion met with a rather different outcome. Smith recalls how at the time he was with his particular mate, the Armoury Corporal, a rare character known as 'Jeep' Livesley. They heard an approaching aircraft and immediately recognised it as being German. Livesley, a remarkable marksman, seized a Lewis gun, rushed out and fired a burst at the plane as it flew overhead. He was immediately placed on a charge by the C/O, Flight Lieutenant Quinlan, something of a martinet in character, for breaking regulations, firing recklessly without permission. This might appear puzzling, unless, one may suspect, it was policy to give the Germans no indication that the Ness was in any way an operational station and hence a suitable target for attack. Evidence of guns fired in its defence could well undermine its innocent appearance. The charge was dropped when it was later learned that the offending plane had indeed been hit and had crash-landed. The pilot had revealed that he had been shot at as he crossed the coast. He was thus in no position to get back to reveal the true, albeit modest, nature of the Ness's military capacity. In fact, the defence of the Ness against enemy attack during the Second World War was at best rudimentary, and for much of the war, well-nigh nonexistent. Initially, a small detachment of RAF regiment was deployed. These men appear in the station photo of 1942, their motley assortment of weapons on display. Their station post was on Orford Quay, somewhat remote from the site of any enemy landing on the beach! Shortly after this picture was taken, these men were replaced by Military Police on the Quay and ORS service personnel were deployed for guard duties.

The outcome of the raid on Orford was that quarters were provided on the Ness for the NAAFI staff. This must have made romantic contact the easier, for in 1944, Miss Gilbert became Mrs Nutman and in 1945, both husband and wife were posted to India. Like so many who worked there, she recalls the real element of secrecy that prevailed. 'We had no idea what was going on. If anyone knew anything it was never mentioned. Secret it certainly was. We just served the boys and got on with things. They made their own fun with impromptu concerts, dances etc. Liberty runs to Ipswich on Saturdays. Everything so normal but so secret.'

Ivan Garwood was the Orderly Room Corporal at this time. The C/O was, for Orford Ness, an unusually strict disciplinarian. This may well have been a response to the tensions of wartime, coupled with the fact that the establishment provided for no other officers to give him moral support. Yet Garwood confirms that comradeship and morale were always good. They appeared to get extra rations too, and the NAAFI was well stocked.

The social life on the Ness must have been quite lively. Garwood records the familiar round of football and cricket matches, singsongs in the NAAFI (which apparently inspired the Irish-born C/O to tear-jerking renditions of 'The Mountains of the Mourne'), and a more formal station dance. For this, an appeal to the young ladies of Ipswich resulted in the recruitment of a couple of coach-loads of welcome guests. The Army provided a live band, and a grand time was had. A strict rule was enforced by service police: no couples permitted to stray more than ten paces from the hall! Such dances became regular events, made all the easier after the WAAF girls had arrived on the Ness and links with the Forestry Commission's Land Army girls were established. Dancing classes were organised and local families entertained visitors in their homes.

Garwood describes 'Liberty Bus' runs to Woodbridge or Ipswich in pursuit of whatever beer was available. Another rather delightful event, with a similar objective, was the Bicycle Treasure Hunt, where participants moved from pub to pub in the locality, in search of liquid treasure.

Garwood was succeeded in his job by one of the WAAFs, Margot Jackson, known as 'Jackie'. The C/O by now was Flight Lieutenant May, who was still the only commissioned officer on the Ness. He would not normally be entitled to command the services of a secretary. Orford Ness was never a normal circumstance! Margot was proficient at shorthand, so Orderly Corporal incorporated the functions of a personal assistant. A consequence of this, as happened on most very small units, was a much more relaxed relationship between officers and other ranks. The C/O was readily available to join in with recreational activities, acting as referee in crazy football games, for example. Mrs Sheppard, as 'Jackie' became, has recalled that in the popular informal dances there were insufficient WAAFs available for the 100 or so men, who had to queue up for partners. A source of imported young ladies would be the Churchman's cigarette factory, which then stood beside what is now the Portman Road football ground. Clearly something of a relationship developed here. An archive photograph has survived of the ORS cricket team at the Churchman's cricket ground.

As the C/O's personal assistant and secretary, 'Jackie' had a close insight into what was going on around her. She recalls the work done by the photographers recording every bomb drop, most of them with dummies. 'One bomb' she writes, 'which held incendiaries dropped several feet before opening like an umbrella to cause as many fires as possible on German cities. One day one of these dummy incendiary bombs accidentally went through the roof of the bath hut and unfortunately one WAAF was having a bath in the next cubicle. You can imagine the noise this bomb made on a cast-iron bath. She shot out of the hut with very little clothing on!'

It was cold on the Ness and it always seemed to be blowing a gale. Leather jerkins were issued to everyone. Life was energetic, since getting down to the jetty involved a long walk or an awkward ride on the crossbar of a bike. The experiments were noisy, with engines running, constant gunfire, petrol tanks exploding and over-flying aircraft releasing their bombs, all evidence of, in Jackie's words, 'a very active

Research Station'. After eighteen months she contracted shingles and was sent to Martlesham to recuperate, by which time the war was over. Her first return to the Ness was over sixty years later, to a reunion in July 2006.

The daily routine would be enlivened by various arrivals on the shore. Bert Smith recalls the occasion when an RAF Air-Sea Rescue launch mistook the Ness Light for the Cork Light, 3 miles offshore. It swung westwards and at full speed shot straight up the beach. Another rescue involved a Supermarine Walrus amphibian out of Martlesham, which rescued the soldiers from a crashed glider, out to sea off Slaughden. Heavily overladen, it was quite unable to take off, and so motored back towards the Ness, where RAF personnel were available to complete the rescue. The wheels on its 'oleo' legs promptly sank into the shingle and only with great difficulty and by employing US Army equipment, was it retrieved. Apart from macabre items, like corpses of German aircrew, there were some welcome arrivals on the beach. The flotsam washed ashore from ships lost on the North Sea could be the source of unexpected additional income. A cargo of timber was loaded on one of the barges, and taken up to Aldeburgh where salvage was claimed. No less popular was the large consignment of Guinness which floated up the river on the tide. It rapidly disappeared, before the excise officers could intervene.

Hardly surprisingly, shooting was a much-favoured activity. The marshes towards Aldeburgh provided a plentiful bag of wildfowl, hares and rabbits. These too could prove to be good little earners for the marksmen. Local butchers welcomed whatever was on offer. The Armoury Corporal, 'Jeep' Livesley, was also the station gamekeeper. Dressed in scruffy uniform, leather jerkin and wellington boots, Corporal Livesley had all the air of the highly enterprising poacher. The sport on the Ness was sufficiently well known for parties of Army officers to come over specifically. Those RAF NCOs who had their own guns would join them, while other Ness personnel acted as beaters. Hares were driven up from North Weir Point towards the airfield site. With other items – pheasant and wildfowl 'poached' from sites in the battle training area on the mainland – the volume of game must have been pretty spectacular.

The only problem arose when the marshes were used for exercises in battle area training. One Sunday, Bert Smith and half a dozen airmen sought permission to go shooting. He describes being used as a target for an artillery unit:

We were standing in a loose group fully exposed to view and the first shell went through or just over the group. We went to ground but the gunner knew his fall of shot to yards and put down several rounds where he thought we were heading, that is, back to base behind the shelter of a bank. We realised his game and stayed put – I think he only intended to frighten us as he used practice shells, not high explosive, but they played rough in the battle area. How many men died or were wounded in training I have never heard, but in these conditions there must have been some.

It is a wonder any wildlife survived on the marshes at all.

Two of the RAF corporals were extremely proficient gunsmiths. One of these was Bert Smith, who with a colleague set up a nice little business. 'Various archaic and frequently illegal weaponry was overhauled and reconditioned', he recalls. As a consequence, several of the airmen became crack shots, capable in competition of out-shooting any Army team. 'Jeep' in particular was a star. In a match against a squad drawn from the neighbouring Tank Corps, firing rifles, the RAF wiped the floor with the Army men, who, chastened, issued a challenge with revolvers: 'The challenge was accepted and they shot first, shoulder to shoulder with well drilled procedures to the officer's orders.' The RAF of course had no officers. They opted to shoot singly, with 'Jeep' their opening shot. He ambled up to the firing point, a cigarette in the corner of his mouth and with one hand in his trouser pocket put six shots into the target, bettering the combined Army score. 'Jeep' and Smith were both the proud owners of a Luger pistol. How legally they had been obtained, or from what source, no one was particularly anxious to enquire.

'Jeep' Livesley subsequently married a Cynthia King and settled down as a farmer at nearby Theberton. He was like so many who having enjoyed their time on the Ness, never left the locality.

The last few years of ORS operation were to witness a closer liaison between the Ness boffins and the inhabitants of Orford itself than ever before, which was in fact to persist throughout the remainder of 'secret' occupancy of the 'island'. In 1951, the terrace of coastguard cottages were vacated and made available for research staff from the Ness. In fact ROC coastguard services continued until the early 1960s. In 1948 a new Cold War unit was established, going into an underground bunker at the nearby Richmond Farm in 1961. The last C/O of this 'Atomic Weapons Detection, Recognition and Estimation of Yield' unit for Suffolk and Essex was Christopher Howard, whose job it was to conduct exercises to test operational efficiency. 'This complicated kit was' he remarks, 'a bit different from the "Mark 1 Eyeball" exercise with a Bristol Blenheim'.

The location of boffins from the Ness in the village led to them becoming partially absorbed into the local community. Ken Daykin was the leading light in the local cricket club, for example. This was the successor to the pre-war Country House club based on Sudbourne House. The team was now called The Avocets. The ground they used was at the hospital at Melton, St Audries. This concession was achieved by a useful deal. The ground was available if, somehow, petrol for running the mowers could be 'won' from the Ness. It could be!

Frank Tanner, living in one of the former coastguard cottages with his new wife, confirms how fortunate he felt to be part of a village community. The place was then still little changed from what it had been fifty years before. It had a full range of shops to meet local needs and was not yet the congenial retirement haven for those keen on sailing and golf; it was moreover too remote to be the tourist attraction it was to become.

Evident from the experience of so many who worked there was the unwritten pact between 'island' and village. Everyone largely tolerated the bangs and roars from bombs and planes. The village suffered in resigned silence the enormous volume of traffic that moved to and fro through the unsuitable streets. They respected the 'privacy' of those working across the river and apparently entered into the conspiracy of silence that accompanied the myth that these folk were merely 'men from the ministry'. People kept their own counsel as to what they were up to. This is well illustrated by an observation by Tanner:

Everyone in the village took a keen interest in the goings-on on the 'Island' and to illustrate the depth of knowledge, consider this: at lunchtime before going back to the Island, I would usually call at Mrs Brinkley's shop, mostly for pipe tobacco and she always had a chat. On this particular day we had dropped the first of a new series of trials involving the 10,000-lb LC [Blue Danube] bomb, just before lunch. I think it was from a modified Lancaster. Anyway, having weighed out my tobacco Mrs Brinkley said: 'I see you dropped that old atom bomb this morning.' Lifting my jaw back to its normal position, I think I managed to say 'Oh!' before going back. Back on the 'Island' I went to see our boss, Stan Price, and told him the story. 'Oh, didn't you know', he said. Collapse of uninformed party!

The war in Europe ended on 8 May 1945 and the following Sunday, National Thanksgiving Day, was marked by a march past through the Market Square by an RAF detachment from the Ness, led by its C/O, Flight Lieutenant A.R. May. Many lining the route that day would have been amazed to realise that secret military occupation was destined to last another fifty years.

The Ness Post-War

RAF ORFORD NESS?

When the war ended, there was just a chance that the RAF might find new uses for the airfield part of the site. Farnborough was of course still directing its ORS trials, which were continued almost without interruption. There was however the briefest of flirtations with the thought that RAF Orford Ness should assume overall authority for the station, displacing the Ministry of Supply. This would see it providing existing trials facilities, but also, as a separate and additional entity, would make it available to the Air Ministry (later, in 1971 to become the Ministry of Defence).

The only surviving example of an Orford Ness Operations Record Book (in the National Archives) opens on 1 October 1946, and ends, on a sad note, with a bleak announcement of the decision to close the unit down. This entry is dated 29 March 1947. This book was effectively a diary of all RAF activity on the station, naming all visitors and the purpose of their visit.

The entries are tantalisingly brief. It notes that there were still several aircraft on the site, a pair of Spitfires, two Harvards, a Tempest and a Thunderbolt. It records a rocket firing trial on the range on 2 October. However an inspection in November by Military Police to assess security suggests that other developments were in mind. Mentioned in this regard is the possibility of a new meteorology unit on the Ness and a new radar centre. The idea of a special Air Ministry Constabulary Unit is also mooted. On 23 October 1946, a meeting was held at the Ness to discuss the state of the vehicles used by the RAF, described as being 'deplorable'. On 12 December there was an official visit by Lieutenant-Colonel Chang of the Chinese Air Force. There is reference too to a medium frequency radio beacon.

At this point, the bleakest winter weather in living memory descended on a Britain already afflicted by the impact of post-war austerity. RAF Orford Ness froze. The station became increasingly cut off, and when the water supply was seriously threatened, it was decided to evacuate. The RAE trials team was not resident on the island at this point and was only affected to the extent that all trials were suspended. The Commanding Officer and six airmen remained for a few more days until no water was left. They then joined their RAF colleagues at RAF Felixstowe. By 29 March, the water supply was restored, but no RAF staff returned. Responsibility for running ORS was restored to the Ministry of Supply and its principal Scientific Officer, J. W. Frame, was placed in charge.

BOMB BALLISTICS AND FIRING TRIALS

There was an understandable reduction in any real sense of urgency in the work being done by the RAE's outstation. Interesting confirmation of a certain post-war ennui is provided by Clifford Rayner's oral archive account in the Suffolk County Record Office. Rayner was a teenage apprentice at RAF Halton[*] when in July 1945 he was despatched to what he understood to be RAF Orford Ness. None of his instructors had ever heard of the place.

Coming from a large and important training station, young Rayner found conditions at his new posting primitive and spartan, the weather unfriendly and the routine somewhat casual. Water for washing was cold, and firing the boilers necessitated wheeling up coal – if available – from the jetty. He was billeted in a partitioned wooden hut. Only slowly did some of the charms and merits of the place begin to manifest themselves. In the charge of a Corporal named 'Chick' Hensall, he was able to opt for a trade of his choice. This was as a sheet-metal worker and welder. A skill which proved quite useful, as it had for Haynes before him. He was able to make utensils like kettles and shovels for trading off with colleagues or neighbours. After three months of apparently trivial assignments, Rayner had become a skilled welder.

He recalls using the railway. It was a preferred way to transport the acetylene and oxygen cylinders up and down from the jetty. No mention is made of the locomotive and he clearly had to be prepared to 'pole' the trucks along a happily level track. Gordon Kinsey describes how it was during the Second World War:

Four-wheeled flat trucks were usually manhandled, but an ancient diesel [sic] locomotive occasionally made an appearance, driven by an equally ancient driver with a permanent 'fag' drooping from the corner of a heavily nico-tine-stained moustache. He also drove what must have been one of the first mechanically propelled rollers for road surfacing and filling in potholes.

---

[*] Halton, part of the Rothschild's Waddesdon estate, shares with the Ness very early RFC origins. The RFC aircraft first landed there in 1913. It became a major technical training station for the RAF.

Which of the two locos this was is not recalled, and, of course, they were petrol driven. The line was facing closure and was pulled up in 1955.

With the pressure of war absent, and, one imagines, a real degree of 'demob' fever among service personnel, a free and easy regime prevailed. The fact was that this unusual establishment was effectively 'officered' by civil servants. Direction of what they were to do came not from the RAF but the Ministries of Supply and of Aircraft Production. They found they were almost in a position to 'please themselves what they did'. Rayner explains that 'the orderly room, the stores and the cookhouse were the three lots of people that it was best to get on well with': he could get a thirty-six-hour leave pass merely by asking, and stores could be traded almost without question. He tells of a colleague, a public school educated REME technician working the SCR 584 radar, who rang the Army central stores at Sudbourne Hall and, in his posh accent, put in a request for some replacement underwear. Realising that the storeman assumed that it was an Officer speaking, the resourceful Corporal requested a complete new outfit of clothes and said he would send a man for it. He switched his accent to cockney as he himself went to collect his loot.

Clifford Rayner seems a trifle vague about what work was going on, but he was of course a very junior airman. As a metal operator, he was involved in elements of lethality and vulnerability testing, including shooting at fuel tanks. He recalls a Derwent jet engine being shot at with a German 24-millimetre gun to test the outcome. Constructing the means of securing this powerful engine to the ground seems to have made a great impression on the young apprentice. Hundreds of hacksaw blades were employed. To his untrained eye, the outcome of the trial was something of a disappointment.

Rayner spent exactly a year on the Ness and his account is valuable for the very fact that he speaks from the viewpoint of junior serviceman. One suspects he learned a great deal about the practicalities of making the best of things. He remarks on the notable role played by a good NAAFI. He left armed with an impressive purloined pile of bed linen! He even put in a request to be posted back to the Ness, but not long after his departure, the Ness ceased to have any formal RAF status. He was demobbed in 1948 and, like a remarkable number of people, he was to return.

Meanwhile, from 1945 Martlesham reverted to its former pre-war role as an experimental station. For two years it hosted the Blind Landing Experimental Unit, which expanded with further flights, the purposes of which were evident from their titles: the 'All-Weather Flight' and 'Rapid Landing Flight'. The RAF at Martlesham were at this time involved in pioneering research on instrument flying, with all that this implied for handling aircraft under adverse conditions. This had no immediate bearing on the Ness, but also set up at this time was the Bomb Ballistics Unit, which did.

In 1950, all Martlesham experimental work was coordinated under a new operational title, the Armament and Instrument Experimental Unit. For everything requiring access to a bomb range, ORS was used. The primary, though not sole, function of the Ness range was defined in a report stemming from RAE Farnborough, dated June 1948. This indicated that the Ness was the place where 'all bombs for which accuracy of aim is required are finally tested, for consistency of flight and for determining the ballistic constants required for bomb sighting ...'

For over ten years after the war, RAE operated two parallel areas of research on the Ness site. The Bomb Ballistics section, for which a staff team was to grow to a fair size, including mathematically expert ballisticians, radio communicators and radar technicians as well as a number of locally recruited assistants. In addition, there was a firing trials section. This involved a rather smaller group of primarily engineers and practical 'experimenters'.

Bert Smith had had outstanding experience in precisely these fields on the Ness during the war. As he has already described, he resumed this career in 1946. The circumstances were significant. Government policy at this time was to encourage suitably experienced demobilised servicemen to take up places at universities for specially abbreviated honours degree courses. Many hundreds did. Smith was planning to read Mechanical Engineering at Cambridge. His curiosity, which took him to make that return trip to the Ness, changed his life. He was immediately offered a job, to carry on in many respects from where he left off two years before, but now as a civilian Assistant Experimental Officer in His Majesty's Civil Service. He remained in this service until retirement.

From 1949, government defence policy changed. This was the year of the Berlin Blockade. The Cold War was proving sufficiently threatening to warrant expenditure on new hardware. Research was rapidly accelerated, and rather than just tidying up projects launched in haste without due attention to detail during the war, serious development and expansion was set in motion. New equipment was installed. It was observed that until then, anyone working on the bombing trials in 1918 would have recognised the equipment and techniques still being employed. That was rapidly changing. In addition, a decision was taken to set up new ranges in southern Australia, at British expense. The objective here was to provide facilities for testing more advanced rockets and bombs. The assumption was that this new location would provide more favourable weather conditions. In fact, heat haze and other atmospheric conditions, including difficulties in identifying stars in the southern hemisphere, presented unexpected problems.

Rather than secret testing being undertaken mainly by the military or under military control in the late '40s civilians were recruited for the task. By 1948, RAE Farnborough was advertising for suitable young people to train. A local boy, Frank Tanner, had completed his National Service and was debating whether to take up his university scholarship place. He accepted an invitation to go over to the Ness to join the Ballistics team. He was interviewed by the Officer in Charge, John Frame, a man he recalls as fulfilling every imagined characteristic of the wild boffin. His hair stood out sideways rather like Einstein's, and he wore sandals on bare feet. This was quite something, as his daily travel to work involved a bicycle ride from Thorpeness to Slaughden. He then would walk the 5 miles or so along the shingle to his office. His uniform appeared to be a white overall, a garb the point of which Tanner never did discover. The interview was cursory, and appeared to hinge around Tanner's ability at cricket (they had a wicket laid out on the northern airfield). This test he passed, and his future career was settled. After seven years working on the Ness, he decided he needed a complete change and attempted to find a new role within RAE. However, Farnborough thought otherwise and he became a seriously important and internationally respected authority on the ballistics of bombs, artillery shells and missiles.

When Tanner began work on the Ness, the ballistics operations were still relatively crude. He recalls that he was instructed to test the optimum shape for a new 25-pound incendiary. Models of fifteen different styles were supplied by RAE:

We made stability tests on them by dropping them from an Avro Anson. The technique required a Martlesham Warrant Officer Armourer to lean out of the aircraft door, supported by a webbing strap and drop them at a vertical angle of about 40 degrees to the airflow… The technique for these trials would be seen as amazing today.

Writing almost fifty years later, he observed that this was little different from the method of the very earliest ballistics and flight tests by Lindemann who leant over the side of his cockpit and dropped his bombs, timing their flight with a stopwatch.

Another beneficiary of the post-war policy for civilians to help with research was Brenda Carter. In 1950, Brenda Fitch, as she then was, was appointed to be one of the operators on the kine-theodolite stations. The remarkable fact is that she was only seventeen when the recruiting officer from the Ministry of Supply visited her grammar school in Framlingham. Her headmistress recommended her for consideration because she was clearly very bright but was already outgrowing school and impatient to move on. She had not even completed any 'A' levels when she joined the ORS team. Her technical expertise developed on the job and her higher professional qualifications came through training courses at Ipswich College. 'How lucky I was to work in a place like that', she later admitted, a place that 'just gets to me'. Later, promoted to work at Aldermaston while her husband took up an AWRE scholarship to university, she found life far less fun, not least because she often felt she was being 'under-employed'.

Brenda Carter helped to operate the kine-theodolites in support of the bomb ballistics researches. She and her colleagues then had to analyse the film, working out the trajectories and speeds of the bombs. Their job was effectively to be human computers, coordinating the results from the various stations, located by the jetty, by the lighthouse and on King's Marsh.

Over the years she was involved, it might be thought that there was monotony in the work, for what she had to do altered little, but the aircraft and their weapons were always developing and changing. The tasks required quite sophisticated understanding of the mathematical problems involved. For example, Brenda had to read the film and calculate the results from the ground speed cameras. These pointed upwards, and this meant there was no terrestrial object in the field of view with which to establish the focal length or orientation of the camera. This would necessitate astronomical focusing, which Brenda's boss, Frank Tanner, describes as being 'a difficult calibration process'. One suspects a degree of understatement here. This was all to become even more demanding when, during the '50s, the operational extent of the range had to be increased.

In its early days, the principle was that the weapons were dropped from above the Ballistics building, to fall into the sea or the shingle down the range. A complex array of lights and mirrors located beside the Ballistics building had coordinated the signalling and marking of the release time for the aircraft. When this was accidentally damaged, it was abandoned. This array was the so-called 'field of mirrors'. Its very name seems to have captured outsiders' imaginations, as if it were the key to all the secrets of the island. It appears that this was not how the Ballistics team referred to it. Even Sir Andrew Motion was taken in, attributing to it magical powers: to 'see beyond the Alps'. Its true function was much more modest. Its proper name was an array of Hills' mirrors. What is perhaps surprising here is that so much of this obsolete piece of equipment has survived as one of the only relics of the wartime bombing range. The small enclosure that housed it still stands a few yards to the south of the Ballistics building.

Distances involved in the operational length of the range had to grow as speed and performance of aircraft increased. The problem was that to release a bomb from above the Ballistics building was no longer practical. In simple terms, rather than operate with a fixed dropping point and ever lengthening splash points, it was much preferable to establish a fixed zone for splash and make the drop zone moveable, to a point further to the south. The result was the setting up of the baseline camera at the southern tip of the Ness, opposite Shingle Street, at what is confusingly called North Weir Point. A bomb release was now possible several miles down the range and the operation could be monitored by radar from Martlesham. However, this new small facility was to provide its own set of problems.

Calibration of the cameras now involved venturing onto a remote part of the range during the hours of darkness as and when cloud cover was such that stars were clearly visible. The stars were needed for providing a fixed and known point of reference for directing the cameras. Setting up the North Weir Point camera would necessitate a long river trip and was not without hazard, especially if the weather conditions deteriorated. Frank Tanner has provided vivid accounts of hazardous trips down the river, especially when the weather turned nasty. The ferrymen, two of whom were members of the Brinkley family, never objected to the antisocial hours involved since they were paid generous overtime and permitted to claim additional hours of operation for mooring duty. One problem remained: the vulnerability of the remote, substantial camera station to interference. Another Orford Ness subterfuge was employed: a warning notice was prominently displayed, alleging the danger of very high voltages. It worked to confirm local rumours of just what 'went on over there'. The threat was droll, given that it had no such power supply.

Accurate weather forecasting was indeed a crucial element in all this work. Conditions needed to be at least reasonable for setting up the instrumentation as much as for running the trials. These might last for quite some time while the bomber made a series of passes over the range. The meteorological station at Felixstowe played a vital role in guiding the team. It is a not entirely surprising fact that on average, the weather was favourable for full use of the range for only forty days a year.

Towards the end of the life of the range, some new staff were recruited, among whom was John Backhouse, a local lad from Sudbourne village. After some months as a labourer with the Ministry of Works department of the RAF, working on rebuilding the river defences following the flood in 1953, he transferred to employment by the Ministry of Supply as part of the Bomb Ballistics team, operating the kine-theodolites and cameras. This would include lonely and bleak stints at North Weir Point, managing the camera station. His favoured kine-theodolite post was by the lighthouse and it was from there that he would be instructed to monitor the passage of Sputnik in 1957. The optics on these German-made machines were, he has recalled, truly outstanding.

Frank Tanner was the principal Ballistics Officer. A trial would see two radio communications staff, a photographer and at least two of the ballistics officers, all crammed into the small space of the operations room, made the more confined by its low ceiling. Not surprisingly, visitors were not welcome.

Tanner worked out where he expected the bomb to land, making allowances for any small alterations to the aircraft's height and speed, and shifts in wind speed and direction. The central focal point of the whole trial was still a large *camera obscura*, a crude but remarkably effective tool for the purpose. An arm stretched from its centre, with the estimated splash point marked on it. As the aircraft approached, its shadow was plotted moving across the table, and a string stretched taut by weights followed its track towards the predicted target. As the bomb was released the pilot would fire a smoke signal. This smoke cloud (pyrotechnic was the technical term they would use) was also tracked by the *camera obscura* to indicate the wind speed and direction. A periscope projected from the metal turret located on the building, to monitor the predicted impact point. In this turret were no less than three super high-speed Vinten cameras, operating 35-millimetre film at over 100 frames per second. Not the least of the team's tasks was to ensure that the very short running time involved coincided with the falling of the bomb and the splash into the sea. The key to getting all this right was a central timing chronograph, which gave pulses to all the linked cameras and to a Teledeltos recorder. During the hectic rush to get all this equipment working and results recorded, someone had to remember to scramble onto the roof to measure ground surface wind speed.

Initially, aircraft attached to the Martlesham Bomb Ballistics Unit were used for these tests. The Avro Lancaster had to have adapted large bomb bays, capable of holding the vast 10,000-pound Blue Danube, one of Britain's first atomic bombs which was over 6 feet in diameter. From the early '50s, these weapons were being dropped purely for ballistics purposes. Soon, the converted Avro Lincoln, equipped with a pair of jet engines, was introduced. A Short Sperrin was an additional type, used solely for trials purposes, an interim jet-engined design intended as a stopgap until the V-bombers came into service in the mid-'50s.

The aircraft were controlled by the radar station at Martlesham and directed to fly to Saxmundham. From there, a fixed course on a bearing of 170 degrees would take the planes over Iken and the Ness. From its site by the jetty on the Ness, the SCR 584 radar would track the plane and monitor the drop of the weapon into the North Sea.

Tests on the various types of bomb case, suitably weighted as 'inert' dummies, continued for many months, and it is a sobering thought that several hundred of them lie out to sea off the Suffolk shore. Very occasionally, a particular weapon had to be retrieved. Tanner recalls how, shortly before he left the Ness in 1957, he was asked if his team would identify the precise location of a particular Blue Danube which had encountered serious problems with the outer casing. The team had photographic records of the whole sequence of the bomb being dropped. Tanner did some mathematical calculation and notified a waiting destroyer of the exact coordinates of where its diver might expect to find the weapon in question. It was a tribute to Tanner's skill and, as he would admit, good luck that the diver descended directly onto his target.

All the while, one-off trials were also undertaken for working on other airdrop operations. The Ness instruments were used for measuring the trajectory of lifeboats dropped into the sea. Likewise, a Short Sunderland Mk V flying boat was employed to drop anti-submarine detection sonobuoys.

The purpose of these trials was to create a stable and reliable casing design, especially for the three projected types of British nuclear bomb. In due course, a shift in requirement arose as it came to be recognised that Russian air defences were formidable and a low level approach to targets had to be considered. During the 1950s, with ever-higher speeds of aircraft, air turbulence problems were encountered for bombs as they left the bomb bay, which might vary depending on the altitude. The behaviour of the weapon in flight had to be analysed, and the effects of adjustable fins or rocket-assisted power were also studied. One particular discovery was the need to slow down a bomb dropped from high altitude to prevent it approaching supersonic speed. The precise configuration of the blunted nose cone required detailed research, conducted on the indoor range being operated by the firing trials team on the Ness.

Other special trials at this period might simultaneously involve both the ballistics and the fuel tank vulnerability expertise of Ness boffins. P.G. Seaward was sent up to ORS from Farnborough to find out what would happen to a fuel tank ruptured at very high altitude. Would there be significant difference to a rupture at low level? An initial problem was solved: how to explode a fuel tank suspended from a Canberra bomber at high speed. It was evident that, for aerodynamic reasons, the tank would have to be carried inside the bomb bay. A test tank was constructed in the shape of a bomb, and to detonate it at relevant altitude and speed, a 20-millimetre high explosive shell was attached to it, fired by remote control from the ground and designed to puncture the tank/bomb in as realistic manner as possible.

Naturally, the system had first to be tried out at ground level, on the beach, to check that the firing mechanisms would work. A brick enclosure was built on the foreshore, several test 'weapons' brought across, and a first firing duly initiated. It worked a treat, and the observers casually wandered over to inspect their handiwork, having dowsed the tank with foam, so as, in the words of the report, 'to save expensive fuel'. This immediately proved to be a mistake. The tank suddenly re-ignited and exploded, blasting the metal container high above the onlookers' heads. Nevertheless, it was judged that the idea worked, and a series of airdrop trials were undertaken, with, it appears, perfect success. Again, boffins flirted with calamity and seem to have enjoyed a charmed existence.

All these operations, some involving quite crude DIY and others sophisticated technology, made the post-war Ness bomb range both a model for inventive ingenuity and a 'state of the art' facility. Its know-how was transferred to other ranges. Most notable of these was the Weapons Research Establishment at Woomera in South Australia. George Hicks, who was a particularly well-respected Officer in charge at ORS, was sent to Australia to set up the Range 'A' at Woomera. Australian staff were brought over to the Ness for preliminary training. When RAE closed the Ness range down, the instrumentation and methodology was likewise transferred from the Ness to the new RAF test site at West Freugh, in south west Scotland.

Summing up the importance of the role played by the Ness range, Tanner observed from his position as an international expert in the field that: 'as a result of the work at ORS, the UK was years ahead of the US and the rest of Europe in the derivation of ballistic data for the bombsight.' Carrying on from a pre-war tradition, lethality and vulnerability tests and trials with fuel tanks conducted by the firing trials section continued throughout this period.

The arrival of jet engines provided a constant need to solve the problems that they created. In 1945, even though hostilities were over, enemy aircraft had been brought over for vulnerability assessment. One new type in particular was of interest. That October, a German Messerschmitt Me262 jet fighter, a type that had made a fearsome impact during its brief appearance earlier in the year, was taken over the river to the Ness.

In one particular matter, the Ness vulnerability testing facilities were especially useful. It had always been a practice to shoot at engines while they were running to identify just how robust they could be to such damage. Smith confirms that the place was littered with an amazing and fascinating assortment of aero-engines. With turbine engines, it became particularly important to discover the effect of shedding turbine blades. Ness boffins were experienced in this sort of research.

ROCKETS

The use of rockets had been investigated at the Ness from the earliest A&AEE days. They returned with a vengeance from 1945. This clearly confirms that 1945 was not being seen as the year that marked the end of a war to end all wars. An illustration of this was the renewed research on 3- and 5-inch ground-strike rockets. These had been highly effective in RAF ground strafing during the latter part of the war in Europe. The need now was to produce the data on ballistics and performance for the next generation of rockets, fitted to high speed jet aircraft. The RAE's Gloster Meteor fighter was brought over to complete these trials.

J.M. Tomlin worked at the post-war ORS on rocket tests. He explains the background to the need to keep research very much alive. 'After the war', he writes, 'it was decided that many of the weapons systems that had been developed in haste during the war, very often on a trial and error basis, should be subjected to a more detailed analysis which would form a sound basis for future development.'

A site was selected for a rocket range, from the north side of the airfield, across the remains of the old Chinese Wall, out over King's Marsh, down to the track that skirts the present Cobra Mist building. Some of the initial tests were for developing instrumentation necessary for tracking rockets flying at heights from 50 to 100 feet. Tomlin has described in some detail how he and his colleagues set up the ranks of single-shot high-speed cameras designed to record the flight of the missiles The problem facing them was the coordination of the total of fifteen cameras to capture the flight, when the exposure time was only 1,000th of a second. It was eventually decided to use suitably sensitive infrared cells, which could pick up the heat given off by the rocket motor. The pulse from these would be amplified in such a way as to trigger the cameras. Five such cells were used, being positioned so that the amplified pulses would trigger in turn each of the five banks in sequence.

Initially, Bert Smith rigged a launch platform at the northern end of the airfield site, near the plate store building, to provide for ground-fired trials. Setting this platform up was in fact one of the last tasks for which Smith was responsible before he was posted to continue his career at RAE Farnborough in 1953.

After ground trials were completed satisfactorily, the air trials commenced using three De Havilland Mosquitoes from the Bomb Ballistics Unit at Martlesham, and then, a Gloster Meteor Mk 9 at maximum permitted speed. This was no mean task for the pilots who were required to position the aircraft very accurately and at very low level.

All the information supplied by the cameras was fed back by landline to a control centre close by the roadway to the Bailey Bridge – a structure that no longer survives. Indeed, the sole remaining evidence of the trials carried out on this site are some of the low posts that carried the cameras, standing forlornly in the middle of grazing marsh and flooded lagoon.

This research, which ran for two or so years during the 1950s, also saw the first experiments on airborne heat seeking missiles, military hardware that was to become standard for the RAF. The closure of these trials coincided with an unfortunate accident. The Meteor aircraft managed to return to RAF Woodbridge, with its wheels still retracted! Frank Tanner recorded just how noisy and disruptive these flights could be, so that he could provide a first-hand report back to RAE Farnborough:

I stationed myself roughly level with the ground cameras but slightly higher, on the shingle and behind a low shingle bank. When the first rocket was fired it seemed to come straight at me and I could not avoid ducking behind the bank even though I had chosen an obviously safe spot. I managed to convince myself after that and watch all the others. The noise as the rockets went past was quite impressive too. What really took my imagination was that if I was worried knowing that it must miss, think of the effect on the morale of a soldier on the receiving end, particularly if a salvo of twelve rockets was being fired. [1]

In the event, this sort of weapon was already becoming obsolete and Tanner's final report to Farnborough was never published or distributed. Tanner does relate how a number of rocket motors had been delivered to the Ness for vulnerability testing. Some had been dumped on the edge of the bomb range and Tanner and a colleague, Eric Drake, picked one up to look at it more closely. Bringing it back to their office, they participated in a practical experiment. Bruce Gordon, the Director of the section, tried to set fire to it, without success. Taking it outside the HQ building, they wedged it against the railway line and again tried to set fire to it. By now a small crowd had gathered. Ignition eventually occurred spectacularly and the crowd disappeared as quickly as it had formed. After trying in vain to move the railway line, the rocket motor took to the air and executed a rapid loop before exiting stage right. Peering around the ends of all the buildings in the row from the machine shop to the canteen were a number of goggle-eyed heads – a superb introduction to the 3-inch rocket motor.

THE GREAT FLOOD

The vagaries of English weather, which play a constant part in the Ness story, shaped events in 1947. They did so again almost six years to the day later, when the Ness suffered a second and more calamitous natural disaster, one that struck the coastal regions of East Anglia and Holland. A storm surge down the North Sea, coupled with atrocious weather conditions with winds that reached hurricane force, swept in flood water 2 feet higher than ever recorded before, and more importantly, 7½ feet higher than was being forecast. The peak water level marked chest high on Orford Quay never ceases to amaze visitors.

There were many drowned up and down the coast that Saturday, the last night of January 1953. Happily, none of those that worked on the Ness were among the casualties, although the two Air Ministry police constables on duty only narrowly escaped. One of them, Harry Brown, had the following experience to relate:

I arrived at the quay with Bill Riches to go on duty at about 5.30 pm and there was quite a wind blowing, but the thing that seemed strange was the high level of the water in the river. The ferryman who took us over remarked that although it was only low water, it was almost the level of high tide and added: 'It's going to be a big 'un tonight, Harry.' On reaching the jetty we set out across the site to our guardroom and apart from the wind there was an eerie feeling about the place.

We carried out our rounds of the establishment, inspecting all the buildings, and by now a watery moon had risen and was giving a pale light through the scudding clouds. When we did the midnight round, I went to the bridge over Stony Ditch and the water was level with the bridge decking and in the pale light I could see the water foaming and breaking on top of the river walls.

Calling my mate I said that I thought we ought to make for somewhere safe and as we were going towards the buildings on the higher ground, the banks broke and the waters roared across the 'Island'. I ran to the toilets that were situated on the top of the bank, while Bill Riches could only get as far as a building lower down.

Bill found himself trapped inside and with water rising fast, realised that he must escape through a window and haul himself up onto the roof. Harry meanwhile was sitting on top of the exposed and far from salubrious lavatory block, exposed to the elements and decanting its effluence somewhat crudely into Stony Ditch. *

---

* The floods led to its replacement, as the sea-wall embankment along the whole length of Stony Ditch was raised to its present height.

For the next five hours they shouted to each other from their respective rooftops, to keep awake and to attract attention. It was bitterly cold and very windy, but the water had stopped rising. Just after 5 a.m. they heard a shout in response to their calls.

The rescuer was John Partridge, RSPB Warden on Havergate Island. He took with him an experienced local boatman in Vic Brinkley. They had realised that the two policemen would be on duty somewhere on the Ness. They managed to rescue both in turn and get them back to Orford. The quay itself was still under deep water, and so they landed direct onto a high point on the riverbank by a resident's house. Harry ends his account:

Bill was greeted by his wife with the remark, 'Why have you come home early from work?' For a week after the flood we did the rounds of the Island by punt. For his wonderful night's work John Partridge was awarded the British Empire Medal.

He neglects to mention that Brinkley was also rewarded, with a Queen's Commendation for Bravery.

Bert Smith for example quickly realised that 'all was not well in the coastal areas'. That Sunday morning, he joined up with Ken Daykin at Martlesham and organised a Lancaster bomber to fly them over the Ness.

They could see where the water had come straight through the site, breaking the wall near the jetty. He describes how the place was awash with only the tops of the sea (he really means, river) walls and roofs of the buildings showing. Their first task was to contact all the RAE trials staff and warn them not to attempt to return to work on the Monday morning. Brenda Carter recalls that for three months, she worked with the Blind Landing Unit team at Martlesham. On her return to the Ness, it was to find that the hut she had used for her work was no more. She and her colleagues were transferred to the former Officers' Mess, the building used eighteen years before by Watson Watt's radar team.

Frank Tanner and his family were living in one of the former coastguard cottages. Tanner has described the night of the flood. The previous evening they had visited Ipswich, and their return bus journey had been marked by the atrocious weather:

We fought our way to the house, and once in, had no intention of emerging again. When we went to bed the wind was still fierce and rain lashing down. We were wakened by shouting and banging on the door at about 3 a.m. and, on pulling back the curtains, there was an amazing change. Instead of our garden, a brick wall, the YMCA hut and fields to the river wall and beyond that, the shingle bank of the 'Island', there was unbroken North Sea and buildings surrounded by water. The whole scene was calm and moonlit and could have served as a setting for the 'Moonlight' Interlude from Britten's *Peter Grimes*. From then on our story was like the others. That first swell just failed to enter the house and after people from the village helped us move furniture we just had to watch the next tide creeping across the fields, into the garden, and rising against the house, lapping both front and back steps before withdrawing. If it had exceeded the height of the steps there would have been a catastrophe because the floor level was below the steps. Other people in the village nearer the quay were not so fortunate.

A couple of days later one of the boatmen rowed Tanner across to his office on the Ness. One wall of the building was missing and he discovered that most of the contents had been washed away, including a rather massive film reader, which had needed a heavy-duty mobile Coles Crane to install it originally, and which was never found!

By 25 February, RAE had produced a long report on the post-flood situation, recording the facts and analysing the consequences. The long and short of all this was that, while ORS was fit to continue, any future for an RAF Orford Ness station was out of the question.

Members of the RAE staff returned to the Ness as soon as the Tuesday after the flood to assess damage and rescue records. Sensitive equipment like cameras were found largely to have escaped the worst impact of the seawater, being installed on posts above ground level. This relative escape from destruction was because the chief impact of the flood was on the airfield side of the Ness. It was the river walls, including those along Stony Ditch, which had failed. Much of the shingle beach where the cameras were located was sufficiently high to be above flood level. The radars by the jetty and on King's Marsh were not so lucky and three of them were replaced by loans from other RAF stations. The kine-theodolites on the airfield were also affected and other recording gear was lost. The guns in the vulnerability and lethality range areas were salvaged, soaked but unharmed. All the ammunition however had to be replaced. Happily, all the targets being set up for forthcoming trials were quite useable.

More worrying was the need to replace most of the electrical cabling and laboratory equipment. In the offices, where destruction had not been cata-strophic, many reports could be retrieved from their locked and fairly watertight containers, but large quantities of manuscript material and photographs were lost forever. Not least among these were files containing reports written during the First World War, particularly those bearing the signature of Lindemann. The RAE report concluded: 'Although losses have been heavy and it will take some time before the Ness is fully restored, sufficient has been salvaged and obtained on loan for trial work to be resumed within a few weeks.'

Meanwhile, repairs to the washed away river walls had urgently to be under-taken. For this, the RAF was alerted and men were hastily brought over from Martlesham to help.

Two 'flights' of men from the Airfields Construction Unit, based at Church Lawford, near Rugby, were despatched to Felixstowe to repair damage there and to provide a team for Orford Ness. This particular assignment was to prove physically very demanding, involving a full two-month long repair.

It was to be tough work on the Ness. The weather, Bill Roberts (Engineer in charge of the East Suffolk and Norfolk River Authority (ES&NRA)) recalls, was awful. They had to use military flame-throwers to destroy the corpses of cattle drowned on Gedgrave Marshes and the sheep from the Ness. The smell created a lingering atmosphere. They had bulldozers, driven down the spit from Aldeburgh, and they could fill their sandbags with dry concrete mix on the quay, and then transport them over to the major breaches just across the river.

One Corporal was hit by a flying cable and knocked into the river. He and the airman who plunged in to rescue him were escorted off the Ness to the home of a retired Air Commodore in Orford who insisted that they both were given hot baths (by the family nanny) and then were served large sherrys before being allowed to return to work. Roberts comments that his men worked so effectively that the whole unit was provided with complete new sets of uniform to replace everything ruined by the saltwater and spray.

The time came for Roberts' men to pack up and depart. Assembled in the Town Hall, they were asked if any of them had seen the priceless collection of the town's ceremonial silver. At the back of the stage area was an unlocked cupboard. No nosey or speculative airman had thought to open it. There lay a veritable treasure, quite untouched.

River rather than sea walls were clearly shown to be the vulnerable element in the defence of the Ness. Work on shoring them up was not halted after the departure of the RAF team. The Ministry of Works recruited a labour force to continue reinforcement work. In autumn 1953, John Backhouse, made his first appearance on the Ness, working on the protection of the flood defences.

Tanner was soon back at work on the Ness, in a different office, and gradually, relative normality was restored. He stayed there for a further two years. Farnborough appeared confident in a report in mid-April 1953 that the site would remain fit for purpose. It required that anti-flood precautions were taken in hand, with walls up to 6 feet high. Tidal surges have occurred regularly over succeeding years, but never anything remotely matching what happened on the night of 31 January 1953.

There is a footnote to the story of the flood damage. Stuck fast into the mud on the eastern bank of Stony Ditch midway between the Bailey Bridge and the First World War ammunition store buildings is the wing of an aeroplane. Quite how or when it got there is a mystery. It is generally supposed that the flood washed it over from the area on the airfield site immediately opposite, where self-sealing fuel tank trials were taking place. One such tank remains in view, nestling within the girders that comprise the central part of a wing; but of what aircraft? Various suggestions have been made, including a Short Stirling, or a Short Stranraer flying boat. One visitor to the Ness has been firmly of the opinion that it must be a Handley Page HP42, a pre-war four-engined transport. However, the judgement of Harry Holmes and Gordon Bruce, leading authorities on the Avro Lancaster, is that this is indeed a flexible or bag tank in a specially constructed replica of the central section of a port wing of either a Lancaster, or its almost identical civilian version, a Lancastrian.*

Enthusiasts would like to see this, the only surviving piece of ORS trials material, extracted and placed on display. In 1995, The National Trust did attempt to lift it from its muddy bed, but short of power hose blasting, there is no means of pulling it clear without severe damage. So, here it must remain, admired from afar and a continuing source of speculation.

SPARK-PHOTOGRAPHY RESEARCH

The unreliability of English weather has been a recurring factor in the Ness story. It was just one of the reasons for setting a major project indoors. This project was to monitor the flight patterns and corresponding airflow of bullets, shrapnel fragments and then, in model form, complete bombs and ballistic missile re-entry vehicles.

Preliminary research in design and basic ballistic characteristics was needed. The plan was to develop on a far more sophisticated scale the technology first devised for wartime lethality and vulnerability trials. On his return to the Ness in 1946, Bert Smith resumed his partnership with his wartime colleague, Bruce Gordon. By now the object of their researches was the effect of all sorts of projectile hits on higher performance aircraft, often operating at high altitude (and hence, at very low temperatures), including shrapnel damage from exploding guided missiles using proximity fuses. A direct hit was no longer necessary: a near-miss burst could be just as lethal.

Their initial trials took place in a specially constructed firing range in miniature in the plate store in 1946. A stop-butt was built at its southern end. Their problem was how to replicate the effects of firing at operational distances when shooting down a miniature range. This they did by reducing the propellant charges, to achieve an equivalent result. The other pioneering idea then was to record the flight of the missile and the surrounding air turbulence by tracking it with a series of high-speed cameras, pictures captured by means of what was defined as 'spark-photography'.

---

* A serious area of vulnerability to attacks by German night fighters during the latter part of the war was the Avro Lancaster bomber's completely unprotected underside. Many return-ing Bomber Command aircraft were found to be riddled with bullets being fired upwards at the exposed belly of the plane. Enemy fighters' guns were being angled upwards, in just the manner that RFC fighters had trialled for dealing with Zeppelins almost thirty years before. The possibility was that this wing had been rigged onto its edge so that guns could be fired across Stony Ditch directly into the exposed flat surface of wing, to replicate the angle of fire being encountered in action over Germany. Perhaps, when the remains of aircraft parts were cleared off the site after the war, this wing, lying forlornly on its own on the eastern side of the Stony Ditch, was forgotten.

The idea here had been pioneered in US ballistic laboratories, but the way this was developed and, within its inevitable limitations, perfected by the ORS team was nonetheless very remarkable. It came to be used for testing the flight characteristics of bombs and rockets for Aldermaston. The principle here was to generate a powerful spark or flash created by passing a current over the gap across a high voltage capacitor. A number of problems had to be solved to make the system work and ensure that the missile itself triggered the flash and the linked camera. A rather mean trick in the early days was to invite unsuspecting visitors, ideally imposing dignitaries from the Science Research Committee, to pass their hands across the gap and thereby create the spark, to their distinct alarm.

Smith had a lathe brought over from the workshops in the large hangars so he could manufacture the models of the missiles or shrapnel fragments under test. He also created the launching sabot, a shoe-shaped container from which the missile was launched. The initial experiments, involving just fragments of metal, were conducted with a simple twelve-bore shotgun. A single spark-photography station – by all accounts, something of a Heath Robinson contraption – was set up.

The successful outcome of the first experiments led to the firing trials team setting up a fresh multi-station range in the former WAAF's quarter, Hut 9, to the south of the southern great hangar. This was the direct prototype of the major facility, begun in 1955: the full-scale Indoor Model Bomb and Missile Range. Members of the Ballistics team were now moved off the shingle to a new site on the edge of the southern airfield, opposite the recently established AWRE workshops building.

The very sophisticated range was the culmination of all the work done over the previous ten years. The facility comprised a Nissen hut some 50 metres long, with a substantial control room and a firing chamber at the northern end. Every 5 feet along the tunnel-like hut, there was a spark-photography station. A 17-pounder smoothbore gun was located outside the hut, to fire through the firing chamber. A miniature model of the weapon was placed on a sabot-shaped tray. When fired, the sabot would exit at high speed, to strike a butt in the chamber and fall into a settling chamber. The missile would then shoot off down the range at high speed in free flight to another stop butt at the far end. As it flew, each camera would photograph its shadow and the surrounding airflow. The model was made roughly 3.4 inches in diameter and 7 inches in length, weighted to ensure a stable centre of gravity. The equipment for recording and analysing the missiles in flight was amazingly complex. Furthermore, in replicating a flight that in reality would have probably been vertical, they had to allow for the model flying in the horizontal, with a 'sagging' trajectory. Designing a sabot that released the model projectile smoothly was not without problems.

A variety of bombs and missiles were involved, including Sea Slug for the Navy. The chief use to which the range was put was on behalf of AWRE's two current weapon systems, the air-drop Yellow Sun nuclear bomb with its blunt nose and the projected Blue Streak medium-range Inter-Continental Ballistic Missile. This latter was to be a possible candidate for providing the delivery system for the British nuclear deterrent. Field trials in Cumbria and at Woomera were later terminated when the whole Blue Streak programme was cancelled in 1960.[2] Likewise, the Yellow Sun bomb was obsolete almost as soon as it was operational and from the mid-'60s was replaced by the WE177. The model bomb range was employed for just two years. Enquiries were made to see if anyone might be interested in making use of it. As Director of the facility, Laurie Porter wrote in his final report: 'So far only bomb and missile re-entry shapes have been fired through the Range, but there is no reason why information should not be obtained on any shape which could be launched.'

No one was interested in using the range. Equipment was stripped out and the buildings handed over to AWRE for recreational use as a shooting range. Derelict remains still stand, enough just to give quite a good impression of what went on. A rather battered square sheet of metal was left behind to hang precariously on the end wall. The pockmarks made by .22 slugs provide evidence as to its use up until AWRE's departure.

The closure of all the ranges marked the end of RAE involvement with the Ness. Use by the RAF for any experimental work was also over. As events unfolded during the next twenty years, only a periodic, small-scale and transient RAF presence was to recur.

9

Atom Bombs Over Suffolk

AWRE TURNS SUFFOLK NUCLEAR

New Year's Day in 1946 was a Tuesday. Not in those days a public holiday, the nation returned to work. At its Cabinet Meeting that morning, Attlee's government had before it a formal report from the Chiefs of Staff indicating their future requirements for the provision of atomic weapons.

Britain had contributed significantly to the Manhattan Project, which produced the two atomic bombs dropped on Japan in 1945. Once the war ended, the spirit of cooperation seems to have cooled and it was evident that America might well deny Britain any further access to ongoing research. This was in fact to happen, with the passage of the so-called McMahon Act in 1946, as a mood of isolationism and later McCarthy paranoia swept the States.

This was the background to the policy adopted in the immediate post-war years. So far as weapons development was concerned, Britain decided to 'go it alone'. Atomic weapons research was a complex and controversial matter, not least because of the financial implications of what this involved. At the time, the nation was effectively all but bankrupt, yet faced a host of major commitments at home and abroad.

Successive governments were determined to see Britain retain its place as a major world power. It concluded that this would be assured by holding, or perhaps just appearing to hold, a significant nuclear arsenal. If the actual means of achieving this was a matter for debate, the ultimate purpose and indeed, the strategy for achieving it were clear. In essence, it was to focus on quality rather than quantity, and by various means to suggest that Britain's military might was greater and more advanced than was in fact the case. Britain was a member of the 'Nuclear Club' but, as an article published in the magazine *Air International* in 1994 indicated, it was 'More Bark Than Bite'. There was a further long-term objective too: to win back United States favour. This could and would be achieved because of the quality and nature of the work done by British scientists. The trials and tests on Orford Ness were to be key to the success of this policy.

In early 1947, Dr William Penny was invited to set up a new branch of nuclear research, under the auspices of the Ministry of Supply. Having been a leading member of the Manhattan Project and a witness to the Nagasaki A-bomb detonation, Penny played a crucial part in setting in motion this new work. By now, precise service requirements for aircraft to deliver a new and heavy design of atomic bomb had been defined. In January 1947, the Cabinet committed the country to a nuclear weapons building programme with the design and supply of aircraft to deliver them – what came to be known as the V-bombers. The Atomic Energy Research Establishment, recently set up at the former RAF airfield at Harwell south of Oxford, was directed to supply a sufficiently large additional quantity of fissile materials for bomb making.

The scale of operations inevitably grew rapidly, and by 1950, another former RAF station at Aldermaston, just a few miles to the south of Harwell, was taken over as the new Atomic Weapons Research Establishment, known for many years as AWRE.

While it still remained the centre for pure research, the need arose for a series of out-stations for manufacture, storage and trials. Sites in Cardiff, Burghfield and Foulness, already in government hands, were quickly brought under Aldermaston's wing. This last was a remote bombing range, but it lacked certain qualities apparent in the by now under-used Orford Ness site. From the outset, the Ness was seen also to have the advantage of its 'privacy'.

This was of course in the era when the true significance of the Iron Curtain threat was widely accepted. The nation was relatively tolerant of military secrecy.

The basic principles of atomic weapons construction would pose no serious problems for British scientists. Perhaps the most significant thing they could do was to make the system neater and more efficient, especially given the limited resources at their disposal. Meanwhile their American rivals were rapidly moving ahead, with, by 1952, the testing of a plutonium thermo-nuclear device at Eniwetok Island in the Pacific. A year later, Russia joined the 'Nuclear Club'. Britain had to show it could create a bomb to match the Americans in reliability and power.

These were not the only factors that had to be taken into account however; another factor could be added, namely, safety. A bomb had to be guaranteed not to be liable to any sort of accidental or premature detonation. In this particular area, the Aldermaston teams proved to have a clear lead; and the Ness was the place where this leadership was to be demonstrated.

In October 1952, the UK's first nuclear device was tested in Operation Hurricane in the Monte Bello Islands, off the north-western coast of Australia. Much of the work that made this possible was undertaken at Fort Halstead, the explosives research station in Kent. Foulness was also used at this stage for a variety of purposes, including testing air-blast, vibration, underwater shock and climatic effects.

However, Foulness was not fully suitable for the sorts of test Aldermaston required. Its geology was such that any substantial building work would require major underpinning. Constructing the necessary deep piles would cause serious delays and involve unpredictable cost. As a site, the Ness had an additional major asset, an operational and highly sophisticated Bomb Ballistics range. A decision to move trials there was taken in 1953. From 1954 for over fifteen years, Orford Ness was to be a major player in the story of creating Britain's nuclear deterrent. Hence, it helped in the successful outcome of the third of the global conflicts of the twentieth century: the Cold War.

Until 1955, when the property was officially taken over by AWRE, the Ness remained under the control of the Ministry of Defence. It was still being called the Orford Ness Research Station, administered by the Ministry of Supply and hence in the hands of RAE Farnborough. Such confusions seem forever to have been a feature of the place. It was to take some time for the legal procedures to be completed. Eventually, AWRE took over some 1,200 acres of King's Marsh and 'beach' by the sea. The Ministry of Defence kept back Lantern Marsh up to Aldeburgh. The Nature Conservancy remained responsible for the area of shingle to North Weir Point, opposite Shingle Street. Technically, the Ness was about to cease to be a military site, but technicalities never seemed to prevail over what might be regarded as expediency. RAF personnel would be drafted there as needed.

Throughout the process of these changes and the arrival of AWRE staff, RAE civilian personnel continued to run the Bomb Ballistics range. For the next four or so years, there were two distinct groups of boffins on the Ness, working both separately and together. AWRE and RAE were both under the umbrella of the Ministry of Supply. In effect, the one was providing a service for the other. The Aldermaston bombs needed ballistics tests, while the aircraft involved in all this experimental work were flown, of course, by RAF pilots, directed by Farnborough. All this explains the somewhat tortuous chain of communication between the AWRE staff on the ground and the aircraft overhead.

Those first men from Aldermaston must have faced a daunting task when they arrived on the Ness. A major building programme would be needed. Only a few of the primitive, largely wooden, huts had survived the flood of 1953, and these were occupied by RAE staff. The 'Chinese Wall' flood barrier would need replacing too. When eventually a new one was built, it was significantly higher and stronger than its predecessor, but it retained the name. A substantial brick building, with workshops and offices, was shortly constructed in the area previously used for airmen's accommodation, by the southern airfield.

The first tests on the Ness involved only the bombing range. This was while the various research buildings were being constructed. Up until then such work had taken place on the RAF range at Aberporth in west Wales or at Jurby on the Isle of Man.

Indeed, following the 1953 flood, there had understandably been real doubts about the Ness range. Part of the problem in Ministry of Defence minds was its relative vulnerability to Soviet intelligence operations. A working party was set up to review the case for reconsidering its future. It seems to have worked at snail's pace, with no sense of urgency, and only reported in 1957, well after the nuclear bomb trials had begun. It recommended a postponement of any move, for the time being. The cost of transferring facilities to an alternative range, at West Freugh in Scotland, was thought excessive and the Martlesham runways were regarded as better suited to the V-bombers.

The research to be done by AWRE at this recently acquired property had two distinct purposes. The first was to test the ballistics of the bombs when dropped from the operational height of the day – up to around 40,000 feet. This work was combined with the testing of the trigger mechanisms by sensitive radio telemetry to check that the very elaborate firing relays would work correctly under actual flying conditions. Put simply, a credible nuclear deterrent could only be effective on the supposition that the bomb would fly reliably and detonate if and as required. Only full-scale dropping exercises could supply the evidence.

The ballistics tests conducted on the early nuclear bomb cases were directed towards developing a weapon that would fall accurately and at not too great a speed. The most obvious outcome here was the alterations to the nose cone of the bomb case, making it sufficiently 'blunt' to slow it down. Yellow Sun was the resulting weapon, in service during the 1960s.

Initially, and before more elaborate facilities were available, a temporary station in a small hut in the middle of the southern airfield was set up for the telemetric monitoring of the trigger mechanism inside the falling bombs. No records of this unit survive, beyond the recollection of the staff who operated it, and the remains of a short tower and a nearby brick building. It also became the headquarters of the scientific and technical operations for all AWRE research work. This was located beside the existing Black Beacon and Power House, which dated back to the pre-war era. The Beacon (as it was then called) would house the radio monitoring and recording equipment. Alongside it a slender 100 feet high lattice mast was erected. This was therefore taller than the lighthouse. The base remains, just feet from the stairway up to the porch entrance. The mast took the various transmitting and receiving aerials. To the east, a substantial single-storey building was constructed, containing offices and stores, workshops and laboratories, a photographic processing lab and a set of four 'trials rooms'. A new boiler house was added. This was the Technical Headquarters for AWRE – known as 'Tech HQ'.

The whole U-shaped complex, which operated for nearly fifteen years, was demolished in 1994. Its footprint is still evident for visitors to see – and perhaps wonder at. Behind it remains just one structure from this period, a rather forlorn relic, with no apparent use other than to serve as a shelter for visitors. This is what was variously known as 'a garage' or as 'the model room'. Here, models of various pieces of equipment could be tested in miniature, prior to full-scale construction. A photograph survives of this building in use, with its 'garage' doors then in place.

A piece of equipment is being tried out, an adaptor designed to give mobility characteristics to a conventional mechanical vibrator.

A scientist involved in this work was Don Revett. A Suffolk man, from Ipswich, Revett worked initially at the Marine Aircraft Experimental Establishment at Felixstowe, and at Martlesham with the Blind Landing Experimental Unit, under the leadership of Keith Wood. On its transfer to Bedford, Revett eagerly sought to stay in Suffolk and in 1958 happily accepted Wood's invitation to join his team on the Ness, following his transfer to the AWRE.

Revett worked on the environmental testing, as it was called. To start with, this involved ensuring that the various electronic components used for the telemetry transmitter would work. These relayed the performance of the trigger firing circuits back to base via the Black Beacon as the bomb was dropping. He has provided a vivid picture of what went on, in what he referred to as a 'more exciting event', a weapon drop over the range:

> The electronics boys would be busy for days beforehand preparing and testing the receiving and recording equipment housed in rows in one of the labs...The bomb (a 'dud' of course) would be dropped from an aircraft to descend over the range and fall into the sea off Orford Ness. On its way down, information about the internal electronic firing systems that triggered the ultimate atomic explosion would be telemetered back to the trials buildings for recording and subsequent analysis. (An atomic weapon needs very precise triggering pulses of microsecond accuracy to initiate the explosion). The bomb itself would be tracked during its fall by operators using steerable helical aerials mounted on a gantry above the building. This ensured the best possible signal level for the transmitted information.

Those free to do so would rush out to watch the drop, from a V-bomber flying at about 40,000 feet. They would see the aircraft, gleaming white in a blue sky with its bomb bay open and an orange-painted weapon clearly visible. It was released well before it was overhead and seemingly far too early, and made a rumbling sound as its blunt nose (this would be a Yellow Sun) buffeted the air until with an enormous splash it hit the sea about 400 yards offshore, where it would disintegrate. There would then follow days of analysis of high-speed camera film taken of oscilloscope traces to ascertain the performance of the weapon's electronics.

The boffins used various euphemistic terms. The bomb was called 'a store'. When it was 'dud' it involved just the casing and all the internal workings but without any nuclear material. The whole thing was correctly weighted with material called 'placebo'. This substitute took the space and weight of the fissile material, which we have every reason to feel assured was never used in these tests. It was after all the high explosive initiating charge and all the electronics that detonated it that were the required objects of the tests. Keith Wood, the renowned Director of the station, described the telemetry involved in this work as 'probably some of the most advanced in the world.'

Another aspect of these early tests was the effect on the bomb of its impact. Instrumentation would be fitted to measure the timing and extent of 'warhead damage'. Pieces of bomb were washed up from time to time on beaches as far away as Thorpeness and Aldeburgh. Occasionally steps had to be taken to retrieve any evidence of a mishap, as Tanner has already described. Curiously, at this juncture no particular fuss over security or danger seems to have arisen.

The first of these British atom bombs was dropped over Suffolk on 11 June 1955 from a Vickers Valiant flown out of RAF Wittering. The weapon was an inert Blue Danube which, if armed, would have been in the 20 kiloton range, much the same power and strength as the Hiroshima bomb. Over the next six months, nine more drops were made. In this period, the total arsenal of 'live' Blue Danube bombs held by the RAF probably exceeded no more than twenty in all. Of course, many dozens of 'dud' bomb cases were available for trial purposes.

For the members of the small teams operating the recording stations, the chance to watch the bombs as they fell was seldom possible. One such member was Jim Drane. Located in the Beacon, his job was to operate the high-speed cameras. These recorded the readings of the oscilloscopes, which measured the various relays operating within the falling bomb. One of the items to be tested was the altitude firing fuses. Of the two types tried, one was barometric, the air pressure indicating the height above the ground selected for detonation. The other worked by radar, where a signal was bounced off the ground, the time taken for it to return back to the bomb again providing the means of measuring height.

Other research positions were involved in testing the ballistics of the bomb. All the stations were linked together by phone. The one element in the whole procedure over which the scientists could not have direct control was the actual aircraft. This would be directed entirely by its two traffic controllers, one at Martlesham code-named Orford 1 and the other in the Ballistics building, Orford 2.

Drane worked in a darkened space, the screens providing the only light, the camera reeling away, the noise of the approaching aircraft the sole means of knowing what was happening. He was never able to observe the dramatic splash. So dramatic was it, that on one occasion the Aldeburgh lifeboat was launched, supposing that it had been a light aeroplane that had crashed. Once the passage of the trial was complete, Drane had to unload his camera and race to get the film processed and a new reel loaded ready for another flight, perhaps within the hour.

The pressure on the team was uneven. At times, trials seemed to come thick and fast, relating to some imminent overseas tests or more probably to suitable weather conditions. At others, things could be pretty relaxed. On one such occasion, when he thought he had leave of absence, Drane was enjoying himself at the Aldeburgh

Carnival, when to his horror, he spotted a trial aircraft approaching the range. There were times he recalls when there was not enough work to keep them fully occupied. They contrived to look as though they were!

Tests were being increasingly held at ever-lower levels. High altitude bombing was regarded as too exposed to enemy detection. It was of course radar that was the problem. Soviet rocketry was seen as increasingly lethal, as the Gary Powers' U2 incident demonstrated in May 1960, when his high-flying U2 'spy-plane' was unexpectedly and embarassingly brought down over a Russia by a missile. As a boffin safely sheltered by RAE employment, Frank Tanner has expressed the deep admiration he held for those V-bomber crews. Had 'the balloon gone up' and they had been directed to make a retaliatory attack, they and everyone else knew that they had very little chance of being able to return alive.

The solution was a low-level approach and bomb release. From 1958, a major shift in tactics was introduced. Low-level drops were extensively tested on the Ness range. This was referred to as LABS (Low Altitude Bombing System). Because the Navy had the fastest attack fighter-bomber then in service, the Scimitar, it was principally Fleet Air Arm aircraft involved. The RAF was disenchanted by this state of affairs and their remarkable workhorse, the Canberra bomber, was also pressed into a service for which it was less suited. Revett describes these bombing trials:

> More spectacular were the low-level bomb drops made by Scimitar and Canberra aircraft. These planes would approach very fast and low over the range in a shallow dive to 500 feet or so and then climb rapidly away, releasing the bomb as they pulled up. The bomb would lob away in a trajectory towards its target. Meanwhile the plane would go into a loop, roll off the top and scoot off on a reciprocal course to be miles away by the time the bomb exploded.

This was indeed spectacular stuff. The Scimitar would exert forces of 4g (four times the force of gravity) on the pilot as it turned on its loop and tore away. Development of LABS, a US concept, was supposed to be highly secret, as was the performance of the plane that made it possible. Copies of the magazine *Flight International*, available to Drane and his teammates in their canteen, described in detail just what was going on, somewhat to their incredulous amusement. They had been told that the Scimitar aircraft flying these missions was top secret. Yet full details about them, including diagrammatic drawings, appeared in the children's comic *The Eagle*. The official approach to security must have seemed somewhat ambivalent. Never in doubt was the remarkable skill and dedication of the pilots. Several people have described just how low these bombing runs were, claiming that they could see the upper surface of the aircraft. Those who worked for the manufacturers have confirmed that the airframes of the Canberra in particular were subjected to mammoth stresses for which they were not designed. It is amazing that no serious flying accident ever occurred. Two test pilots of the highest calibre were employed, Flight-Lieutenant Tony Picking from the RAF and Lieutenant-Commander Paul Millett from the Fleet Air Arm, Tanner has described how the Scimitar would make its way at a reasonably high level from Farnborough to Orford, and then, picking out its flight path, would dive to achieve speed, low altitude and accurate line of approach.

The other and more extensive trials related to safety. It was essential, for obvious political reasons if for no other, that the bomb should be seen to be totally secure from any possible unintentional detonation. As Gordon Simkin, one of the senior contract managers on the Ness, later observed, 'the Yanks had got nothing like it'.

This project necessitated an enormous and highly costly building programme however. In the event, this was undertaken in two distinct phases. The first was associated with testing the British bomb mechanism, fitted to weapons given an assortment of somewhat colourful names such as Blue Danube, Yellow Sun and Red Beard. The second phase related to the WE177 bomb, a British casing which, from the 1960s onwards operated with an American system. The purpose of this work was always the same: what came to be defined as 'environmental testing', and what in contemporary common parlance was referred to as 'shake, rattle and roll'.

For each of these two phases three test 'labs' or cells were built, designed to provide an artificial replication of every conceivable operational circumstance. Vibration in transfer to the bomber or in flight, extremes of temperature and humidity and of speed or of deceleration, were all skilfully imitated.

A curious fact emerges from investigating the sequence of events that led to the building of in all, six labs. Just at the time when AWRE had finally acquired the lease for the property, which was finalised on 1 October 1959, and perhaps rather surprisingly, Aldermaston seemed to indicate that it might close down the whole facility. The chief reason seems to have been that it was looking to transfer to a location for these tests closer to its Berkshire base.

A circular was put about that AWRE was seeking a suitable disused military property. There was an immediate and eager response, since the government had a veritable stockpile of such places now surplus to its requirements. What was needed was a site about 1 square mile in extent, secure from any possible local opposition and situated within about 60 miles of Aldermaston. Suggestions in Yorkshire and Cheshire, Staffordshire, Shropshire, Northants and north Norfolk all showed willingness to be of assistance, without demonstrating much geographical awareness! AWRE consulted the Forestry Commission, the Admiralty and the Ministry of Works. Existing ranges at Foulness, Shoeburyness and Bulford were all considered and rejected. A very possible site, in civilian ownership, at Wing, in leafy Bucks, was seriously favoured, but here, a need for planning approval and local opposition problems which would have delayed matters by months – if not years – ruled out the idea

Documents in the National Archives show that AWRE was simultaneously concerned at the possible problems arising from their acquisition of the Ness. Mainly due to the implications of the dangerous ordnance still remaining on their property: what was referred to as 'clear range liability'. In January 1960 yet another worry had to be resolved. It concerned the notorious Crichel Down case. This had involved the unlawful disposing of military land without giving the owner, from whom it had been taken by compulsory purchase, any opportunity to buy it back. As recently as 1957, there had been the latest of a series of rulings over the correct interpretation of the law. In early 1960 the government was able to confirm that there could be no possible case for liability so far as the Ness was concerned. The whole property had been freely sold to the state in 1914. No previous owner could make any legitimate claim. In the light of this ruling and the fact that no alternative site was found, AWRE decided to stay on the Ness and promptly authorised a second phase of construction work.

Gordon Simkin had come to Orford Ness in the late summer of 1955. He was the site agent for the main contractors, Howard Farrow Ltd, of Golders Green, London. His job was to supervise the whole of the first phase building programme. Over the next three years, a remarkable range of structures appeared on the AWRE property. Only one of them remains in use, an open-fronted garage by the jetty, originally put up to shelter the buses used for transporting staff around the site. It was taken over by the BBC for its staff from 1975 and is still used as a garage by their successors. Of the rest, many are now no more than shadows on the ground, all that remains of buildings too damaged to warrant repair and of no possible practical use, architectural merit or historic importance.

Simkin managed the construction of the first of the two substantial bridges over Stony Ditch over which all building materials were transported by lorry from the jetty to the shingle.* The only other standing memorials to Farrow's labours are the ruins of the first three labs, and their various support buildings, now slowly decaying and scarcely safe to enter, but nonetheless so robustly built that they may survive as empty shells for decades to come.

One piece of infrastructure that Farrows were not required to provide was the network of roadways. These were built by a firm of specialists, Roadworks, using foundation aggregate taken especially from a quarry in nearby Hollesley. This was mixed with cement before being rolled into the shingle to form the foundations for the concrete road surfaces, which have survived for over fifty years, with only slow signs of decay.

Simkin's job was to ensure that AWRE's requirements were being met. He recalls that the chief supervisor from Aldermaston had an imposing military manner. He was Major Harrison, who treated the whole thing as if it were a military operation. Entering into this spirit, his assistant, Roy Billington, used to call himself 'the lance-corporal'. Simkin regarded AWRE as 'a good client' with whom he seldom came to blows. Any friction there was seems to have occurred within the AWRE team.

The workforce was, in his judgement, admirable, chiefly because it was reliable, resourceful and adaptable. They were all under very considerable pressure to

---

* This bridge was condemned as unsafe by the National Trust and pulled down in 1995.

complete on schedule and yet were constantly faced with alterations and additions to the specifications. Simkin's men seemed to revel in helping to solve problems. There were no labour disputes and no demarcation issues. Perhaps their pay kept them happy: they were being given 1*d* an hour above the going rates. It is interesting to note that he found his electricians the most resourceful of all, a particular joy for him in view of the reputation of their union (the notorious ETU). Simkin put it down to the fact that they came from the East End of London. The secret, he found, was to get them to laugh. The conditions could indeed test their good humour. The snow drifting across the site in February 1956 was such that the bulldozers had to dig themselves out. Water pipes froze solid, yet the 'team spirit' was admirable. He had only to hint that painting needed doing, and men from every trade would appear in suitable overalls to give it a go. They did a good job, for evidence of this paintwork remains over fifty years later.

The Tech HQ building for AWRE, located alongside the Beacon, was erected simultaneously with the work on the much more elaborate Lab 1 and its neigh-bouring control room. A row of trailers stood by the side of the roadway between the two construction sites. These provided for the contractors' offices. In the face of gale force winds, wire hawsers were used to strap them down. Opposite stood a mighty concrete mixing machine. The chief ingredient for this might be thought to be lying around in abundant supply. The problem was that the shingle's saline content did not make for the best quality concrete. A special machine was brought over to pump and spread the liquid cement. It is thought that it dated back to before the war and had been invented for the construction of the RAF station and Fighter Command HQ at Bentley Priory. It was needed for depos-iting great quantities of cement at considerable speed. When the third lab was built, its lightweight barrel-vault roof required a special mix of cement, posing a very significant challenge to the contractors.

The designers of these first three labs were C. W. Glover & Partners. Their resident representative on site was the twenty-three-year-old Jim Brown. He later commented that relations between scientists and designers were sometimes quite tense. His task was to ensure that the scientists were being given exactly what they required. The problem seems to have been that the physicists claimed to know the answers to structural issues – design specifications for the walls and imperviousness to radioactivity, for example – better than the engineers.

Brown referred to the nuclear weapons as the 'cans of tomatoes', perhaps a reas-suringly casual description of what were in all conscience most sinister objects. The possibility of an accident can never have been entirely ignored. Brown could not avoid speculating what would happen to the more bulky items inside the labs, such as the cranes, had a bomb blown up. 'Probably hit the Crown & Castle' he surmised. The evidence is that such thoughts had also occurred to the engineers when the style of roof in the so-called 'pagodas' is compared with that of the first three labs.

Of all the actual constructions, Lab 1 was the biggest because it involved a vast concrete raft on which the whole building had to rest. Some sixty concrete piles had to be driven into the shingle, down as far as the water table. The raft itself was 2 feet thick, with asphalt insulation. The walls had to be reinforced to take the weight of the internal gantry crane. The pit, designed to replicate the size and shape of an aircraft bomb bay, needed heavy reinforcement to take the strain and stress of the vibration equipment. In the midst of so much subsequent decay and demolition, this pit remains on view, a telling reminder of what went on within the building from the summer of 1956. It is the only interior feature that is still available for the general public to see. For reasons of safety, entry into all the other labs has to be restricted to controlled visits with a National Trust warden in attendance.

The mighty walls of Lab 1 were constructed by a process of pumping concrete into a cavity created by shuttering, in a continuous flow. They were then heavily reinforced, using a pair of bulldozers to push up great shingle abutments. This feature gives these labs their lasting appearance of vast burial mounds, as Sebald remarked on his visit in 1992.

The construction of the roofs required special consideration. The danger of an accidental explosion was very much in the designers' minds. It is useful to recall that the immediate purpose of these trials was to test a possible detonation by accident of the high explosive charges in the bomb, not the fissile material. The initial solution to venting a blast was to provide a 'soft' roof made of corrugated steel, which would direct an explosion upwards. A similarly lightweight 'asbestolux' false ceiling hid the roof structure. This was necessary to secure an enclosed environment, capable of variable control so that different climatic conditions and atmospheric pressures could be replicated. An air-conditioning unit was installed and at the time of the lab's inauguration a 28-day test was set up, at a temperature of 70 degrees and with 100 per cent humidity. This established a fully unified, stable and steady temperature throughout the whole building and its surrounding shingle walls.

The last part of the Lab 1 building was the so-called 'drop test' unit, a chamber at its western end in which a bomb could be hoisted up and physically dropped onto the concrete floor, to replicate an accident on the runway. Soon, other sub-contractors were on site, to fit specially dedicated equipment. Most significant of these were two large mechanical vibrating machines built by the sports car manufacturer, Frazer Nash. The instrumentation for monitoring the vibration tests came from the well-known instrument makers Nigretti & Zamba. A plant room, a heating boiler house, workshops and stores soon completed the complex. By early June 1956, the whole building was ready for handover. Despite a contract that had all but doubled in size and complexity over the previous nine months, and all the difficulties of access to the site and unhelpful weather, completion was just one week late. With becoming modesty, Simkin understates the general satisfaction that was expressed with what was a major achievement: 'everyone was quite pleased'.

Work for the contractors immediately switched to Lab 2, in which a large centrifuge was fitted, and Lab 3, with its thermal chamber. The centrifuge was reputed to be the most powerful in the world at this time. The method of construction of these next two chambers was similar to Lab 1, although no great concrete raft or piles to support it were needed for either.

There were no serious disasters during the construction period, though inevitably minor crises occurred. A summer gale blew over scaffolding around Lab 2. A human skull was discovered in the shingle near Lab 3. The foreman dealt with what could have caused a tiresome delay had the police or a coroner's court been involved. It was summarily reburied in the concrete mix being applied to the building of the walls.

Once completed, Simkin and his fellow workers were never permitted to see their handiwork in action. It might now seem strange how little people working on the Ness knew about what their neighbours on site were up to; or how little curiosity drove them to poke their noses into intriguing places with which they had had such intimate contact. A case in point was a small unit constructed for the Royal Navy in autumn 1955, just after Simkin arrived. Because they were already 'on site', Howard Farrow was commissioned to build a concrete platform on which was to be placed a metal hut, located to the side of the coastguard lookout. The hut itself was sent up from the Underwater Countermeasures Unit at Havant in Hampshire. The project was supervised by a clerk of works from Chatham. Cables arrived by sea and electrical power was supplied by an extension from the AWRE headquarters building, then in the course of construction. As Simkin observed, 'this was the Silent Service'; neither he nor anyone around had any clue as to what went on there. No further detail of this particular project has emerged since. The hut has long since been removed but the concrete blocks and base on which it rested remain, seemingly as good as new. Howard Farrow's concrete was high calibre!

In 1957, a man whose career had run a course curiously parallel to the story of the Ness arrived on the island as the new AWRE superintendent. He was to be in charge of the whole operation of the place and answerable to his superior, the Head of the Trials Department at Aldermaston, Dr Ewan Maddock. By any measure, Keith Wood was a very remarkable person. An expert radio technician by training, he had been recruited in 1936 to join the Bawdsey radar team and joined at the same time as Hanbury Brown, Preist and others, to work on the airborne radar experiments. He may well have visited the Ness at this time, though in his memoirs, he never says so. In 1941 he was seconded from RAE Farnborough into the RAF so that he could fly with aircrew as they wrestled with aerial arrays to make long-range air-to-surface vessel (ASV) radars work. Such was the role of the true boffin. He soon found himself travelling around the USA and elsewhere, an acknowledged expert in radar technology. After the war, he was appointed to the Blind Landing Experimental Unit at Martlesham, which worked on ever more advanced developments in instrument landing systems. Here, he was so close to the Ness, but again had no occasion to use its facilities. This work was initially directed towards military operations but of course had immense implications for civilian use. His team was involved in trials, for example, for landing civilian aircraft in real-life fog conditions at Heathrow. By 1956, however, Wood was threatened with an enforced move away from his beloved Suffolk. He had achieved the status of Senior Principal Scientific Officer and was shortly awarded the highly prestigious Wakefield Gold Medal for his work as a research scientist.

Just at the moment when he faced the possibility of a self-imposed redundancy, the post of Superintendent at AWRE Orford Ness was advertised in the *East Anglian Daily Times*. The notice was deliberately placed in a local paper where Wood would see it. He was AWRE's intended and preferred candidate. Though his expertise did not lie in handling explosives, it did lie in dealing with radio electronics, a field that covered the telemetry being conducted at the time. He was duly appointed, and ran the station for over four years, his departure coinciding with the decision to proceed with the second phase of building and research.

On arrival some months after the telemetry trials facilities had been set up, Wood commented on its advanced sophistication. He was well qualified to judge. Explaining the significance of this he writes that the secret of success was to ensure that the relays within the bomb worked in precisely the right sequence and timing. In order to achieve the all-important critical mass to bring about a nuclear explosion the core was surrounded by explosive material, the 'tamper', in the form of a number of small sections all of which had to fire almost simultaneously. In practice that meant within very small parts of a second. If the explosion was not symmetrical there would be a 'blow-out' and critical mass would not be achieved.

Wood's boss, Maddock, was by all accounts a vibrant character. It was he who took the initiative over Russian launch of Sputnik, the first Russian communications satellite, in 1957. Wood recounts how, pointing out what a nice quiet site they had from an electrical and electronic interference viewpoint, Maddock suggested that 'we prepare a system to receive and examine the signals it would be transmitting'.

Together, they had ample experience in radio propagation and in the design of aerials. Wood 'acquired' an old gun mounting from the Ministry Maintenance Unit in the Midlands and had his workshops whittle into shape a pine tree trunk 40 feet in length from a neighbouring Forestry Commission plantation. Wood was a life-long sailing enthusiast and his expertise was useful in devising the rigging to brace the 'mast' around which a suitable helix aerial was wound. A gun mounting proved ideal for 'steering' the aerial. Tracking the Sputnik required rotation and elevation, and the Ness's contraption was known as the 'Sputnik Chaser'. The results were admirable. Wood reflects on this rather extraordinary achievement: 'This work, I believe, is typical of the enthusiasm and innovation one can achieve with small teams in a small unit away from the main large establishments.' Wood and his men received many plaudits from the government departments concerned.

Not long after this, Wood was again approached by Maddock for another similar project. AWRE was concerned about the trials the French were promising to conduct with their nuclear bomb, to be detonated in the Sahara. The Ness site was deemed ideal for detecting the effects of this explosion on the ionosphere. This might well have had a serious impact on vital communications signals in the high frequency band. It was therefore extremely important to monitor the results of the French test. Wood set his team to work again. This was 1959.

It was decided to set up three large Rhombic aerials on the northern airfield by what is referred to as the Plate Store. These were erected by the GPO (General Post Office), using poles made of pine trunks from the same source as before. The resulting aerials were 80 feet long and fixed 15 feet from the ground. One of Wood's team came up with a suggestion that the frequency of the monitoring signal transmitted from the Ness should be adjusted to a critical level that would duct along the ionosphere, rather than wastefully penetrate it.

The outcome was a complete triumph for the AWRE boffins. On 13 February 1960, a pulse signal was received which showed that the ionosphere was, in Wood's own words, 'suffering severe and widespread activity comparable with occasions when large auroras and sun flares occur and so disrupt communications'. This of course had grave implications for understanding the working of defence communications generally. Wood and his men were again the object of official satisfaction.

Part of the success of Wood's management of the AWRE work must have arisen from the fact that so many of his team joined at his invitation. Don Revett certainly felt that as a relatively junior Scientific Officer, he was often given tasks of daunting responsibility. His own job centred on leading a small team required to fit the test instrumentation to the weapons.

The science of vibration impact was a rapidly developing one at this time. 'It could be useful in deciding where to mount a vibration-sensitive piece of equipment in an aircraft or ship,' Revett writes. Many errors were made through ignorance of the issues involved. He and his team designed a special multi-channel vibration controller. There being absolutely no commercial equivalent on the market, they were able to manufacture a number of them in their Ness lab, using the drawing office and other AWRE facilities. These could be offered for sale to other test agencies. Indeed, 'our expertise in this field was such that we were being consulted by other government agencies over the drawing up of vibration test specifications'.

As time passed, the AWRE work on the Ness tended to diversify. The priorities for bomb testing became less intense, even leading to a slowly growing doubt as to the very need for the Ness facility at all. Wood had an overall brief, which took him off-site, notably to Australia, where much of the bomb and rocketry range technology devised on the Ness was to be transferred to new ranges based at Woomera. The principal weapon involved at the time was Blue Streak, shortly due for trial firing. His account of his trip reads very much like a diary of a holiday expedition, and in view of the fact that the Blue Streak project was about to be abandoned, this in the event is what it proved to be. Notice of the cancellation was given the day after his return to London. Shortly after that, Wood left the Ness for a variety of significant posts in the public service, in recognition of which he was awarded an OBE in 1980.

Wood makes no mention of AWRE's attempt to move its operations from the Ness. Perhaps he was kept largely in the dark over what would be a very unsettling decision, since he was known to be a Suffolk man, unhappy at the thought of having to move. However, by 1960 it was decided after all to stay put and to proceed with the second phase of trigger safety research. New labs would be required in conjunction with the decision to use American bomb designs. It was just at this crucial juncture that the highly capable new Superintendent, Harry Weeks, arrived to take over from Wood.

THE WE177 ATOMIC BOMB

For more than ten years, AWRE had experimented with a bewildering array of nuclear weapons. Most were discarded while still on the drawing board or cancelled because they were clearly inoperable. They were given a colourful gallimaufry of codenames. Those working on them must have had ample cause to resort to a glossary to be sure of the current name of the item they were researching. The chief colours used were blue, red or yellow, but brown and green, orange and purple, indigo and violet were also featured. Some of the names to which the colour was attached were scarcely such as to strike terror in our opponents' minds. These names and the occasions for changing them were due to a climate of apprehension over security. Big Bertha became Brown Bunny and in turn Blue Peacock turned into Blue Hare, supposedly because its name had been compromised. There appears to be no indication of whether or not Russian intelligence was confused. Going by the names given to the project – it was a Blue Danube-based nuclear landmine – they may well have been unimpressed. Seen as a whole, the list of codenames adopted for many of these trials was hardly intimidating.

The new bomb, which came to acquire the generic title of WE177, had as its explosive mechanism an adaptation of the American W47 system. This was the original weapon designed for the US Polaris missile. The W47 presented a serious problem however: until, about 1965, it was never what was called 'single-point safe'. This meant that the conventional explosive in the core of the weapon was liable to detonate prematurely in the event of an accident, and do so moreover with a modest radioactive fallout. This was highly unsatisfactory. It is in this context that the high priority attached to this second phase of testing at the Ness is to be seen, especially as the US/USSR test ban treaties were in operation from 1960.

Farrows were not awarded the contract for the new series of labs. Gordon Simkin's time on the Ness was over. The preferred contractor this time was Cubitt and Goff from Ipswich. Glover & Partners were again the designers for the two principal 'cells' – as they called them – the buildings known ever after as the 'pagodas'.

The problem of containing blast and consequent 'missile' or shrapnel damage from disintegrated material following an accidental explosion, remained very much in mind as work on the design proceeded. The original hope was that a simple 'shoe box' shape, without any allowance for venting the blast, would be sufficient so long as the concrete walls and roof were thick enough. The engineers were dubious. To put the issue to the test, a trial was conducted at Foulness, with a one-tenth-scale model to be blown up. Its resulting total demolition, with debris scattered far and wide, proved dramatically that the engineers were right and the scientists less so! A similar model with a vented roofline window – a precursor of the 'pagoda' design – survived its explosion with scarcely a mark.

The result was a design given robust walls and an enormous roof, supported on strong pillars, allowing a substantial window between the two, through which venting could occur. Debris would be directed downwards onto the shingle by a wide overhang. The roof was a concrete tray over 3 feet thick, loaded with a further 7 feet of shingle. The pillars were never fixed to the walls: they merely rested on them. Had a fearful accident occurred, the roof would have lifted and then crumpled the pillars as its mighty weight fell back, burying the chamber beneath and limiting the spread of blasted material.

The labs had to be totally insulated. Effective glazing of the vent windows required some very special design features. It was necessary to retain various internal environments, including atmospheric pressure. Glass was rejected because in the event of blast, shards would shower far and wide, compounding the hazard. The ideal material should be transparent, light in weight, and capable of tearing quite easily when so required, yet robust against exterior weather conditions. The result was the use of double layers of plastic sheeting, mounted into frames fitted into each section of aperture. The plastic was tensioned, with a central rod, to which sharp cutting blades were attached. In the event of an explosion, the plastic would be pressed against the blades, making the splitting of the plastic almost instantaneous. Happily, no blast ever occurred in Labs 4 or 5. Harsh weather over the years has insured that almost none of these window frames or their plastic inserts have survived the passage of time.

The pagodas were much more elaborately fitted than the earlier labs. Evident to this day are the slits in the side walls and floor to which could be attached the rigs for the vibration equipment. These could be precisely focused on all or any part of the bomb. The vibrators themselves were electronic, not mechanical. Vibration was generated by enormously powerful amplifiers. The specifications for them were so demanding that the British manufacturers, Goodman's, professed themselves unable to meet them. Special equipment, the Ling 249, from America, was supplied via the agency Pye of Cambridge, so that the cost, an estimated £88,000 a unit, could be paid in sterling rather than dollars. Later, one technician visiting the site remarked that given a comparable set of speakers, the amplifiers would have been perfectly capable of blasting a sound audible in Ipswich!

Hot or cold environments were created out of mobile trucks parked outside each lab. The external tubes to which the thermal generators were attached have survived. Ducts to the control building erected about 200 yards to the west carried CCTV and other control cables. These were covered in plastic protective coating, which rather alarmingly were very much to the taste of the rat population. As a consequence, trials could be threatened by tiresome interruptions caused not just by intrusive Russian 'spy' trawlers or by technical mishaps, but by hungry rodents.

As to serious mishap, none of any consequence is recorded. Occasional alarms there were, however. On one trial, the Lab 2 centrifuge was rotating at full speed when it began to suck up the linoleum floor covering, pulverising it and causing a terrifying roar and an impenetrable cloud of thick dust. A shattered staff team immediately shut down operations and waited in trepidation for quite some while for the cloud to disperse so that they could discover the source of the noise and the nature of the damage done. It proved to be minimal.

The building programme in this second phase was completed by about 1965, with Lab 6, a small centrifuge, designed chiefly to test the warhead for the Polaris submarine ballistic missile system. This was something of an afterthought for AWRE. It was only in November 1962, at the Nassau Conference, that Kennedy and Macmillan agreed to focus the UK's nuclear deterrent on the Royal Navy. The Resolution class of nuclear powered ballistic missile submarines followed, from 1966. The Ness meanwhile was made ready to perfect their operating systems. This marked the beginning of the total transfer of nuclear weapons from the RAF, which culminated in the abandonment of the WE177 air-drop bomb in the late 1990s.

The control building, referred to above, contained offices and workshops and a canteen; attached was a fire station with a large water storage tank. The AWRE fire officers would conduct periodic exercises with Suffolk firemen from the mainland. These were very popular events, giving the men from Orford a grand opportunity to play around with the AWRE equipment, including driving the landing craft. Much of this range of buildings survives. The architectural style for all of them was in some contrast with everything else built for AWRE in the locality of the test labs. They were totally unprotected against blast.

HARD TARGET TESTING

During this period the last of the major structures was added to the AWRE complex. This was the large barrel-vault shaped ammunition store where bombs were kept before and after trials. It seems somewhat ironic that having gone to such trouble to protect the local civilian population from an accidental explosive blast, this store was located significantly closer to Orford than any other AWRE structure on the shingle. The truth was that, by the mid-1960s, the likelihood of any serious accident seems to have receded. The high explosive charge by now involved in detonating a chain reaction was reduced too. All in all, these factors were contributing to all the many good reasons for closing down the whole nuclear weapons testing operations on the Ness. The need for such a place, however useful its reputation for 'privacy', had all but disappeared.

This work came at a price. Subsequent generations, with the many advantages of hindsight, cannot be blamed for speculating just how much all this effort cost, and indeed whether it was really worth it. National Archives files hint at great sums involved, at the bickering with the Treasury and at the uncertainty in the minds of AWRE and of the Services as to whether they should be proceeding on the site at all. The Treasury in particular were quite tiresome in querying the need for the second phase of buildings, arguing that Foulness should be quite adequate as a site for tests. They even raised the almost outrageous idea that Suffolk County Council should pay for the sea defence work. On the other hand, those who recalled the parsimony of wartime funding commented on the total change in attitude by the authorities during the Cold War. Money was never seriously denied AWRE.

The value of having done this research was well illustrated many years later. In August 2007, *The Times* published a news item under a somewhat sensational headline, 'Britain drops nuclear bomb. Fortunately it doesn't go off'. Referring to recently released information about two incidents, in Germany and at the Faslane submarine base during the 1980s when bombs were accidentally dropped, it quoted MoD sources as denying that these were anything but minor affairs, asserting that there was never any risk to the public. The tone of the article was not totally convincing. Reassurances came not from Aldermaston but from Orford Ness. A letter to the editor from a volunteer warden was published a few days later. Describing just what was being tested on the Ness in the 1950s and '60s, it stated that 'the safety of our trigger mechanisms was brilliantly proved... Such regrettable mishaps as you describe should not be used as a reason for questioning the validity of the British nuclear deterrent... No one in Germany or Scotland was in any serious danger...'

As to the cost of this whole project, the figures in archive reports were batted to and fro between various departments of government, with some evidence of calculated obfuscation and deviousness. Truth to say, a high price had to be paid for essential work on what was a key element in Britain's Cold War deterrent.

On loan to the Trust for display is an example of a WE177 case on its trailer. This sinister item, resplendent in bright white paint is a relatively small version of an air-drop weapon, designed for use by the Royal Navy as an anti-submarine nuclear depth charge. It was just the sort of weapon to be subjected to the severe testing now described.

This was the last test facility that AWRE constructed. Rather less elaborate or costly, it was located near to Lab 1. This was an impact testing facility, or 'Hard

Target' as it was generally described. It is now entirely ruined but enough of it remains for the passing visitor to gain a clear understanding of what it was all about and how it worked. It was simultaneously a simple and yet a sophisticated facility for 'crumple testing'.

The reason for adopting the tactic of low altitude approach of a nuclear attack bomber was to try and approach a target 'under' the radar, flying at a low level. Only as the WE177 system was perfected did the need arise to allow for the bomber to escape the explosion into which it was inevitably going to fly. The solution was to delay the explosion. The question then was – would a bomb that had hit the ground or its target, even at reduced speed, survive the impact without compromising its trigger mechanism?

The Hard Target was the test site designed to prove the technique. A large and imposing reinforced concrete block still stands and behind it, the rusting remains of a tower that stood above the block. From the tower projected a wooden gantry, housing very high-speed TV cameras. On the apron in front of the block there once stood a trestle trackway five feet off the ground and about 25 yards in length. A rocket was attached to a sledge upon which the bomb under test was placed. In actual operational use, a network of cables would be connected to the bomber to initiate the firing sequences. These were replicated in the rig by a sort of umbilical cord slung from a wire cable, which was stretched immediately above the track. The ignited rocket would project the whole contraption down the track, to smash into the wall at about 150 miles per hour, simulating the impact of an air-drop weapon hitting its target when retarded by a parachute. The sledge was fitted with a retro-rocket, which would brake it violently just short of the block, allowing it to drop into a container slung underneath the track and permitting its load to shoot ahead into the concrete. The object here was to test the delayed action facility built into the trigger mechanisms. Detonation had to occur at least 10 seconds after impact, allowing the dropping aircraft to escape the result of the explosion. It was of course essential that the inevitable crumpling of the nose and casing that would occur did not affect the various functions required for firing the bomb.

Subtle variations on a simple crash test were involved. This permitted the differing styles of bomb-drop methods to be simulated. These could be as depth charges, as air burst bombs or as ground burst. A variant, the so-called 'laydown land', was where a bomb was dropped via the low-altitude (LABS) technique to slide along the ground. For these situations, the rocket-launching rail could be swung round to an oblique angle for an impact up to 40 degrees from the vertical.

Thermal testing was also involved in these tests. This could add just another complication to this difficult work. Les Armer was one of the technicians involved in setting them up. He has described the acute discomfort from operating in partnership with a mobile freezer unit capable of blasting air at -40 degrees centigrade. Fingers could get stuck to the weapon, so great care had to be used.

Armer explains that the original intention during the period of peak test activity had been to conduct a trial every four days. This implied an enormous volume of smashed bomb nose cones! They quickly realised that the damage done to the concrete block was sufficient to require at least five days for the cement to harden, so these tests ran from 1965 to 1967 at a rate of one per week. They were ended only when AWRE decided to wind down its work on the Ness.

All the tests had to be recorded for analysis of the weapons' systems. Initially, an inboard recorder was used, but this proved to be slow and was constantly damaged by the impacts. An American Consolidated Dynamics (CBR) 50-channel recorder was then introduced, a most highly sophisticated piece of equipment, designed as an event recorder for the USAF. So complex was it that it could monitor every single function, taking the team at least twelve hours just to set it up for each trial. The impacted weapon would be returned to Aldermaston for analysis and the statistical results sent to a facility in Stevenage. Armer himself would drive to Watford with what he termed 'key components'. The most important factor in triggering the WE177 was the exact sequence of timers, which relied on in-board 24-volt batteries coming live at the right moment and at the correct power.

This was all highly technical work and Les Armer recalls with evident pride that he and his colleagues – Williams, Humphries, Ballard, Ives and Goss – celebrated the completion of what they clearly regarded as highly satisfying research, with a dinner party at The Captain's Table restaurant in Woodbridge.

AWRE BOFFINS' TALES

At the height of the tests, AWRE had to expand the workforce to around 350 personnel on the site. There was also a small RAF detachment to deal with matters requiring service know-how. For AWRE however, the recruitment of sufficient specialist scientists and technicians was quite a considerable challenge. One significant area of recruitment – given that the date was March 1958 – was revealed in an internal AWRE memo, indicating the urgent need for what were quaintly described as 'computresses'. Of course, these so-called computers were sadly crude: they were in fact no more than mechanical number crunchers, that speeded the calculation of the vast array of figures that the trials were generating.

The Ministry of Supply and RAE Farnborough found bright sixteen year olds and gave them what most freely admitted was an amazing opportunity. 'How lucky I was to work in a place like that' is a not uncommon comment. David Warren was just such a youthful recruit, brought in by AWRE as a promising school-leaver and assigned the problems of attaching workable strain gauges to the instrumentation involved in the vibration tests. These had to be inserted into the narrow spaces inside the bomb case. Special types of soldering iron were needed to prevent the whole installation from being cooked. Warren recalls that this was exciting because here he was, still effectively a schoolboy, involved in high security work for Queen and Country.

Understandably, it made him feel rather important. There was a great sense of teamwork. What he had to do was scarcely pioneering stuff but it gave him unique experience at a very early age, which was to lead to his ultimate achievement of a Physics degree and a career in industry.

Another unlikely recruit to the ranks of AWRE technicians was John Backhouse. He was transferred from the Bomb Ballistics team in about 1958 and for the next ten years was based in the Tech HQ building. His workshop was at the northeast corner of the complex, with pleasant views of the seashore and lighthouse. Here he was allotted a whole variety of construction jobs, often involving the creation of complex circuits. He was never given any idea of their purpose, and in common with everyone else, was unable to enter any buildings without authority or enquire what his colleagues were up to. One project allotted to his team led by Charlie Taylor and Dave Pool was for what was described as a 'mobility meter', a gadget for detecting weaknesses in joints of welded metal plates. He was given the impression that their success in making it work had highly significant commercial implications, though he personally was in no position to claim patent rights.

Some of these scientists spent relatively few weeks on site, undertaking a particular project. One such was John Bleach, who was sent from Aldermaston in the summer of 1959 to conduct a trial involving a 3,000 hour-long vibration test on the current phase of the Yellow Sun bomb. Recalling what he was to describe as 'incredible times', Bleach gives a vivid picture of what it was like for these talented men working in the labs. He writes:

> The trial was to be conducted by staff working 12-hour shifts and I think perhaps it had already started as I seem to recall a preliminary visit to the site. I drove up from Berkshire in my newish Austin A30 and stayed the night in Woodbridge. It was not restful as the US air base nearby flew frequent night exercises.
>
> Next morning at Orford Quay I was met by a courteous Atomic Energy constable armed with a Sten gun. A small landing craft took me over to the Island where the current duty officer was waiting for me. I was then taken to a group of caravans parked on the shingle a short distance from a heavily banked bunker and was duly briefed...

The shift comprised an explosives specialist, a health physicist and two or three weapon/instrumentation technicians. During the shift a constant watch on instrumentation and television cameras was maintained and all conversation within the caravans was recorded on huge tape recorders.

As has often been observed 'health and safety' as later understood, seldom featured in the work done on the Ness over the years, but the presence of a technician specialist to check radioactivity is significant.

Two shifts were allocated to operate the trial, on a fourteen-day tour of duty. At 4 p.m. every day the trial was temporarily shut down and after a brief delay, the team would enter the chamber to check that all was going according to plan. They then reassembled the apparatus and restarted the test.

John Bleach was kept very busy, but not overwhelmingly so. He was not alone among the AWRE staffers in referring to a particular recreation that was enjoyed with evident pleasure: what may be termed the Orford Ness Grand Prix:

> Time speed trials between shift teams in driving our site vehicles over a measured section of quite twisting concrete roads enlivened quieter moments. The presence of a neutral invigilator with a stopwatch ensured the veracity of these competitions. The nearby police studiously looked the other way.

Like many others working on the site, the LABS bombing runs by Scimitars and Canberras were inescapably impressive. Unlike most of his colleagues, Bleach seems to have struck up a useful contact with the lighthouse keepers 'who proudly demonstrated to us their own special instruments'. Staying in the pub in Orford in what he described as 'affable disarray' – shifts that ran from 7 a.m. to 7 p.m. made for certain difficulties over feeding arrangements – he clearly had an agreeable time on the Ness. It was summer, and 'we all appreciated the stunning beauty of the area'.

Not all the AWRE employees were boffins. Indeed, without the technicians – electricians and mechanical engineers – the experts could never have accomplished what they did. Alec Wiseman was one such 'techie'. He describes himself as 'an experimental mechanic'. He and his resourceful colleagues made the trials work. Wiseman was the second in command of the team that fitted the vibration machinery to the test bombs in Lab 1. This often involved extraordinary improvisation and imagination. Making the gauges for monitoring the multi-directional vibration movement required finding appropriate materials – like resin-bonded fibre – and then machining it to shape. All the while, no possibility of a spark or static electricity could be permitted; special tools made of bronze had to be used. Immense care had to be taken; short cuts or sloppy workmanship could have been fatal. Furthermore, they had to ensure total cleanliness. Concern over safety was very evident. None of Wiseman's team was permitted near the labs during the running of a trial. Whenever they did enter a lab, they had to leave behind an identity tag on a board outside it. Yet he recalls not a single accident, apart from a Kelvinator freezer unit blowing up.

Wiseman was one of the longest serving and most versatile of all AWRE staffers, remaining there from 1956 to 1971. Clearly he came to enjoy being in Suffolk, so much so that he declined the offer of further employment at Aldermaston and stayed on in the county.

Wiseman is not alone in mentioning how versatile the labour force was. A member of his team was Colin Ault, who served for just two years, as a fitter, who, in his words, 'did everything'. He recalls Wiseman as his foreman with particular affection.

His job was to set up the tests in Labs 4 and 5: the pagodas. This meant fixing the vibration rigs onto the walls of the labs in the slots, which remain in evidence to this day. He might equally be directed to install the heater or freezer units, or work on setting up trials at the Hard Target site.

Ault was still a very young man, and his employment was in the nature of an apprenticeship. Security and discipline were very tight. Ault suggests that this was quite accepted. He felt he was doing vital work and contributing to the waging of the Cold War.

Soon he realised that work on advanced weaponry was being run down. Some trials he was involved in setting up were for items like the rocket motors for ejector seats. As for so many, his experience on the Ness stood him in excellent stead. He felt AWRE were good employers, and though no redundancy arrangement existed in those days, he was easily able to return to his former employer, Cranes of Ipswich.

Following his year as an RAF apprentice, already described, Clifford Rayner was working in Ipswich when in 1956 he was invited back to the Ness, to work as a 'techie' – or as he described himself, an 'industrial'. He was employed by the Ministry of Supply, later transferring to AWRE.

His first job as an engineer, working in his old trades in sheet metal and welding, was to construct the cover for the kine-theodolites. He made ventilation ducts for the labs, including the pipes for the thermal units in the Kelvinators and manufactured the mountings for vibrators. He was a long-serving jack-of-all-trades and became a much-appreciated employee. His work was essential for the effective conduct of the various trials described above. What is apparent from his account of his life on the Ness was how little he understood the purpose of the tasks he was assigned. The prevailing policy of 'need to know' was, he confessed, 'something of a menace'. It might explain why in his reminiscences he never once mentions the nuclear bombs he must have witnessed falling into the sea. He assisted in building the spark-photography model bomb range but again neglects to explain what it was for. He was involved too in the construction of a 'universal gun mounting', designed to enable a variety of calibre of guns to be used from a single site in lethality firing trials. He may have felt uncomfortable speaking about the precise, highly secret, purpose of it all. Meanwhile, he freely appreciated the liveliness of the social and recreational life on the island. Rayner perhaps realised that activity was running down when in 1968 he took a job as a Technical Lecturer in Bury St Edmunds. He had thoroughly enjoyed his time on the Ness and was genuinely sorry to leave.

COMMERCIAL TESTING

Towards the end of the period of nuclear weapons testing, and anticipating signs of decline in activity, AWRE recognised that continued operations on the Ness could only be justified by widening the 'customer base'. It could provide test programmes for civil purposes and for military clients other than the MoD. To advertise what was available, a comprehensive brochure was produced. 'If you have a trial requirement that cannot be handled in a conventional, locally controlled laboratory,' it ran 'or if it needs sophisticated control or analysis techniques – or if it is just a straight forward environmental trial which you want efficiently and promptly done – you are invited to ring ORFORD 345 and ask for David George, the Senior Trials Officer'.

The Ness was venturing into the industrial and commercial world. Don Revett has already indicated that this development in the use of the AWRE facilities was very much on all of their minds. 'We had the biggest test facility of its type in Europe so we actively went out seeking work, even to the extent of publishing a brochure and inviting possible customers to the site.' In fact, there was never a great take-up here; indeed the brochure it seems was never widely distributed.

However, this promotional document headed 'WHAT ORFORD NESS CAN DO FOR YOU' offers a rare and comprehensive insight into all the work that was done in the various labs from 1956 and the increasingly elaborate tests that could be undertaken. It emphasises the high calibre of the staff, qualified both to run tests and to design and construct any special test rigs that might be needed. Security could be provided even for what it refers to as 'stores'. The disposal of small quantities of explosive could be dealt with on the establishment's burning ground. That the AWRE had in mind clients involved in developing munitions is not in doubt: 'A heated magazine, with a capacity up to 3,000 lb of explosive is available for storage of test specimens and bulk explosive'. Was AWRE indeed offering its services to foreign governments for testing their weapons?

In his memoirs, Don Revett reveals a further element in the 'commercialisation' of the Ness operations. He was sent up to Cheshire to assist the Atomic Energy Authority with its problems in developing a new method of enriching uranium. The use of a centrifuge for this process was novel, being cheaper and quicker than the diffusion method. But vibration damage was inhibiting progress. Revett's intervention appears to have resolved the difficulty. 'It did mean', he wrote, 'that developing countries could have a ready source of enriched uranium for peaceful or weapons purposes.*' Although the project was supposed to be secret, an article at the time we were doing this work appeared in the *New Scientist*, describing the whole process in detail!' This was not the first example of such a 'leakage'.

Such vibration tests were all part of a wider use of the Ness facilities at this period. Among items tested were black-box recorders for civilian aircraft, including Concorde. Not the least of these were tests involving motor vehicles on varied rough terrains. Revett was asked to assess vibration impact, including a hair-raising drive in a fully laden 3-tonner Bedford army truck over continental pavé, at a test

---

* The aspiration of countries like Iran to join the race to acquire its own nuclear weapons arose from the development of this technology.

track at Chertsey. His days on the Ness were coming to an end, however, and the idea of work at Aldermaston was, as for so many, unthinkable. Revett quit government service and assumed a new career, inspired partly by his feeling for Orford Ness. He took employment with the Wildfowl Trust near Ipswich.

The opportunities for doing civilian work in the labs proved to be limited and never alone could justify keeping the establishment running. It amounted at most to about 15 per cent of operating time. The economic impact of AWRE's final departure in 1971 was of course cushioned by the intense activity on King's and Lantern Marshes. Many of the local civilian workforce switched from one employer to the other.

The full consequence of an almost total shutdown of military activity was still many months away. The uncertainty over the options for future uses of the Ness were to cause some local dismay. The presence of AWRE, nuclear weapons notwithstanding, was generally welcomed in the locality, for good reasons, and Aldermaston's skill in ensuring this should perhaps be recognised.

Meanwhile, it is pertinent to reflect that this major enterprise had to be administered and secured. The employees too, who were not, by and large, servicemen, had social lives on the Ness, and this is the subject of the next chapter.

SECURITY

As the Ness grew more and more into a civilian operated station, with sevicemen present only to supply technical expertise where needed, so certain areas of activity changed. Notable among these was the provision of security. Thus, guard duties were no longer a responsibility for military staff on site. During the war, as Ken Daykin recalls, a solitary policeman might be stationed on the Orford Quay. Now that it was peacetime, a new regime was required. A separately recruited Military Police detachment had to be expanded to provide security and if needs be, discipline. One of those recruits, Cliff Caley, has provided memories of his long service as a Constable on the Ness.

Caley was brought to the Ness in the summer of 1953 as part of the process of police expansion. He was a local Suffolk man, coming from Butley, and like the majority of his colleagues, he had served as aircrew in Lancaster bombers. On arrival, he found the police team comprised a Sergeant and five Constables. By 1955 and AWRE's formal occupation, the complement had risen to an Inspector, a Sub-Inspector, four Sergeants and no less than sixteen Constables. Caley was a handler for the three dogs on site. By 1961, the police presence extended to armed night patrols. The job was taken seriously and was important. Equally, not a shot was fired and not a single serious security incident was recorded during Caley's entire time on the Ness.

The importance attached to this aspect of AWRE occupancy may be measured by the fact that no less than eight married quarters were built in Orford. A local builder was employed for the work. This was just one example of the way Aldermaston demonstrated its social responsibility to the local community. Such consideration was never to be forgotten. Moreover, the Air Ministry police were made available to support the civilian police whenever needed, as happened when any form of demonstration took place, notably at nearby RAF Bentwaters.

This service police performed when shipping ran aground on the fickle coastline. In February 1954, a collier, *Kentbrook*, was wrecked between the lighthouse and Martello Tower during a winter storm. Rescue was carried out by the Aldeburgh lifeboat, with the assistance of the Orford Life Saving Association. The role of the police was to prevent looters from stripping the ship before it was eventually cut up and trailered off the beach. Three years later, a modern trawler, *Faithful Star* out of Lowestoft, suffered a similar fate. This time, two members of the crew managed to scramble ashore. This was over a year before the security fence was built, so they were able to reach Lab 2, where they contrived to set off the alarm, bringing police scurrying to the rescue.

The vast bulk of the work done by Caley and his fellows was very routine and very boring. A police post was established on Orford Quay. Initially this was a modest affair, but in 1955, the building now used by the National Trust as its office was constructed. It was known as the 'clocking station' and it fulfilled a double role, for security and workers checking in. Another police point was located on the jetty and for random searches of staff as they departed to prevent anyone removing any 'contraband' material. At issue was common theft of tempting items of equipment: very occasionally, someone was caught. Whereupon dismissal would be immediate. No case of any breach in security was reported. These police searches were naturally unpopular: not because the need for them was doubted, but because they held people up from catching their buses home.

Originally, the security team occupied part of the First World War headquarters, or 'station office/guard room' building. From 1960, the need to step up security was met by encircling the central part of the site with 8-feet high wire fencing secured to concrete posts. Many of these posts still stand – strange symbols of a former state of security. Gates were installed and these were guarded. The chief point of entry to the secure site was at what was the Second World War building works office, now the National Trust's information building. It housed offices for the two Inspectors, a locker and cloakroom for the men, a Mess room and a waiting room for visitors. Plus a small telephone exchange at the rear. A 'young lady' from the Post Office was appointed to operate this during office hours.

Life was now tougher for the Constables, night duty in particular. AWRE staff left by 5.30 p.m. and the police would find themselves effectively locked into the site for what was a fourteen-hour stint. A Sergeant was on hand to check that the Constables religiously patrolled as required, on a constantly changing pattern, signing in at various checkpoints. It must have been quite a daunting task in that bleak environment, lonely, boring and devoid of any enlivening incident. Caley appears never to have complained, though he recalls that he and his colleagues devised an early-warning system to ensure that they were never found to be anything but exemplary in their duties.

This was a period when the police tower, now no more than a striking silhouette was in constant use to check on unwelcome visitors from the sea. None of consequence were reported, but Aldeburgh fishermen came close, looking for sea bass. They were required to give notice of their intention to approach the shore.

Security for the AWRE staff was stricter too. Entry to the site was closely controlled, with formal passes required. These had to be carried at all times, including during rest or 'off duty' periods, in the canteen for example. Even when permitted entry, visitors would always be escorted to their destination. Nevertheless, the dull routine of police duty was regularly enlivened by a major task, namely escorting weapons to and from Aldermaston.

Caley shared with so many others on the Ness a sketchy idea of what was going on in the test cells, or why aircraft continuously roared overhead. The national response to Cold War tensions was clearly 'not to reason why', but carry on with a job to be done.

Not everyone quite agreed, where nuclear weapons were involved. A demonstration by the East Anglian branch of the Committee of One Hundred, as the active wing of the Campaign for Nuclear Disarmament (CND) described itself, was always on the cards. On 20 June 1964, threat became reality, albeit on a modest and somewhat lacklustre scale. Gordon Kinsey relates what happened:

... less than a dozen members assembled on the sea-front at Aldeburgh with the intention of setting out on a proposed six mile trek along the shingle beach... At 12.30 the organiser announced that owing to a delay in the arrival of members from London and Colchester ... the demonstration was being delayed and would not start until 2.00 p.m., when it was anticipated that forty people would take part. The marchers had previously stated that on this occasion they did not intend any entry into the Establishment. The sole intention of the march was to publicise its presence to people in East Anglia, many of whom did not know of its existence.

The demonstrators were aware they were going to be stopped at the perimeter boundary, three miles from their starting point... The walk there and back was expected to take them three hours, through thick mud left by recent high tides. Notices were posted along the perimeter warning them that it was an offence to cross the line...

The party was met by a stalwart detachment of police who were able to persuade them of the discomfort as much as the folly of proceeding. The demonstrators trudged back and concluded their day with a meeting in Aldeburgh, which at the time rather was more involved with the 17th annual festival. Joyce Grenfell was due to give one of her inimitable performances in the Jubilee Hall that evening.

The Ness never suffered from the sort of attention that was given to Aldermaston. Moreover, campaigners from CND might well have met with a far from sympathetic reception had they settled in Orford as they were to at Greenham Common. AWRE was seen as a good employer and a sympathetic and generous source of support to the local community. In addition to gestures already referred to, it was policy to purchase local produce from local suppliers; and not far short of 100 of the workforce came from the locality.

From 1959 police on site were employed by AWRE, and remained so until 1971, when it reverted to an Air Ministry responsibility – or Ministry of Defence as from then on it was designated.

STATION SECRETARY

When AWRE arrived, the expanding scale of activity argued for some revision of the management structure; for a brief spell, there were no less than three major employers operating simultaneously. Such military establishments as Foulness or Woolwich supplied the model for this change. The senior officer, reporting to Aldermaston, would be titled the Superintendent. For most of the AWRE years, the holders of this position were Keith Wood and Harry Weeks. They in turn needed an adjutant to run the infrastructure. The title for this job was Station Secretary, a post filled for almost all the period under consideration in this chapter by Peter Broome.

Broome appears to have been ideal for the task. He had held a short-service commission in the RAF and then had joined Aldermaston in 1954 as an administrator. He was transferred to the Ness on New Year's Day 1958 to straighten up a place operating under dual management and without a clear structure of command. He gained an early impression that the place was run by a variety of semi-independent fiefdoms, ordered by seemingly autonomous team leaders. He arrived with phase 1 of the labs building programme complete, and phase 2 shortly due to start. This was in itself a major undertaking, but in addition, there was an increasing amount of wear and tear to the motley assortment of buildings and plants in his charge.

He found himself directly responsible to Aldermaston at this early stage for over 200 employees. This number would increase significantly during his time. His substantial clerical office staff dealt with employment matters and the myriad tasks involved in any large and complex enterprise. He employed the police, over twenty strong, the fire crew of six, the boat and ferry men, at least eight in number, a number of drivers, the catering and canteen staff and all the maintenance workforce. Including the scientists and technicians, the numbers working under his immediate command would swell to around 350. Only service personnel were outside his direct control.

Broome recalls that he never seemed to lack the equipment and materials needed to run the place. It was the height of the Cold War, and this seems to have given the Ness a high priority. There was constant building repair or construction work and Broome provided the liaison between AWRE and the various contractors. Their people seem to have been absorbed into the Ness community. One contractor's resident engineer, Broome notes, was a more than useful cricketer, roped in for the Ness team. A concrete strip was laid down with a matting wicket, but the more elegant venue for matches was the lovely ground in the Sudbourne estate.

Mention of cricket is a reminder that leisure activity was quite an important element in the life of those working on the Ness during this period. In part, this may have been something of a hangover from service days. A post-war instruction from the Air Ministry directed that stations should ensure all personnel had an afternoon per week devoted to sport. A football pitch was created in this period, and a team took part in the local league. But no positive record survives to show whether this was still in place during AWRE occupation.

Provision for varied recreation and sporting activity is often recalled. A badminton court was marked out in the northern large hangar: draughty and incongruously surrounded by workshop equipment, it was clearly popular and well used. Booth explains the significance of these sporting facilities, relating them to the lunch break, the only time when most people could relax. He goes on to explain that '… we had our own canteen run by Miss Baker and Miss Brennen, for the mid-day meal. Some intrepid souls did go home to Orford at mid-day, but after travelling from AWRE site to the ramp, across the river and home, it must have been a very quick meal in order to make the journey back within the hour.'

Having an hour for lunch meant devising some means of passing the time after a quickly taken meal offered in the canteen, which Don Revett describes as 'excellent'. Some of the old disused buildings were brought into use for lunchtime activities. These facilities developed into the widely supported Orford Ness Recreation Society – or 'Rec Soc'. One hut was fitted out as a snooker, table tennis and darts hall. Another piece of recreational equipment was something that might be expected in an establishment that had useful raw materials and advanced engineering facilities to hand. This was a table football game: the pitch was made out of a finely machined and polished block of aluminium. A horticultural shop was set up to bulk-buy fertiliser and other commodities for members. Don Revett and Dennis Jones formed a rough shooting club, the latter a wildfowler of many years' experience whose expertise was to change Revett's future career. The interest in bird watching inevitably grew with such interesting bird life all around. The most popular pastime, however, was putting. After many manhours of work during the lunch breaks, volunteer groups converted a square of grassland into an 18-hole putting green. While not up to park green standards, it was 'sporty'. For this the charge was one penny (old currency) per round, which was used to replenish golf balls and clubs. The par for the course was thirty-six and the course record round was thirty-two, which meant at least four 'holes-in-one'. Revett describes another feature of Rec Soc activity:

I was very involved in the Rifle Club. We converted a disused Ministry of
Supply projectile firing building [see chapter 9] into an indoor .22 rifle range.
The building was a Nissen [corrugated steel] construction, which meant it
wasn't bulletproof, so we had to construct brick baffles inside at intervals to
prevent any stray bullets escaping and endangering our colleagues in the nearby
canteen. Anyhow, it made a superb range and we competed, with some success,
in the Suffolk postal league. The then superintendent of Orford Ness officially
opened the range for us. We arranged that after he had fired the first ceremonial
shot, there would be a great cacophony of sound – *Land of Hope and Glory*, the
sound of gunfire, low-flying aircraft, *Rule Britannia*, the lot! He looked a bit
confused at first, wondering what he had unleashed by pulling that trigger, but
then realised it was our little joke!

This light-hearted prank took place shortly after Harry Weeks's arrival as the new
Superintendent. It typified the carefree attitude of the AWRE staff.

Knockout competitions were held for all these activities, for which trophies
were presented at the Christmas Dinner in the Canteen. Booth also depicts a
lively and positive existence in what he recalls as 'a very close-knit community spirit'. Happily one of these trophies never left Orford. The winner of the
Horticultural Cup for its final presentation was appropriately the keen gardener,
John Backhouse, who was a leading light in this section's activity. In retirement,
he returned to Orford. He has recalled that part of his duties for AWRE included
preparing and mowing the golf greens as well as ironing the snooker table.

The seriousness of the work being done meant that there was never any alcohol
on the Ness, in theory anyway. Parties there might be, as when a significant
member of staff departed. Then, the lunch hour and activities were abandoned
and in Booth's words, 'we would adjourn to the Jolly Sailor on Orford Quay for a
right royal farewell party. This mainland establishment was also the venue for the
Christmas Eve celebrations'.

As for other activities, shooting for game as well as Revett's wildfowl had its
devotees. Broome recalls the enormous and variously coloured rabbit population and the restoration of arable farming on sections of the airfield encouraged
pheasant and partridge, 'which', as Broome admitted, 'improved the quality of
our shoot immensely!' Fishermen had plenty of sport and some people were
able to sail. Swimming was available for the hardy, off the beach, subject to police
permission. A pseudo-lido was set up on the river, south of the jetty, an arrangement that had its origins in the First World War.

It might be supposed that military occupation was inimical to any serious
re-introduction of agriculture. This was the case until about 1947. Thereafter,
grazing in areas not being used for tests and trials was hired out to local farmers.
One suspects that initially the land may have been fairly unmanaged. In 1953,
reports of a substantial number of cattle and sheep drowned on the site would
confirm this. Broome was at pains to restore this facility and arranged a 364 days

a year let; the area reverted to AWRE on Christmas Day. The licence was offered to farmer Sam Cordle of Chantry Farm, Orford for grazing and the planting of wheat, barley and sugar beet. Booth adds the observation that the cost of mowing the grass on the southern field was sufficient to justify this return to agriculture. With a commendable sense of prudent husbandry and an eye to profitable recycling, Broome paid for the fencing costs involved in enclosing 150 acres of land by selling off surplus material that was lying about the airfields. Notable here were the large number of 5 feet cubed concrete blocks scattered over the fields in 1939 to impede any possible enemy invasion by gliders or aircraft. These he had broken up with explosives and laboriously carted up the coast towards Aldeburgh. The East Suffolk and Norfolk River Board needed to supplement the vast loads of shingle being applied to repair the sea walls, between 1963 and 1966.

Although AWRE were advertising for 'computresses', this was still the age when an office employed typewriters and distributed carbon copies. Broome had a pool of four to five ladies working on the written reports for Aldermaston. He also admits that he found he was drafting the final version of technical and academic research documents; he found the boffins were inexpert in the art of writing English.

Broome comments on the fact that not the least attractive aspect of his job was the immense variety of the work he had to do; 'every day was different', he observed. This variety included the matter of running the ferries. A pair of Second World War period small Ministry of Supply landing craft was in constant use and were no less constantly breaking down. These and subsequent vessels were defined as Landing Craft General Freight and named *LCGF* 1 and 2. A vessel with greater capacity was clearly desirable. The acquisition of the larger *Portree II*, (also labelled *LCGF* 3) a former Isle of Skye car ferry involved Broome in seeing to the rebuild and conversion of the craft in Belfast, where she had 20 feet taken off her bow and the forward bridge removed. There followed an epic voyage via the Caledonian Canal to Lowestoft, where her engines were overhauled. This achievement was evidently a highlight of Broome's nautical experiences. The last boat brought in for ferrying work was *LCGF* 4. She remained in operation through to the present century, now rechristened *Guinevere* by her civilian owners.

For both Broome and his successor, Booth, the reliable running of the ferries was always to prove a major concern. Operating these craft and keeping them running on a steady timetable, with crossings every twenty minutes was in itself a source of constant anxiety. Immediate responsibility for ensuring they operated satisfactorily lay with the young MoS Technical Officer Ron Richardson, who was to work in a variety of capacities on the Ness between 1957 and his retirement in 1989.

Naturally, transportation of materials being delivered to the quay would always take rather longer than any contractor had calculated. The weather could at times seriously interfere with schedules. To those managing the building contracts, anxiety over wind, tide, mists or fog seems to be ever-present. 'It never rains at

Orford Ness', one is quoted as remarking, 'The rain goes across at knee level, and doesn't reach the ground'.

The other worry never far from Broome's mind was security. The climate of 'need to know' meant that most people's knowledge was confined solely to their own specific area of activity. Revett confirms this. 'If you were not directly involved in a weapon, you had no special privileges to enquire into it or ask for details about what it was being tested for. The security was so tight that I couldn't go into one of the test cells if there was a classified item in there, unless I was directly involved in that test.'

Curiosity seems to have been less pronounced than in the more inquisitive post-Cold War era. The people best placed to ask awkward questions were the most familiar with activity on the Ness: the locals in Orford and surrounding villages. Taking no chances however, all references to AWRE were suppressed. The duffle coats issued to those working on site were plain, without any identification initials emblazoned on the back. If asked, personnel were instructed to explain that they worked 'for the ministry'. Exactly which one, they were to leave vague.

Les Armer described one episode with rather more sinister implications. It could have led to just what Aldermaston most feared: a security leak to the popular press. Armer recalls how he was once confronted on Orford Quay by someone he was reluctant to engage in conversation. This was none other that the noted investigative journalist, Chapman Pincher. Armer was returning to his somewhat elderly motorcar, when Pincher approached him, enquiring whether he could say what was going on at the Ness. Armer answered perfectly correctly – for like everyone on site, he had signed the Official Secrets Act – that he feared he was unable to reveal anything. Pincher pointed to a particularly smart vehicle parked nearby. 'Is that yours?' he enquired. There followed a clear hint that suitable information would be rewarded sufficiently generously to enable such a car to be his. 'Well, I can tell you' confided Armer, appearing to be taken in by this irresistible offer and pointing at the herd of cattle grazing on the southern field across the river, 'they are trying to develop radiation-free cows'. This episode will have been common knowledge around the site and perhaps explains his colleague, Don Revett's comment: 'We had to be continuously on our guard over conversations on the mainland, particularly in the local pubs as there were almost certainly agents like Chapman Pincher out there waiting for snippets of information.'

Naturally, Broome had to handle a wide range of visitors. Some had VIP status. One such was the Duke of Edinburgh. In June 1965, he came to Snape to assist the Queen at the opening of the new concert hall. During the visit, the royal couple travelled by AWRE launch No. 2 to Orford. The Duke was eager to see what was going on at the secret station.

Some visitors were less welcome, but were no less Broome's responsibility for attention. These included Russian trawlers, in Revett's words, 'bristling with aerials', which had a habit of mooring in Hollesley Bay to observe what they could of over-flying aircraft. It was Broome's task to decide whether to put the radios on hold, or even suspend operations. Indeed, in his mind security was the major problem facing him, chiefly because he could never anticipate whether a crisis might occur.

The attractions of life on the Ness began to deteriorate rather sharply around Christmas 1967 when AWRE gave staff a warning that a closure of the site was imminent. The reasoning was clear. The Ness was a victim of its own success. The lack of any serious accident demonstrated that environmental testing could safely be carried out on a less remote location. The charismatic leadership of Harry Weeks as Superintendent had earned him a prestigious appointment in Washington. His successor was briefed to expedite the return to Aldermaston and the whole atmosphere of enterprise and challenge evaporated. Broome took early retirement, and his deputy, Oliver Booth held the fort, as the numbers were reduced. The final announcement of a decision to move towards the closure of AWRE on the Ness followed some fifteen months later. Booth will have been very aware that this was inevitable. Running the establishment down took two years, the very last trial being completed on 9 June 1971. Staff not wishing to transfer to Aldermaston were largely found employment either on the Cobra Mist site or at the new Post Office establishment at Martlesham. Oliver Booth reflected that: 'Closing down any establishment is a very involved business and the whole process took some two and a half years. I was the last to leave AWRE Orford Ness and finally closed the gates at 12.00 hours on Friday, 1st October 1971.'

The sixteen years of occupancy by the nuclear boffins and their extensive support teams were quite as significant as any in the story of the Ness. The legacy of these Cold War years was the achievement of a British nuclear deterrent that deterred. The purpose of this very costly work was surely to ensure that unspeakable weapons would be so proficient that they could never be used. The principle was that of MAD – Mutually Assured Destruction. The boffins on the Ness saw to it that the Cold War was never to become a hot one.

To succeeding generations, the vast, gaunt buildings that AWRE erected constitute lasting and unforgettable monuments to this work, their silhouettes on the horizon making a unique contribution to the coastline of Suffolk. The people of Orford had every reason too to be grateful to AWRE. Materially, the town gained its capacious car park, which AWRE handed over as a gift. For its employment and patronage, AWRE played a shrewd game. As regards the reaction of the townsfolk to AWRE, Booth concluded:

During the whole period I was at Orford Ness following the closure announcement, I heard nothing from these people other than regret that the AWRE was leaving. We were able to help the local bodies in many ways, one of which was to lift private boats out of the river, free of charge, using our crane on the quay. When we left we presented this crane to the Orford Town Trust.

Cobra Mist:
Over the Horizon Radar

In 1967, AWRE trials were proceeding but no further building work was evident. Peace and quiet was soon to be rudely interrupted. The Ministry of Defence issued a formal press release on 24 August 1967. A news item duly appeared in the *East Anglian Daily Times*, hinting strongly what was in store:

> The Ministry of Defence and the United States Department of Defence have agreed to collaborate with construction and operation of a Radio Research Station at Orford Ness.
>
> The station will conduct joint research into long-range propagation of radio signals. Orford Ness is uninhabited and closed to the public.
>
> The civil and engineering work will be carried out by British firms ... the station should be ready for practical research within two or three years...

Such information made available to the press was typical of what was to follow over the next eight years: half-truths, deliberate and misleading falsehoods, and optimistic expectations jumbled together in a fashion that could only breed speculation. There was rather more to this project than the authorities were letting on. Certainly, the attempt to provide 'cover stories' for this operation was as futile as the one for the rotating-loop beacon in the inter-war years had been successful. Suspicions arose in the minds of the local population in both Orford and Aldeburgh that all this would cause a major upset to the peace and quiet of what had developed into a rather sedate haven for the retired and well-to-do.

The US government saw that a military presence in Europe was essential for its own security, since it offered a forward position for its defence surveillance. While NATO went some way towards providing for this, it felt it needed additional exclusive facilities. The system that was to evolve into what would ultimately be called COBRA MIST was first conceived for operation from a station at Diyarbakir in Turkey. Perhaps understandably, the uncertain security there persuaded the US to switch to a more reliable ally, Great Britain. No archive evidence to show when this project was first discussed has come to light, but it clearly must have been early in the 1960s. Final agreement on the terms for the construction and operation of the Cobra Mist system was reached in principle with Wilson's government in June 1967.

The choice of Orford Ness will have appealed to the Americans since they were familiar with the place, having already quite recently made an approach to set up a surveillance radar station there. In December 1963, at the height of the second phase of nuclear bomb testing, AWRE was asked if it would permit the establishment of a US radar station on its property designed ostensibly to monitor Soviet nuclear test explosions. This would be located on the shingle site to the north of the trial laboratories and close to the lighthouse. It was an attractive deal. The US would supply all the materials for construction and would train the operating staff. The running cost – estimated at about £25,000 a year – would fall to AWRE.

The feeling was that this would not just provide information useful to AWRE and the UK government, but that it would also indicate cooperative goodwill. On two counts, however, the proposal had to be rejected by interested parties. Access to the lighthouse would be impeded and this was unacceptable to Trinity House. More seriously, the US required what they termed 'security of possession'. This seemed to imply the threat of having a sitting tenant with absolute and undefined rights of access and use. AWRE could not accept this condition.

Meanwhile, the deal for the new station to be built on King's Marsh was of course not a matter over which AWRE or Trinity House could complain. This part of the Ness site had never been sold to AWRE and remained MoD property. Ownership subsequently transferred to the Foreign and Commonwealth Office.

Again this proposal was one that seemed highly advantageous to the MoD. The US government would supply and pay for the vast bulk of the materials to be used and four fifths of the running costs. A reassuring clause in the agreement confirmed that there would be no environmental impact on the local population from the enormous transmission power output involved. Shipping and aviation would need to be warned, but again, it was not anticipated that the consequences would be troublesome. In the event, these impact factors were to give rise to constant anxiety.

The willingness of the US to place the construction contracts with British firms was a major consideration in making this American project so attractive to the UK government. Inevitably, it caused periodic problems, particularly when the timetable began to lag behind schedule. No clear definition of what constituted repair and renewal work led to sharp exchanges and throughout construction and operation, some considerable tension was evident. Furthermore, such pioneering technology necessitated constant changes in plan and specification, which escalated costs and caused inevitable delays. The overall cost to the Americans at the time was somewhere between £35 million and £55 million.

It will almost certainly never be entirely clear what the final total was. The UK government paid out about £1.4 million.

The mighty project about to involve the Ness for the next six years was officially designated by the Americans as the System 441A, operating the AN/FPS-95 OTH (Over The Horizon) radar. Its original code name was SENTINEL FAN, which in fact rather neatly describes both its purpose and its characteristic shape. During 1968, the more secretive MIST replaced FAN. In the summer of 1969, the name by which it was finally described was adopted, COBRA MIST. The prefix COBRA has been attached to a variety of associated projects since.

Information from the Pentagon now reveals exactly what Cobra Mist was intended to achieve:

> The missions of the back-scatter radar were to detect and track aircraft; detect missile and earth satellite vehicle launchings; fulfil current and critical intelligence requirements; and to provide a research and development test bed for determining optimum back-scatter techniques for other operational missions.

Entering into a more detailed description of its purpose, the Pentagon document explains that it was built to 'overlook air and missile activity in Eastern Europe and the western areas of the USSR'. It was hoped to 'detect and track (a) aircraft in flight over the westerly part of the Soviet Union and the Warsaw Pact countries and (b) missile launches from the Northern Fleet Missile Test Centre at Plesetsk'. Further functions included 'aircraft detection and tracking at ranges of 500 to 2,000 nautical miles, corresponding to one-hop ionospheric range from the radar'. It was explained that 'a searchlight mode was provided for high-priority targets whose approximate locations were known a *priori*'. The expectation was that:

> ... these targets could be single aircraft, compact formations of aircraft, or missile launches. In this mode, the radar continuously illuminated a small geographical area to obtain the maximum data rate on the selected targets. As an alternative, a scanning mode was provided, which allowed the radar to search in maximum azimuth and range over any chosen sector of the radar coverage.

The claim made by the Pentagon that Cobra Mist was 'the most powerful and sophisticated backscatter radar of its kind up to that time' cannot be questioned.[1]

The design was based on a system devised by US Naval Research Laboratories. Their concern was with the analysis of oceanic wave patterns. This was clearly related to similar patterns in atmospheric radio waves. The problem that had to be overcome to make the system work was the creation of sufficient transmission power to ensure that the return signal could separate the required message from the massive background 'clutter'.

Cobra Mist would need to exceed 80-decibel response to be successful. With refreshing candour, the Pentagon report affects to admit that it never reached much more than 60. The daunting fact was that hitherto, no radar had been able to achieve more than what was defined as '60 or so decibel sub-clutter visibility'. In an attempt to achieve sufficient signal to noise ratios against the predicted noise background, the Cobra Mist was capable of very high transmitted power output. A peak power of 10 megawatts and an average power of 600 kilowatts were what had been specified.

The main contract for the technical equipment was awarded to the US electronics giant, Radio Corporation of America (RCA). For currency reasons it was handled by the subsidiary, RCA (UK). There was a widely held view that this award owed not a little to political expediency: RCA was believed to be in trouble and to need the work. The construction contract went to Balfour Beatty Ltd, who naturally sub-contracted much of the specialist work. The employment opportunities this afforded the locality were highly significant. The building of the Nuclear Electric Magnox Power Station, Sizewell A, had been completed only some months earlier, and there was a skilled labour force anxious to find construction work. Since the pay rates were generous, this was to be a far from unpopular venture.

The 150-strong labour force was bussed in to Orford each day from the start of building operations in 1968. An extension to the car park had been created for the project's use, a valuable asset for the Orford Town Trust to this day. The fleet of landing craft was kept on. Five in all were employed at one time or another, ferrying men and materials. Work went on day and night, seven days a week. The schedule was extremely tight, and only the weather from time to time brought work to a halt.

The first problem with this site, which in terms of radio transmission was ideal, was the two-fold unsuitability of the land. This was marsh, and a presence of excessive water had to be sorted out. Pumping stations had to be constructed. More importantly, the site had been a dumping ground for ordnance and military rubbish, as well as part of a bomb and rocket range. Intensive bomb disposal work had to be a vital component of the preparation of the several hundred acres involved in the project. This was conducted with speed and success, and no record exists of any accidental explosion. Likewise, both drainage and flood barriers were essential. In 1964, there had been a major breach in the sea wall just south of the Martello Tower, and the threat of flood cannot but have been brought to mind. This work all took time and it was several months before the site was ready for actual building work to start.

It was calculated that about 75,000 tons of material would need to be moved onto the Ness. This prompted very serious misgivings among the local population. In both Aldeburgh and Orford, it was rightly anticipated that there would be enormous volumes of heavy traffic moving through their narrow streets. Local anxieties had to be prevented from growing into outright opposition. The Mayor of Aldeburgh, Air Vice-Marshal John Marson was quoted in the local press: 'Aldeburgh shakes like a jelly when anything big drives through'.

The cudgels were taken up in March 1968 by a resident of Aldeburgh, a retired senior civil servant with contacts in high places. Sir Anthony Wagner also carried the prestigious title of Garter King of Arms. He was President of the Aldeburgh Society, a function of which was to guard the traditional interests of a proud and ancient borough. His letter to the Permanent Under-Secretary of State to the Ministry of Defence warned of 'a seething population', concerned at the likelihood of massive convoys rolling down the high street, and the possibility of the unacceptable disturbance to cherished properties and institutions, notably, the golf club, the yacht club and the internationally renowned annual Aldeburgh Festival. He was concerned that serious damage would be done to roads and drains and was unhappy at the prospect of any relief roads cutting across valued property. Planning permissions for Cobra Mist had been rushed through, at too short notice for any coherent local comments. This was because the MoD, betraying perhaps a degree of geographical unawareness, had contrived to send their applications to West Suffolk County Council, rather than East. 'We do not want to be a little Stansted', wrote Sir Anthony, referring to the difficulties that arose when planning was first sought for the London northern relief airport in Essex.

Sir Anthony came up with a positive suggestion. Why not use the river? Barge traffic both up from Felixstowe and down from Snape Bridge quay could ease pressure on local roads. It was an indication of MoD sensitivity and perhaps of the clout that a civil servant could exercise when dealing with a former colleague that this idea was gratefully and speedily accepted. By April, signs of cooperation and support from Aldeburgh became quite marked. Both yacht club and festival authorities indicated willingness to be unobstructive and indeed, where possible, helpful. The Nature Conservancy also expressed its satisfaction that environmental implications were being recognised. Aldeburgh appeared to be 'on side'.

A few months later, the voice of Orford was to be heard. The local MP was Sir Harwood Harrison, who was always to take a close interest in what went on at the Ness. In October, he was complaining that the contractors were exceeding the agreed volumes of traffic through the town and down to Orford Quay. There was more than a little merit to his objections. By the following February, some 11,200 tons of material had passed through Orford. By barges meanwhile, 5,000 tons came down from Snape and 23,000 tons up from Felixstowe. Charlie Underwood recalls the burden imposed on the patience of the villagers. A queue of lorries would stretch all the way up Quay Street, waiting to unload onto the ferries. The worrying problem was that this was little more than half the anticipated total expected volume.

At this point, a formidable 'big gun' from the Orford community stepped into the fray. The National Archives contains a letter dated 18 May 1969 from the British Embassy in Moscow. It was addressed to the Secretary of State for Defence. Without any preamble or prior explanation, it opens: 'I apologise for worrying you on the subject, but I think you should know that all is not well and that some action is needed if the situation is not to deteriorate further.'The letter soon makes it clear to Denis Healey that the 'subject' in question was not Anglo-Russian relations but Orford and Cobra Mist construction work.

Tom, later Lord Bridges, was unashamedly using his influential position in the diplomatic service to bring pressure to bear over a domestic matter that concerned the village to which in due course he intended to retire. He had a number of grounds for complaint, chiefly over the planning procedure, the secrecy of the project and the excessive traffic. He also expressed his concern at the threat to the natural history of the locality, especially with reference to Havergate Island, lying just to the south of all the building operations. He suggested that the MoD should be creating a new quay away from the town, with its own roadways to service it. He, like Sir Anthony, raised the spectre of Stansted-type local protests.

The files contain no copy of the MoD response. But there were even bigger problems, the contractors were failing to keep up to schedule and the Americans were growing impatient over the delays.

Any MoD station that was occupied by US forces retained a British title and service presence. Hence, it was RAF Bentwaters that hosted the USAF. Likewise, RAF Orford Ness needed to be revived, although any serious military presence was pretty notional. The first C/O of the newly established RAF station was the youthful Flight Lieutenant Alistair Taylor, justly proud and surprised to be given such an important post so early in his career. He rapidly discovered that his 'command' was limited. On his arrival, he himself was the sole member of the RAF contingent. His home-base station was RAF Bawdsey, from which he commuted daily. His delight at being allotted a rather grand staff car for the purpose proved short-lived. The C/O at Bawdsey decided that it was far too grand for so small a unit! Taylor was there for only a few months during the early construction phase. The liaison role was to grow increasingly important. A swelling contingent of RAF personnel followed, with a Wing Commander in charge. Their role was to coordinate the various clearance and other service activities, including dealing with the press.

In July 1969, Sir Charles Cunningham, Director of AWRE, indicated that the requirement to operate on the Ness would shortly be coming to an end. Because they would consequently wish to relinquish their lease, he wanted to discuss the future of the property. It had belonged to AWRE for over a decade now, but clearly the MoD would wish to have first option on purchasing it back. Did they want to do so?

Arriving at this precise moment, the news must have come as a severe irritant. Indeed, the MoD expressed the view that AWRE might have notified them of their intentions somewhat sooner. The shingle 'beach' site might have been more suitable for Cobra Mist had they only known it could have been made available. Now, they were faced with having to decide whether to negotiate a reasonable buy-back price – £160,000 was mentioned – coupled with a debate over whether they really needed it at all, and if so, for what purposes.

The tension in the air was not confined to the higher echelons of the ministries involved. It was evident that Cobra Mist was regarded by AWRE people as the reason for closure. Cliff Cocker was a Supervising Engineer employed by the Ministry of Public Buildings and Works, who worked on the site from September 1969, just as the vast concrete platform that constituted the floor of the main building was being installed. He and his colleagues found themselves meeting the AWRE staff in such places as the canteen and the ferries and became all too aware of the tensions between AWRE staff and those working on Cobra Mist.

Any prospect of the work being completed within a year of commencement was proving increasingly unrealistic, as the programme was falling months behind schedule. The Americans grew impatient and even threatening. The MoD became genuinely concerned that the whole thing might be cancelled.

Throughout this period, Greville Beckerton was employed by Balfour Beatty as their Site Engineer. His job was to ensure that all materials arrived on time and at the right place. He was in a unique position to see the various difficulties that were impeding progress. Constant modifications to the design and building specifications led to inevitable delays and inescapable cost increases. His position also made him appreciate that there were valuable openings for specialist sub-contractors. He set up his own business to lay out the network of timber supports for a metal aerial screen on the north side of the site. He later worked for an American firm, Filtron, a sub-contractor to RCA (UK), which, under the pressure of the task, went bankrupt. His experience in so many areas of the construction gave him special insight into what happened in creating Cobra Mist between 1968 and 1972.

It is quite clear that American impatience arose in part because of the nature of the contract with RCA. The technical equipment for the radar system was being manufactured in the States very much quicker than the buildings to house it. No delay in paying RCA could be entertained. Yet payment was out of order until the material had been accepted.

Conditions in Suffolk made this impossible. As early as March 1969, a secret memo from the MoD to the Ministry of Buildings and Works, responsible for managing the construction contract on its behalf, stressed that it was 'essential that everything be done to relieve the Americans' present anxieties'. These anxieties were not helped by some evident uncertainties over the original contract's terms, in respect of liabilities over any changes in the specifications of the building plans. By September 1969, the US side faced up to the realities of the situation and agreed to slow down the timetable and spread their own budget costs. The MoD had to pay for some of the added expenditure. Both parties accepted that this was all to be preferred to any watering down of the system's specifications. By now, it was understood that it would be 1972 before trial operation could begin, a far cry from the original expectation.

As the Supervising Engineer, Cocker and his steadily expanding team of Monitors and Inspectors had to check the installation and operation of the complex equipment the system required. From the time in 1969 when the great concrete raft of the vast floor was being constructed and the main building was rising on its stilts, Cocker and his men could work only at the pace this was happening. Hence, he personally recalls little sense of pressure arising from US impatience, because it was never being directed at him.

His responsibility was to check that all installations were up to the requirements of safety and operational efficiency. Because of the immense radio frequency (RF) power and high voltages being employed, effective earthing was vital, as well screening and shielding of the transmitters. 'Everything over 18 inches long made of conductive metal had to be earthed', he explained. This required the closest of supervision. If any of the walls round the transmitting hall permitted excessive 'leakage' of signal they had to be replaced.

He was no less involved in construction of the aerial masts. The problem here was the nature of the ground, the subsoil of which comprised large areas of coral crag with empty pits, which all needed to be filled with limitless quantities of concrete. The taller masts supporting the aerial array were made of a series of concrete pipes, which were slotted together up to the required height. A significant number of these remain on site to this day, by now attractively decorated by the lichens and the stains of passing years. The actual aerial cables ran up these pipes, which were installed in a sealed environment of ultra-dry compressed air. This atmosphere would not conduct any RF or electricity. Given that the lesser blacked-back gulls regarded this as their chosen habitat, construction was very far from straightforward.

Provision of compressed air was not the only special facility required. The transmitters were cooled by demineralised water. Because local water was extremely hard, a substantial softening plant had to be installed. Again, this soft water would not conduct electricity. Cocker and his team had to monitor the installation, the operation and the maintenance of all the plant involved. The electrical supply was 'filtered' to prevent power surges. Only on one occasion did a filter explode!

Cocker's responsibility ran to checking on the pumps that operated the sewage outflow into the river. On one occasion, a MoD policeman heard a suspicious clicking noise by the riverbank. He had not realised that a special irrigation sprinkler had been erected to fertilise the marram grass being planted on the river wall to help bind it together. The clicking was the time clock: the unfortunate Constable was suddenly and comprehensively showered. Another worker at this time has described how some of his fellow labourers would break through the perimeter fence to take an illicit recreational swim in the river during their breaks.

Accidents of course were inevitable on such a large-scale project. In 1971, fire broke out in the contractors' cabins and the Orford Fire Brigade was summoned. Charlie Underwood was a member of the crew that successfully dealt with a blaze that, with large propane gas cylinders involved, could have been quite serious. There were big explosions, which those on the mainland recall as representing an entertaining fireworks display. Some of the equipment destroyed contained radioactive materials. The appearance of a hastily summoned special hazardous substances team in its sinister-looking garb caused some alarm. Happily, nobody was injured, and the firemen's efforts were recognised by the award of the Chief Fire Officer's Commendation for their work.

Security was naturally very tight, but it seems that the 'privacy' of the site continued to prove its worth. The CND protesters who had rather sadly failed to get even close to the AWRE fences in 1964, threatened to repeat their efforts against Cobra Mist. Rumour spread that an incursion was planned. Cocker does not recall the exact date, but remembers the place being on high alert, with county and MoD police guarding the quay and lining the roof of the main building. No one appeared. Suddenly, an emergency report: a party waving banners had somehow emerged on the roadway leading over the Chinese Wall. The 'protesters' turned out to be a mischievous group of contractors' men, airing their demands: 'More sex and free beer'. Alas, neither was ever in plentiful supply on the Ness. Somehow, threats of serious protests seemed to evaporate. Indeed, work on Cobra Mist was positively welcome in the community, and when the Royal Corps of Transport brought up an army landing craft, *Eden*, to operate the ferry while the regular boat, *Portree*, was undergoing survey and repair, the lusty young squaddies who resided aboard just added to the attractiveness of the whole project in the minds of the young maidens of Orford.

The Pentagon Cobra Mist files describe in technical detail just what Beckerton and his fellow engineers and builders were erecting:

System 441A comprised a huge fan-shaped array of aerials supported on masts from 42 feet to 195 feet high. The antenna consisted of 18 'log-period' [sic] antenna strings, which radiated like spokes in a wheel from a central hub. Each string was 2,200 feet in length and carried both horizontal and vertical radiating dipoles. The strings were separated by 7 degrees in angle and they thus occupied a 119-degree sector of a circle. The complete antenna was located over a wire-mesh ground screen, which extended beyond the strings in the propagation direction, to an underground chamber, lined with copper, in front of the array. [This was called the Ballun Pit.]

This aerial was a mammoth, fan-shaped spider's web of antennae, occupying around 135 acres in extent, and tilting down from the landward side towards the sea (see Plate Section). In 1969, Beckerton became the sub-contractor for building an important element in this construction, a single filament aluminium wire earth screen to reflect the radar pulse signals and complement the vitally important natural reflection caused by the sea a few hundred yards to the east. This job was to take eighteen months to complete and involved erecting wooden posts with the many miles of wire stretched between them. The environment for making such a structure was far from friendly. The capacity for shingle and sand to shift uncooperatively was just one of a number of handicaps faced by contractors. The fact that every mast or stay required intensive pile driving to secure it just added to the time taken. In order to obtain sufficient tension on the wire, tractors fitted with specially designed tyres had to be used.

The so-called 'blockhouse' building was the last part of the system to be erected. It is the sole element that has survived, apart, that is, from the scars and stains in the marsh and parts of the mat of wire that remain embedded there. Mindful of the floods of 1953 and 1964, the building was on stilts 8 feet above ground level. To ensure total security from any sort of intelligence penetration, it was given three skins of wall and provided with no external windows. To accommodate the banks of transmitters, receivers and processing computers, as well as the operational control and other more domestic facilities, it was built on two floors. Its flat roof and dull grey colour does make it appear like some gigantic wartime pillbox. Its forecourt contained some brick buildings, for stores and for emergency generators. The ground was – and largely remains – paved with railway sleepers, which were seen as the ideal material for covering the marshy surface.

Security, provided once the system was running by armed US Marine guards, was highly visible. A 6-foot fence surrounded the entire 700-acre site. Surveillance was such that a 40-yard *cordon sanitaire* was maintained beyond this fence. Intruders would have found it extremely difficult to penetrate the defences surrounding Cobra Mist.

A further barrier was provided. A local contractor, C.A. Blackwell, was hired to create a shingle bank. His men worked in close liaison with the RAF bomb disposal team to ensure that the shingle was free of ordnance. It seems that they succeeded in making it so. No one is recorded as having been hurt in this work, apart from one man, who ill advisedly leapt from his Land Rover without looking to see that the drop was some 5 feet. To his dismay and his colleagues' immense amusement, he emerged with a broken leg.

Access from Orford was by a roadway from the Ness jetty and the landing craft ramp, running parallel with the river. Initially this road was paved with sleepers. A new and handsome bridge lifted the road over the reconstructed Chinese Wall, the view from which is still one of the most advantageous in the whole of Orford Ness. A second and similar bridge still spans the drainage ditch by the main entry gates to the site. Ditch, bridge, fence and shingle bank, the whole scene is somewhat reminiscent of the site of a medieval castle.

Work on construction continued through 1970 and into 1971. It was non-stop, seven days a week, and, with the whole site floodlit, operated right round the clock. Apart from severe weather conditions, only one thing in Beckerton's experience would bring work to a temporary halt. These were the glory days of Ipswich Town Football Club, shortly after Alf Ramsay's departure. A home match would cause all operations to cease.

Beckerton leaves a happy impression of his life working with Cobra Mist on the Ness. He recalls how even hardy labourers became entranced by the wildlife all around them. The camaraderie and nature of the site were such that these were very special times. There was a great feeling of 'let's get the job done'. Worry at the Russian threat at this time was very real. One particular feature of work was the means of transport adopted on site. Many men used old 'banger' cars, scrap at £25, driven around until they disintegrated and then bulldozed into the shingle. Often they were run on their rims.

A particular creature mentioned only by Cliff Cocker was the handsome and dangerous pest, the coypu. A species introduced from South America for its pelt, they were at this time proving harmful both to other native animals and to the integrity of river walls into which they tunnelled. They found happy accommodation under the contractors' huts and cabins. A policy of eradication has since removed the coypu threat from the Ness.

TRANSPORT SOLUTIONS

Greville Beckerton confirms that access for materials was now largely by river, from Snape or Felixstowe. The experiment of trying to land loads from Army landing craft directly onto the beach was rapidly suspended when it was realised that unless tide and sea conditions were ideal it could not be done and hence much valuable time was being wasted.

Despite the anxieties of the Aldeburgh townsfolk, some loads of heavy plant were brought down past the Martello Tower and along the shingle track. They would be conveyed on trailers fitted with vast low-pressure tyres, designed to avoid any damage to roadways as well as to negotiate the soft shingle.

In 1964, a major breach in the sea wall south of the Martello Tower led to substantial flooding of the Lantern Marsh. In 1953, both river walls at Orford and the sea wall south of Aldeburgh had breached, but railways were not seen as providing a means of introducing repair materials. It was to mark the end of the old military 1918 line. Repair to the damage to the sea wall from Aldeburgh was the responsibility of the East Suffolk and Norfolk River Authority (ES&NRA). Bill Roberts was the engineer in charge. In 1953 he hired a fleet of bulldozers to restore the shingle. When eleven years later another major breach occurred a more measured programme of reconstruction was adopted. Roberts was again in charge. Repairs involved the transfer of some 300,000 cubic yards of shingle to reinforce the area around the Martello Tower and the shore for some 3 miles towards the lighthouse.

This time a new railway was introduced to shift materials. In October 1964 the River Authority ordered no fewer than four small diesel locomotives from Motor Rail Ltd of Bedford. These were standard four-wheel machines, fitted with Dorman motors, and weighing some 4 tons each. They were painted in a green livery with the letters ES&NRA on their sides. At the same time, at least forty side-tipping hopper wagons, four of them fitted with hand brakes, were ordered from Allens of Tipton, Staffordshire. This provided for four distinct rakes of ten. The repair work continued along the vulnerable stretches of coastline throughout 1965 and '66. The rolling stock was removed on completion of the work and transferred to Haddiscoe in Norfolk for work on riverbanks.

The works in conjunction with Cobra Mist brought the railway back into use to reinforce the riverbank in order to prevent flooding of the site. Work began in July 1969, with the chief contractors, Balfour Beatty, acquiring three of the original Haddiscoe locomotives to shift clay and gravel. A mile long track stretched from the Cobra Mist building site up towards Aldeburgh.

Repair work was not the only function served by this newly re-laid line. At the same time, the American authorities were very unhappy with the continuing presence of the wrecked collier, SS *Kentbrook*, which went aground back in February 1954. Seventeen years later, it was still lying there, exactly opposite their new project. It was feared that it might interfere with their transmissions. It was decided to cut it up into small sections for scrap. The railway was used for transporting it to a collection point north of the Martello Tower at Slaughden.

Once the riverbank repairs were complete, the MoD appears to have made no effort to rescue its equipment, which was left to decay, abandoned to the elements, which could be very damaging. One loco was left in the salt marsh, and soon began to deteriorate beyond recovery. A number of hopper wagons littered the river bank, but the other two engines fared much better. They were 'parked' on dry land on a short spur, a few yards north of Cobra Mist. A decade on, and a slightly more responsible owner appeared, the Property Services Agency, which assumed responsibility for all such items from the DoE and MoD. On discovering that it was the proud owner of a railway, it promptly sought to find a purchaser, advertising in the local press.

The immediate destination for the two survivors was to be the Imperial War Museum at Duxford. Given grand names, appropriately *Orfordness* and *Thorpeness*, they were briefly in service to transport visitors before finding a final resting place at the Suffolk Transport Museum by Lowestoft, where they continue useful work, hauling visitors round a small circuit of track.

An aerial photograph taken in 1971 shows the principal means of shifting heavy loads. There was a small jetty on the river at the spot called Pig Pail. Among the consignments delivered this way were the railway sleepers, which were stacked in gigantic piles in front of the Snape Maltings buildings, awaiting transit. Typical of the maddening hold-ups that had to be faced was when the load from across the North Sea arrived it was so closely packed together in the hold of the steamer that no crane could be used to extract them.

PROGRESS SLOWS

Another difficulty arose with the making of the very high-grade cement that the contracts stipulated. It was hoped that pre-mixed cylinders of cement might speed things up but these were found to be too unwieldy to be workable and too inconsistent in quality.

If the contractors had to contend with tiresome irritations, the government were facing issues that gave rise to serious debate up to Cabinet level. The path to a successful completion of a working Cobra Mist was proving far from smooth.

The original agreement with the US government had reassured the MoD that there would be no environmental threats to the local population arising from the operation of very powerful electronic equipment. Serious doubts were emerging, however, that various forms of radiation could result once the system was in full operation. The issue that faced the UK government was what to do about this: it would be impossible and wrong not to notify the public. However, such warnings would inevitably arouse the unhealthy interest of the press. This in turn could well undermine support for an American venture at a time when the Vietnam War was already damaging confidence in the United States. The MoD was determined to sustain the cover story, that Cobra Mist was no more than an advanced experimental radio transmission system. Any suspicion that it was more than this could well have had a serious impact on popular sympathy for it. The controversial issue now emerging was this: were Cobra Mist to constitute any sort of strategic military installation which might antagonise the Russians, Orford itself might immediately become a legitimate target for Soviet retaliation. This was all the more sensitive at a time when Strategic Arms Limitations Treaties (SALT) were being negotiated.

In the autumn of 1970, a full year before any attempts at preliminary operation of the radar, the first serious query about radiation was raised, initially over the possible interference with television and radio signals in East Suffolk. While the military might regard this as trivial in the circumstances of the Cold War, no politicians could afford to duck the issue, with its direct impact on the electorate.

By 10 November 1970, it was admitted that there could be quite serious problems of interference, although this was as yet no more than a possibility. Early the following year, a question was raised about whether there would be any impact from radiation on heart pacemakers? By now, the effects on aircraft flying in the locality and on shipping and smaller craft in what was a popular and well-frequented area for recreational as well as commercial purposes had to be understood. Suitable warning notices could scarcely avoid exciting again the interest of the press. To say nothing – a proposition that had its backers – would have been immoral. To say anything could spark unwelcome attention. By the spring of 1971, the media in general was starting to show tiresome interest.

Cobra Mist was an exclusively Anglo-American enterprise, with no immediate link with NATO. When operating, it would inevitably have had an impact on European air space of our allies but without their knowledge or say-so, Sweden in particular was likely to have been affected.

The cover story was maintained. Here was a station researching 'long-range radio propagation': ionospheric radio research, in other words. This explanation was exactly the same as that given during Watson Watt's radar trials.

Preliminary trials began as early as March 1971, with tentative full power tests to follow in July. These were early days, but TV interference seemed manageable. However, the local population was very much on its guard and the blowing of a cathode ray tube, in those days a very much more common occurrence than subsequently, was immediately and directly attributed to the machinations of the Yanks down on the Ness. The correspondence of a Mrs Strowger of Lee Road, Aldeburgh, claiming for an entire new TV set, complete with a quotation from Messrs G.A. Hubbard Ltd of Saxmundham, appears in the files of the National Archives. Perhaps it was something of a 'try on', but the very fact that this claim has been lodged in files as part of the Public Record suggests that the MoD was happy to settle such matters without undue fuss: a new set was duly provided. The authorities could not appear to be taking a casual attitude to this issue however, and commissioned British Telecom to investigate the idea of placing protective filters on TV receiver circuits to protect them from destructive surges.

The matter of the pacemakers was far more serious and sensitive, chiefly because so much was at risk. It was taken up by the American authorities and subjected to a research programme at the Brooks Air Force Base in Texas. The initial thinking was that the threat of radiation was directional: the people at potentially serious risk would be mariners sailing close inshore immediately opposite the transmitting aerials. It so happened that Air Vice-Marshal Jackson, RAF, was a consultant and expert on cardiac arrest. His recommendation, in the light of US research, was that only one type of pacemaker was liable to any trouble, the Meditonic 5841, and that so long as all users of this particular type were warned, and kept clear of the locality, no threat existed. What should be admitted in the notices to mariners and airmen, which didn't say more than was strictly needed? Anything that might persuade people to take the warnings seriously would appear too alarmist, arousing public apprehension and generating a torrent of press speculation. On the other hand, a bland statement, seemingly discounting any significant possibility of danger, could lead to no one taking any notice of the warning at all. No one quite knew for sure just what hazards there might be once the system was running at full power.

In early 1971, the first draft of the notice to aircraft spoke of some potential radio interference 'of short duration, within a radius of 3 miles and up to an altitude of 6,500 feet'. This interference could cause damage to HF/MF receiving equipment, the notice went on, adding, somewhat alarmingly, the possibility of 'triggering the accidental operation of electrically initiated explosive charges'. The parallel notice to mariners offered clear and public warnings of possible hazard within a defined distance of the station. It directly implied that the dangers generated by the transmission would be similar to those created by any normal electric storm.

Perhaps these matters caused more anxiety than they warranted. While there were tales of local offshore boats seeing their aerials spark and flash, no serious damage was ever reported. As for aircraft, amateur pilots entering the Ness airspace were subject to RAF Bentwaters traffic control. One such aviator who used to fly over the site at quite low level at this time has recalled that he seemed to be under no restriction over the course he took. He was certainly not made aware of any possible danger.

Soon a decision had to be taken over the contents of general press statements about possible threats to public safety. Since low power signals only were by now being tested, no great immediate problem was anticipated and it was decided to issue no warning at all and avoid arousing needless curiosity.

Parliamentary questions however were always liable to be asked, and while there was not exactly a conspiracy of silence, certainly a policy of very low-key reassurance was evident. This policy was not easily sustained however. The US Embassy stepped in, insisting that it should vet any press statements. Its intention was positively to suppress any alarmist stories.

The press release of 26 February 1971 was bland enough to satisfy everyone and no one. A single-page document was issued, confirming the story of 'research into problems of long-range radio propagation'. It went on: 'There is no question of any biological hazard outside the boundaries of the station. The remote possibility exists of occasional mild electrical side-effects in the near vicinity of the high-powered radio system.' The release confirmed that notices to airmen and mariners were being issued by the Department of Trade. The statement concluded:

> Though extremely unlikely to occur, the possible side effects are as follows:
> – Mild and harmless electrical shocks from metal rigging or metal structures, accompanied by slight sparking.
> – Damage to radio equipment if connected to an external aerial.
> – The spontaneous operation of certain kinds of electrically initiated devices which are normally carried only by commercial and military vessels and aircraft.

The ringing of alarm bells could not long be avoided, for in March 1971 the *Observer* newspaper published an article by the investigative journalist, Peter Wilbey. With an accompanying photograph, a headline blazed the message: 'It's getting a bit like Doomwatch around here'. (*Doomwatch* was a contemporary sci-fi television programme.) 'Local residents claim it's an early-warning station, which by using OTH will give better warning of any Russian nuclear attack', he wrote. A local inhabitant was quoted: 'I don't think the scientists themselves know what the effects will be yet.'

The genie was out of the bottle. Worse was to come, some of it caused by an extraordinarily careless American lapse in security. In no time, intrusion by television was threatened. A request came from the BBC to make a TV documentary. A long debate arose in MoD circles as to the pros and cons of permitting cameras anywhere near the place. To keep them out could provoke even greater curiosity; the solution lay in careful and discreet handling.

The senior RAF spokesman contrived to manage brief and controlled access while hiding behind the not unreasonable screen of security requirements. He sent the BBC team away with 'an answer answerless'. Wing Commander Donald Evans was the C/O at what was grandly termed 'RAF Orford Ness'. It was the first time such a description had been publicly attached to the place since 1947 and it was to be the last. The archive memo records that he earned high commendation for the skill with which he charmed his way through what could have been a difficult assignment.

A week or so after transmission of the ensuing programme in early May 1971, the *Daily Telegraph* published a large aerial photograph of the Cobra Mist station, similar to that in the Plate Section. Low-flying aircraft had no trouble in entering the supposedly restricted airspace. An even more serious breach of confidentiality arose in an article in the *Daily Express* on 1 June. Chapman Pincher, the investigative journalist specialising in defence issues, already described as displaying persistent curiosity about the Ness, was at it once again. His argued that Cobra Mist would provide Russia with a valid reason for retaliatory attack. He wrongly claimed that this new facility could give the US surveillance capability for the whole of the USSR and that it was contrary to our treaty obligations. This argument created mounting suspicion and anxiety among local inhabitants, in just the manner the government was most determined to avoid.

The most serious gaffe in sustaining any credence in the radio research cover story, still being stoutly maintained, arose in December 1971. An article appeared in the prestigious US journal, *Aviation Week*. Describing Cobra Mist, it quoted a Congressional Committee Minute on the progress of the project, which accidentally failed to delete the passage that described its true purpose. A hastily convened MoD meeting was held to decide what to do. It was agreed that the cover story should stand and that the policy would be to 'bluff it out'. It was debated whether to employ Chapman Pincher (no less!) to cover over the cover up.

The rumour and counter-rumour continued throughout 1972. Perhaps the most disturbing pieces to appear in the press were articles in both *The Times* and *Daily Telegraph* on 28 August 1972, both quoting 'US sources'. It stated that the System 441L was now operating to detect Soviet aircraft. They specifically raised the issue of the SALT agreements and hinted that, over the cost of the whole thing, the American government might even then be considering its abandonment. The significance of this transatlantic leak – if such it was – was the use of the description 441L, which was the code for fully operational radar, rather than 441A, which was the research and trial label. This in itself hinted at a significant breach in security. In MoD minds it further suggested a mounting lack of Anglo-American cohesion. New bland statements were issued and reassuring answers prepared for 'friendly' Parliamentary questions.

The trouble was that the cover story in itself was posing its own problems. One arose over public advertisements for the recruiting of suitable technicians for the maintenance of the radar equipment in the blockhouse building. RCA (UK) was required to sustain the fiction that it was radio research they were conducting. They could therefore never advertise for the radar specialists they needed.

With full power trials starting in the late summer of 1971, there were now about 200 service personnel on the site. The bulk of them were American. The nearby RAF Bentwaters was a fully operational USAF station, which acted as their base. The RAF detachment, involved in liaison duties, grew to about forty-five, which included crewmen for the ferries. They were all attached to RAF Bawdsey or briefly, to Martlesham. In addition there were around 100 UK civilian technicians and operators, employed by the MoD. The contractors' staff still on site numbered about 130. The Ness was indeed a hive of activity.

LOST IN THE MIST

Despite all the troubles it was causing, there is good evidence that the British government was keen for Cobra Mist to work and valued the input the MoD might expect to gain from its success. The Under Secretary of State at the MoD wrote to his boss: '... if the system works as it is meant to, it will be of inestimable value.' This letter was dated 5 November 1971. The trouble was that the system seemed very reluctant to work. By mid 1972, the US authorities were beginning to look distinctly disenchanted.

The year had begun badly. There was a crass example of seriously crossed wires, when a projected MoD exercise, codenamed POLEX, came to everyone's notice. This was intended to trial a system for supplying fuel across an open beach in support of a military landing. It was very much a successor to PLUTO, the supply system for the Normandy landings in 1944. The Ness was seen as a highly suitable location. In the very nick of time, the whole thing was aborted. It seemed to have escaped the organisers' notice just how close this would be to Cobra Mist transmissions. It was also felt that the local Orford population had enough on their plates without such a potentially dangerous exercise on their very doorstep.

A secret memo of 19 September 1972, to be seen as a briefing document for any high-ranking official visitors, presented an outline history of the Cobra Mist project to date. Among a number of admissions were references to the brittle nature of the cover story, the worrying problem of making the system work at all, and an acceptance of the possibly embarrassing question of a breach in SALT commitments. It had to be recognised that the US might well back out and leave the whole operation in UK hands – at UK expense. The memo quoted a rough estimate of the cost involved in remedying the perceived causes of the current failure: the figure was reckoned at £12 million.

There was indeed increasing evidence of American impatience. Communications between the two governments over the future of the project were growing obviously more strained. The MoD was being given no clear idea of what the long-term prospects and plans for Cobra Mist might be and Edward

Heath's government was disinclined to offer any sort of financial commitment. The memos of the day suggested that the UK had already set up its own OTH radar research stations, with mention of current projects in both Hong Kong and Cyprus. The latter would be British-built, which with the Americans, operated forward-scatter coverage across southern Russia and China, with its US receiving station on Okinawa. The occupation of Allied military bases on Cyprus posed increasing diplomatic problems from 1964. Ten years later, with the Turkish invasion of the island, the issue was even more acute, but in 1972, the British made it clear that they had no need to rely on Cobra Mist.

As for any record of the actual operation of the OTH system 441A, a brief Pentagon statement has already been mentioned. The equipment was in place and ready for trial by September 1971, but so far no meaningful signal returns were being received. The report admits that 'most of the problems appeared to be in the receiver and signal processing areas, since it was known that the transmitters were working and the antenna was radiating at expected power levels.' Attempts were made to get things ready for the next phase, a crucial test for what was called the 'Reliability and Maintenance Trials'. These were all part of the preliminary programme in preparation for the operational handover. RCA fitted what were described as 'modification kits for the screen regulators'.

John Backhouse enters the story yet again here. Following his realisation that work for AWRE was running out, he moved up the island to take up employment with RCA (UK). Initially, he was involved in the assembly of the large concrete tubes that had to be glued together to form the larger aerial masts Some of them already needed some repair work, which proved only possible during daylight hours. Backhouse latterly was part of the maintenance and repair team, operating an eleven-hour day to install and sustain the equipment.

There were mounting delays – the result of which was that the final acceptance process of the radar was not begun until 9 February 1972, with a target date for what was termed 'the system turnover' set for 1 July 1972. A fudge was agreed. By combining various evaluation and design verification tests, it was hoped to telescope these processes and have the whole thing satisfactorily in operation by January 1973.

By 29 December 1972, it was evident that the 'background noise' problem which obscured any discernible signal had not been cured. A crisis meeting was held. It was agreed to assemble a joint US/UK team of OTH radar experts to determine the cause of this failure and recommend what they termed 'appropriate fixes'. This Cobra Mist Scientific Assessment Committee included academic and service experts from Britain and America, including Ramsay Shearman, Professor of Electronical Engineering at Birmingham. It was chaired by a Dr M. Balser of the American Xonic Corporation, and included British radar specialists from both Cambridge and Malvern. The C/O from RAF Orford Ness, Wing Commander D.R.J. Evans was included as Secretary.

Professor Shearman was a radar expert of the finest provenance. For a number of years, he was employed at the Radio Research Laboratory, specialising in wave theory and ionospheric researches, and had as his supervisor none other than Arnold Wilkins of radar fame.

The report the committee drew up for the US and UK governments produced four pressing recommendations in some attempt to keep the project alive. Material that was declassified some thirty years later demonstrates how detailed was their analysis of the problem. It is equally fair to conclude that while they were very unsure as to the causes of failure, they were very anxious to conceal the fact. This is demonstrated by a very remarkable quotation from Shakespeare's *The Tempest* with which they concluded their list of proposals.

> This is as strange a maze as e'er men trod.
> And there is in this business more than nature
> Was ever conduct of: some oracle
> Must rectify our knowledge.

The finest minds in the field were prepared to admit that only an oracle could resolve their problem. Perhaps this was deliberate obfuscation. A brief summary of this report concludes:

> Much work was done to establish the source of this noise and to try and elimi-
> nate it, but the source of the difficulty that caused Cobra Mist's demise was
> never found. The noise problem could be overcome by certain system modifi-
> cations ... with limitations on its expected capabilities. In the end it was decided
> that the economics of the situation were unjustifiable and the project was
> terminated. On 19th June 1973, the UK was advised that the US had decided to
> close down the site and de-activate the system on 30th June 1973.

Why did Cobra Mist system 441A fail to become the operational system 441L? Why did it prove so hard to cure the faults in it? A host of possible explanations have been put forward over the years. Practical and physical factors, like the wet nature of the marshland site, may well have caused corrosion and deterioration of the wiring or chemical reaction to the various materials being used, which may have affected reception. Certainly, the damp/wet issue is one BBC engineers inheriting the site have subsequently taken very seriously. Their pumps operate without ceasing, in order to lower the water table so that all their cables and connectors are secure.

Another possible technical problem arose over effective screening within a single building of the signals between transmitters and receivers. A similar diffi-culty arose in the early days of Watson Watt's radar experiments. It was for this reason that the two buildings used for these purposes on the Ness site were 150 yards apart. Certainly, subsequent OTH radar stations in the US placed the receivers up to 100 miles from the transmitters.

Perhaps various political issues with reference to arms reduction treaties (SALT) and NATO left the US administration disinclined to pour even more money into a project too sensitive to warrant the expense. Perhaps the closure was part of a diplomatic tactic; abandonment was a bargaining counter with the Russians. Cocker commented: 'We knew the Russians knew what we knew.'

This view is supported too by an article that appeared shortly after closure, in the November 1974 issue of the prestigious *New Scientist* magazine. The author, Peter Laurie, explained that it would be inconceivable that the Russians were unaware of the enormous bursts of radio signals being beamed over their territory.

As to discovering the precise location of the technical failure in the system, a strong hint is provided by the Pentagon report of September 1972. They could transmit, but the computers could not decipher. Computer technology of the late '60s was simply not up to the job. A visitor to the Ness had worked some years later on OTH at the Pentagon. He was adamant in his judgement: the principal behind Cobra Mist technology was fine. It worked and still works. It just needed computers with the capacity to cope with the enormous demands required of them. Indeed, it might be, he argued, that it was too efficient, capable of detecting more information than it could handle.

If, by chance, conditions in the ionosphere had changed radically during the late '60s, reflections off it would have become unreliable. It is unlikely that at this juncture there was very much the Americans could have done. Another informant has confirmed that the Russians were very adept at jamming any troublesome signals. He had been responsible for setting up BBC World Service shortwave transmission to Russia from Skelton, Cumbria, during this period. It was routinely jammed by a counter-signal. Such jamming would have had an effect similar to a disturbed ionospheric layer.

All the above causes for the abandonment of the enterprise are valid possibilities, but why did the assessment committee members allow themselves to appear so feeble? Was it perhaps because they could not admit to their true ambition for Cobra Mist? Reports from US sources indicate that Cobra Mist's transmitter was faultless and that the power achieved was up to the required level of 90 decibels. What is also evident is that it was so sensitive that it was picking terrestrial signals in plenty but also astronomical radio noise. It was effectively operating as a radio telescope. All these signals combined to create an undecipherable complex of noise.

The only obvious solution would have been to lower the power of the signal. Why was this option rejected? A very feasible explanation lies in the politics of US intelligence gathering, which has persisted into the twenty-first century. The US Air Force and CIA were and are bitter rivals. The latter controlled the satellite programme, which at the time was loaded with practical problems. The Pentagon's USAF wished to acquire via Cobra Mist the facility to monitor not only what was in the air – missiles and aircraft – but what was on the ground, and thereby steal the CIA's thunder. To operate it at a reduced level of performance would have been to miss its point. It would have reverted to just another successful aerial surveillance system, which they already were operating. Cobra Mist was just too ambitious to work as hoped.

This interpretation of events is mere speculation, of course, and no concrete evidence exists to confirm it. However, it does explain to a great extent why the Americans so summarily washed their hands of the whole project, and appeared to cover up their explanation for this decision.

As a footnote to the 'failure' of 441L on the Ness, it can be argued that the various protagonists in this venture emerged happy enough. The US had valuable trial experience; the UK had important employment in a locality that needed it and at modest cost; the Russians, who happily parked their 'spy' trawlers off the coast to monitor what was happening, could feel satisfaction at the thwarting of their foe's intentions.

Writing at the time of the thirtieth anniversary of the decision to abandon the project, Dennis Skeat recalled the day he learnt that he was about to lose his job. Skeat describes how very rewarding it was for him and his colleagues to be working on Cobra Mist, both for the good wages paid and for the advanced technical experience gained. Operating in three shifts, they were, in his words, 'a merry band of workers'. He provided a unique account of 'the sombre building', with the radar transmitters 'housed in six large metal-cased rooms with internal observation windows'. The secrecy and the daunting power output involved made it seem like Fort Knox. Several locks had to be manipulated before a giant door swung open. This could only be done when the power was turned off. If a fault occurred which could not be rectified from the control panel, it was a technician's job to investigate the problem. A brave soul would be 'locked in' with the lights out, to determine the source of an electrical arc or possible component burnt-out. Other technicians worked on receiver maintenance or operated the radar consoles. Significantly, he hints at the computer problem. 'Those who understood them worked on computers, which analysed the echoes returning from possible targets.' They were given no reason to doubt that it was working, and that giving up Christmas Day or New Year's Eve when on shift was indeed worthwhile.

Only whispers filtered through to the men that all was not well. They knew that a joint US/UK Scientific Committee was meeting regularly up until May 1973, when it issued a series of recommendations for enhancing the performance of the system. Skeat explains that early one morning in June 1973 a technician boarded the mini-bus at Ipswich for the journey to Orford. Ten minutes later he glanced at his newspaper – its headlines announced the immediate closure of the Orford Ness secret radar site! No warnings, no meetings, no consultation – stunned silence on the bus. Forty minutes later at Orford, the RCA management denied any such action would take place.

Skeat has described the tense stand-off that followed. The day-shift workers were very dissatisfied with the situation and anarchy momentarily raised its head. The red emergency button, used to shut down the radar, was pushed and the transmitters summarily ground to a halt. Managers raced down from their offices and demanded that work continue. After technicians expressed their thoughts in no uncertain terms it was agreed to bring the transmitters up to working order. By midday it was official – Cobra Mist was to cease operation. On 29 June it was confirmed publicly by the Ministry of Defence and by midnight on 30 June, Cobra Mist closed down. This was a devastating blow to all who worked there.

Dramatic scenes resulted, as the press rushed in to report the ensuing staff and management confrontations. The day-shift workers were approached by a crowd of what were taken to be tourists who magically transformed into reporters from the national daily press.

These events seem in retrospect to indicate seriously flawed management and lack of administrative coordination. Gordon Kinsey commented that:

> On 3 July 1973, after their demands regarding notice, guarantees of alternative employment, enhanced redundancy pay and relocation grants, had not been met, the staff staged a 'sit-in' strike. Employees were told by officials of the Society of Scientific, Technical and Management Staff that their negotiations with RCA, who had supplied the bulk of the equipment, had failed.

Three days later, angry technicians besieged the Cobra Mist station. It was claimed that two of their number had locked themselves inside the building. A decision was taken to establish eight-hour long pickets on Orford Quay, which resulted in extended redundancy agreements being offered by their employers, RCA:

> Some days later an announcement in the papers stated that disgusted technicians at Orford Ness Early Warning [sic] had reluctantly accepted a redundancy agreement with their employers, RCA. The company extended the notice period by paying an additional sum for eight weeks while the men were still unemployed and much feeling was expressed, as it was virtually impossible for the men to find alternative work in the area.

In the House of Commons Mr Ian Mikardo MP expressed his anger at the poor treatment of the workforce and loss of the equipment.

The Defence Secretary, Lord Carrington, had to deny that there was any sort of conspiracy between America and Russia, which might be at UK expense. Nor did this decision provide evidence of some sort of sinister new Russian jamming device. In the Commons, the local MP, Sir Harwood Harrison, who had already taken such interest in the project, now sang a rather different tune. 'This staggers me' he fumed, referring to the closure, 'considering that there was so much rush and hustle to get this project finished only three years ago.' He announced that he would be seeing the Minister 'to see if the installation is going to be left to go to rack and ruin'.

Feelings in the locality were, in the short-term, very mixed. Local employment had benefited from the existence of such a very large enterprise. The Orford Trust revenues had gained much from the rents charged for the quay and the slipway ramp, as well as the car park and other buildings. Prudently, the US authorities at RAF Bentwaters quickly stepped in to offer alternative employment opportunities for around forty locals.

An article in the *New Scientist*, just a year later, speculates over what was to be made of this 'cloak and dagger' episode. Appreciating that Britain's Cold War antagonists were well aware of what Cobra Mist was about, it wondered whether it had been little more than 'another expensive toy for the military'. Equally, there was an argument that it was a good thing 'that the Super Powers should know as much as possible about each other's capabilities, and it is presumably useful that a small amount of tax-payers' money should be spent to this end.'

The aerial array was dismantled, with the dipoles disposed of in the locality, to be seen, in Gordon Kinsey's words, 'in many a local garden, as pea and bean sticks and supports for the taller flowers'. Many of the larger concrete posts were left in the shingle, to gather colourful crops of lichen. With the equipment shipped back across the Atlantic, an empty shell of a building was left, with its vast forecourt of railway sleepers.

While speculation arose as to what might be done with the remnants of Cobra Mist structures. The solution to the problems over what to do with the property as a whole would exercise the MoD planners for the next twenty years.

Was Cobra Mist the end of OTH radar? During the period that followed the Orford Ness experiment, various long-range stations continued to operate. Satellite surveillance made their need less acute, but US authorities came to find it useful for monitoring shipping round their coast, especially where drug smuggling is concerned. Australia has operated a successful JORN system. The most significant development, however, has been French. Built to the north of Paris, NOSTRADAMUS became the nearest in style to Cobra Mist. Its vast aerial comprises nearly 300 Pan-Polar arrays, with its transmitters and receiver equipment located below ground in three 80-metre length tunnels. It surveys both the Atlantic and Mediterranean. It can claim to detect aircraft at up to a range of 2,000 kilometres in all directions and at any elevation. While it has a military surveillance capability, it has serious applications in the fields of maritime safety, weather projections and radio research. It does seem that the pioneering work on the Ness has not been entirely in vain.

AN UNEXPLAINED RING

A few yards from the Bomb Ballistics building lying in a desert of shingle that stretches towards the lighthouse tower are the scattered remains of what was once obviously a substantial installation. Aerial photographs indicate that the date of its construction must have been sometime between 1959 and 1965. The remains consist of a large circular concrete ring with the remnants of fixing bolts protruding from it, a plinth on which some sort of building had been placed, the traces of a powerful electrical supply and an apparently random spread of large concrete anchoring blocks with rings for securing stays. No oral or documentary evidence has come to light to explain its purpose and it continues to be one more tantalising Orford Ness mystery. The timing of its appearance on the Ness gives the clues to its probable function or functions.

It seems likely that it was used for more than just one experiment. One obvious line of speculation might suggest that it was associated with Cobra Mist, constructed only a mile away to the northwest. Yet the ring had clearly been built some time before any final decision to go ahead with Cobra Mist.

It is now possible to benefit from the expertise of well-informed visitors to the site. Geoffrey Taylor has brought to bear his knowledge of post-war military technology, including British and US radar systems and can offer some sort of educated guess as to what went on here. His conclusions are entirely based on material now in the public domain, suggestions represent an 'informed deduction and if generally correct, must in detail be wrong.' Little remains to provide the basis for his deductions, and his conclusions are a supreme example of twentieth-century industrial archaeology.

The period 1958 to 1965 marked perhaps the chilliest period of the Cold War, peaking with the 1962 Cuban Missile Crisis. The Russians' ballistic missile station at Plesetsk, near Archangel, was operational. Britain, having abandoned its Blue Streak programme in 1960, relied on its V-bombers as a nuclear deterrent retaliatory force. Meanwhile, the US long-range distant early warning stations, located in Greenland and Alaska, offered no assistance to Britain. The base being built at Fylingdales, Yorkshire was only operational from January 1964.

Taylor concludes that 'the Orford Ness Ring and the platform behind the Ring was an experimental Over The Horizon Radar (OTHR) facility. It was probably built *c.* 1963/4 and was originally used for European–Far Eastern research for the System 440L, Forward Scatter OTHR.'

System 440L was being developed at Stanford University in 1962/3, and by 1964, part of this development had been transferred to Europe for test transmissions to the Western Pacific. Taylor surmises that the Ness transmitter, using sloping Rhombic antennae, operated to the Philippines. This system 440L was not a long-term success, for it became clear from 1971 that signals could be faked and results invalidated. Its working life on the Ness was even briefer.

There is clear evidence that the site was used for a second distinct, though clearly related, purpose. The array of antennae which is evident both from aerial photographs taken in 1965 and from the bits of 'Orford Mess' still lying around the site to this day. It exactly coincides with the fan-centre bearing of Cobra Mist aerials. Both pointed directly at Russian ballistic missile silos at Murmansk and Plesetsk. Such a choice was not without precedent; Keith Wood had been asked to monitor the Russian Sputnik satellite only a few years earlier.

Professor Ramsay Shearman has stated that it had 'nothing to do with Cobra Mist'. He believed that it was 'an experimental trials location', and observes that at the time AWRE 'were active in studying any technique which could detect atomic explosions as background to the Test ban treaty'. His interpretation is in accord therefore with the project, mentioned in the previous chapter, which AWRE and Trinity House rejected and which is documented in the National Archives.

Only one other source of information has come to light. Ron Richardson returned to Orford Ness in 1967 as a Mechanical and Electrical Engineer, employed by the Air Ministry Works Department. He remembers vividly the concrete ring and recalls that at the time it was thought to be an experimental aerial array in preparation for Cobra Mist. He never worked on it and his lack of definite knowledge confirms how little those who worked on the Ness knew of the research they were not involved in.

There may have been a third possible explanation; that it was a radio monitoring station. During the last years of AWRE occupation, employees were sent to the control station by the ring to operate radio receivers. Their task was to record propaganda and military broadcasts transmitted by Radio Tirana, from Soviet-controlled Albania. Two of the men involved in weekly twelve-hour overnight stints were John Backhouse and Fred Tricker. Backhouse was aware that there was a parabolic aerial located within the ring and that the equipment was for radio reception; he was not aware of any transmitters. One can but wonder who AWRE was working for.

THE PLUGS ARE PULLED

In the midst of all the other issues plaguing the MoD, the question of the future of the Ness site still had to be resolved. The AWRE had ceased operations and by 1971 had moved from the site. Despite the many months that had elapsed since Aldermaston first gave its notice, there was continuing indecision.

In August 1970, the idea was mooted that a satellite tracking station might well be established on the Ness. Nine months later a decision in principle began to emerge. While still very uncertain quite what use it might have for the shingle 'beach', the MoD accepted that the 1,900 or so acres used by AWRE should be purchased back. This would effectively include all of King's and Lantern Marshes not occupied by the Cobra Mist project. Ownership of the southern part of the shingle spit, leased to the Nature Conservancy, would be transferred to it.

The prudent thinking behind this decision was that MoD ownership would act as a buffer zone for the radar site, making security much easier. Concern over the possibility of flooding remained. For what would be effectively government property, ownership in MoD hands seemed to offer the best safeguard here. It was felt that a number of the surviving buildings could still be useful for an as yet undefined purpose, including a possible radar outstation for the Telecommunication Research Establishment at Malvern – the successor to nearby Bawdsey Manor. A final and inevitable reason for keeping control of the whole property was the matter of unexploded ordnance and other similar hazardous military detritus. Orford Ness would make a suitable training and exercise area for bomb disposal teams. Retention would also be more economical than enforced clearance, which would be required before placing it on the open market.

There seems to have been little sense of urgency over the protracted negotiations with AWRE and it was not until 24 July 1972 that the MoD resumed ownership of the Ness. With it came a motley assortment of facilities, a situation that appears to have prompted a number of improbable suggestions for future uses. One of these was to reopen the range for bombing. Blowing them up was seen as a way of removing some of the more unsightly buildings and AWRE labs. In the event, no such plan was adopted and a period of slow but inevitable deterioration and decay was to follow.

Orford Mess

WHAT TO DO WITH THE NESS

The MoD may have seemed unclear over their plans for their 'new' property in East Suffolk. There was considerable debate relating to what its future might be in the early 1970s, and letters, meetings and column-inches were devoted to the discussion. The detail is not strictly relevant to the history of the Ness and the political wrangling that went on is well-documented elsewhere.

In the summer of 1971 AWRE sold the full freehold of the southern strip of shingle to the Nature Conservancy, who acquired the lease to the area in 1953. In October 1971 that AWRE handed over their site to the MoD on the last day of the previous month.

In the meantime, East Suffolk County Council had decided that the pagoda labs were 'an eyesore on the coastal skyline' and required their removal. AWRE had estimated that demolition would cost around £50,000, a sum which the MoD declined to spend, retaining ownership and control for another twenty-one years. The pagodas remained, to become an iconic landmark on the Orford Ness skyline, but the authorities clearly felt it would be prudent to investigate what it referred to as 'Proposals for Rehabilitation'. Through the Property Services Agency, which was responsible for government building works, the Department of the Environment conducted a project survey on behalf of the MoD. Their conclusions were published in July 1973. Their instruction was to investigate the possibility of restoring all of that part of the site now in MoD hands to its status as in 1913, including in their researches the cost implications. The consequent report is interesting for the insight it offers into contemporary understanding of the history and significance of the Ness. The costings were for total removal of all buildings, either to ground level, or, as a cheaper option to avoid very expensive demolition of the exceptionally robust reinforced concrete foundations, to 0.5 metres above ground level, with shingle 'mounded' over what was left.

A total of £1.8 million was suggested as the possible cost, but it is clear that this was a quite meaningless exercise, because it excluded any reckoning of the difficulty in dealing with the unexploded ordnance or the consequent cost involved. While it anticipated that Cobra Mist might well be closing down, it could only guess at the implications of an American departure. It also recognised the need for what was termed 'Continuing Maintenance Commitments': this included in particular the reinforcement of sea and river walls, which would clearly be required if full reinstatement was contemplated.

In these distinctly lacklustre years, the Ness came under the direct management responsibility of the Property Services Agency. Their man on site was Ron Richardson, who as he has admitted, became so identified with the place that he was referred to as 'Mr Orford Ness'. After Army service in REME, he became a civilian Technical Officer, working as a Mechanical and Electrical Engineer initially at Martlesham with the Blind Landing Experimental Unit until its move to Bedford in 1957. He had two years on the Ness during the early years of AWRE occupancy, employed by the Air Ministry Works Department, returning in 1967 for a final stint of twenty-two years from 1967 until retirement in 1989. His job was to maintain infrastructure and carry out the management instructions of whichever government department chose to send them.

The MoD could not consider a quick disposal of its property until it was rendered safe, so understandable delay surrounded any decision over what long-term use it might have for the Ness. Events would resolve matters in due course. Meanwhile, there occurred a strange episode, which came to nothing, but might have transformed the face of Orford Ness – indeed, not just Orford itself but also the whole locality – had there been a decision to proceed.

THE NUCLEAR MIGHT-HAVE-BEEN

Within months of the Cobra Mist closure, the Central Electricity Generating Board came on the scene, showing a very real interest in taking over the site for the construction of a vast nuclear power station. The subsequent report on the scheme indicates that serious local obstructive protests could be anticipated.

The consulting engineers, L.G. Mouchel and Partners, based in Weybridge, Surrey, were commissioned to undertake an extensive feasibility study. Their terms of reference included a physical survey of the land and review of the access, as well as availability of natural resources, especially cooling water. They were asked to supply cost estimates, with special reference to comparable costs at Sizewell and the Isle of Grain. They appear to have worked with amazing speed and thoroughness. A report was published in January 1975. It concluded that Orford Ness was a perfectly feasible location and projected costs involved would be 'quite in line with the scale of the development proposed'.

It all came to nothing. The project was taken no further. It was all perhaps in the nature of a 'stalking horse', designed to push the authorities in the direction of settling on Sizewell 'B'. Sizewell was eventually selected as the preferred choice, but it was to be delayed by the most protracted planning enquiry of the era. Work did not begin on its construction for over a decade more, and power generation began only in 1995.

However, the detail in the Mouchel report is intriguing, not least for confirming just how massive the AWRE's building programme was and how complex was the legacy it left behind when it departed.

The survey looked at the concrete labs in the context of demolition and removal, which they estimated would cost £200,000. The scale of the foundations for Lab 1 came as a surprise, with over 100 concrete 0.5-metre diameter piles at least 16 metres deep. Buried ordnance was such a major problem that no figure for clearance was even suggested, presumably because it was considered to be a matter for the MoD to deal with, at its expense. However, the engineers recommended that this clearance should extend to a depth of 6 metres. The current policy was just 3.5 metres, too shallow for safety.

The weather characteristics, seismic record, tidal patterns and rates of coastal erosion were all reviewed. The geology of the Ness with its base of London clay was considered perfectly suitable for the construction of power station buildings on the shingle side of the site, subject to an inclusion of £4.8 million expenditure for piles. This would be cheaper than comparable foundations at Isle of Grain. The possibility of flooding was covered by waterproofing any subterranean working to a depth of 6.5 metres, which, by a rather amazing calculation, it reckoned would secure the power station buildings against a one in one million years chance of flood.

Availability of cooling water and the impact on both the river and the seashore of hot water outflows was reviewed, and no serious problems envisaged. What was less obviously apparent was suitable access, both for bringing in construction materials and for operating what could have evolved into a vast complex. In the drawings, three power station units are depicted and a fourth pencilled in. For all this, a possible new dock on King's Marsh was considered, with a proposal that a smooth flow of river traffic might be guaranteed only by complete control of the mouth at Shingle Street. This would seem to imply a need for its acquisition by a compulsory purchase or lease.

Of even greater impact on an unsuspecting local population would have been the report's recommendations for improved communications. British Rail was consulted over a possible spur from the East Suffolk line from Ipswich. Beyond offering private sidings facilities at Melton or Wickham Market, British Rail was unwilling to promise any help, since they were in the process of cutting back services on the line. So an improved road scheme was suggested, with two alternative routes, either from the Wickham Market bypass via Tunstall Forest, or from Woodbridge, via Melton and Chillesford. Nuclear Power would construct these new roads, something that over its sixty years of occupation, the military had not even considered.

The major and most obviously contentious element in this scheme was the means of crossing the river Ore. Here indeed would have been an issue to cause the sailing community to rise in protest. Either a tunnel would have to bore under the riverbed, closing down all traffic during its construction. Worse would be the alternative, a bridge, albeit a handsome span as the drawing depicts it, bringing the projected road over to King's Marsh. The pros and cons of these various suggestions are carefully analysed in the report. It is admitted that resolving the communications problems would add significantly to the costs and increase seriously the likelihood of objections. This would lead to unpredictable delays. The conclusion of the report confirms the seriousness of this issue:

> Having considered the major civil engineering problems associated with devel-
> opment of the site for about 10,000 megawatts of nuclear generation it is our
> opinion that the site is suitable for development using any of the reactor systems
> proposed without undue problems. Estimates of cost of development have not
> been possible, but as a generalisation, we would suggest that this site might
> be between Grain and Sizewell in order of cost of development for the main
> structure, once road access has been built...

All this provides a fascinating insight into what might have been. It is perhaps clear in retrospect that this project was never a serious contender as an answer to the 'what to do with the Ness' question. Clues as to its solution have cropped up more than once. Building Cobra Mist was possible only because in 1967 a squad of a dozen members of No.2 Explosive Ordnance Disposal Unit arrived on site to clear swathes of King's Marsh of a fearful crop of unexploded weapons dating back to 1916. Only ten years previously, as has already been described, this area was part of a rocket-firing range. Never could all the missiles be accounted for. During both wars, checking on the fall and detonation of every single bomb, shell, bullet or missile was quite impossible and represented the lowest of priorities. The work done in making the Cobra Mist site safe was the vital preliminary to the construction workers being able to enter it. It is remarkable that this was achieved so speedily and without a single serious accident.

In making it all safe, around 800 separate borings were made on King's Marsh, every other one of which successfully yielded the discovery of something that needed dealing with. The records indicate that 188 of these 800 separate borings were live, dangerous and to be destroyed.

This was a relative tip of a sinister iceberg. The power station survey above indicated that clearance of the shingle area would be the prime condition for beginning any work there. The MoD had its answer. Ordnance clearance would be the essential precondition to any other use for its property.

OVER TO 'AUNTIE'

Meanwhile, with the great fan-shaped aerial removed, the Cobra Mist building still stood. By a happy coincidence, a ready use for it immediately offered itself. The BBC's Overseas Service was due to lose its long-standing medium-wave transmission station at Crowborough for its broadcasts to central and eastern Europe. Via its paymaster, the Foreign and Commonwealth Office, the BBC World Service (as it has come to be called) was offered use of the giant building and the extensive King's Marsh site for its aerials. Ultimately, twelve slim masts were erected. First exploratory tests indicated that the location was incomparably more suitable than the one in Sussex. In 1975, broadcasting began, and the Cobra Mist site came alive again, with a tiny team of engineers, managers and ferry staff. Under a subsequent change in the ownership of the transmitting company, the BBC handed on responsibility to Merlin Communications, which in turn was taken over by Vosper Thorneycroft. New high-powered digital technology permits automated transmission, run by a small team of just six, who occupy perhaps 20 per cent of the enormous building and take proud care of the remaining empty cavernous chambers.

The Cobra Mist site is not part of the National Trust's property, remaining in government hands, but the staff are the Trust's close neighbours, sharing basic infrastructure services. They still own the last of the landing craft, *Guinivere*, formerly *LCGF* 4, and thus the VTM staff can provide vehicle ferry services for the Trust and indeed, for Trinity House; they also share a common interest in operating in a remote and at times environmentally unfriendly place.

Is this all there is to be told of the Cobra Mist story? It is hard to say for sure, since the Official Secrets Act still retains its grip. The property remains in government hands. Permission for erecting short-wave aerials was granted in the late 1970s, and there is some residual evidence that a part of the building has had a secret use, and may indeed still be used for undisclosed activities.

THE RENDLESHAM UFO

The Pentagon's report on the working of the Cobra Mist radar project concludes with a remarkable statement. 'Cobra Mist' it blandly reports, 'is well known for its association with Unidentified Flying Objects' – UFOs. Perhaps here is just another of those inspired Orford Ness 'cover stories'. In the depths of Rendlesham Forest, about 5 miles inland from the Ness, on Boxing Day night, 1980, there was a spectacular 'happening' some hundreds of metres from the end of the runway of the USAF airbase at Woodbridge-Sutton Heath. Brilliant lights and evidence of damage to trees indicated that something abnormal in the nature of a large crash had indeed occurred. Exactly what has ever after remained clouded in doubt, although both service personnel and civilians supposedly witnessed its aftermath.

The authorities, British and American, responded in a secretive fashion and all attempts to deny fanciful stories were so clumsy that they merely provoked suspicion that the facts were being suppressed. Tales of landings from outer space, with aliens climbing out of a spaceship, were denied, but only in such a way as to raise doubts and scepticism in many minds.

A high-ranking officer from a neighbouring base, the Deputy Commander at RAF Bentwaters, was assigned the task of making an official report on the incident, despite not witnessing it himself and working at a base a mile or so away from the scene of the affair. USAF personnel who had witnessed what happened were promptly returned to the US to appointments that effectively scattered them. The behaviour of the civilian police as well as the USAF was coy and vague, serving to provoke the rumourmongers and conspiracy theorists. What actually happened was effectively hidden behind a smoke screen of obfuscation.

Jenny Randles, a noted UFOlogist has researched this episode, and speculated that the vehicle that crashed into the forest that night was part of a Russian 'Cosmos' satellite. The sinister aspect to this was the way she imagines it was brought down. Supposedly, the US National Security Agency (NSA) had set up another secret radar apparatus in the old Cobra Mist building. This was, she claimed, a new system codenamed 'COLD WITNESS'. Its purpose, as she understood it, was to operate some sort of 'death ray' to incapacitate a satellite.

As Alan Clark (grandson of Mackenzie Clark of Sudbourne Hall) admitted to Parliament when Defence Minister in April 1990, there was indeed a system codenamed Cold Witness, a successor to Cobra Mist. The project was abandoned and it supposedly never operated from the British Isles, most certainly not from Orford Ness. Had it ever been set up, it would have been located in Pembrokeshire, at RAF Brawdy. Equally, the possibility cannot be entirely ignored that the government might have retained some corner of the Cobra Mist building for its own purposes. There is some circumstantial evidence that the MoD continued to operate some sort of surveillance from the Ness during the 1970s, but any corroborative evidence is likely to still be subject to the Official Secrets Act.

The release by the MoD of files on UFOs in August 2009 raised again the issue of sightings during the previous forty years. Included was a statement by a former Chief of Defence Staff, Lord Hill-Norton, dated 1985, confirming that there was no case for denying any 'defence interest' in the Rendelsham incident. Either there had been a serious breach of national security; or some US servicemen played an unacceptable prank. This latter view was confirmed in 2003 by the claim of an ex-security policeman, Kevin Conde, that he and colleagues had concocted the whole thing, using car headlights and a loudspeaker.

SCRAP AND DEMOLITION

From the completion of the first King's Marsh clearance in 1968, the bomb disposal team of RAF personnel became a permanent fixture on the Ness, remaining on site until after the National Trust acquisition in the mid-1990s. It cannot have been at first sight an entirely agreeable posting, being dangerous, uncomfortable and somewhat tediously repetitive. Yet no single example is on record of anyone seeking to be posted elsewhere.

The men of No.2 Explosive Ordnance Demolition Unit (EOD) had to dig deep into marsh and shingle. The one was always liable to flood with water as the tide came in while the other saw the sides of the pits they created with inevitably unstable walls of stones cascade back. They had bulldozers to assist them, required when a 'target' was so deep a trench had to be dug to reach it. The essence of the work was backbreaking investigations of what could be extremely unpredictable and hence volatile weapons. Some of them were hard to identify because they were very ancient, very experimental or of enemy origin. Many were dummies, with no explosive content. Others required a laborious process of extracting the explosive charge. However, there was a small consolation for all this: No.2 EOD Unit was unique: it was the only one in the RAF to have a routine rum ration, prescribed by the Medical Officer (MO) after a wet or cold day's work. But as David Andrews, who was in charge of the team from 1983 to his retirement in 1985, this was scarcely practical. The nearest MO might be 100 miles away and in practice, he was the one on site to take the decision. Gordon Kinsey had described their operations:

> After a bomb had been located, usually by means of a detector, it had to be exposed and then identified to determine the disposal procedure. If it was a common type and did not weigh more than 190-kgs it was blown up after being removed to a desolate area of shingle reserved for this purpose. Should the discovery be in excess of 190-kgs and of a type that would be of interest to one of the Service Museums, the fuses were removed and the explosive content heated by steam to render it into a semi-liquid state when it could be drained from the bomb casing. It was then burned off without fear of explosion and the casing disposed of to its final resting place.

The detectors scanned to around 35 feet, and bore holes were made to 30 feet, using water-jets to aid penetration by telescopic tubes. Square-shaped boxes were used to hold up the sides of the pits. 'All the work had to be carried out with hand tools ... as the pit digging proceeded and the water level rose, so the personnel laboured on, often waist deep in murky water', writes Gordon Kinsey. They had specially adapted Land Rovers, so-called Cuthbertson Conversions, mounted on four triangular-shaped caterpillar tracks, designed to ease movement over the shingle.

The Ness had been used as a dumping ground for certain types of ordnance, like rocket booster motors and butane gas canisters. These would be piled up and then blown to bits with explosive charges. Andrews remarked that the team 'never knew what you'd find' and this seems to have made the job that much more interesting. On occasions minor mishaps occurred. A rocket motor would be imperfectly dismantled and would blast off across the shingle. In Andrews's time, none of the RAF personnel was injured. Certain types of weapon were notoriously dangerous, like the 30-pound 'J' type incendiary. At the other end of the scale were the 1,000 pounders, jettisoned offshore by Allied bombers limping back to their bases or hoping to make it to the 'Crash Base' at RAF Sutton Heath, by Woodbridge. These bombs were often jettisoned into the sea, but have proved particularly elusive since they continue to be washed in and out by the tide.

It was hoped that perhaps by 1982, the whole site would be cleared. In the event, much remained to be done. After the property ceased to be MoD responsibility, RAF units had to be on hand to finish the job. Even then, from time to time, 'something nasty' would emerge from the depths of marsh or shingle, or be washed ashore, necessitating an emergency summons of disposal squads. What cannot be denied however is that the No.2 EOD team did a phenomenal job, quite in the tradition of the Orford Ness boffins: they were professional, persevering and very brave. As Gordon Kinsey observed back in 1981, when the work was very much still in hand: 'it is doubtless the wish of many that in the future they may be able to stroll along the bare shingle of Orford Beach. If their wish is granted, it will be the endeavours of the men of No.2 EOD who will have made it possible and safe.'

By the 1980s, scrap merchants and vandals were reducing the buildings to a state of dereliction. Not a pane of glass survived. This was to prove the most inglorious decade of the Ness' existence. A property that is unguarded and clearly uncared for is a sitting target for such treatment. Both Andrews and Richardson, on the site at this time, confirmed that the scrap contractors took the most valuable and easily removed material, leaving an open invitation to their men to 'take for themselves what they could find'.

However, one last trial was known to be held on the Ness. Strangely, it was set up by the Royal Artillery on behalf of the Royal Navy. After the Falklands War, the Navy had good cause to be thankful that its inability to destroy the French designed skimming missile, Exocet, had not proved fatal to the Task Force's operations. An American-designed weapon, the Phalanx 'Goalkeeper', was a five-barrelled radar-directed gattling type of gun, firing sprays of solid titanium-tipped shot in short bursts, creating a blanket that no low-flying missile could penetrate. A preliminary trial site was set up on the shingle to the south of the Ness light-house in the autumn of 1982. During its Christmas leave period, a 'Goalkeeper' was fitted to the aircraft carrier HMS *Invincible*. Late the following January, as a guest of the Commanding Officer, Captain Jeremy Black, the author witnessed the first sea firing trial of the gun off the Isle of Wight.

Yet again, but for the very last time, the Ness could claim to have offered 'some service' to the nation's armed forces. What was to lie ahead was a transformation, which saw swords rapidly turned to ploughshares.

The Military Departs

By the late 1980s, the MoD had ceased to have any interest or even concern for its Suffolk property. Finding the appropriate organisation to take it over was going to be far from easy, however. The National Trust alone had available a sufficient breadth of experience and skill to cope with what was simultaneously a nature reserve and a site of rare historic significance. Their Properties Committee was chaired by Sir Marcus Worsley, who in 1990, while in East Anglia, paid Orford Ness a special visit. The ensuing report in June that year confirmed the interest the Trust ought to be taking in acquiring the place as soon as the MoD confirmed it was ready to part with it. Later in 1990, the Trust's Director-General, Angus Stirling, also came over to the 'island' to see it for himself. A year later, the Nature Conservancy Council, as one of its last moves before it was reconstituted into English Nature, formally recommended that the Trust should be the body to take over and promised to offer its official support in any application the Trust might make. This proposal was presented to the Properties Committee in early 1992 and things began to move, at last.

Lord Chorley, National Trust Chairman was in no doubt as to the merits of purchasing the Ness. He had two vital supporters in Angus Stirling, and in the Regional Director for East Anglia, Merlin Waterson. This acquisition was going to prove a highly contentious issue in many directions. Some in the management of the Trust had grave doubts about the wisdom of being saddled with such a 'difficult' property, and perhaps rather sadly, they anticipated only tortuous and protracted negotiation with government departments, notably the Treasury and MoD, before any headway could be made.

The enthusiasts for the venture themselves had to justify to their colleagues the importance of the Orford Ness property. Among the experts commissioned to supply evidence in support of the purchase was Professor Keith Clayton, from East Anglia University School of Environmental Sciences. He was of course not the first academic to point to the unique features of the shingle spit. Professor Alfred

Steers had conducted pioneering research work on the Ness's accreting ridges during the 1920s (at a period one must presume when trials on the site were at a relatively modest level!). Steers had established that the spit was physiographically one of the most important in Europe. He also confirmed just how exceptional was its wealth in plant and bird life. Clayton merely echoed his illustrious predecessor's opinion but added his own commentary on the fearful damage done by military and civilian occupancy since Steers had visited. This judgement on the Ness's merits had been reinforced in 1977 when it was designated a Grade 1 listed site following a Nature Conservancy review. It does seem that very little notice of this rating had been taken by the MoD.

Sir Marcus Worsley soon strengthened his opinion that the Ness should be acquired. He saw it both as a nature reserve of great importance and as an addition to the Enterprise Neptune coastal rescue campaign.[1] His formal report presented to the Properties Committee was a curious mixture of somewhat bland naivety, factual inaccuracy, illuminating foresight and evident enthusiasm. The question of visitor admission was glossed over and he was wrong to imagine that the Trust would obtain control of land that was not in the event for sale, such as the lighthouse and the BBC building. He was right in imagining that what he called 'an incredible litter of derelict buildings, Nissen huts, cook houses etc. etc.' would need careful expert scrutiny to ensure that none of value was demolished. He hoped this would be undertaken by the MoD, before the Trust were to assume ownership, 'so that we would not get involved in arguments in the future about retaining them'. This somewhat cautious recommendation could not in the event be met: demolition was left to the Trust.

Worsley's attitude to the AWRE derelict labs was significant, even visionary:

One needs to see them in the context of Orford Castle on the mainland as an aspect of defence over the centuries. The 'Trigger Buildings' are anyhow much too solid to demolish. What is needed is to assess what costs are involved in making them safe and if possible visitable, either under supervision or by open access.

Sir Marcus's judgement was not infallible. He looked for 'a centre for refreshment' in the Black Beacon, an idea that was rejected as being quite alien to the spirit of the property. The Worsley report concludes: 'I hope we do get an offer of this property and that we can raise the funds to accept it, though they would not be inconsiderable.'

This hope was duly realised, but not without several headaches. Finding the money was just one. By chance, earlier in his career with the Trust, Lord Chorley, who was so in favour of acquiring the Ness, devised the formula governing how to calculate the total sum of money a property should require to fund the purchase, the restoration and the management 'running costs'. Almost without exception, a Trust acquisition had to carry a substantial endowment so that it never needed to rely solely on the income it could generate from its visitors. Orford Ness was to be no exception.

In the rough and tumble that was to follow, Merlin Waterson was a highly interested party. There were grave misgivings within the higher echelons of the Trust. The Properties Committee was understandably alarmed at the possible hazards to visitors in such an extreme environment and with so much uncertain military detritus all around. It was also anxious about the Trust assuming liability for sea and river defences, and the consequent impact on the population of both Orford and Aldeburgh.

It was the mention of Aldeburgh that swayed the argument in favour of acquisition. Landowner, environmentalist and farmer, Sir John Quicke reminded his colleagues on the Properties Committee that this very stretch of coast 'reverberates with the music of Benjamin Britten'. Waterson reinforced the argument, suggesting that, having been 'for long influenced by the gentle harmonies of Wordsworth, the Trust also needed to have regard to the more brutal realities that concerned Crabbe and Britten'. For, as he observed, Crabbe's view of nature is somewhat less benign and forgiving than his romantic contemporaries. As for Britten, the 'Sea Interludes' from his renowned opera *Peter Grimes* spring to mind at every step along that long beach from Aldeburgh to Orford.

Negotiations over a National Trust purchase began in December 1991. The most serious issue was obviously the whole matter of legal responsibilities relating to possible hazards, both unexploded or uncleared ordnance and harmful materials, notably asbestos. Argument was to rage for many months over both government liability and financial support.

By January 1992, a preliminary analysis of what needed to be done, with outline estimates of possible costs, had been prepared. Two distinct phases of operation were envisaged. The first would be to clear the site, making it safe for visitor access. The second phase would be what was termed 'wilderness management', which foresaw a policy of deliberate low maintenance, to permit 'natural decay' of the military buildings. The implication of this policy was that the Trust was giving higher priority for the future of the Ness as a wildlife and nature reserve than as a place of unique historical importance. This was perhaps understandable. The Trust enjoyed a long-standing expertise in running the former, from its earliest days when it had first acquired Wicken Fen. It was from this property, not entirely by chance, that the Ness's first Property Manager, Grant Lohoar was recruited. The Trust had relatively no experience of running a property with such extensive military significance. Perhaps only the Imperial War Museum did. It was evidently assumed at this stage that such a relatively remote place would attract few visitors other than naturalists and wildlife enthusiasts.

Some of the early calculations in 1992 were to prove far too conservative. In two matters, the Trust would immediately be disappointed. The large car park by Orford Quay was assumed to be part of the deal. This, it was expected, would provide a good income for the Trust, but of course it was no longer MoD property: it belonged to the Orford Town Trust. It was also anticipated that the MoD would be selling a site with the demolition work already completed prior to handover. In their disappointment over this issue, the Trust was strongly advised by English Heritage not to permit the MoD to undertake such work. The military was simply not professionally competent enough to conduct such sensitive undertakings without a risk of doing serious damage to the place, which was by now designated a Site of Special Scientific Interest.

Waterson and Stirling had to conduct multi-sided negotiations, some of them, within the Trust itself. The Treasury held the purse strings, the Department of the Environment exercised judgement over whether relevant criteria for the award of grants were being met, the Treasurer of the Trust guarded his limited funds and the enthusiasts for purchase were increasingly pressing for an acceptable deal. By the summer of 1992, with tension between all parties noticeably rising, it reached the point where ultimatum was met by counter-threat, including pulling out of the discussions. This threat was more effective than might be supposed. The MoD had made heavy weather of disposing of the Bawdsey Manor site and was anxious that history should not repeat itself.

Stirling determined to continue his policy of courteous patience and diplo-matic conciliation, which included the pleas that, during the current recession, the Trust was totally reliant on the generosity of others.

The strategy worked. The Department of the Environment was persuaded, and confirmed the offer of very substantial grants, including the one from the Derelict Land Fund specifically designed for this sort of purpose. A few days later came the reassuring news from the Trust's Controller of Finance that the Enterprise Neptune Fund would indeed contribute to the purchase of the Ness, indicating that the record sum would total £549,000.

Shortly before the Trustees of the National Heritage Memorial Fund (NHMF) agreed to support the venture, Waterson had gone onto the offensive. He took the initiative, offering to invite them to come over and see for themselves just what this appeal for help was all about. If necessary, he would arrange a visit by helicopter. To clinch his case, Waterson also wheeled in some powerful 'big guns'. Lords Rothschild and Cranbrook, both very eminent naturalists, made clear their support for the Trust's bid on environmental grounds.

In mid-November, Waterson produced a substantial memorandum, which summarised the reasons why the Trust could claim to be better placed to take over the site than any other body, notably than English Heritage or Suffolk County Council. It laid particular emphasis on its appreciation of the Ness as a nature reserve and its unique geophysical significance as 'the most important shingle spit cuspate foreland complex in Britain as well as being one of the few examples of its type in Europe'. It drew attention to the initiative the Trust had taken in securing an academic report from Professor Clayton to confirm its judgement. Reference was made to the significance of the military experiments that had been conducted on the Ness. Mention was made, more than a little questionably, of an association to research done by Barnes Wallis on the Ness.

This document did the trick. NHMF allowed itself to be persuaded and the grants were authorised, albeit delayed until the New Year and to a figure well short of what was hoped. The Trust gratefully accepted £388,900 for capital works. It needed to spend about £500,000.

This prompted the County and District Councils to make small but no less significant grants towards the land purchase. This, however, left unresolved the last stubborn barrier in the way of ultimate progress: no agreement was yet reached with the MoD. Detailed discussion continued over removal of fencing and asbestos hazards, essential under health and safety requirements. This rumbled on until 9 February 1993, when the deal was struck. The final purchase price was to be £292,500, which was £7,500 less than the asking price. This was in recognition of the decision that the cost of asbestos removal would lie with the Trust and not with the MoD (in line of course with English Heritage's most solemn advice).

Orford Ness now belonged to the National Trust. It had raised £3.5 million to purchase and endow what was clearly a major acquisition. It was less than had been hoped for and considerably less than would be needed, especially if it was to attempt to restore some of the most historic buildings. It also faced a quite indeterminate potential liability for sea defence. At last the deed was done and the ambition of all who fought a long and tough battle had been realised.

It was naturally intended to make it available to the public as soon as reasonably possible. This last process was to take well over two years to fulfil. Some tiresome loose ends that plagued the Trust during the spring of 1993 provide a clue as to why this should have been so.

The first burning issue concerned liabilities. Despite the best efforts of the No. 2 EOD team and other bomb disposal personnel to make the place safe, it simply could not be denied that for the foreseeable future hazardous items were bound to exist. The MoD was as a consequence adamant that it would not accept a 'Hold Harmless' status for the sale. In other words, they would not offer any guarantee that every bit of dangerous ordnance had been cleared. Their argument seems to have been bolstered by the thought that as so much government money had been supplied to acquire the place, the Trust should in turn take a share of the implications of liability. There was a nice loophole that enabled both parties to reach a compromise.

It was self-evident that the sale did not intend to include bombs and similar material. They were therefore not 'expressly conveyed'. A UXB (unexploded bomb) certificate dated 17 March 1993 confirmed that the site had indeed been cleared and that the MoD had 'no reason to believe that unexploded bombs will constitute a serious hazard'. The MoD was willing to concede that they could not guarantee to have cleared every single one, nor could it 'eliminate the risk of UXBs', but it gave 'an undertaking to clear any which might be found, at their expense'. Another MoD memo is on file, confirming that 'to the best of their knowledge and belief, there are no hazardous substances on site, other than asbestos'. A further note in this file asserts that 'the Trust has identified where this is and it will be dealt with by the National Trust itself, using licensed contractors'.

Another worry was over possible flooding and consequent liabilities arising from damage to the shingle caused by factors outside the Trust's control. Of greater concern were the conditions imposed by the Trust's insurers for cover for visitors. In April 1993, this was fixed. It was to be provided on an assumption that public access was restricted to specific controlled routes. An additional clause confirmed that because of potential damage to plant and animal life, 'individuals will not be given freedom to wander at will'. In the event, this was entirely in accord with the Trust's site management policy. Restoration of the flora and fauna of the Ness would rely on denying visitors an unrestricted 'right to roam'.

On 26 April 1993, Stirling wound up the whole operation with a letter to the Department of the Environment thanking it for invaluable help over the previous eighteen months of protracted negotiation. Was everything settled, though? At the eleventh hour a new and unexpected shadow emerged. Just as it was thought all had been agreed, the Treasury announced a ruling over the money for an endowment grant from the Countryside Commission, which had been awarded via the Department of the Environment. It was to be understood that this was for a restricted period of 80 years only. Thereafter, it might want to claim its money back. The Trust meanwhile had accepted responsibility in perpetuity for a property, which by the terms of all its acquisitions was inalienable and *sine die*. The implications of such a restriction were very grave, for it cast serious doubt over the value of government grants at all and posed a threatening precedent for all future Trust purchases. It was so serious that it could have led to a complete withdrawal from the Orford Ness project. The files do not indicate how this potential threat was handled. One may suppose that it could be regarded as an issue too remote to bother with. Sufficient unto the day...

Two years of hectic planning and activity followed, during which decisions were taken over how to treat this extraordinary place. Demolition, restoration, refurbishment, construction and clearance all were urgently required. With this flurry of work, the past history of the Ness moves imperceptibly towards the present, as it was made ready for its first visitors.

THE NATIONAL TRUST ACQUISITION

By December 1993, the Trust's Historical Buildings Adviser, Jeremy Musson, had supplied an early appraisal of the policies that should direct the management of the site. He clearly saw the array of derelict buildings as having significance as monuments and memorials to the wars of the twentieth century, comparable with ancient houses or castles in the Trust's care. He noted in this context that the loss of the great hangar blown down in 1987 would make 'evidence of the airfield's use harder to appreciate'. This was a very shrewd observation and it was sad indeed that the brick-built part of this historic building was not left standing. He referred to 'the feeling of mystery and secrecy created by sound, silence broken by gulls and wind in rattling buildings, by dilapidation of ruins, and by incomprehension as to what happened here'. At the same time, he could not but be aware of the awesome natural environment of the place.

He felt that the survival of the property would be best served by making public access so difficult as to deter all but the persistent. Hence pedestrian access should in his view be via Aldeburgh. After 5 miles of walking along the shingle path, few would have any energy left to want to explore the buildings. This was a remarkably reactionary and erroneous proposition.

Other observations however were accepted. That no intrusive signs or notices should be introduced and any tidying up of the site or clearance of weeds from around buildings could only be justified on the grounds of safety or management efficiency.

The Trust meanwhile employed the surveyor Martin Williams to investigate every single surviving structure, to assess its value and the feasibility of repair or conservation. By February 1994, this considerable investigation was under way. There were over forty assorted buildings, ranging from wooden huts in a state of collapse to massive concrete blockhouses. In addition there were nearly thirty small huts, store buildings, observation posts and such facilities as dog kennels and lavatory blocks. The report presented to the Trust the following September described the most recent use to which every one had been put, so far as was known. Many, of course, were 'recycled' from earlier times. Attached to each was the surveyor's proposal for what work, if any, should be undertaken on them. These recommendations were usually, but not always, followed.

Work that anticipated the arrival of the general public was to involve the total rebuilding of the jetty and setting up of facilities for handling and providing for the visitors. The ferry, to be christened *Octavia*, was purchased. Those buildings that were too derelict to merit repair or preservation were pulled down. Others for which good use might be made were renovated. All the bridges over Stony Ditch were clearly too dangerous to be left standing. A new Bailey Bridge replaced one of them, on fresh foundations a few yards upstream of the original. Buildings with historic significance were protected with new roofing, pending decisions as to their future. In some cases, positive steps were taken to investigate the cost of full repair and utilisation for an appropriate purpose.

The so-called Maritime Navigation Beacon – now referred to as Black Beacon – was the most obvious case in point here. It was to be beautifully restored as a focal point for visitors' information on what clearly was to be seen as the prime location on the shingle. The Victorian Coastguard lookout was less lucky. Initially, it was hoped that funds could be found for total restoration. However, it was felt that its increasingly precarious location by the rapidly eroding shoreline made any long-term future too uncertain to warrant the very substantial expenditure involved.

Five significant structures dating back nearly eighty years to the First World War also had to be considered. One, the repair workshop/motor transport building was so well built and so potentially valuable it was restored for use by the Trust's staff for maintenance work. The two wooden buildings, the former Officers' Mess and regimental institute, used in 1935 by the radar team were so historically significant that they had to be preserved, although structurally they were in a decrepit state. The question of complete repair as the home for a radar museum would have to await future developments. The great prefabricated barrack, which in fact was not erected on the site until about 1924, was architecturally valuable as a unique survivor of its type. A fresh roof was all that could be considered. The RAF itself had relegated it to the status of store building. The Trust raised this standing by designating it a prime habitat for barn owls. One last sad remnant from RFC glory days remained for consideration. The station headquarters/guard house, with its veranda facing across the roadway to the airfield, was in a sorry state. Perhaps too hastily, the decision was taken that it should go. No sign of it remains apart from the concrete foundations. Yet, here was the building that above all others might have provided a real feel for that early air station. It would have made a grand focal point for a museum and display of the artefacts, which would soon increasingly come to light.

Another military site disappeared as a consequence of a land management programme. This was the gun range along the river wall at the southern extremity of the grazing marsh. Although it was known from wartime plans of the site that a target butt existed, the significance of the 800-yard long range where Spitfire and Hurricane Browning .303 machine guns were first trialled was not appreciated. A major element in the Trust's strategy for the area was the creation of new reedbeds, which were excavated and planted down at each end of the airfield site. The gun range disappeared beneath the newly planted reeds. This in turn necessitated a complete refurbishment of the whole irrigation system. New sluices and pumps were introduced and substantial channels opened up. Gradually, the two airfields became flooded by winter and during the summer were crossed by ditches, which aimed to replicate what might have been there in the past.

One other major land management project had to be undertaken. This was the repair of the river wall, which in some stretches was in a parlous state. The material for this work was to hand. The rubble from the demolished buildings and bridges was piled on the hard base of the southern hangar, ready for transfer to be recycled into the new walls. This work was done entirely by Trust staff and without external contractors. Further north, in Lantern Marsh, the Trust took a bold and somewhat controversial course. They decided that 'managed retreat' was the preferred option, allowing deliberate tidal flooding through breaches in the wall to create a natural flexible barrier of salt-marsh flora. Northey Island in Essex was a Trust property where this technique had been successfully introduced. Despite alarm in some minds in Aldeburgh, it was adopted for this northern part of the Ness. Time will surely tell whether this proves to be the right option.

The biggest and most perplexing issue concerned the fate of the mammoth nuclear bomb labs. The eventual decision was to leave them untouched. The actual proposal from the surveyor adopted the phrase 'leave to crumble'.

The Trust has described the policy as a matter of 'gentle decay'. The cost of demolition and the whole problem of the disposal of the rubble seemed quite out of proportion to any benefit gained. They were increasingly coming to be seen as iconic symbols and an essential part of the coastal landscape. Only the first lab was to be included in the visitors' route however, because the entrance lobby could be gated off from the dangerously precarious interior chambers. It was possible therefore to exploit the historic significance of that first environmental trial of August Bank Holiday weekend, 1956. The remaining labs, once cleared of dangerous asbestos, were even then too insecure for unsupervised entry. They were to become an irresistible attraction for the increasing number of guided tours the Trust was to arrange.

Designated a National Nature Reserve within a crucial section of Suffolk's Heritage Coast, the Ness accumulated a string of classifications as a Site of Special Scientific Interest. It became a Special Protected Area under a European Union designation for sites for conservation and protection of bird life. From 1996, it was designated a Ramsar Site. This is a worldwide classification for exceptional wetland areas for bird conservation.

Not surprisingly, the Ness was classified as an Area of Outstanding Natural Beauty. So, a place that had endured for eighty years a series confusing initials around its name – A&AEE, ORL, ORS, RAF or AWRE – settled now to one with which it could confidently and proudly feel secure for its future: it is now just Orford Ness, NNR (National Nature Reserve).

In many respects it was these various designations governing the managerial thinking of the team that directed the work of restoration and rehabilitation. The popularity the Ness was to gain for its military associations came as a happy bonus, ensuring that visitor numbers for such a relatively remote location were to prove greater than was anticipated.

Curiously and sadly, the National Trust's wisdom in undertaking this project, with its high cost, was questioned in a number of quarters. In response, a quite powerful voice spoke out. Sir John Tusa, former Director-General of the BBC World Service, was very familiar with the place. In a letter to *The Times*, he deplored the 'woeful ignorance' of the Trust's critics. Orford Ness 'is eerily beautiful and historically significant' he wrote, 'set on ancient shingle banks that have their own geological value…'. A visit offered 'a fascinating trip through recent industrial/military archaeology'. With a flourish, he concluded with the heartening words: 'If this is the 'modern' National Trust at work, they are being as imaginative as they should be in broadening their portfolio of properties.'

The Ness could now extend a welcome to a stream of visitors flocking over to see what it was that no one had been allowed to see for so many decades. During the previous year, on top of all his other work, including writing a book to mark the Trust's Centenary, Merlin Waterson, who had patiently laboured to see this whole project come to fruition, summed up his feelings:

As the decision to acquire Orford Ness demonstrates, the Trust has not in the course of the last 100 years turned away from what is difficult, harsh or unglamorous. Orford Ness will be open to the public in 1995, the year of the Trust's centenary. Exactly a hundred years earlier Octavia Hill had wondered whether its first property, Dinas Oleu, would also be its last. The protection of Orford Ness has assumed a much wider significance. Once again it is to be an area of wilderness, valued as the habitat for the yellow poppy and sea pea growing on the shingle; for its breeding avocets, marsh harriers, terns and short-eared owls. What was until recently a testing ground for weapons of mass destruction has become a symbol of what is worth conserving. The pagodas are now stark monuments to the futilities of the Cold War. The great vacant spaces within them are a chilling reminder and a symbol of hope.

OPEN TO THE PUBLIC

On the day of the official opening on 6 June 1995, *The Times* made it a main front-page story. The journalist Libby Purves, a Suffolk resident, wrote of the significance of the place, '...symbolic of the conflicts of man and nature, and of nation with nation...'. Quite correctly, she observed that 'Orford Ness will always be an uncomfortable and untidy place to visit'.

The actual opening celebration was done in style. Apart from local and national dignitaries and Trust people who had played such an important part in the acquisition, the guest list included some of the heroes who had actually worked on the Ness. They were welcomed back to see just how the Trust was 'turning swords into ploughshares and pruning hooks'. For some, this represented a first visit for as much as fifty years.

One such was especially notable, for he was indeed the world's very first boffin. Professor Robert Hanbury Brown's pioneering work on airborne radar led not just to a crucial advantage in aerial night fighting but also to the victory over U-boats in the Battle of the Atlantic in 1943. He above all others was entitled to regard himself as 'the man of bombs, beams and boffins'. Like so many of these great people, his outstanding contribution to victory in the Second World War was never publicly acknowledged[*]. Having played a major role in the creation of Joddrell Bank telescope, he moved to Australia to pursue a career in optical astronomy. Most wonderfully, his wife Heather recorded the events of that day in June 1995. Her account provides an apt conclusion to the story of the military site on Orford Ness.

---

[*] This lack of honours for those so clearly deserving them was the subject of correspondence in the *Daily Telegraph* in 2005. Lord Howell of Guildford described Hanbury Brown as 'one more of those heroes to whom we did not give the thanks deserved.'

À LA RECHERCHE DU TEMPS PERDU
(IN SEARCH OF LOST TIME)

We've just been back to Orford Ness – a nostalgic visit – as my husband began working on the development of radar there 60 years ago. He was, so Watson Watt tells us, the original Boffin for whom the word was coined later. Of course we compared 'Then' with 'Now'. So, what's changed?

In August 1935 Sir Henry Tizard snatched Hanbury from University and sent him to join the radar team working at Orford Ness. The group was small, select and highly secret. His Bawdsey Manor pass was number 14 and, being the baby (he was only 19), he was allowed to take his dog along too.

In June 1995, Emeritus Professor Robert Hanbury Brown, FRS etc. joined the large, select and highly publicised jamboree celebrating the opening of the Ness to the public. His pass was now an invitation from the National Trust and being a venerable 79, he was allowed to take his wife along too.

Sixty years is nothing to the weather; on the party day it was its usual self, changeable, cloudy and unseasonably cold. 'In the old days we had to gather firewood before we could light a black-bellied stove in those huts. It was nearly always blowing a gale and usually raining. We ate our sandwiches over flickering cathode-ray tubes.' Typical boffins' lunch.

On this Celebratory Day however, we stood elegantly sheltered from the drizzle in a marquee lined in billowing silk. We drank pink champagne and ate smoked salmon with silver forks over starched white napkins. Typical VIP's lunch.

You still have to cross the river to get to the Ness itself, but not for us an Air Ministry boat with a taciturn boatman suspicious of all 'foreigners'; our freshly painted Trust launch shuttled us courteously to and fro with a friendly hand to help the aged on and off.

Once up the iron steps on to the 'island' itself, we found things were not so different. The muddy channels and desolate marshland were as unwelcoming as ever, and the endless shingle made it just as difficult to get about on foot despite our sensible shoes. ('Footwear should be suitable for country walking'). Only the nesting gulls looked comfortable, squatting among the pebbles, smug and proprietorial; this was their sanctuary, part of Neptune's kingdom, and I felt an intruder on Nature's preserve.

We searched for the hut where the vital radar experiments were done. 'This one. No, this one – or is it that?' Landmarks have disappeared; blocks of concrete foundations are all that is left of the wooden masts on their 70-foot towers. 'Once we'd got used to the height it was tremendous fun climbing about on them putting up antennae.' Some of the huts have later additions from the MoD's missile testing days. 'We used to be able to see Orford Castle from a window here.' Some, mercifully, have been demolished. 'That's better – you can

really appreciate the radio lighthouse now'; others remain energetically vandal-
ised, standing among the shards of their shattered glass – 'to decay naturally'. *

Trying not to decay naturally ourselves, we watched Lords Chorley, Bridges
and Hemingford** demonstrate their skill at raising a windsock to mark the
auspicious occasion. 'When I demonstrated radar here I had Lord Swinton
[the Air Minister] breathing down my neck – and not a photographer in
sight. We weren't even allowed to keep a diary.' Their present lordships, aided
and abetted by a host of green-wellied wardens, took less than a minute to
get the orange emblem aloft and then did it all over again for the benefit of
the cameras. Second time round it caught the wind and fluttered nobly over
the National Trust's island HQ. This is the one hut so far renovated…

It's an odd acquisition for the Trust. Wildness and wilderness are understandably part of our heritage and gathering this unique bit of coast into the
Neptune project was very reasonably their main concern, but the weird debris
of the Ministry of Defence that comes with it presents a problem. If you can't
take it all away how do you use it to delight or educate the public? Can you
really convey the urgency and excitement of those young scientists through a
collection of derelict buildings? Can you recreate a sense of their desperate race
against time on a stony shore swept by the timeless sea? Can you even begin to
explain the dynamic science behind all this dead technology?

The Trust is famous for restoring the physical fabric of its buildings, but as
Lord Bridges reminded us, this is an exercise in restoring the '*genii loci*' of an area
used for widely different purposes. I only began to get the feel of it through the
people involved, past and present. In the face of those young men ferrying us
about in Land Rovers, I found the same enthusiasm for saving a bit of Britain
as Hanbury's bunch had for saving all of it. Behind them the Establishment is
probably no wiser in the fine detail of the enterprise than it was in the radar days,
but, like their predecessors, they have the wisdom to recognise expert advice.
As for the visitors, now welcome, Orford's strange mix of beauty and desolation
must make them ponder our history as surely as any great house might do. Not
much has changed after all: the young have a project, the promoters, prestige,
and the public have something to grumble about: 'What, no shop?'

Our pilgrimage proved its point: Orford Ness remains remote, secret and
contradictory. Its wide sky has been a painter's delight and a pilot's nightmare.
Like many before, what you find there depends on what you seek. Over the
door of Bawdsey Manor is carved the motto: '*Plutot mourir que changer*'. On
Orford Ness I would prefer the stones to say:

'*Plus ça change, plus c'est la même chose*'.

Heather Hanbury-Brown, 1995

---

* The radio lighthouse must have been such a more accurate and appropriate description of
Black Beacon: for that is just what the rotating loop beacon was.
** Lord Hemingford was Regional Chairman.

13

Epilogue

The Anglo-Saxon Chronicle tells of a battle recorded in the Icelandic *Saga of Olaf the Holy*. A thousand years ago, and over fifty years before the Conquest, the teenage Olaf Haraldsson, future king and patron saint of Norway, fought the ninth of his great battles here as part of a campaign to gain strategic control of key areas of East Anglia. The local authority on Anglo-Saxon history, Dr Sam Newton, asserts that the location is the so-called Crouch, the area opposite Havergate Island at the mouth of Stony Ditch.

Wars and skirmishes will have been conducted over the centuries on this prominent coastline. The Dutch Wars saw naval engagements and threats of Napoleonic invasion prompted the building of the mighty Martello towers, of which the one at Slaughden is the northernmost and biggest. During the nineteenth century, schemes were mooted for recreating substantial naval anchorages at Orford and at Aldeburgh, which would have necessitated the cutting of a canal through the Ness. For many and good reasons, these came to nothing.

The Ness is notable for much more than its association with matters military. In 1555 occurred the famous 'Miracle', which saw the shore along the whole Ness sprout such a plentiful crop of sea pea (*Lathyrus japonicus maritimus*) that serious famine was averted.

Maps over the decades show movement of the point of the Ness down the coast, just as the shingle spit has taken the mouth of river Ore further and further to the south. During the twentieth century, a slow but steady process of erosion has continued, with the point of the Ness growing blunter and less pronounced and the shore shifting unpredictably. The survival of both the Trinity House lighthouse and the National Trust's neighbouring coastguard lookout building has become a matter of real concern. The iconic lighthouse is doomed and will be removed. What, if anything, will replace it is yet to be decided.

The story of Orford Ness would be incomplete without reference to the property as a twenty-first century Nature Reserve. The National Trust is in no doubt as to its responsibility. With its impressive list of wildlife designations, the property is managed throughout the year with due attention to the wildlife as its first priority. The Ness is perhaps chiefly important as a leading site in East Anglia for migrating birds. Some of these visitors are precious rarities.

The Ness is noted for the vegetation that flourishes in the shingle. Each spring, the whole area goes green. Plant growth is visibly expanding from the ridges down into the swales. The quantity of plants and the area covered are both increasing.

The Ness, then and now. What of the Ness in centuries to come? While forecasting the future is scarcely the stuff of a history, the facts are that the very survival of fragile and positively volatile coastal areas is a subject for legitimate speculation. These pages have spoken of constant changes in usage and uncertainties over sustaining the status quo. An era of global warming and accelerating erosion must create for the Ness grave apprehension. Thus, in planning for the management and development of this property, the Trust has to take into account the grim possibilities of radical and far from predictable changes.

The truth is, however, that in the decades ahead, a harsh change in this shoreline must be a distinct possibility. Any breach in the sea wall at Slaughden would have an unpredictable impact on the flow of the river in and out of its existing mouth at Shingle Street. What would happen at Orford? Will erosion and deposition be affected by a serious rise in the sea level? How much more of the river wall will be overwhelmed as a result? Will Orford Ness, so long described as an 'island', in the event, actually become one? As to the impact of climate changes on the flora and fauna, and indeed, on the Trust's whole management programme of its historic property, who can tell?

The story of Orford Ness over the past 100 years has shown how this remarkable place has witnessed the creation of myths, mysteries and legends. It has told of the making of history, surrounded all the while by clouds of deception and subterfuge. Its unique atmosphere has inspired truly remarkable loyalty and affection from those that worked there, from those who allowed their creative imagination to be stimulated by the place, or from the swelling stream of visitors who cross the river to enjoy its open spaces and unpredictable climate. Perhaps its ultimate miracle will be that over the next 100 years it succeeds in coping with any and every adversity that may arise to threaten it.

GLOSSARY

AA	Anti Aircraft
A&AEE	Aircraft and Armament Experimental Establishment
AI	Air Interception (radar)
AFC	Air Force Cross
ARP	Air Raid Precautions
ASV	Air to Surface Vessels (radar)
AWRE	Atomic Weapons Research Establishment (subsequently AWE)
BBU	Bomb Ballistics Unit
CBE	Commander of the Order of the British Empire
CIA	Central Intelligence Agency (US)
CND	Campaign for Nuclear Disarmament
CPO	Chief Petty Officer (Royal Navy)
CSSAD (Tizard)	Committee for the Scientific Survey of Aerial Defence
C/O	Officer in Command
D/F	Direction finding
DSIR	Department of Scientific and Industrial Research
DSO	Distinguished Service Order
ENSA	Entertainments National Service Association
EODU	Unexploded Ordnance Demolition Unit
ES&NRA	East Suffolk & Norfolk River Authority
FRS	Fellow of the Royal Society
G-force	Force of gravity
GPO	General Post Office
HF/MF	High and medium wave (radio) frequencies
IFF	Identification Friend or Foe
LABS	Low altitude bombing system
LCGF	Landing Craft General Freight
LMS	London, Midland & Scottish (railway)
MoD	Ministry of Defence
MoS	Ministry of Supply
MAP	Ministry of Aircraft Production
MC	Military Cross
NA	National Archives, Kew (formerly the Public Record Office)

NATO	North Atlantic Treaty Organisation
NAAFI	Navy, Army & Air Force Institute
NCO	Non-Commissioned Officer
NHMF	National Heritage Memorial Fund
NNR	National Nature Reserve
ORS	Orford Ness Research Station
OTH	Over The Horizon (radar)
PLUTO	Pipe line under the ocean (fuel supply)
POW	Prisoner of War
PSA	Property Services Agency
QC	Queen's Counsel
RAE	Royal Aircraft Establishment (formerly Royal Aircraft Factory, Farnborough)
RCA	Radio Corporation of America
RDF	Radio Direction Finding (code 'cover' for Radar)
REME	Royal Electrical and Mechanical Engineers
ROC	Royal Observer Corps
RFC	Royal Flying Corps
RADAR	Radio Aid to Detection And Ranging
RAS	Royal Aeronautical Society
RNAS	Royal Naval Air Service
RNLI	Royal National Lifeboat Institution
RNVR	Royal Naval Volunteer Reserve
RSPB	Royal Society for the Protection of Birds
SALT	Strategic Arms Limitations Treaties
SNO	Senior Naval Officer
SSSI	Site of Special Scientific Interest
TRE	Telecommunications Research Establishment (Malvern)
UFO	Unidentified flying object
USAF	United States Air Force (USAAF during the Second World War)
UXB	Unexploded bomb
V-bomber	Victor, Valiant and Vulcan, nuclear bomb carriers
VC	Victoria Cross
VHF	Very High Frequency
VTM	Vosper Thorneycroft Merlin (Communications)

Endnotes

CHAPTER 3 — WARTIME PIONEERS

1 As a postscript to the story of parachutes, Melvill Jones father and son were to conduct further important research work on parachuting techniques from very high altitude shortly after the Second World War. Bennett Melvill Jones' son, Geoffrey, became a research physiologist, investigating the impact on the human body of very low air pressure at great height and the absorption of oxygen into the bloodstream. Bennett supplied his expertise on falling aeroplanes to develop the best sort of drone chute to maximise safe rapid descent to the point when the main chute would be released. Together the two wrote the definitive chapter in the *Textbook of Aviation Medicine*, entitled 'Aerodynamic forces and their effects upon man'.

2 The idea of confusing the enemy by dazzle should be understood in its context. By 1917, camouflage techniques adopted by the Royal Navy and Merchant Marine were designed to confuse the image of a ship as seen through a submarine periscope. The designs being devised by artists, notably by Norman Wilkinson, were effective enough and used for well over 2,000 vessels. Clearly, this idea was simply inappropriate for aircraft, but since such a technique was being adopted by one branch of the Services, it was almost inevitable that the others must try it too. The Royal Academician, Solomon J. Solomon was made an honorary Colonel to lead the programme for army camouflage on the Western Front. Orford Ness was the obvious venue for such trials for the air arm.

CHAPTER 4 — WIDENING HORIZONS

1 This idea of an aerial gramophone may seem somewhat bizarre. It was to be resurrected over twenty years later. The family archive at Tatton Park, Cheshire, reveals

that Lord Egerton was in touch with the Air Ministry in 1940 with a somewhat far-fetched suggestion: to confuse enemy anti-aircraft gunners by broadcasting the noise of British aero-engines from amplified gramophone records suspended in self-destructing balloons dropped from Allied bombers. Egerton, a pioneer pilot with his own private airstrip, had served in the RNAS from 1914. His idea was not adopted. However, his Lordship's estate at Tatton did provide the facility for Second World War training with a strange link to Orford Ness, where early para-chuting had first been tested during the First World War. It was the dropping zone for training military parachutists from the nearby No.1 Parachute Training School, based at RAF Ringway, now Manchester Airport. Once the RAF had accepted that parachutes had an important role to play in warfare, they quickly evolved a landing technique so much better and safer than any other anywhere, including in the USA and Germany, that they were assigned the job of training all military parachutists.

2 The Gotha bomber was a formidable weapon of its day, unmatched by any aircraft in the RAF. The so-called 'England Squadron' enjoyed great prestige and gener-ally high *esprit de corps*. Its chief purpose was to so 'blitz' London as to undermine British resolve to continue the war, and its ultimate method of attack was the incendiary rather than high explosive bomb. It never succeeded in creating the massive firestorms that were intended. The aircraft seemed to suffer from uncer-tain engines and other mechanical problems, which seriously undermined the confidence of pilots. The concept of bomber attack was never fully embraced by German High Command and the squadron suffered from lack of supply. In 1918 they were diverted to supporting the army in the field. In damaging civilian morale they were effective. They were far faster and better armed than Zeppelins and more than capable of resisting the RFC and RAF fighters sent against them. Only twenty were shot down by aircraft or anti-aircraft fire, the latter in spite of the enormous quantities of shell expended, the shrapnel from which did serious self-inflicted damage. Gothas were not robust and the Germans lost forty either crashing on landing or lost over the North Sea. The Gotha blitz nearly succeeded, but strangely, Britain learned more from the experience than Germany. The RAF developed the concept of the heavy bomber to destroy enemy cities. The Luftwaffe never took its bomber force much beyond what it conceived during the 1930s.

3 This curiously pusillanimous step by the War Office is explained by the 1899 Hague Conference on the conduct of warfare, and which banned the use of 'expanding' – or presumably, exploding – bullets. This convention was allowed to lapse in 1907, although it was still supported by Britain. The government must have questioned in its own mind whether the exigencies of war should override this policy, bearing in mind that the Allies were eager to be seen as the civilised contenders in this war who abided by the 'rules'. Interestingly, another convention from 1899 banned the projection of missiles from balloons. Was a Zeppelin 'a balloon'?

4 Readers interested in discovering the realities of life in a frontline Sopwith Camel fighter squadron in 1918 are recommended to read perhaps the finest novel about First World War action, written in 1935 by V.M. Yeates from his first-hand experience. *Winged Victory* graphically describes the terror pilots experienced from the danger of being hit and especially their horror of being set on fire, without parachutes or means of escape.

CHAPTER 5 — INTER-WAR YEARS

1 The radar project was, from August 1935, given a formal 'cover' name, a portmanteau creation that combined Radio Detection and D/F (direction finding): RDF was the result. It remained the British name until July 1943, when somewhat surreptitiously, the American name Radio Detection and Ranging – RADAR – was officially adopted. The word has become part of international vocabulary ever since. Watson Watt claimed in his autobiography that he had been responsible for this, following a visit to the US. It is interesting that at the time, the US Army were calling it DERAX – for Detection, Elevation, Range, Azimuth and Experimental – which could possibly have provided an alternative to the word radar.

2 It is easy to suppose that British radar was crucially superior in 1940. Luftwaffe fighter ace, Adolf Galland admitted as much, suggesting that 'we had nothing like it'. This was the claim made by historian George Millar, who graphically describes Chain Home as 'invisible walls twelve miles high and one hundred and twenty miles thick', in his book *The Bruneval Raid* (Cassell & Co., 1974). He was not altogether correct. German *Freya* and *Würzburg* radar systems were brilliant. But the Germans never accorded them high priority and the success of the 1942 raid provoked Hitler to divert resources to V-2 rocketry.

CHAPTER 6 — PRE-WAR RESEARCH

1 Not all historians agree. Professor Niall Ferguson in his study of twentieth-century conflict, *The War of the World*, (Allen Lane, 2006) argues that Germany was still too weak economically and diplomatically to risk war. Had Britain taken a robust line at Munich, he suggests, Hitler would have backed away. However, in purely military terms, the RAF needed every moment of respite to catch up with the Luftwaffe. Even in the late summer of 1940, the Germans enjoyed a five-fold numerical advantage.

CHAPTER 7 — THE RESEARCH STATION AT WAR

1 Any successful intelligence and propaganda ploy needs to remain undisclosed for as long as possible. In 1918, Britain had openly boasted of its intelligence successes,

notably over the achievement in breaking German naval codes in Room 40 at the Admiralty. This prompted the Nazi regime to develop their Enigma machines, to ensure that history would not repeat itself. Of course, the genius of Turing and his many colleagues at Bletchley Park confounded the enemy, and history did repeat itself. After the war, the truth of Bletchley was not revealed for over thirty years. Winston Churchill once described these Bletchley Park cryptoanalysts as 'the geese that laid the golden eggs'. He was a member of a Cabinet in 1923 that ill advisedly 'cackled', revealing the contents of a Soviet Russian coded message which immediately compromised an invaluable intelligence source. The Russians changed their codes and for twenty years, Britain was no longer able to read secret Soviet communications.

2 One enemy weapon defeated by Tallboy was the so-called V-3, Hitler's battery of long-range 150 millimetre guns, designed to fire relays of 6 feet long rocket-assisted shells targeted at London, 100 miles distant. The 420 feet long guns were being constructed in a bunker buried deep beneath the hamlet of Mimoyecques, between Boulogne and Calais. The 21-feet long 12,000 pound Tallboy bomb alone had the force and, with its Ness-designed fins, the accuracy and penetrative power to cause a subterranean earthquake. It is estimated that 10,000 workers were killed by drowning when the whole site was demolished by a direct hit from Lancasters of 617 (Dambusters) Squadron. This attack was launched following the failure of the USAF ill-fated Operation Anvil, which planned to drive Liberator bombers packed with explosive into the target area. Sadly, an accident led to the death of Joseph Kennedy Jnr when his plane prematurely exploded over Blythburgh. The German's V-3 project was abandoned. It was probably unworkable anyway, but the prospect of enormous shells hitting London at the rate of 5 per minute, as was intended, would indeed have been unthinkable.

3 Barnes Wallis was surely an inventor of pure and creative genius, whose contribution to technical development in aviation from the days of early airship design through to the era of supersonic flying was astonishing. He was the victim of rather miserly treatment, partly because he was seen as an employee of an industrial giant, Vickers, rather than as a 'public servant' and partly because he was not the sort of man to push himself forward. He also suffered severely from a sense that his inventions, however valuable, had inevitably led to excessive casualties particularly in Lancaster bombers' aircrews. He was made to believe that he was due to receive an award of £20,000, but when he revealed his intention to keep none for himself, the sum was halved – surely a strange response to generous altruism. His award went to his special charity at his old school, Christ's Hospital, to provide scholarship for the children of RAF personnel killed on active service. His knighthood came no less reluctantly, long after the war and more than twenty-five years after Watson Watt's. Wallis went on working creatively into the era of supersonic aircraft. Watson Watt achieved nothing of note after the early 1940s, and after the

break up of his marriage, he emigrated to Canada. He eventually died in 1973, seemingly almost forgotten and unrecognised, in an Inverness old peoples' home in his native Scotland.

CHAPTER 8 – THE NESS POST-WAR

1 The achievement of the rocket-firing squadrons of Typhoons during the Normandy campaign is described in *D-Day: The Battle for Normandy* by Anthony Beevor (Viking, 2009) His conclusions reflect tellingly on the post-war Ness trials. The rockets proved to be very inaccurate and an average of only 4 per cent of those fired hit the tanks that were their principle target. The evidence supplied by the Operational Research Section shortly after a battlefield was vacated showed that the RAF wildly exaggerated, on occasions up to ten-fold, their scores of hits on German Panzer tanks. Analysis of the battle scene showed that many more vehicles were destroyed by canon and machine-gun fire than by rockets. This is not to reflect on the decisive impact of rockets as a form of aerial bombardment. The most telling impact on the Germans, especially when counter-attacking over open country, was exactly what Tanner experienced. Swooping aircraft created a real sense of terror. Far more tanks and half-tracks were immobilised by their crews abandoning them than by strikes by the sixty-pound high explosive warheads of rockets. This inaccuracy explains the necessity for Ness trials.

2 This research work on Blue Streak was not entirely in vain. In 1961, the European Launcher Development Organisation was set up. Blue Streak was the UK contribution and full-scale launch tests of it were conducted over the next few years. This was all to become the precursor of the European Ariane space rocket. About ten firings of Blue Streak were undertaken, but from 1971 it was finally abandoned and Britain surrendered its rocketry expertise to continental rivals.

CHAPTER 10 – COBRA MIST: OVER THE HORIZON RADAR

1 Backscatter radar involved bouncing the transmitted signal backwards towards the source of the transmission. Cobra Mist therefore comprised a system where transmitter and receiver occupied the single site. Forward-scatter radar on the other hand projected its beam onwards to be received on the opposite side of the world. Its potential for monitoring aerial traffic was thus twice as great, though inevitably less sensitive. It seems the Cobra Mist system was over ambitious, but subsequent backscatter radars benefited from the lessons learned on the Ness.

CHAPTER 12 — THE MILITARY DEPARTS

1 The Neptune campaign was launched in 1965, to raise money so that the Trust could purchase coastal rescue properties without having to open time-consuming appeals. It was a great success, although at the time a major controversy arose over the Appeal Director and his reforming views. The total mileage of coast acquired rose from 150 to 550 miles by 1995. This also saw the Trust itself change dramatically into a more openly popular and democratic organisation, with membership soaring from just over 100,000 to over 3.8 million in 2010.

Index

A little b

Sussex

Personal memories inspired by The Francis Frith Collection®

THE FRANCIS FRITH COLLECTION

www.francisfrith.com

A Little Book of Sussex Memories
Personal Memories inspired by the Francis Frith Collection

The Francis Frith Collection
6 Oakley Business Park,
Wylye Road, Dinton,
Wiltshire SP3 5EU
Tel: +44 (0) 1722 716 376
Email: info@francisfrith.co.uk
www.francisfrith.com

Printed and bound in Malaysia
Contains material sourced from responsibly managed forests

Front Cover: Littlehampton, "Gee Whiz" c1960 L58087p
Frontispiece: Horsham, West Street 1959 H119122

The colour-tinting is for illustrative purposes only, and is not intended to be historically accurate

A little book of Memories – A Dedication

This book has been compiled from a selection of the thousands of personal memories added by visitors to the Frith website and could not have happened without these contributions. We are very grateful to everyone who has taken the time to share their memories in this way. This book is dedicated to everyone who has taken the time to participate in the Frith Memories project.

It is comforting to find so many stories full of human warmth which bring back happy memories of "the good old days". We hope that everyone reading this book will find stories that amuse and fascinate whilst at the same time be reminded of why we feel affection for Britain and what makes us all British.

Francis Frith always expressed the wish that his photographs be made available to as wide an audience as possible and so it is particularly pleasing to me that by creating the Frith web site we have been able to make this nationally important photographic record of Britain available to a worldwide audience. Now, by providing the Share Your Memories feature on the website we are delighted to provide an opportunity for members of the public to record their own stories and to see them published (both on the website and in this book), ensuring that they are shared and not lost or forgotten.

We hope that you too will be motivated to visit our website and add your own memories to this growing treasure trove - helping us to make it an even more comprehensive record of the changes that have taken place in Britain in the last 100 years and a resource that will be valued by generations to come.

John M Buck
Managing Director

www.francisfrith.com

Memories of a war time evacuee at Milton Street

I spent 3 years during the Second World War at Dumbrell's farm at Milton Street, a small hamlet near Eastbourne. I was a little Birmingham evacuee, aged 9 years old when I first arrived there, and it was three wonderful years of my life I shall NEVER forget. I went to school at Alfriston, my 'Uncle John' took me fishing in the River Cuckmere (Dumbrell's farm belonged to his father) and we went shooting wild duck at night. It was an unbelievable experience for me, as I had never been out of Birmingham before.

A particular memory of that time is of one dark night in 1940 when I was alone at home in Pond Cottage. My 'uncle' had gone with his wife for a drink to the Royal Oak pub. The German bombers were going over all night to bomb London. Suddenly, there was a knock on the door. I went to the door and opened it – and stood there in the doorway was a German Luftwaffe airman, who had baled out of his crashing Heinkel. He had his hands above his head, showing that he wanted to surrender. I just ran past him, and ran as fast as I could to the pub, where I screamed out "There's a German at our cottage!". Everyone ran down the lane, some with shotguns, and he was still there, with his arms in the air, BUT he had turned all the lights on, so everyone could see he wanted to surrender. The police came and took him away, and one of the policeman said to me "Well done, son". I felt very proud, and my Uncle John bought me a new bike as a reward. I often think about that German airman though, and I hope he got home safe to his family after the war.

Gordon Cooper

Sussex

Alfriston, View of the Cuckmere Valley from High and Over c1960 A33044

Does anyone else remember this forgotten piece of Netherfield history?

On 4th October 1940, during the Second World War, a Heinkel He 111 H-2 bomber crashed near the Mountfield gypsum mines, near Battle. Only one crew member survived, his parachute had caught in a tree and he was rescued unhurt. I was only five years old and still remember the event vividly. Due to the threat of enemy invasion my mum and I had gone to live with my gran and granddad (Charles and Sara Crouch) on Netherfield Hill, and late that night we heard the bomber crash over by the gypsum mines. The plane came down close to the miners' path that leads from the 'shooting box' near Netherfield church close to the mines, only about 700 metres, as the crow flies, from the church.

We got up very early the next day so we could go and look at the crash. There was the parachute, still hanging from the tree. The gypsum mine workers, including my uncles, were stripping what useful items they could from the wreckage. They thought at the time the aircraft was a Junkers, but records now confirm that it was a Heinkel. My uncle, Jim Crouch, known locally as 'Tubby', stripped lovely soft leather from the self-sealing petrol tanks. Later on we all had some items made from this leather, and we also made rings out of perspex taken from the wreck. My gran's brother, 'Ashie' Jennings, was the gypsum mines' blacksmith. He and his wife lived near the Netherfield Arms, and they kept one of the wrecked plane's propellers in their garden.

I would not like this crash to be forgotten as the dead crew members were all someone's loved one. The crew members' names were:

Unteroffizier Hildebrand – killed, Unteroffizier Bauer – killed, Gerfreiter Tschop – killed, Gerfreiter Zuckriegel – survived unhurt.

Peter Venner

Yes, we do...

I too remember the German plane crashing near the
Mountfield gypsum mines during the war. I came home on
leave shortly after the crash and went to see it. I actually got a
souvenir from the wreckage, the helmet of one of the German
crew members that was still there. It cleaned up well and I
used it after the war on my motor cycle, it was really good,
beautiful soft leather. I used it for several years.

Eric Saunders

> "Late that night
> we heard the
> bomber crash
> over by the
> gypsum mines."

I too as a child remember finding many pieces of the German
bomber that crashed near the Mountfield gypsum mines in
1940, on the crash site and around the surrounding area. This
was in the late 1960s. I still have them, bullets, fragments with
paint on, electric parts and so on. I worked in both mines and
was told about the crash by others that remember it.

Tim Willett

Growing up in Brighton during World War II

I was born to Jewish parents who had a ladies' clothes shop in
Kensington Gardens (The Lanes) in Brighton. My father died in 1941,
during the war, and my mother, now a very young widow, decided
she wanted us all to live above the shop. It had 2 rooms upstairs
which we used as bedrooms, and a small room which we used as a
dining/living room with a gas fire. She told us that if the Germans
invaded we would sit in front of the gas fire and turn it on, because
she was terrified of what might happen to us then as we were
Jewish. We had no bathroom, we went once a week to the public
baths, ugh! There was a toilet outside in the yard next to the coal
cellar, and a kitchen downstairs. I remember running to the air-raid
shelter during the night when Brighton was being attacked, which
was around the corner in another street. Everyone took something
down there to eat, it was like a picnic. However we eventually got
tired of doing that and stayed in bed during the air-raids and just
hoped for the best. I remember, of course, the local sweet shop,
and the rationing books coupons we had for everything. I used
to dream of when the war was over and I would go and buy such
a lot of sweets and just eat and eat. I also remember going to the
pictures, and the weekly serials we all looked forward to. When
an air-raid warning was shown on the screen a lot of people left
but my mother always told us never leave the cinema but to take
shelter under the seats – she was worried the people in the cinema
would panic as they were leaving and we might get trampled on.
Of course during the war the beaches had barbed wire all across
them, so we couldn't go to the beach, so we didn't go swimming at
all. School wasn't too bad. The Hippodrome Theatre was opposite
the school where we took shelter during air-raids. At first it was
fun because it meant we missed lessons, but then the teachers got
clever and took work with them for us to do whilst we were there.

After a few years of living above the shop we moved to a house in Hove. We had a Morrison shelter in our lounge, an iron contraption with a gate in front where we used to sleep during the air-raids. It wasn't big enough for all five of us so my mother and I slept on top of it, which wouldn't have been much help if a bomb had hit our house. When I grew up I asked my mother why she had made me sleep on top of it with her, she said she had no idea why, and we used to laugh at this.

Anita Lewis

Brighton, The Clock Tower
c1942 B2085008

ENGLAND
STILL
EXPECTS
YOU
TO DO YOUR
DUTY.

"Have you got any gum, chum?"

I was born in 1938 at Drewetts Cottage at Warninglid, a small village between Haywards Heath and Horsham. Dad was the head chauffeur to the Erricsons. By the time I was born, Dad was out swimming at Dunkerque and we never met until 1947. During the war years Mr Erricson died and the estate was sold up, leaving me and Mum homeless, but we must have lived there until just before D-Day in 1944 because I remember lots of soldiers, Canadian or American, walking past the house during the evening. I suppose they went to the (now closed) Rifleman Arms. We used to ask them for fags or matches, no wonder I had a 20-a-day habit by the age of 6! We also used to say "Have you got any gum, chum?", this was usually more successful than asking for fags. I often wonder how many of them survived D-Day.
Roy Hunnisett

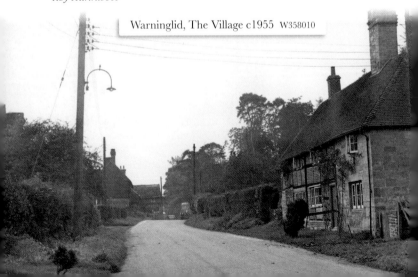

Warninglid, The Village c1955 W358010

Home to Eastbourne after the war...

From 1945 until around 1960 my family lived at 5 Wellesley Road at Eastbourne, at the rear of All Souls' Church. We got back to Eastbourne after being evacuated away during the Second World War to find it pretty much a ghost town. It took ages for the bomb damage to be repaired, and numerous unexploded bombs were excavated over the next 10 years. Every street corner you turned around revealed more damage, it seemed.

David Patterson

> "It took ages for the bomb damage to be repaired, and numerous unexploded bombs were excavated over the next 10 years.'

Eastbourne, The Bandstand and Pier 1947 E5105a

Bonfire night at Battle

One of the many memories I have of Battle from my childhood in the 1950s is of Bonfire Night, November 5th. Every year Battle had one of the best November 5th bonfire celebrations in Sussex, it was lots of fun. I remember Battle Rousers (home-made fireworks), they were awesome. They were arranged in circles and then let fly, they would run and explode with a huge bang, very scary. On Bonfire Night there was a huge parade down the High Street before a 'Guy Fawkes' was placed on top of the big bonfire that had been prepared in front of Battle Abbey. Then the fire would be lit and a rousing cheer would erupt, "Thanks to the Battle Bonfire Boys!". What a memory. The Abbey Hotel across the street always did a huge trade that night!

Eric Saunders

Battle, The Abbey Gatehouse 1927 80411

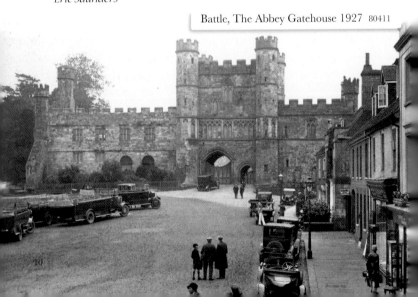

10

Looking for King Charles

When I was little and we went shopping in Chichester, I always liked looking for King Charles on the medieval Market Cross in the city centre. One of the niches on the Market Cross holds a bronze bust of King Charles I, who was executed in 1649 during the Civil War. Chichester's Member of Parliament at that time, William Cawley, was a signatory on the king's death warrant, and had to flee the country after the dead king's son was restored to the throne in 1660 as King Charles II, and he lived abroad for the rest of his life. Chichester's city fathers made sure that the new king could be sure of the city's loyalty in future by having this bronze bust of Charles I put on display on the Market Cross!

Julia Skinner

Chichester, The Market Cross from West Street c1955   C84024

"This is Worthing seafront, Sir, not a race-track."

In about 1935, when I was 5 years old, my grandfather used to take us all on gentle rides into the South Downs from his home at 11 Gaisford Road in Worthing in his circa 1930 Hillman Minx car. The beloved Minx was not turbo-charged and could probably manage to reach 50mph downhill following a scintillating acceleration to 40mph in about 5 minutes. My grandfather was well into his seventies and had only learned to drive following his retirement to Worthing. 'Taking it gently' was his usual driving style and, perhaps anticipating my later BMW 3-series boy-racing in London, I used to sit in the lovely rear leather seat secretly urging him on.

On one lovely sunny day my grandfather decided to live it up a little and ventured into downtown Worthing, where the Minx got caught up in the roaring traffic and ended up travelling the seafront at an unaccustomed and decidedly uncharacteristic speed. Very soon a large member of the Sussex constabulary raised a white glove and brought the Minx to a juddering halt. Peering through the window at my grandfather he observed: "This is Worthing seafront, Sir, not a race-track." For once my learned grandfather was speechless and all the passengers in the Minx erupted in laughter. "Ah well, Sir", said the constable, "they are all obviously on your side, but do watch your speed in future."

So my grandfather got away without receiving a speeding ticket and spent the rest of his life burning up the tarmac on the South Downs. Somewhere up there, an old black Hillman Minx, registration number PO 7764, is looking down and chuckling.

Cedric Marie

A near-death experience at Swan Hotel Corner

I nearly died here at Fittleworth in 1956, when I was seven
years old, after being sent on an errand for a quarter of
ham from Picknell's, the village shop at the top of the
hill above the Swan Hotel. Dodgy brakes on my bike led
me to come down the hill and emerge from the blind
corner created by the hotel across the main road without
stopping. I coincided there with Mrs Morley Fletcher who
was moving probably at only 20mph in her grey A30 car,
so I was saved.

Paul Barry

Fittleworth, The Swan Hotel c1950   F29003

Watching the signalman from the school bus

Between 1964 and 1966 I used to travel by bus from Haywards Heath to school in Burgess Hill, going over the railway level crossing at Keymer twice a day. If we were lucky a train would be coming and we would get to see the crossing in action. This photograph was taken looking south, towards Burgess Hill, and the signal box is visible on the far side of the crossing on the left. We would watch the signalman through the windows of the signal box as he operated the gates by turning what looked very much like an old-fashioned ship's wheel. On one occasion the train, instead of being the usual rather dull electric multiple unit, was hauled by a big mainline diesel (possibly a Class 40) in BR blue and yellow, which was much noisier and more impressive!

Mike Brown

Burgess Hill, Keymer Crossing 1966 B284128x

Helping the signalman on school holidays

Friends of our family once lived in Railway Cottages on Bexhill Road at St Leonards-on-Sea, their names were Harry and Rene Eaton. In those days when you were young and your families were friends you tended to call the adult members 'uncle' and 'aunt', and I used to stay with 'Uncle Harry' and 'Aunt Rene' during school holidays in the 1950s – and what fun it was, because Uncle Harry was a signalmen at Bo Peep Junction. I used to go down to the signal box when he was on duty and he would sometimes let me pull the signal levers, under his supervision of course. The next duty would be to log the passing train in, what a treat, I never wanted to go back home when the time came. What hazy happy days they were, gone forever into the mists of memory. I wish I could travel in time and go back there now.

Colin Apps

> "I used to go down to the signal box when he was on duty and he would sometimes let me pull the signal levers."

The Bury ferryman

In this old photograph (opposite) you can see the steps that were used in the past by the Bury ferryman, who used a pole to steer the punt from the Bury bank of the River Arun to the Amberley bank on the opposite side. The punt was attached to a chain which stretched across the river, lying on the bottom. The ferryman from the 1920s to the late 1940s (when the fare was three pence) was my 'Uncle' Bob Dudden, who took up the duties of ferryman when he left the Navy after the First World War. Bob was not really my uncle, but he and my grandfather were friends who ran away to join the Navy together in about 1912. Sadly, my grandfather was severely wounded in the First World War, but Uncle Bob came through it safely, having had the job on board ship of barber! Uncle Bob also took care of the grassy area behind the steps. He and his wife 'Aunt Min' lived in the house you can see on the left of the picture. You can see a bench dedicated to Bob Dudden near the ferry today.

Wendy Carey

> "The ferryman from the 1920s to the late 1940s (when the fare was three pence) was my 'Uncle' Bob Dudden."

Delivering smuggled goods up the Arun...

My grandmother Hannah Burchell came from Bury and was married at the church seen in this view, St John's. Next to the church is Bury Manor, which is now a school but in the past it was where the local 'bigwig' lived. My grandmother told stories of her youth in the 1890s of smugglers coming up the River Arun and delivering goods to the Manor. The smugglers' friends used to pretend to be ghosts in the churchyard to deter unwanted people from getting near.

Wendy Carey

Bury, The Church from the River 1898 42556

A little book of memories

Kirdford School in the 1960s

I went to school at Kirdford for a couple of years in the 1960s and have fond memories of it. The headteacher then was Miss Dunsmore, and other teachers I remember were Miss Dadswell and Mrs Heaver. The toilet block was outside, as is was at most schools in those days. The classrooms were heated in winter by big old coke-burning stoves with a metal guard round them. The headteacher's office was a room off the top classroom.

I used to travel to and from school on a school bus from Ifold that we called 'Ken's Camel' – probably because it was owned by Ken Scammel.

I recently went back to Kirdford and couldn't find the school – it must have been demolished – but the village itself hadn't changed much. I approached the village on a road that passed the old school playing field which was probably the village playing field. I was really pleased to find this photograph on the Frith website showing the school I remember so well.

Carol Evans

Kirdford, The School 1950 K118012

Fond memories of Whincroft School at Crowhurst

I was at Whincroft School for Girls at Crowborough as a 7-10 year old, from 1959 until 1961, when it closed. I have fond memories of the school, but I was a quite mischievous and naughty little girl who was often in trouble with Miss Vyse, my teacher! Having taught myself now for nearly 39 years, I realise that the naughty lively chatty ones quite often become teachers themselves, having driven their own to distraction!

Some of the most exciting events I remember from those days were Miss Vyse's dog swallowing a drawing pin and then being given a cotton wool sandwich with mysterious effects, having to sleep on an army bed in a classroom for one night as a punishment because I had been talking after lights out,

> "I was a quite mischievous and naughty little girl who was often in trouble with Miss Vyse, my teacher!"

and the week we managed to secrete a guinea pig or something similar in the wood (my weekly boarder friend had brought it back to school from her weekend home). I also recall the 'Back of Beyond' – a glorious place of confusion and oddity near the kitchen. But best of all were Miss Cholmley's wonderful reading evenings round the fire, which inspired me with the tales of 'The Borrowers', 'Pilgrims Progress' etc. It was a school with a wonderful atmosphere and worth fondly remembering.

Caroline Nias

Happy memories of
Warnham Court School

Warnham Court near Horsham was bought by the London County Council in 1947 and (under the LCC's successor, the London Borough of Lambeth) was run as a residential school for 'Delicate Children' from London until the school closed in 1997. This often meant children with asthma or those recovering from tuberculosis, who were sent to Warnham Court School to benefit from the country air of Sussex and the facilities the school and its extensive grounds could offer. Many former pupils have recorded happy memories of their time spent at Warnham Court School on the Frith website – here are just a few:

Warnham, Warnham Court from the South East c1924 75343

I was only at Warnham Court School for six months in the 1950s, but they were the best six months of my life. I loved the post coming because I had a large family, two brothers and six sisters, so I got lots of letters and Mum and Dad always sent me some money for the tuck shop, going to town etc. I remember one particular girl who was there, I think her name was Maggie, she was our age but her asthma was so bad that one of the lads had to give her a piggy back so she could come wherever we were going. That's how nice everyone was.   Pat Lewis

What a year 1961 was for me. Like others before me I arrived at Warnham Court School not knowing what to expect but found a place of peace for the first time in my life where I was treated with kindness. When we arrived, the headmaster Mr Ernest Savage and his wife greeted everyone in the hall and then we were whisked off by Miss Western and Miss Bedford for something to eat and then a bath before being given our school uniforms. I was the Captain of Bodiam House but I lost the Captaincy for a month after being caught smoking, and I haven't smoked since! I wrote to Mrs Savage many years ago just to say how wonderful I thought she and her husband were to everyone who was there.   Jacqueline Davey

I was privileged to teach at Warnham Court School in 1966-7. It was my first year of teaching and although I found the days long – from breakfast supervision to 'lights out' on the dormitory floor in the evening – I have fond memories of my time there. I spent a lot of time with my pupils exploring the countryside and doing things like pond dipping – getting our wellies good and wet! I can still remember the aroma of Mr Savage's cigars…   Dr David Ford

A little book of memories

Boring History!

I attended Storrington Primary School in Spierbridge Road in the 1980s. We all looked forward to our last year at the school, because during the summer term the seniors were taken to Church Street as part of a local history lesson. Of course, we all thought it would be a great excuse to lark about and pop into the sweet shop which used to be on the corner of Church Street going into the High Street. How disappointed we were when we realised we would have to work! After the shock of the realisation we were actually having a history lesson, I thought it became quite fun, learning about the monastery and the old buildings – but I didn't dare tell my mates that!

Ashlea Shaw

Newhaven, The Harbour c1960 N20054

Fun on the Newhaven-Dieppe Ferry in 1960

When I was at Pinner Grammar School in the 1960s the school had a student exchange programme with Annecy in France, and every year a party of 4th- and 5th-formers from the school travelled over to France on the Newhaven to Dieppe Ferry. When I was in the fourth form I joined the school party, which was very exciting as I had never previously travelled abroad. We sailed on the 'Arromanches', a cross-channel ferry that sailed on the Newhaven to Dieppe route until 1964 (although the large ferry ship seen in this photograph is the 'Londres'). I still remember my channel crossing in her one sunny day in May 1960. A group of us got into trouble for playing with the ship's manual steering gear at the stern!

> "A group of us got into trouble for playing with the ship's manual steering gear at the stern!"

John Howard Norfolk

Andreadswald

In ancient times the great primeval forest of 'Andreadswald' covered much of Kent, Surrey and Sussex and gave its name to the Weald, a flattish region of heavy land between the forest ridge at the northern border of Sussex and the South Downs. The Weald remained heavily forested and was not perceived as an area to be farmed until the Middle Ages, with only a few small clearings made in the woodland for habitation – the 'hursts' of the region, such as Ticehurst and Wadhurst – but is now an agricultural region. The remains of the huge Wealden forest of the past are now split up into separate patches of woodland in both East and West Sussex. Ashdown Forest in the north-west corner of East Sussex is the largest, and includes tracts of heath, moorland and rocky outcrops as well as woodland. Many of the forest hamlets, such as Chelwood Gate and Coleman's Hatch, take their names from the old 'hatches', or gates, into the forest in past times.

Ashdown Forest,
From Colemans Hatch 1928 80763

Life in the Forest, from the 1940s onwards

My family moved to Colemans Hatch in East Sussex in 1940,
when I was 20 months old, and my father finally sold up in the
early 1980s. We lived at Yew Tree Cottage, out in the Ashdown
Forest. I loved the Forest, and was allowed to roam free from an
early age. I have many memories of the wide open spaces (yes,
they were then, when the smallholders cut and gathered the
vegetation for their animals' food and bedding, and cut birch for
firewood). Once, when I'd wandered off (aged about 4) to meet
the postman, who came from the Forest Row direction, when
he didn't come I apparently just kept on walking. I remember
feeling sleepy and lying down by a bridge to sleep, and being
woken by the search party, led by my dad (Tom Townsend) I
wasn't at all bothered, I just loved the attention.

Vivien Barber

Colemans Hatch, Newbridge 1928 80771

I was a choirboy at St John's

I first attended the church of St John the Baptist in Hove in 1958 as a Cub Scout and went to the children's Sunday service at 9.40am. The 'grown-ups' service at 11.00am seemed very serious to me as an 8-year-old! I joined the church choir as a choirboy around 1960. Mr Clifford Roberts was a charming but very serious man and a brilliant organist and choirmaster. The range of pieces we sang as anthems was truly amazing, and the choir of about six ladies, four boys, and six men took on and performed every Sunday a different anthem as well as psalm chants and all the hymns (in full harmony, of course!). We used to practice every Friday evening, and Mr Roberts laid out all the music for the coming weeks on chairs in front of the chairs that the choir would sit on. Each chorister had their own hymn book and psalter with their names on them. It was just before the choir practice one night in 1963 that we heard that John F Kennedy had been shot and when my father came to pick me up for the walk home, he notified us that the President had died. So I really do know where I was when I heard President Kennedy was shot!

It was an honour to be chosen to carry the cross in front of the procession, comprising the clergy and the choir, as we emerged from the side door to the church, which always seemed to be full for the 11.00am service. We also sang for the 6.30pm evensong, and memories of the sun flooding through the west window during the service stay with me still. I stayed in the choir until 1968. I spent a very happy 10 years singing at St John's during my teen years, a period that laid down a passion in me for music that has remained with me ever since. In this photo of the church, the small door on the extreme left was the entrance to the church hall, and the door next to it, to the choir robing room and side door to the church.   *Tony Hagon*

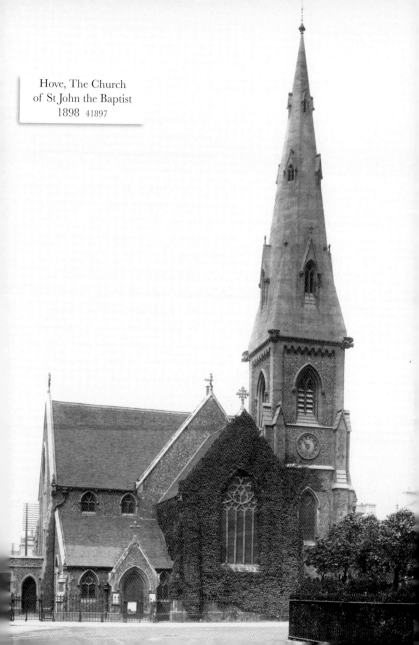

Hove, The Church
of St John the Baptist
1898 41897

My teenage years at Sompting, near Worthing, in the 1950s and 60s

My family lived in Orchard Cottages on West Street in Sompting. I have many happy memories from my childhood and teenage years in the village, include going to Mr Atturbury's shop to buy sweets. Near his shop was the Salvation Army Hall, which a lot of the village children attended on Sunday afternoons. On the right of the photograph S148004 of West Street is the Smugglers Restaurant which is where I gained my first employment after leaving school, but sadly it didn't quite work out. My dad wouldn't let me carry on working there because he thought the hours were too long for a 15-year-old! Just further along West Street was (and still is) the Gardener's Arms pub where my friend Sally and myself would sit and pretend to like lager and lime, but when nobody was looking we threw it out of the window – the money we wasted!

Linda Milburn (née Reardon)

Sompting, West Street c1955 S148004

Uncle Bonnie's Chinese Jazz Club

Around the time this photograph was taken, the Aquarium at Brighton was the venue for Uncle Bonnie's Chinese Jazz Club, which ran all-night sessions on a Friday night, from 11pm until about 6am the next morning. All sorts of jazz was played there, including trad jazz. Drinks were served most of the night, and of course there was a smoky atmosphere from cigarettes. It was great music and a great atmosphere, and afterwards you all went home for breakfast – unless you could find a café open somewhere.

Dave Wright

> "It was great music and a great atmosphere, and afterwards you all went home for breakfast."

Brighton, The Aquarium c1955 B208502

An embarrassing incident on Kingston Beach

In the late 1960s I lived opposite the lighthouse seen in this photograph. I remember one occasion when a friend and myself decided to go 'skinny dipping' late one night. When we got in the water and turned round, to my horror I found that my mother was following! The silly woman dropped her towel half way down the beach and as she went to walk to the water's edge the light from the lighthouse came round! There was my blessed mother making a complete idiot of herself – naked – fully lit up – and trying to crouch down and hide herself. I was mortified!

Another embarrassing memory is of the day I came home from school and was furious to find that the local lifeboat crew had been allowed to bunk down in my bedroom (a really Heath Robinson loft conversion!) after a very late call to sea. How embarrassing that was for a teenage girl – all my frillies were on view, and I had really sad posters on my wall! I loved living there though – our house was dead in line with the harbour entrance and we had a great view. I remember once looking out of a window of our house and seeing a ship stuck right across the harbour entrance.

Paula Kinsella

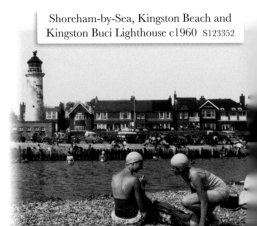

Shoreham-by-Sea, Kingston Beach and Kingston Buci Lighthouse c1960 S123352

Bass fishing at Southwick

I turned eighteen in 1965. It was around this time that I
had a tendency upon coming home from the pub (in the
summer) to have a black coffee,
tie a fishing rod onto the bike,
and head off for Southwick via
Brighton (about 35 miles from
Reigate). Such energy, at that
age! Upon arrival at Southwick
I'd catch shrimps from the
walkway using a drop-net and
kippers for bait, then when dawn came (and a suitable tide),
I'd float-fish for bass from the power station outflow, the
output being gentle at that time of day. (Bass: stupidly called
'sea bass' on menus these days.) Those were the days.

> "I'd float-fish
> for bass from
> the power station
> outflow."

Stephen Grieve

Southwick, The Harbour and
Power Station c1950 S477037

A little book of memories

This was my grandfather

The boy standing in the road in the 1908 photograph of Park Avenue at Arundel (below) was my grandfather, Joseph Smith. He was about 12 when this view was taken. The two little girls sitting on the roadside were his sisters (and my two great-aunts), Kathleen and Josephine Smith. They lived just a few yards from where this photograph was taken, in the lodge at Arundel Park gates. My great-grandfather, William, was a groom to the then Duke of Norfolk (Henry) of Arundel Castle, and his wife Kate, my great-grandmother, was a domestic.

Nicholas Seward

Arundel, Park Avenue 1908 60166

The people in this photo are...

My mother has a copy of this photo of Rustington on her wall. I am told that the two ladies pushing the prams are my grandmother (Peggy Prebble) and her twin sister (Elsie Cheshire). The little girl in the middle is my mother, Patricia Margaret, and the girl sitting in the pram is her sister Joyce. My mother remembers the photographer asking permission to take the photo of them all, and then he sent them a copy that was printed as a postcard – and she still has that original postcard.

Dave Turnbull

Rustington, Broadmark Parade c1950 R81035

A little book of memories

This might be me...

I am wondering if the child bending down and putting his wellies on in this photograph is me, as I spent every minute I could of my childhood down on the shore at Itchenor, especially as my dad's boatyard, Haines, was right there. I had a bobble hat and jacket exactly the same as the boy in this view. I would have been 9 years old at the time.

Andrew Haines

Itchenor, Yachts on the Water c1960   I46045

This is me and my mum

The lady seen in the foreground of this photograph of Newhaven is my mum, with me walking to her left, and my sister is one of the children in the pushchair. We lived locally and went to the beach all the time. My favourite memory of that time was the excitement we felt on arrival, smelling the familiar smell of seaweed draped all the way up the concrete steps leading on to the sand, and the lovely feel of sand under your feet as you padded down them.

Terrie Leach

Newhaven, The Promenade c1965 N20071

35

Polegate Windmill

North of Eastbourne is Polegate, where the oldest tower windmill in Sussex can be found. When it was built in 1817 it was in the parish of Willingdon and known as Willingdon Mill, but since the creation of the Civil Parish of Polegate in 1939, which included the mill, it has been known as Polegate Windmill. It was restored in the 1980s by the Eastbourne and District Preservation Society and it is open to the public every Sunday afternoon during the summer from Easter to the end of October. For more information see the Sussex Mills Group website www.sussexmillsgroup.org.uk where there is a link to Polegate Windmill.

Plump pigeons from Polegate Windmill!

I remember when Polegate Windmill was still a commercial working mill, and I recall watching the millstones grinding the grain. This was in the 1950s when the Council houses were starting to be built there. Later the mill closed and went into decline for some years until the decision was made to restore it. I knew the gentleman who was given the job of cleaning out the resident pigeon population and so secured quite a few very plump pigeons which were delicious, they having been so well fed on the grain that had been left stored in the mill.

Polegate, like Willingdon, has grown considerably over the last 60 years or so. In the 1950s when I used to walk to Polegate from Lower Willingdon there were few houses between the two villages, whereas now they are practically continuous.

Jeff Miller

Polegate, The Windmill c1965 P259030

Wannock Tea Gardens

Wannock Tea Gardens near Eastbourne were created in the 1930s. The gardens included various attractions including a model village.

I was very familiar with the Wannock Tea Gardens as a child, as I used to walk through them on my way to The Glen on Jevington Road which was a favourite play area for me and my friends. We used to look for eels in the creek that ran through The Glen. On one occasion we took a picnic with us and on the way home I was carrying an empty lemonade bottle. As we went through the gardens we passed a silver globe known as 'The Witches Circus'. It was entertaining in that it would distort reflections, and I was putting it to use with my lemonade bottle when I accidentally hit it. The globe shattered into numerous pieces and I was promptly apprehended by Mr Wootton, the proprietor, for wilful damage. Then police got involved but I convinced them that it was an accident and no further action followed apart from the confiscation of the bottle (and there was a 3 pence return on that!).

(Honest – it WAS an accident.)

Jeff Miller

Wannock, The Tea Gardens c1950 W372005

Hazelwick Mill

I remember the draining of the mill pond at Three Bridges, near Crawley. My family were the last occupants of the old mill, which was lost to the Crawley New Town development. We children used to play on the mill pond, making rafts from the old oil barrels that the contractors left. We used to wait for them to pack up for the week and then start up the little engine and dump trucks, having a wonderful time. We also had the keys to the RB 49 caterpillar digger that we would start but were too small to drive, although we could make the dig bucket at the front go up and down.

Edward (Ted) Miller

Three Bridges, Hazelwick Mill 1906 55387

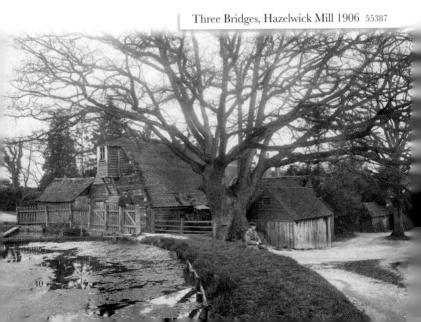

40

Playing by the River Mole

I too remember playing by the River Mole at Three Bridges
as a child. My parents ran the (now demolished) Fox Hotel
close to the river at Three Bridges for most of the 1950s and
60s. When the new estate at Three Bridges was being built,
the construction company had a narrow gauge railway for
moving stuff around. We used to ride on this at evenings
and weekends after the builders had gone home! My love
of railways came from the Loco crew who drank at the Fox
and gave me (unofficial) footplate rides.

David Randall

Three Bridges, The Fox 1905 53311

Fun and frolics with my grandmother at Bognor Regis

When I was young my family lived in Nyewood Lane in Bognor Regis, but I used to stay frequently with my grandmother in her flat a couple of hundred yards from the Royal Norfolk Hotel near the seafront. One of my earliest memories, from the late 1940s, is of her taking me out of bed one summer dawn for a walk down to the beach in front of the Esplanade Theatre. We both went skinny dipping, for it didn't matter to her that the classy hotels on the Esplanade overlooked the shore!

Bognor Regis, The Promenade 1949 B130048

The pier at Bognor was on my parents' list of forbidden places, but my grandmother and my old aunts took me there after it had been rebuilt after the Second World War. (The long deck of the pier had been cut so that it wouldn't be so easy for Hitler's troops to use it to come ashore.) I remember there was a miniature train that took adults and children from one end of the pier to the other. As a young child, I soon learnt that if I put a penny into the slot of one of those little crane booth amusements on the pier, there was only the remotest

> "The pier at Bognor was on my parents' list of forbidden places,"

likelihood of the crane picking up anything, and if it did, its jaws were so slippery that it would drop the cheap toy. Hence, I have never bought a lottery ticket.   *Josephine Hammond*

Bognor Regis, The Pier, c1960   B130158

My great-great-grandparents had this pub in 1871

My great-great-grandparents Mary and William Street had the Sussex Oak pub in Warnham in the 1870s and my grandmother says she used to have to get up at 5am to go and clean for them. She was told by her grandparents that she'd better do it properly or there would be trouble, she was only 8 years old then. Her own parents had the Greets beer-house in Friday Street in Warnham.

Sandra Baldwin

Warnham, Warnham Corner and the Sussex Oak pub c1955 W28009

Working at the Drawing Office

From 1962 to 1966 I worked in the drawing office of
Horsham Urban District Council, which was in the first
floor extension to the right of this picture. This was
my first job and my boss was Deputy Engineer and
Surveyor, John Sheldon, and the big chief was John Ridd,
Engineer and Surveyor. I used to park my motor-scooter
in the stable block at the rear of the building. A source
of amusement was to launch paper planes down to the
schoolgirls who used to sit on the park benches below!

Richard Scullion

Horsham, The Council Offices c1955   H119073

Turning the gas lights on and off at Hassocks Station

I was born in Burgess Hill in 1955. I attended Oakmeads County Secondary School, and when I started work I got an apprenticeship with South Eastern Gas and worked out of the workshop and stores at the back of the showroom in Church Road in Burgess Hill. This was in 1971 when the gas board only had 2 vans, one was a Ford Anglia and the other a Ford Transit. The rest of us had to use trade bikes, with a tray on the front where we put our tool bags, and cycle round to the customers' houses. One of our jobs was to turn the gas lights on (last job of the day) and off (first job of the day) on Hassocks Station railway platform – not a job anyone enjoyed when it involved cycling to Hassocks on a heavy bike, especially in the pouring rain.

Paul Smith

> "In 1971 the gas board only had 2 vans, one was a Ford Anglia and the other a Ford Transit."

My dad sold flowers at the Black Swan pub at Pease Pottage...

In the late 1940s my father and our neighbour, Mr George Lee, used to sell flowers outside the Black Swan pub at Pease Pottage, south of Crawley. The pair of them would bunch flowers picked from their respective gardens and take them up to the Black Swan on a Sunday evening to sell to trippers homeward bound from a day by the seaside on the Sussex coast. The flowers were kept fresh in stone jars.

Eileen Cook

...and so did mine!

My dad, Sid Sargent, also sold flowers at the Black Swan at Pease Pottage in the 1950s. He grew dahlias and golden rod in our garden at Truggers in Handcross, bunched them up on Sunday afternoon and biked up to Pease Pottage to sell them to the Londoners going home after a day in Brighton.

Penny Smith

Woodhurst Hospital

I was a pre-nursing student in 1962 at the South London Hospital for Women. As part of our course I was sent to work at Woodhurst Hospital at Pease Pottage in Sussex for 6 months, prior to beginning my SRN training. Woodhurst was the convalescent home linked to the South London Hospital, where ladies were sent for a couple of weeks to recover from surgery. They had excellent care from the nursing staff and the local GP called regularly to monitor progress. The beautiful grounds and gardens of Woodhurst were a great place to recuperate. Visitors were allowed at strict visiting times at weekends. When discharged, the patients were transported back to London by ambulance. As staff, we were very well treated. We lived on the upper floor (the old servants' quarters) and we had our own private garden. I well remember camping out in the garden on warm summer nights, as the rooms were small and hot. There were several of us pre-nursing students there at the time, as well as the permanent staff. One of our jobs at weekends was to remove the small wooden blocks under the feet of the hospital beds and wash them in carbolic and replace them – there was no MRSA then! I went back to the South London Hospital to do my SRN and then Midwifery training, and retired in 1999 after a 30 year career as a Midwife. I have often driven past Woodhurst and reflected on my time spent there.

Valarine Cooper

Pease Pottage, Ward 3, Woodhurst Hospital c1955 P252010

My grandad looked after the Eastbourne flower gardens

My grandad was foreman of the Carpet Gardens on Eastbourne seafront. He took over from his elder brother who had taken over from their father. They had, as a family, looked after the Carpet Gardens for over a century. The family name was Cottington. Grampy always told us that when the Carpet Gardens were first laid out and they were digging over the flower beds they uncovered Roman mosaics. As a tribute to those long-ago craftsmen who had made them, they copied the design in the flowers.

Just a simple family memory from long ago.

Yana Askaroff

Eastbourne, The Carpet Gardens 1912 64974

I was a postman at Bolney

In 1957, having just completed my National Service, I was living at home in Lindfield. Whilst looking for a permanent job I took up a part time job at Haywards Heath Post Office. Each day for 6 days a week, after reporting to H H Post Office, I was driven out to Bolney Post Office with two others plus the mail. On arriving at Bolney we set about sorting the mail and delivering the same by bike. This was done twice a day, with sometimes only up to six letters to deliver in the afternoon post. At the furthest point a post box was emptied which usually only contained 2 or 3 letters, plus some coins for me to purchase the required stamp.

Stanley Wood

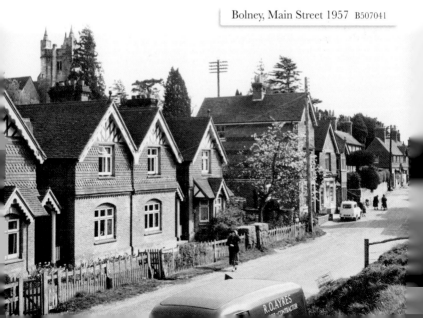

Bolney, Main Street 1957 B507041

My grandfather was the head gardener at Bateman's

My grandfather, A J Hurd, was Rudyard Kipling's head gardener at Bateman's for a time in the 1920s. He, my grandmother and my mother and her sister lived in one of the cottages (which still exists) near the mill adjacent to Bateman's. In addition to his responsibilities in the gardens, Grandpa also worked with the private hydro-electric turbine generator (which also still exists) which provided electricity to the house. That work is referred to in a letter of reference Mrs Kipling wrote for Grandpa when he moved on, which my mother still has. She also still has the letter Rudyard Kipling wrote to the local education authorities explaining to them that my mother was too young to have to walk the considerable distance to the local school, and was so bright that waiting another year wouldn't hurt!   *Ian Richardson*

Burwash, Bateman's, Rudyard Kipling's House c1960 B291030

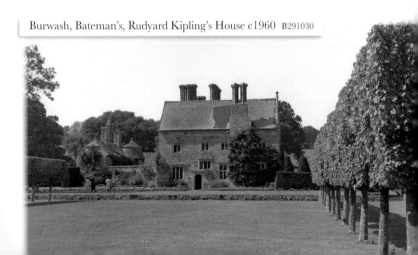

A little book of memories

Mrs Rapley's corner shop at Crawley Down

The shop seen on the corner on the right hand side of this 1960s photograph was called Rapley's Corner Shop when I was a child in the 1950s. It was owned by Mrs Rapley, and as a child I used to help her there after school and on Saturdays, serving in the shop and re-stacking the shelves with stock. I loved doing it and enjoyed spending time talking to people as they came in for their groceries. In those days the sweets were in huge jars and were measured out by the ounce into brown paper bags. I remember eating dairy ice-cream blocks in between wafers, the ice-cream was really creamy and came wrapped in paper then and the wafers were kept in big glass jars. Cigarettes came in small packs of 5 and 10 then, too!

Elizabeth (Liesel) Walters

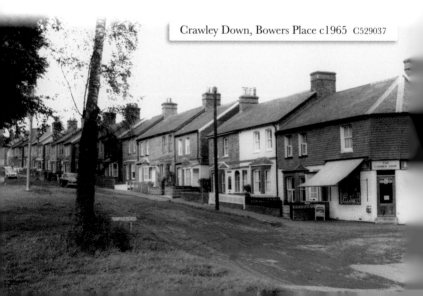

Crawley Down, Bowers Place c1965   C529037

My father worked at this shop

My father, Ron Burchell, worked in the village shop at Bury seen
in this photograph. The Burchell family had lived in the village for
generations. The owners of the shop then were Edward Grinsted
and his wife Millie, who was my godmother. We lived at the
thatched Old Cottage behind the hedge on the left of this view. My
dad had been a shop boy here before he joined the RAF in the 1920s,
and when he left the RAF in 1946 he worked there again. The shop
sold a wide range of food and hardware, and was also a Post Office.
Sugar, rice and so on would be weighed out and wrapped up in
'sugar paper', often in a deep pink or purple colour. Just after the war
we had to take our coupons to the shop and the amount needed
were cut out of our ration book with a big pair of scissors which
were kept on a string by the till and the fearsome bacon slicer. The
shop was the hub of the various social groups and activities of the
village, such as the folk dance group, the Women's Institute and the
Flower and Produce Show. Notices about what was going on, items
for sale and suchlike were hung on the door.   *Wendy Carey*

Bury, The Village Stores c1955   B509017

FRANCIS FRITH

PIONEER   VICTORIAN   PHOTOGRAPHER

Francis Frith, founder of the world-famous photographic archive, was a complex and multi-talented man. A devout Quaker and a highly successful Victorian businessman, he was philosophical by nature and pioneering in outlook. By 1855 he had already established a wholesale grocery business in Liverpool, and sold it for the astonishing sum of £200,000, which is the equivalent today of over £15,000,000. Now in his thirties, and captivated by the new science of photography, Frith set out on a series of pioneering journeys up the Nile and to the Near East.

INTRIGUE AND EXPLORATION

He was the first photographer to venture beyond the sixth cataract of the Nile. Africa was still the mysterious 'Dark Continent', and Stanley and Livingstone's historic meeting was a decade into the future. The conditions for picture taking confound belief. He laboured for hours in his wicker dark-room in the sweltering heat of the desert, while the volatile chemicals fizzed dangerously in their trays. Back in London he exhibited his photographs and was 'rapturously cheered' by members of the Royal Society. His reputation as a photographer was made overnight.

VENTURE OF A LIFE-TIME

By the 1870s the railways had threaded their way across the country, and Bank Holidays and half-day Saturdays had been made obligatory by Act of Parliament. All of a sudden the working man and his family were able to enjoy days out, take holidays, and see a little more of the world.

With typical business acumen, Francis Frith foresaw that these new tourists would enjoy having souvenirs to commemorate their days out. For the next thirty years he travelled the country by train and by pony and trap, producing fine photographs of seaside resorts and beauty spots that were keenly bought by millions of Victorians. These prints were painstakingly pasted into family albums and pored over during the dark nights of winter, rekindling precious memories of summer excursions. Frith's studio was soon supplying retail shops all over the country, and by 1890 F Frith & Co had become the greatest specialist photographic publishing company in the world, with over 2,000 sales outlets, and pioneered the picture postcard.

FRANCIS FRITH'S LEGACY

Francis Frith had died in 1898 at his villa in Cannes, his great project still growing. By 1970 the archive he created contained over a third of a million pictures showing 7,000 British towns and villages.

Frith's legacy to us today is of immense significance and value, for the magnificent archive of evocative photographs he created provides a unique record of change in the cities, towns and villages throughout Britain over a century and more. Frith and his fellow studio photographers revisited locations many times down the years to update their views, compiling for us an enthralling and colourful pageant of British life and character.

We are fortunate that Frith was dedicated to recording the minutiae of everyday life. For it is this sheer wealth of visual data, the painstaking chronicle of changes in dress, transport, street layouts, buildings, housing and landscape that captivates us so much today, offering us a powerful link with the past and with the lives of our ancestors.

Computers have now made it possible for Frith's many thousands of images to be accessed almost instantly. The archive offers every one of us an opportunity to examine the places where we and our families have lived and worked down the years. Its images, depicting our shared past, are now bringing pleasure and enlightenment to millions around the world a century and more after his death.

For further information visit: www.francisfrith.com

INTERIOR DECORATION

Frith's photographs can be seen framed and as giant wall murals in thousands of pubs, restaurants, hotels, banks, retail stores and other public buildings throughout Britain. These provide interesting and attractive décor, generating strong local interest and acting as a powerful reminder of gentler days in our increasingly busy and frenetic world.

FRITH PRODUCTS

All Frith photographs are available as prints and posters in a variety of different sizes and styles. In the UK we also offer a range of other gift and stationery products illustrated with Frith photographs, although many of these are not available for delivery outside the UK – see our web site for more information on the products available for delivery in your country.

THE INTERNET

Over 100,000 photographs of Britain can be viewed and purchased on the Frith web site. The web site also includes memories and reminiscences contributed by our customers, who have personal knowledge of localities and of the people and properties depicted in Frith photographs. If you wish to learn more about a specific town or village you may find these reminiscences fascinating to browse. Why not add your own comments if you think they would be of interest to others? See **www.francisfrith.com**

PLEASE HELP US BRING FRITH'S PHOTOGRAPHS TO LIFE

Our authors do their best to recount the history of the places they write about. They give insights into how particular towns and villages developed, they describe the architecture of streets and buildings, and they discuss the lives of famous people who lived there. But however knowledgeable our authors are, the story they tell is necessarily incomplete.

Frith's photographs are so much more than plain historical documents. They are living proofs of the flow of human life down the generations. They show real people at real moments in history; and each of those people is the son or daughter of someone, the brother or sister, aunt or uncle, grandfather or grandmother of someone else. All of them lived, worked and played in the streets depicted in Frith's photographs.

We would be grateful if you would give us your insights into the places shown in our photographs: the streets and buildings, the shops, businesses and industries. Post your memories of life in those streets on the Frith website: what it was like growing up there, who ran the local shop and what shopping was like years ago; if your workplace is shown tell us about your working day and what the building is used for now. Read other visitors' memories and reconnect with your shared local history and heritage. With your help more and more Frith photographs can be brought to life, and vital memories preserved for posterity, and for the benefit of historians in the future.

Wherever possible, we will try to include some of your comments in future editions of our books. Moreover, if you spot errors in dates, titles or other facts, please let us know, because our archive records are not always completely accurate—they rely on 140 years of human endeavour and hand-compiled records. You can email us using the contact form on the website.

Thank you!

For further information, trade, or author enquiries please contact us at the address below:

The Francis Frith Collection, 6 Oakley Business Park, Wylye Road, Dinton, Wiltshire SP3 5EU.

Tel: +44 (0)1722 716 376 Fax: +44 (0)1722 716 881
e-mail: sales@francisfrith.co.uk **www.francisfrith.com**